CHAOS

IS A GIFT?

ENDORSEMENTS

Written for multiple sectors from diverse voices; this book illuminates the importance of self-leadership in a VUCA world.

Cynthia Cherrey, President & CEO, International Leadership Association

CHAOS IS A GIFT? Leading Oneself in Uncertain and Complex Environments is essential reading during these volatile, uncertain, complex, and ambiguous (VUCA) times in which we must now navigate how to live, work, and survive. The 17 chapters from international authors guide leaders from business, education, nonprofit, and public sectors on utilizing self-leadership in multiple contexts toward reduced conflict. The book offers foundational information on self-leadership and VUCA theories, provides in-depth standout chapters on topics such as stillness by Adrienne Castellon and liminal leadership by Randal Thompson, and concludes with strategies and recommendations. Chaos can be a gift if you have the right tools such as this indispensable book.

Dr. Chrys Egan, Associate Dean of the Fulton School of Liberal Arts at Salisbury University (USA) and the Chair of the International Leadership Association's "Women and Leadership"

CHAOS IS A GIFT?: Leading Oneself in Uncertain and Complex Environments, raises provocative questions and alternative perspectives on the nature of leadership in an era of paradigmatic change, uncertainty, and chaos. As Kuhn noted "it is rather as if the professional community had been suddenly transported to another planet where familiar objects are seen in a different light and are joined by unfamiliar ones as well." *CHAOS IS A GIFT?* provides new insights into accelerating challenges and the emerging opportunities for leading oneself in times of turbulence. Even as economic disasters, social upheavals, and virus pandemics swirl throughout world, those who dare to develop new ways of seeing and of leading will help create this as-yet unknown future. The authors who contributed chapters to *CHAOS IS A GIFT?*, provide a dynamic mosaic of ideas, insights, and practices for Leading Oneself through today's turbulence into a generative, more equitable and sustainable future for organizations, education, governments, and societies.

Dorothy Agger-Gupta, Professor, School of Leadership Studies,
Fielding Graduate University, Santa Barbara, USA

Educator Parker Palmer wrote in Let Your Life Speak (2000, p. 77): "We have a long and crippling legacy of believing in the power of external realities much more deeply than we believe in the power of the inner life... But the great insight of our spiritual traditions is that we are its co-creators. External reality does not impinge upon us as an ultimate constraint: if we find ourselves confined, it is only because we have conspired in our own imprisonment."

While reading *CHAOS IS A GIFT?* I was struck by the authors' warning that today's leaders are ill prepared for leadership of current external realities, which they characterize as "Volatile, Unpredictable, Complex, and Ambiguous." Indeed, the authors claim that the gap between today's leaders' preparedness and readiness for addressing today's external realities is constantly widening, and that conventional leadership theories are no longer adequate. The book presents a number of insightful life-stories of effective leaders and intrigue us with innovative theoretical proposals for addressing today's thorny societal and institutional issues, including the proposal to view leadership experiences as liminal encounters with others, transforming both leaders and their followers in the collaborative pursuit of peace. Yes! *CHAOS IS A GIFT?*, inviting and challenging every leader to dig deep for spiritual renewal and to collaborate with others for the betterment of our world. I highly recommend this book!

R. Ray Klapwyk, Ph.D., Educational Consultant Instructor in Educational Leadership
at Trinity Western University, Langley, BC

Although the notion of VUCA (volatility, uncertainty, complexity, ambiguity) has been around since the end of the Cold War and popularized by the terrorist attacks of 9/11, the advent of the disruptive technologies and trends of the Fourth Industrial Revolution combined with the trauma surrounding the COVID-19 pandemic, have made *CHAOS IS A GIFT?* a must read for leaders in all contemporary and future organizations. Reliance by leaders solely on their traditional skills are no longer adequate for leading an organization through the chaos of an uncertain and unknowable future. As the multiple authors in this book make abundantly clear, one has to learn how to lead oneself before becoming successful at leading an organization. These authors masterfully combine theory with practical examples of leaders in many countries and disciplines who have been successful in navigating through the VUCA environment. Fourteen of the most needed leadership skills for leading in these times are categorized as decision-making, inner, emotional, and social skills. A unique feature of this book is that it does not just deal with the usual political and economic environments but adds in the academic where future leaders in this chaotic world must come from. This book shows you what you must learn and model in order to lead in todays' world.

Don Page Ph.D. is a former foreign policy analyst in the Canadian federal government and
academic vice president at Trinity Western University who has been a leader and leadership
developer in multiple organizations for more than 50 years.

We live in a tremendous VUCA World, characterized by volatility, uncertainty, complexity and ambiguity. This book, authored by several scholars reflecting on (self)-leadership from their respective fields of expertise, provides novel and stimulating perspectives. After having read the book, I am convinced that leaders are called in a VUCA time like ours, to lead themselves and others by finding vision where others only see volatility, to gain understanding where others are caught up in uncertainty, to find clarity and courage where others only see complexity, and to become agile and adaptable leaders in the face of ambiguity.

Prof. Dr. Jacobus (Kobus) Kok, Co-Director RCEC, Leuven,
Contributing Editor of the book "Leading in a VUCA World"

CHAOS IS A GIFT? addresses the question of how to lead oneself in the context of today's increasingly complex VUCA world. As such, it could hardly have been more timely in this era of coronavirus, which compounds already existing crises, such as the climate crisis; it is an era of chaos, indeed. The various contributors to this volume consider the question of how we are to comport ourselves, in this era of chaos; the various answers they give to it are both wise and important. To survive and thrive in these times, it is essential to look beyond ourselves; thriving can only be done in relation to others and to nature. The authors that contribute to this volume all share this fundamental realization, and seek to respond to it. The resulting skill-set (well-summarized in chapter 17) is a crucial resource for people looking to lead themselves in today's VUCA world.

Steven C. van den Heuvel (Ph.D.) is Associate Professor of Systematic Theology at the
Evangelische Theologische Faculteit (ETF), Leuven (Belgium), as well as Director of the Institute
of Leadership and Social Ethics, a research institute of the ETF.

There are various books on leadership, but this book, in navigating today's volatile, uncertain, complex and ambiguous (VUCA) environment, presents chaos as both an opportunity and possibility in developing 'selfcare practices' in leading oneself. Leaders must have the cognitive flexibility to adapt to the unknown in the midst of chaos (and a crisis). Through making sense of leadership approaches in different environments, including the business, private, academic and public sectors, as well as in conflict/post conflict situations, the book provides a deep insight into leading oneself effectively, with innovation and empathy in a VUCA environment – an excellent contribution to self-leadership.

Francis Petersen, Rector & Vice-Chancellor: Top Management,
University of the Free State

As of 2020, the world is changing dramatically, requiring a profound reexamination of what is required to lead effectively. Choosing to title a book with a question (*CHAOS IS A GIFT?*) combined with a subtitle emphasizing the importance of *Leading Oneself,* signals that prospective readers can expect out-of-the-box insights applicable both to individual leaders and to the field of leadership studies. That promise is delivered upon in cutting-edge ways through this provocative new contribution to the literature. Choosing descriptors to position this new volume brings to mind the following: paradigm-shifting, globally-oriented, provocative, and yet intensely practical for both aspiring and seasoned leaders. The various chapters, which are instructive singly or when taken as a whole, draw from leadership theory and lead into applicable recommendations for practice (e.g., the importance of leaders practicing "stillness" in the midst of the chaos). At the same time, readers will face the reality that the tectonic plates that have undergirded the leadership field are being upended in the world's current VUCA context. This book has the potential to play a key role in bringing critical conversations front and center in the minds of leaders both individually and collectively.

Karen A. Longman, Ph.D., Professor and Ph.D. Program Director, Azusa Pacific University (CA)

Leadership is without a doubt one of the key determinants of the degree to which enterprises, regardless of sector or industry, will be able to craft and implement a new economic, social and way of work set of principles and practices. *CHAOS IS A GIFT?: Leading Oneself in Uncertain and Complex Environments* takes a slightly more "serious" approach to this topic, which is refreshing as there are many publications that focus more on the "surface" issues of leadership.

The fundamental philosophy of "inside-out" makes perfect sense in that personal mastery is a key determinant of the ability of individuals to play a meaningful and impactful leadership role, regardless of their organisation level.

Dr Anton Verwey, Executive Chair, inavit iQ (Pty) Ltd

CHAOS IS A GIFT?: Leading Oneself in Uncertain and Complex Environments contradicts, screams, objects against all logic, as chaos is not necessarily associated with a gift i.e. something positive, something nice. However, this catching phrase is sure to grab the attention of everyone. Chaos creates opportunities, as eloquently addressed in this book. To furthermore have the opportunity to learn something about yourself and how to exert yourself in your work environment, is a bonus.

Prof Hendri Kroukamp, Dean: Faculty of Economic and Management Sciences, University of the Free State

CHAOS IS A GIFT?: Leading Oneself in Uncertain and Complex Environments offers a fresh, interesting, relevant, true-to-life and fascinating alternative. The structure of the book promotes its relevance to the private, public and academic sectors. Furthermore, the range of international contributors from no less than seven countries increases its relevance to a more global context.

Prof Roelf van Niekerk, Director: School of Industrial Psychology and Human Resources at Nelson Mandela University

As a teacher and a parent who is seems involved daily in the engagement of chaos, I love the idea of a book titled *"CHAOS IS A GIFT?: Leading Oneself in Uncertain and Complex Environments."* The optimism alive in this book's topic is an invitation to be nudged from our complacency and comfort to see the taken-for-granted with new eyes. I'm engaged by that invitation.

Specifically, the fear humans are engaging as they face the COVID-19 pandemic is palpable. Instead of an event that sees an opportunity, there seems to be a collective capitulation to what seems inevitable – as if we have surrendered agency to thoughtfulness.

The book offers us individual pause and collective conversation about possible next steps – not just for the moment, but for the future. The Table of Contents presents wonderful choices – from individual quietness to business ethics. As always, I immediately want to create a graduate course on the topic of "Celebrating Chaos" that might use this book as a core reading. What a conversation the book might engender. It's hopeful, which is something we need.

The book also seems an invitation to shape ourselves for projects of opportunity. Certainly, leadership must consider the event chaos might offer. I look forward to reading the book more fully and conversing with others about the possibilities of action it invites.

Jim Parsons, Professor Emeritus, Faculty of Education, University of Alberta, Canada

True to its title, *CHAOS IS A GIFT?* is a must read for leaders in both public and private sectors. More than ever, the 21st century is yearning for leaders who can help their people flourish and provide credibility that can engender trust. The principles of leadership presented are truly blocks that help in building trust, reducing conflict, increasing effectiveness, quality leadership skills and effective communication. As a diplomat reading this book, I have been reminded that being a leader isn't about ability, it's about responsibility, and when we understand that in these challenging times, we are in the world to make paths easier for others.

Dr. Imbenzi George, Honorary Consul General, Vancouver Diplomatic Corps

First published in 2020.

ISBN: 978-1-86922-860-6 (Printed)
eISBN: 978-1-86922-861-3 (PDF ebook)
eISBN: 978-1-86922-862-0 (ePub)
eISBN: 978-1-86922-863-7 (Mobi)

Published by KR Publishing
P O Box 3954
Randburg
2125

Republic of South Africa

Tel: (011) 706-6009
Fax: (011) 706-1127
E-mail: orders@knowres.co.za
Website: www.kr.co.za

Printed and bound: HartWood Digital Printing, 243 Alexandra Avenue, Halfway House, Midrand
Typesetting, layout and design: Cia Joubert, cia@knowres.co.za
Cover design: Marlene De Lorme, marlene@knowres.co.za
Cover Illustrations: Dr Erna van Zyl, erna@kremetarte.co.za
Editing and Proofreading: Jennifer Renton, jenniferrenton@live.co.za
Project management: Cia Joubert, cia@knowres.co.za

CHAOS
IS A GIFT?

Leading Oneself in Uncertain and Complex Environments

Edited by

Ebben van Zyl

Andrew Campbell & Liezel Lues

publishing

2020

ACKNOWLEDGEMENTS

I want to thank the following people:

- Dr Andrew Campbell who initiated the idea of this book.
- Ronel Kleynhans who suggested the title of the book.
- My lovely wife Dr Erna van Zyl (who did the painting of the spiral on the front page) and Prof Liezel Lues (who helped with the designing of the front page).
- All the contributors, including the authors and proofreaders, as well as to the publisher (Cia Joubert in particular), for their professionalism.

Ebben van Zyl

TABLE OF CONTENTS

ABOUT THE EDITORS

Professor Ebben van Zyl is currently Professor in the Department of Industrial Psychology (University of the Free State, South Africa). Professor van Zyl has published 48 scientific publications, 39 research projects and has presented 45 papers at national and international conferences with regard to industrial psychology and leadership-related topics. He is also the editor and co-writer of the book, *Leadership in the African Context* (2009; 2016), co-writer of the chapter, 'Leadership in South Africa' in *LEAD: Leadership effectiveness in Africa and the African Diaspora* (2016), and co-writer of the chapter, 'Cultural intelligence as a way for organisational leaders to enhance peace' in *Global Leadership Initiatives for Conflict Resolution and Peacebuilding*. He received awards for 'Top Performer: Research' in the Faculty of Economic and Management Sciences (1999 and 2015, University of the Free State) and 'Research Excellence' from the University of the Free State (2004). His book, *Leadership in the African Context,* was nominated as one of the best books at the University of the Free State (2017). Professor van Zyl is co-editor and co-writer of the book: *Peace Leadership: Self-transformation to Peace* (2019) which was launched in West Palm Beach (Florida) and in Johannesburg. He also acts as a consultant for various companies in the fields of medico-legal investigations, leadership, conflict and peace management, stress measurement and management, as well as human resource management. Email: vanzyles@ufs.ac.za

Dr. Andrew Campbell is the Director, International Peace and Leadership Institute. He provides emerging leadership research and leadership development and training programmes on a leader's role in international, national and nongovernmental organisations designed for conflict prevention and resolution, specifically for conflict resolution practitioners conducting and executing peace-making, peacekeeping, and peacebuilding activities within post-conflict resolution and peaceful leadership. In addition, Dr. Campbell, as a retired senior military officer, works for the Department of Defence specialising in Counter-Terrorism and Global Security Cooperation. Dr. Campbell possesses a Doctorate in Global Leadership from the Indiana Institute of Technology, Fort Wayne, IN. and a Master's in Diplomacy in International Conflict Management from Norwich University, Northfield, VT. He is an Adjunct Professor for the U. S. Air Force Command and Staff College, Norwich University, and the Federal Executive Institute. Dr. Campbell is a recognised national and international speaker on peace leadership and has addressed the World Society of Victimology at The Hague (2012), the Peace Leadership Conference (2017), the International Leadership Association (2011–2020), and the European Consortium for Political Research (2015–2017). He is widely published in both national and international journals, with book chapters on such topics as 'Leadership Education in Transitional Justice in Promoting Global Peace' and 'Civic Engagement through Education and Forgiveness and

Reconciliation as an Organizational Leadership Competence in Transitional Justice' in the *International Journal of Servant Leadership*. He recently published a book entitled *Global Leadership Initiatives for Conflict Resolution and Peacebuilding* and co-authored *Peace Leadership: Self Transformation to Peace*, which explores leadership theories and practice models to conceptualise the intersection of leadership within conflict management and resolution and peace development. Email: andrew.h.campbell3@gmail.com

Professor Liezel Lues has a Ph.D. in Public Management, and is an Associate Professor of Public Administration and Management at the University of the Free State, South Africa. She previously held the position of Head of Department following a term as Programme Director of the Department of Public Administration and Management. She was respectively the Deputy- and Chairperson of the Association of Southern African Departments of Public Administration and Management. At present, Professor Lues is the co-chairperson of the working group VI – Public Sector Leadership and Governance of the International Associations of Schools and Institutes of Administration.

Her research interests include Public Sector Management Transitions, particularly the role of leadership accountability. She has published extensively in this field (42 peer reviewed papers) and presented papers at 33 conferences. Her latest work appears in the *International Journal of Transforming Government: People, Process, and Policy*. Her latest academic book chapters focus respectively on 'Peace Leadership in the Public and Private Sectors' and 'Leadership in the African Context'. She has been awarded the Faculty Economic and Management Sciences Best Senior Research Award and is an NRF-rated scientist. Email: Luesl@ufs.ac.za

ABOUT THE CONTRIBUTORS

Professor Adrienne Castellon has worked as a secondary school teacher, elementary school principal, education consultant and Director in North and South America, and has presented at conferences worldwide. She is currently the Associate Dean for the Masters of Leadership, Trinity Western University, British Columbia, Canada. Professor Castellon is the author of the resource, *Indigenous Integration: 100+ Lesson Ideas for Secondary and College Teachers, The Role of Wisdom and Spirituality in Leading Self and Others in Peace Leadership: Self Transformation to Peace*, as well as several articles related to gender equity and indigenous and environmental justice in education. Email: adrienne.castellon@twu.ca

Professor Ajay K. Jain is a full Professor of Organizational Design and Behaviour at the Management Development Institute, Gurgaon, Mehrauli Road, Sukhrali, Gurugram, India. He is also a visiting professor to several international universities including Aarhus University, Denmark; IULM University, Italy; University of Free State, South Africa; and the Indian Institute of Management Lucknow and Ranchi. Jain has published 50 research articles in journals, including the Journal of Managerial Psychology; Personnel Review; Journal of Knowledge Management, Psychology and Marketing; Journal of Management History; International Journal of Environmental Research and Public Health, and Leadership. He is a recipient of Best Paper awards from the National Academy of Psychology in India and Emerald for his research papers, and has received post doctoral fellowships from Aarhus University in Denmark and the Indian School of Business Hyderabad. Jain delivers training programmes for companies including ABB, Nestlé, Taijin, Denso and Suzuki, which focus on leading from within and emotional intelligence. He also teaches courses on organisational design, leading transformations, emotional intelligence and research methods. He has research interests in the field of distributed leadership, emotional intelligence, organisational citizenship behaviour (voice and silence) and well being. Email: akjain@mdi.ac.in

Professor Barbara Schellhammer started out in Social Work (specialising in systemic family therapy), after which she earned a PhD in Philosophy and a Habilitation (post-doc) in Cultural Philosophy. She worked as professor at the International YMCA University of Applied Sciences in Kassel, Germany, and now holds the chair for Intercultural Social Transformation at the Munich School of Philosophy SJ, where she also heads the Center for Social and Development Studies. For approximately 15 years Professor Schellhammer lived in Canada, where she worked as associate faculty at the Royal Roads University in Victoria, BC, and conducted research in several communities in the Northwest Territories. Other research projects brought her to Togo and Kenya in

Africa. As Academic Director for Jesuit Worldwide Learning, she also spent time in refugee camps in Northern Iraq. Her current research interest lies in (inter-)cultural philosophy, peace studies, conflict transformation, self-care practices and identity. Her latest books deal with the development of "alien-ability", conflict-coaching, and education for resistance. Email: barbara.schellhammer@hfph.de

Professor Barney Jordaan holds a doctorate in law from Stellenbosch University. Prior to being appointed as Professor of Management Practice at Vlerick Business School, Belgium, in 2014, he held positions as full Professor of Law at Stellenbosch University, Extraordinary Professor at the University of Stellenbosch Business School and Visiting Professor at the Graduate School of Business, University of Cape Town. In addition to his academic endeavours, Professor Jordaan has been involved in private practice since 1985, first as an Associate in a human rights law firm and thereafter as co-founder and Director of a consulting practice that specialises in negotiation, mediation and dispute resolution. He is a senior mediator, having been involved in the field since 1989. He is certified by the International Mediation Institute as well as by the ADR Group (UK), the Centre for Effective Dispute Resolution (CEDR, UK) and Conflict Dynamics, South Africa. Professor Jordaan also served as an external consultant to the World Bank Group's Office of Mediation Services for a number of years. He has been listed in the international *Who's Who of Commercial Mediators* annually since 2011. Email: Barney.jordaan@vlerick.com

Dr. Daphne Pillay is currently a lecturer at the University of Pretoria and a registered Industrial Psychologist with the Health Professions Council of South Africa. After being employed in the private sector and working as an independent consultant, she entered academia to further her passion for research. Her research interests include women in the workplace, leadership and the role of positive organisational behaviour in developing psychological strengths in the workplace. In her PhD, she constructed a model of resilience promoting factors for female leaders in higher education. Dr. Pillay has published and presented papers at national conferences and has been accepted to present at world-renowned international psychology conferences. She is a published scientific scholar with her work featuring in peer-reviewed journals. She is currently working on a research project that focuses on mindfulness-based strengths practice in the workplace, and was awarded a research grant to fund the project. Dr. Pillay holds a PhD from the University of the Free State and a Master's degree from the University of KwaZulu-Natal in South Africa. Email: daphne.pillay@up.ac.za

Professor Erich Schellhammer recently retired from Royal Roads University, Victoria, Canada, after a long career in Justice Studies. He holds a German law degree (Baden-Württemberg) as well as a Canadian M.A. and Ph.D. in philosophy (Queen's University).

His research interests focused on a philosophical justification for the merits of cultural diversity and a phenomenological grounding of human rights in human ontology. He presently uses recent leadership studies to identify a new leadership category – peace leadership. His latest academic interest is in combining modern leadership studies with peace and conflict studies to formulate a framework for peace leadership. He was the inaugural chair of the Peace Leadership Affinity Group of the International Leadership Association and has published articles on peace leadership. Email: erich.schellhammer@gmail.com

Professor Jack Barentsen studied physics, philosophy and theology in the US, before moving back to the Netherlands in 1988 to be a missionary pastor and church planter, with a focus on leadership development. His doctoral research at the Evangelische Theologische Faculteit in Leuven (Belgium) focused on leadership development in early Christianity (*Emerging Leadership in the Pauline Mission: A Social Identity Perspective*, 2011), for which he was awarded the Jablin Dissertation Award from the International Leadership Association. Since then, Barentsen has taught on and researched pastoral leadership in multiple countries, developing a descriptive Integrative Model of Pastoral Leadership. He has also published a volume on evangelical churches in Belgium's cities (*Zoektocht naar hoop voor de stad*, 2019), and is currently investigating cooperative church networks in various cities. He serves as Professor and Chair of Practical Theology and as Senior Researcher of the Institute of Leadership and Social Ethics (ILSE), for which he has co-edited a number of leadership books: *Leadership, Spirituality and Innovation* (2014), *Christian Leadership in a Changing World: Perspectives from Africa and Europe* (2016), *The End of Leadership? Leadership and Authority at Crossroads* (2017), and *Increasing Diversity: Loss of Control or Adaptive Identity Construction* (2018). Professor Barentsen also holds an appointment as Extraordinary Researcher in Practical Theology at the Faculty of Theology of North-West University in Potchefstroom, South Africa. Email: jack.barentsen@etf.edu.

Dr. Maréve Biljohn is a senior lecturer in the Department of Public Administration and Management at the University of the Free State (UFS) in South Africa. Prior to her appointment at the UFS, she worked for local government (LG) in the Western Cape Province of South Africa. She holds a Doctor of Philosophy degree in Public Administration, as well as a Master of Public Administration, an Honours degree in Industrial Psychology, and an Honours degree in Public Administration. In 2015 she was awarded an Erasmus-Mundus EU-Saturn scholarship which she completed in Belgium, and she received the UFS Economic and Management Sciences Faculty Emerging Researcher Award in 2018. Dr. Biljohn's research interests are in the fields of social innovation in LG service delivery, and citizen participation in the governance of LG service delivery. Her work includes publications on social innovation as an alternative approach to South African LG service delivery, determinants for citizen and third-sector participation during social innovation in LG service delivery, as well as considerations for South African LG for using social innovation in open and closed governance systems. Her most recent work is published in the *International Journal of Transforming Government: People, Process and Policy* and the *International Journal of Public Administration*. Email: BiljohnMIM@ufs.ac.za

Dr. Martha Harunavamwe is currently a senior lecturer in the Department of Industrial Psychology (University of the Free State, South Africa). Dr. Harunavamwe has published six scientific research articles and three book chapters, and has presented at eight national and international conferences on human resources management, industrial psychology, positive psychology and leadership-related topics. Dr. Harunavamwe is the co-writer of the chapter, 'Cultural intelligence as a way for organisational leaders to enhance peace' in the book, *Global Leadership Initiatives for Conflict Resolution and Peacebuilding*, and is also a co-writer of the book, *Peace Leadership: Self-transformation to Peace* (2019), which was launched in West Palm Beach (Florida) and in Johannesburg. Email: harunavamweM@ufs.ac.za.

Dr. Randal Joy Thompson is a scholar-practitioner who, for many decades, has worked globally in international development. A former US Commissioned Foreign Service Officer, she is currently consulting internationally as the Principal and founder of the companies Dream Connect Global and Excellence, Equity and Empowerment. She was lead editor for the International Leadership Association's (ILA) 2018 volume, *Leadership and Power in International Development: Navigating the Intersections of Gender, Culture, Context, and Sustainability*, which won the Academy of Human Development R. Wayne Pace HRD 2018 Book of the Year Award. Her book, *Leading Proleptically on the Commons: Ushering in a New Global Order*, will be published in late 2020. She is also co-editing the forthcoming 2021 ILA volume, *Redefining Leadership on the Commons*. Dr. Thompson has published many book chapters on leadership and peer-reviewed articles on women, evaluation, foreign aid, and education. She earned a PhD in Organization Systems from Fielding Graduate University, an MBA and MA in Philosophy from the University of Chicago, an MA in Biblical Exposition from Capital Seminary and Graduate School, and a BA in Philosophy from the University of California, Berkeley. She also holds a certificate in French Civilization from the Sorbonne and in Organization Development Consulting from Georgetown University. Email: rtdreamconnectglobal@gmail.com

Dr. Wesley R. Pieters is currently a Senior Industrial/Organisational Psychology lecturer at the University of Namibia in Windhoek. His research is focused on organisational effectiveness, employee wellness, organisational justice/fairness, effective leadership and healthy job attitudes of employees. He graduated with a PhD in Industrial Psychology from the University of the Free State, Bloemfontein, South Africa. In 2019, he received the Meritorious Award for Research and Researcher of the Year in the Faculty of Humanities and Social Sciences. He was also recognised on numerous occasions as Researcher of the Year in the Department of Human Sciences: Psychology section, for his contributions towards the university's research output. Dr. Pieters has published in regional and international journals and has presented at various regional and international conferences during his academic career. He is passionate about moulding young researchers and guiding his research students to present and publish their work. Email: wpieters@unam.na/.

INTRODUCTION

Welcome to the first edition of *Chaos is a gift? Leading oneself in uncertain and complex environments*. Human nature has not changed since the beginning of time. One of the current global challenges is managing and adapting to the complexity and uncertainty of change and new demands.[1] For instance, the coronavirus pandemic has led to a lock-down of countries all over the world. Many industries and factories were forced to shut down, adversely impacting global markets and economies. Levels of stress are soaring among employees due to rising employment uncertainty. Domestic violence has increased, due to people being confined at home. Mental health problems such as depression and anxiety are escalating due to loneliness and isolation. Having no sense of control over circumstances causes fear of dying, fear of relatives dying, and fear of not knowing how long isolation and physical distancing will be maintained. Besides causing high levels of stress, the current situation has led to posttraumatic stress disorder in some people.

Companies are desperately trying to be proactive by re-imagining the future world and continuously developing new products and services. The decline in economic activity globally has forced private sector companies to do more with less employees, which contributes to the uncertainty in organisations. In the public sector, ineffective political leadership and the constant changing of lockdown legislation has created a complex environment in which employees have to function.

In the academic sector, the uncertain impact of the global pandemic on educational delivery systems has moved academic institutions from being instructor-led to functioning as remote instructional delivery systems. Online training and evaluation methods have been introduced, all of which are contributing to a volatile and ambiguous educational environment. Apart from the volatile, uncertain, complex and ambiguous (VUCA) business, academic and public sectors, the global environment is characterised by regional instability and ambiguity, failed states, increased weapons proliferation and global terrorism, all of which require greater global leadership.[2]

The important question is how leaders and non leaders can lead themselves in order to deal with the changing world and demanding VUCA environments. Currently, some empirical, theoretical and application leadership models are available in the business, academic and public sectors, however there is no empirical, theoretical leadership model aimed at the "leading oneself" role in VUCA environments. This book will play a critical role in expanding leadership skills within the changing global environment we are functioning in.

---

1   Van Zyl and Campbell, 2019.
2   Campbell, 2018.

PURPOSE OF BOOK AND TARGET POPULATION

The purpose of this book is to give deeper insight into the concept of "leading oneself within different VUCA environments." The book provides practical realities and specific recommendations on how to lead oneself in the private and public sectors, the academic world, and conflict/post-conflict environments. Guidelines of how to lead oneself are also provided.

The book is aimed primarily at leaders in different environments, including the business, private, academic and public sectors, as well as conflict/post-conflict environments. The secondary market is anyone who is interested in learning how to lead them-self in a VUCA environment.

STRUCTURE OF THE BOOK

The book is presented in four parts:

Part one: Introduction – Leading oneself in VUCA environments

This section provides introductory discussions on perspectives of leading in complex and uncertain environments, followed by perspectives of leading oneself in VUCA environments.

Part two: Leading oneself in the private sector

Skills of conflict wisdom, self-care, humanness, and stillness are discussed in part two.

Part three: Leading oneself in the academic sector

In this section, some of the significant concepts discussed include resilience, agility, optimism, adaptability, and servant leadership.

Part four: Leading oneself in the public sector

In part four, transformational, relational and participative leadership are scrutinised.

Part five: Leading oneself in conflict and post-conflict environments

This section focuses on conflict resolution, liminal leadership and religious leadership.

Part six: Looking ahead, outcomes, recommendations, and final thoughts

First, future possibilities are discussed with regard to a strategic leading oneself model in VUCA environments. The outcomes of the book (leading oneself skills in general and in different environments) are then set out. Recommendations are discussed and finally, concluding thoughts are given (explaining why chaos may indeed be considered as a gift).

A more comprehensive structure and description of the book are as follows:

Part one: Introduction

Chapter 1: Perspectives of leading in uncertain and complex environments (Andrew Campbell, International Peace Leadership Institute [IPLI], USA)
Chapter 2: Perspectives of leading oneself in volatile, uncertain, complex, and ambiguous environments (Ebben van Zyl, University of the Free State [UFS], South Africa)

Part two: Leading oneself in the private sector

Chapter 3: Conflict wisdom – The ability to change the frame (Barney Jordaan, Vlerick Business School, Ghent, Belgium)
Chapter 4: Leadership by Socrates – Self-care in difficult and unpredictable times (Barbara Schellhammer, Munich School of Philosophy, Germany)
Chapter 5: Humanness in the business and private sectors (Erich Schellhammer, Royal Roads University, Canada)
Chapter 6: Perspectives on stillness for a VUCA world (Adrienne Castellon, Trinity Western University, Canada)

Part three: Leading oneself in the academic sector

Chapter 7: Resilience and agility in Zimbabwean higher education (Martha Harunavamwe, UFS, South Africa)
Chapter 8: Optimism and adaptability within the South African higher education sector (Daphne Pillay, University of Pretoria, South Africa)
Chapter 9: Basic psychological need satisfaction at the University of Namibia (Wesley Pieters, University of Namibia, Namibia)

Part four: Leading oneself in the public sector

Chapter 10: South Africa's surviving VUCA environments (Liezel Lues, UFS, South Africa)
Chapter 11: Leading self in South Africa's VUCA local government environments (Mareve Biljohn, UFS, South Africa)
Chapter 12: A model of leading self in VUCA environments (Ajay K. Jain, Management Development Institute, Gurgaon, Mehrauli Road, Sukhrali, Gurugram, India)

PART ONE

INTRODUCTION

CHAPTER 1

PERSPECTIVES OF LEADING IN UNCERTAIN AND COMPLEX ENVIRONMENTS

Andrew Campbell

ABSTRACT

We live in a world of rapid geopolitical and socio-economic change, spawned by technological innovation and driven by economic inequality and ideological discourse. Rapid change within the global political context and marketplace produces complex and uncertain outcomes which impact the operational environment among transnational corporations. This chapter aims to introduce a conceptual volatile, uncertain, complex, and ambiguous (VUCA) understanding, as well as a brief comparative discussion of traditional to strategic approaches. Secondly, the chapter will present the role of existing theoretical leadership models in understanding the foundational tenet of leadership in a VUCA environment. Finally, a brief discussion of different perspectives of leadership challenges in VUCA academic, business, economic, and peace development settings is offered.

INTRODUCTION

The global transition from agrarian to industrial advancements throughout the 20th and 21st century carried socio-political, educational, economic, ideological, and security challenges that shaped domestic and international relations. Numerous studies suggest a positive association between economic and education inequality and socio-political tension when it comes to the security of nation-states. Shifting from colonialism to state sovereignty created a complex mixture of economic, socio-political, legal, and cultural challenges within the transnational, national, and subnational systems. History shows that within the international system these challenges carried economic disparities between states, both in bipolar and multipolar political and security challenges causing chaos, volatility, and uncertainty within the international system.

After World War I and II, the international community formally created international institutions and treaties between states. The institution of non-intervention and treaties of collective security agreements provided the space for significant technological developments that have altered the international economic system, as well as the world order. As a result, the integration of economic and technological innovation span across territorial boundaries, impacting not only the principal sectors of society, but also the peace and security apparatus. In fact, the interconnectedness of globalisation and technological innovation has changed the organisational and operational environment. The biggest leadership challenge now is how to not only lead in an unpredictable environment, but also how to navigate an organisation when experiencing unanticipated events. The world has become more volatile, uncertain, complex, and ambiguous (VUCA) within the current political, educational, and economic environment.

We live in a world of rapid geopolitical and socio-economic change spawned by technological innovation and driven by economic inequality and ideological discourse. Rapid change within the global political context and marketplace produces complex and uncertain outcomes that impact the operational environment among transnational corporations. Literature shows that the issues of one domain, like volatility, impact other domains, such as complexity, uncertainty and ambiguity, amid chaotic events (uncertainty may, for instance, also include volatility, while complexity may include ambiguity). This chapter introduces a conceptual VUCA understanding and a brief comparative discussion of traditional to strategic approaches. The subsequent chapters focus on complexity and uncertainty within a chaotic context. This chapter also describes the existing role of theoretical leadership models in understanding the foundational tenet of leadership in a VUCA environment. Finally, a brief discussion of different perspectives of leadership challenges in VUCA academic, business, economic, and peace development settings is offered.

CONCEPTUAL UNDERSTANDING

During the 1990s, researchers at the Army War College in the USA recognised that the fall of the Soviet Union had created a security vacuum comprised of wicked challenges for military strategic planners. Given the rise of global terrorism, the rapidly changing socio-ethno-economic and political environments not only made stabilisation and reconstruction activities unpredictable, but also nation-building uncertain. In the same vein, transnational corporations recognised that the challenges the military experiences from internal and external forces can be found within an organisational business context. As a result, national and business leaders were in uncharted waters, and traditional leadership approaches needed to change and adapt to this new environment.[1]

The contextual descriptors of VUCA are characterised below.

Volatility

Kok and van den Heuvel[2] suggested that the speed of technological innovation, the magnitude of political discourse, and the scale of unstable socio-economic events bring not only instability but also volatility within a constantly shifting global business ecosystem. As actions unfold, rapid change and managing unexpected events generate chaos within the operational environment. More importantly, the unpredictable context in the environment brings about a cause and effect that are frequently out of the organisational leader's span of control. According to Landsberg, "leaders are not afforded the luxury of stability and predictability."[3] To illustrate, the introduction of Bitcoin cryptocurrency and blockchain technologies designed to transfer money seamlessly is not only bringing volatility, but is also generating rapid global market fluctuation and instability across the financial ecosystem.

Uncertainty

Globalisation and technological innovation have changed the geopolitical and transnational corporate landscape.[4] Additionally, the increased levels of globalised technological innovation, economic integration, multicultural and social interdependence, and transnational corporate operations frequently bring about an institutional and organisational crisis. Such a crisis event often results in continual change in the political, socio-economic, and security environment. To put it simply, the acceleration of change often brings a lack of clarity in information sharing, a lack of strategic planning capability in managing the unexpected, and a lack of strategic foresight amongst leaders to foresee the outcomes of major change.[5] The uncertainty of governmental policies in economic sanctions, trade embargoes, import and export restrictions, currency manipulations, and increased tariffs on goods and services are uncontrollable events that impact not only the relations of glocalised and transnational business leaders, but also consumers.

---

1   Veldsman & Johnson, 2016.
2   Kok & van den Heuvel, 2019.
3   Landsberg, 2016: 268.
4   Veldsman & Johnson, 2016.
5   Kok & Van den Heuvel, 2019.

Complexity

Global conditions of managing political, diplomatic and economic integration, collective security agreements, and socio-ethnic stability have become more complex than ever before. Veldsman and Johnson[6] stated that "complexity involves navigating situations resulting from the confluence of the many different business, economic, government, and political players." More importantly, the rapid speed of integrating technological innovations, such as robotics and artificial intelligence, into our daily lives and the day-to-day operations of organisations are changing the societal landscape. No longer are agrarian and post-industrial societal challenges single-layered with limited second or third orders of effects. Simply stated, the global ecosystem is dynamic with multiple, interrelated moving parts. In fact, the global demand to both integrate economic resources and leverage interconnective technologies carries multi-layered challenges for leaders. Weick and Sutcliffe[7] suggested that "interactive complex systems possess a more elaborate set of interconnections and nonlinear feedback loops, some of which are hidden or impossible to anticipate." That said, disentangling the interconnective relationship contained within multiple layers makes it impossible for organisational leaders to create and decide on a singular path for a particular action. In other words, navigating the unpredictability and uncertain demands from multiple directions increases the interactive complexity in decision making. Organisational leaders frequently face the possibility of both multiple decision pathways and multiple consequences. The outcome of organisational chaos is only as complex as the leader's decision-making process.

Ambiguity

Leaders are accustomed to solving organisational crises with predictable and certain outcomes. Amid organisational chaos, the leader's decision is only as good as the information presented. The political uncertainty and socio-economic volatility within the global environmental impacts not only government operations and transnational corporations, but also regional and communal entities.[8] In fact, global demands are frequently fragmented, unclear and unpredictable, therefore disentangling those demands frequently generates confusion and a lack of clarity where interconnecting relationships are unknown and undefined. Scholar-practitioners believe the lack of information, predictability, and clarity causes organisational uncertainty and ambiguity.[9] In fact, "ambiguity triggers dependency needs and consequently,

---

6   Veldsman & Johnson, 2016: 485.
7   Weick & Sutcliffe, 2015: 92.
8   Kok & Van den Heuvel, 2019.
9   Weick & Sutcliffe, 2015.

higher levels of anxiety."[10] Given this type of operational environment, the leader's dependency on predictable and certain outcomes are no longer valid.

The challenge for organisational leaders is to examine the global commons, disentangle and make sense of the chaotic interconnective pathways, and develop strategic planning assumptions into a singular direction when the environment is fluid and unpredictable. To illustrate, the negotiated multilateral Pacific Trade Agreement by the Obama administration, later rescinded by the Trump Administration, caused much confusion and uncertainty in trade policy and business development. This impacted international trade, economic stability, and the entire supply chain among nations. To be sure, the unknowns of changing trade policy produced not only chaos and ambiguity within the markets, but also brought forth unpredictability and missed business trade opportunities.

THEORETICAL EXPLANATION

As per the following discussion, literature reveals limited empirical or conceptual studies that link leadership theories with conceptual leadership approaches within a VUCA context. Therefore, a brief theoretical discussion is warranted to illustrate possible interconnected relationships in multiple turbulent contexts. Below, three leadership theoretical constructs are presented that may undergird and provide guideposts as glocalised leaders strategically navigate within a VUCA environment and develop the leadership acumen to lead with a clear vision, situational understanding, clarity of purpose, and adaptability to cope with unpredictability.

Chaos Theory

The chaos theory framework suggests that in an unpredictable and uncertain environment, the leader makes sense of patterns and brings order by directing change to fix an organisational problem or to achieve a goal.[11] According to Galacgac and Singh[12], "chaos theory states that the behaviour of complex systems are highly sensitive to the slightest changes in conditions, which results in small changes to giving rise to more unpredictable, prominent effects on the system." This is visible when leaders in a VUCA environment transform the chaos from uncertainty and ambiguity into a clarity of direction and purposeful conditions that bring organisational change. The challenge for an organisational leader is disentangling not only the connection among multiple variables, but also understanding the cause-and-effect relationship within the decision-making process. Essentially, the idea behind chaos theory is shifting the leader's

---

10 Veldsman & Johnson, 2016: 772.

11 Lichtenstein & Plowman, 2009.

12 Galacgac & Singh, 2016: 517.

mindset to accept and strategically navigate through uncertainty and unpredictability as an emergent ingredient in a rapidly changing technological, political, and socio-economic environment.

Change Leadership Theory

The literature on change leadership addresses how leaders manage complexity, uncertainty, and turbulence to shape organisational change within the global political, socio-economic, security, and academic contexts. Veldsman and Johnson[13] stated that "change leadership is the ability to influence and arouse enthusiasm in others through personal advocacy, vision, and drive, and to access resources to build a solid platform of change." Literature reveals that applying change leadership constructs is a model for leading organisational change by influencing the context in which the change is being implemented. To design and implement, change leaders contextualise fragmented systems by deconflicting and connecting multiple variables in the chaos, anticipating with clarity and purpose, in driving change to solve wicked problems. Moreover, multiple key variables within a complex and uncertain environment rest with changing the organisational culture through altering one's behaviour in a different organisational context that empowers new communication practices, attitudes, goals, and practices.[14] Veldsman and Johnson[15] postulated that "a lack of clarity of purpose by the leader has the potential to make the change process unnecessarily unstable and fearsome for people." In other words, change leadership theory advocates that strategic leaders must lead with clarity of purpose and vision in a VUCA environment. Change leadership theory provides a structural framework to examine, prepare, and garner transformational change at the core level within an organisation.

Complexity Leadership Theory

Researchers note that leadership is a complex interaction, with multiple interactive behaviour patterns impacting organisational outcomes. "Complexity leadership theory is a framework for leadership that enables the learning, creative, adaptive capacity of complex adaptive systems in knowledge-producing organisations or organisational units."[16] While much of the literature points out that complex leadership theory is about organisational leaders' adaptive capacity to deal with complex and uncertain challenges. Scholar-practitioners believe that the construct provides a framework to understand not only how to manage and coordinate activities from the emergent

---

13 Veldsman & Johnson, 2016: 537.

14 Kotter, 2012.

15 Veldsman & Johnson, 2016: 542.

16 Uhl-Bien, Marion & McKelvey, 2008: 200.

complex and uncertain events amid chaos, but also how a leader rapidly responds to organisational chaos.[17] Hence, applying the complex leadership concepts offers a framework that any strategic leader can rely on to deconstruct the multiple pathways and leverage networks to gain new information and agility, creating a singular action that aligns with the strategic vision.[18] The theoretical implication is an understanding of how strategic leaders lead and create tangible solutions in a dynamic VUCA context.

Adaptive Leadership Theory

There is general agreement among researchers that adaptive leadership is radically different to traditional leadership practices. Traditional leadership frameworks within a complex and uncertain environment are proven to be ineffective when responding to the chaos associated with an organisational crisis.[19, 20] Nonetheless, adaptive leadership theory is "the activity of mobilizing people to tackle challenges and thrive."[21] An adaptive leadership framework challenges leaders to think differently about wicked organisational problems amid uncertainty and chaos. Strategic leaders adapt to a set of circumstances with little information, but also respond rapidly by creating innovative solutions to organisational problems in a fluid operational context.[22] Moreover, the adaptive leadership framework posits that for organisations to thrive in a fluid environment, strategic leaders must create learning organisations and communities with deep critical thinking ability toward analysing problems, taking calculated risks, and making decisions. That said, the lens of strategic leaders needs to have the courage, even while taking the heat along the way, to embrace failure. In other words, adaptive leadership frameworks promote the leader's strategic agility to not only deepen their organisational dynamic capabilities and build high-performance teams, but to also drive rapid results by leading their organisation into an unknown future.[23]

PERSPECTIVE

There is a plethora of literature that argues for an emerging paradigm shift with new ways of thinking about leadership approaches amid the organisational challenges in a VUCA context. It is important to note that uncertain, complex, and volatile events

---

17 Uhl-Bien, et al., 2008.
18 Codreanu, 2016.
19 Codreanu, 2016.
20 Heifetz, Grashow & Linsky, 2009.
21 Heifetz & Linsky, 2011: 26.
22 Glover, Jones & Friedman, 2002.
23 Heifetz et al., 2009.

frequently disrupt the status quo and require transformational change. This disruption is particularly true when leaders lack information to make sound decisions and rely on internal and external networks to disentangle the chaos and find a way forward. In fact, the absence of leadership during uncertain, complex, and unpredictable times drives chaos, instability, and volatility in the environment. That said, Ikenberry[24] argued that "if there is one complaint in politics around the world today, it is about the absence of 'leadership' – local, national, global ... no country or national leader seems to be articulating visions of the global leader." The reason is that global and national leaders are unable to disentangle and strategically navigate through the increasingly interconnected, as well as the frequently turbulent, political and economic environment. Thus, the amount of adult leadership requires new knowledge, skills, and competencies to operate in a VUCA world. In the article, *We Need More Mature Leaders*, Davis[25] argued that:

> "In the past few months we've seen [childish attitudes] reflected in the halls of government and corporate boardrooms across the country. Arrogance, pouting, tantrums, personal attacks, and betrayal of trust seem to be the order of the day... [in the international environment]demonstrate the kind of sandbox leadership that is all to prevalent right now. The timing could not be worse. The nation's current problems, vast and overwhelming as they are, appear secondary to the whims of spoiled children, unwilling to play well together. At a time when we need solid, grounded leadership more than ever we seem to be in short supply of adults who act like, well ... adults."

Leaders must give up the illusion of command and control, as well as accept the comfort of being uncomfortable in this chaotic environment. The illusion of predictability in a global context is unattainable within a fluid and complex institutional and organisational environment. In real terms, the pervasiveness of Machiavellian leaders in the present environment has produced a global deficit of adult leadership.[26]

As traditional leadership models focus on individual leaders' characteristics and the leader/follower relationship, they lack the attention to navigate within an unpredictable, ambiguous, and complex environment. Traditional leadership models with predictive decision-making outcomes, such as transactional, transformational, contingency theory, do not adequately address the leadership challenges in an unpredictable VUCA environment. Scholars suggest that, "with the increasingly global environment, leaders are exposed to many complex challenges and what we know about leadership theory and

---

24 Ikenberry, 2001: 387.

25 Davis, 2011: 3.

26 Rayment & Smith, 2011.

development may no longer be effective in this global context."[27] Therefore, traditional leadership models such as transactional, transformational, leader-member exchange, and situational and contingency leadership (where strategic and organisational leaders use command and control measures to leverage follower commitment through positional, personal or coercive power), are no longer effective within a VUCA context. For example, the emergence of applying artificial intelligence into socio-economic, security, financial and other professions is creating organisational chaos, uncertainty, and turbulence within transnational institutions and organisations. Christopher D. Kolenda[28] argued that, "while the technologies have changed, the very human dimension of leadership has remained constant." Rayment and Smith[29] stated that, "with globalization and related developments such as information technology, the complexity, speed, and expectations placed on the leadership role have multiplied to such an extent that it may now be becoming almost impossible for humans to perform a leadership role." Traditional leadership application models are thus no longer sufficient to address the fluidity and unpredictability of an organisational crisis.

Researchers argue that "our world is changing so rapidly that the models for interaction that we've developed over thousands of years of civilization are no longer helpful they cloud our perception of what is needed now."[30] Today's global challenges are dynamic and often unclear, contradictory, and duplicative. Many researchers hold the view that thought leadership will require breaking old leadership paradigms and adopting new leadership constructs, skills, and mental models. First, scholar-practitioners note that future Leadership and Learning Development (LLD) initiatives must develop a leader ability to strategically think outside the box, embrace innovative fresh ideas and accept a new way of performing routine tasks, lead through collaboration and influence, and possess the emotional intelligence to think with clarity in times of chaos/crisis/turbulence.[31] Second, strategic and organisational leaders will require additive competencies such as strategic foresight to detect the emergence of conflicting patterns, navigate through organisational chaos, and have the agility and adaptability to influence the direction of outcomes from uncertain events. Third, strategic leaders need the ability to manage the unexpected, navigate through the complex competing demands among internal and external stakeholders, and resign command and control over events. Finally, organisational strategic planning documents are composed of defined operations, actions, and activities enabling tactical, organisational, and strategic leaders to guide structural actions toward accomplishing pre-defined outcomes. From transnational institutions to corporate organizations, strategic leaders must understand

---

27 Van Zyl & Campbell, 2019: 375.
28 Kolenda, 2001: 4.
29 Rayment & Smith, 2011: 149.
30 Steeffen, Trevenna & Rappaport, 2019: 185.
31 Kok & Van den Heuvel, 2019.

that by the time strategic planning development is completed in a rapidly changing and fluid environment, the strategic document is obsolete. Thus, new ways and means of strategic planning and leading are needed. These examples support that new transformational leadership approaches are required in an unpredictable VUCA environment.[32]

In a fluid environment, transformational change within an organisation remains the strategic leader's responsibility. To put it another way, the organisational leader's responsibility is to explain how transformational change will develop and resolve organisational issues during the midst of uncertainty and chaos. Above all, transformational change is a complex and ambiguous process. The reason is that organisations do not change, but rather that people change. Therefore, leading transformational change needs leaders with the emotional intelligence to lead themselves amid organisational chaos and the agility to adapt within an ambiguous environment. Leadership is an activity and not a person, and that leadership can be exercised by anyone, whatever their role within or external to an organisation. That said, strategic and organisational leaders must give up the illusion of dictating change from the top-down and accept that transformational change is derived from the bottom up. Nonetheless, strategic and organisational leaders must understand that the VUCA environment allows for few errors, as past success does not guarantee future success. Pearse's[33] article, *5 Reasons Why Leadership Is In Crisis*, and Smith's[34] article, *Why Leadership Sucks*, offer the following reasons for why leaders struggle to make a transformative organisational change in a fluid, uncertain, chaotic, and unpredictable context:

- *Outcomes Focused, rather than Cause Focused*: A failure to focus on the internal factors of an enterprise will come at a detriment to the outcome. Among complex VUCA systems, leaders can only control predictability within a range of parameters. With endless opportunities for uncertainty, a leader will fail if he/she attempts to predict outcomes given tremendous variability.
- *Leaders Treat Organisations like Machines to Which They are Not*: It is a mythical belief to attempt to do so, especially among the current VUCA environment. Because the current industrial climate is the antithesis of order and predictability, leaders cannot lead linearly and expect to succeed in a complex system. Rather, they must foster a non-linear and non-deterministic dimension to their organisations.
- *Failure of Leaders to see beyond Ego, Vanity, and Arrogance*: This translates reciprocally to exuding a lack of empathy and compassion. This commonly

---

32 Cashman, 2014.

33 Pearse, 2018.

34 Smith, 2012.

occurs as a result of having leaders considered "experts." When anyone generates challenge crises or threat responses often kick in, and existentially the response is portrayed as arrogant due to the leader's feeling of threat.

- **Lack of Self-Awareness**: This pitfall entails being unaware and not present in the moment, or a leader's own personal beliefs, attitudes, feelings, and emotions that command responses. It is suggested that daily meditation helps keep all individuals, leaders included, present and promoting intelligent, decision-making vice conditioned reactions.
- **Meaningless Achievement:** This speaks to a lack of a work-life balance. Perhaps the adoption of a paradigm is needed to change the old adage that more work equals success, and more time at work equals increased productivity. Conversely, achieving and maintaining a balanced work/life situation has been studied and associated with a more meaningful and fulfilling life, thus becoming an addition to physical and mental wellbeing.

For present and future leaders to succeed in a VUCA environment, strategic and organisational leaders must have the ability to impact the operational environment through personal influence, emotional intelligence, and adaptability. Some researchers believe that the style of leadership of strategic and organisational leaders influences not only the organisational culture in a VUCA context, but also the ability to effectively manage the unexpected. Additionally, leaders with a balance of hard skills and soft skills within a VUCA environment are transformational change agents.[35] The recognition of the importance for current and emerging leaders in a VUCA environment to critically think through the organisational chaos, by acknowledging assumptions, evaluating arguments and drawing conclusions, will require leaders to strategically and creatively think through organisational chaos with clarity. This will require leaders to develop mental flexibility, intellectual curiosity, and intuition for sensemaking. Therefore, the challenge of an individual leading in a VUCA setting will require new ways of applying leadership approaches, briefly identified below, as well as through use of the additive competencies presented and discussed in succeeding chapters:

- **Accountability and Trust**
  - Takes ownership and pride in his/her work and supports others when they make tough choices that are consistent with the organisation's objective.
  - Highly effective at successfully delivering key outcomes in a matrixed environment.
- **Analytical and Inquisitive**
  - Challenges conventional thinking and practical constraints when developing ideas that translate into business results.

---

35 Mendenhall et al., 2018.

- o Integrates facts and data to support decisions from a variety of data sources (internal, external, benchmarking, and best practices).
- o Applies strategic thinking and good judgement when looking for opportunities to innovate.
- **Transparency, Candour, and Openness**
  - o Shares information and ideas across the organisation (upward, downward, and laterally) encouraging learning and shared success.
  - o Communicates both internally and externally to keep others informed, sharing as much information as possible with those affected.
- **Collaborative and Team Player**
  - o Models active listening and cooperative behaviour.
  - o Empowers a high-performing work team by building partnerships and embracing constructive tension to ensure that the best ideas surface.
  - o Encourages integration and cross-functional problem solving to break down silos.
  - o Viewed as a team player.
- **Develops Self-awareness**
  - o Sets high standards for themselves and others to drive results and foster growth.
  - o Models and encourages others' agility to pivot on key organisational or strategy shifts.
  - o Demonstrates initiative to solve problems and launch new projects.

The prevalence of volatile, uncertain, complex, and ambiguous environments produces an organisational chaos that is a gift to current and emerging leaders. These are challenging times with rapidly changing socio-political and economic conditions for strategic and organisational leaders to achieve organisational success. Some leadership scholar-practitioners view that the true test of an effective leader rests with how they handle an organisational crisis; an element of a leader's deepest character is revealed during a highly charged event. In a VUCA context, an organisational crisis can quickly expose a leader's hidden strengths and core weaknesses. It can show the world if the leader has what it takes to function effectively when the heat is on. Will the leader address the crisis head-on, take those actions needed to fix it, and, if appropriate, take responsibility for the crisis? Will the leader freeze, or worse, claim to be a victim and pass off the responsibility to others? What can and should a leader do to find out what went wrong and to ensure it does not happen again? The gift of organisational chaos provides opportunities for the leader not only to develop a broad set of new competencies to think critically, but to also create and test innovative solutions to complex problems and act strategically in a VUCA environment. Essentially, as organisational leaders prepare for new crises produced within a VUCA setting, we need leaders who can learn from their own and others' experiences, adapt to an unstable environment, and strategically forecast future challenges instead of operating in a reactive mode.

CONCLUDING REMARKS

The world that transnational institutions and business organisations operate in is swiftly changing due to global competition, technological innovation, and socio-political disruption. As a result, the challenge for strategic and operational leaders is how to lead in an ever-changing and fluid environment. Leading change in an environment of chaos and disruption is one of the most difficult leadership challenges, if not the most difficult, at the strategic and organisational levels. This chapter presented a conceptual analysis that explored the challenges leaders experience in a volatile, uncertain, complex, and ambiguous environment. Second, a brief theoretical analysis discussed chaos theory, change leadership theory, complex leadership theory, and adaptive leadership theory as proposed frameworks for leading within a VUCA context. Finally, a leadership paradigm shift where past leadership models do not equate to future leadership effectiveness in a VUCA context was described. The exploration of traditional command and control leadership models to provide different perspectives on new and different capabilities for strategic and organisational leaders were also addressed.

In Chapter 2, the solutions to volatility (vision), uncertainty (understanding), complexity (clarity) and ambiguity (adaptability) are discussed.[36] The succeeding chapters will not only address ongoing leadership challenges, but will also explore new ways of leading strategically and organisationally in an uncertain and complex environment.

---

36 Codreanu, 2016.

CHAPTER 2

PERSPECTIVES OF LEADING ONESELF IN VOLATILE, UNCERTAIN, COMPLEX, AND AMBIGUOUS ENVIRONMENTS

Ebben van Zyl

ABSTRACT

The purpose of this chapter is to introduce the concept of "leading oneself" as an important element of leadership in a VUCA world. Crises and new demands (e.g., the coronavirus pandemic) necessitate a new look at how leadership can be improved. The leadership styles of the young and successful world leaders of today are discussed in this chapter as a way to understand how leaders are dealing with the challenges of our time. Current successful world leaders are focusing on giving direction and meaning to their decisions. It is clear that, in the process of giving direction and meaning to decisions, commonality and cohesion should be fostered. This can only be achieved by accommodating the needs of people, which, in turn, requires us to be inclusive, approachable, supportive, transparent, agile/adaptable, empathetic and sensitive towards different needs. The aforementioned might be viewed as a humane-oriented leadership approach. Leading oneself as part of the humane-oriented leadership approach seems to be relevant in our current world. Future leadership developments should emphasise the way in which the quality and availability of humanism can be improved in general. Leading oneself is an important concept as part of the improvement and implementation of the humane-oriented leadership approach. Leading oneself will help leaders to be more effective, which, in turn, will help them lead others.

INTRODUCTION

The leadership strategies of the last 50 years focused on the traits of a good leader and areas of development for leaders to become successful.[1] In the field of leadership, many heroic leaders have been hailed as examples of how to command and inspire organisations and communities. However, in the last 15 years, this approach has become less effective because of new challenges and the lack of appropriate abilities among these heroic leaders to deal with new demands.[2]

Some of the new demands include:
- information overload;
- the dissolving of traditional organisational boundaries;
- new technologies that disrupt old work practices;
- different values and expectations of new generations entering the workplace; and
- increased globalisation creating the need to lead across cultures.[3]

Recently, due to the coronavirus pandemic, countries (and companies) have experienced lockdowns. This necessitated new perspectives of leading oneself in volatile, uncertain, complex, and ambiguous (VUCA) environments.

According to Ledbetter[4], our environment is characterised by rapid change, threats to peace, complexity, uncertainty, and new high-tech, autonomous work roles in the information age. In the business environment, companies continuously have to adapt the products and services they offer, as well as the way they produce, promote and sell these products and services.[5] Companies are desperately trying to be proactive by re-imagining the future and continuously developing new products and services. In the public sector, similar challenges are forcing governments to do more with less.[6] In addition, the ageing population and depletion of natural resources are challenges that governments grapple with daily.[7] The demand for more, better and sustainable services is rising, and places a heavy burden on the shoulders of some public officials to steer clear of corruption and act ethically and professionally.

The academic sector has not been spared from turmoil. In 2016, South African universities saw the rise of the Fees Must Fall protest movement. Classes, tests and examinations were disrupted, which brought a sudden change to the way students

---

1   Petrie, 2014: 7.
2   Van Zyl & Campbell, 2019: 34.
3   Van Zyl & Campbell, 2019: 35.
4   Ledbetter, 2012: 12.
5   Gruwez, 2017: 9.
6   Lues, 2019: 157.
7   Lues, 2016: 298.

were to be trained and evaluated. Innovative ways of presenting classes and assessing students were implemented, and online training and evaluation methods were introduced – all of which contributed to changing the academic sector into a volatile and ambiguous environment.

Apart from VUCA business, academic and public sectors, the global environment is characterised by regional instability and ambiguity, failed states, increased weapons proliferation, and global terrorism, which require greater global leadership.[8] Amaladas and Byrne[9] indicated that, in the last few years, combat fatalities have risen. These mainly occur in civil wars and are often intensified by external interventions supporting different sides. The Middle East has been the primary locations of these wars.

Researchers argue that, in an increasingly VUCA world, people are working longer hours[10], giving rise to conflict and bad relationships, with detrimental effects on their health and relationships in general. There are many reasons for conflict in organisations. Factors such as division of labour, functional dependence, decision-making styles, limited resources, new specialisations, communications systems, and organisational size have all been shown to cause conflict.[11] In addition, more and more people are tending to become depressed and anxious.[12] For example, in South Africa, 62% of employees indicated in a study that they experience stress-related health problems.[13]

Given the abovementioned challenges, there is no doubt that leaders should look at ways to improve leadership. In this chapter, the leadership styles of Emmanuel Macron, Jacinda Ardern and Sophie Wilmes will be discussed as a way to understand how young, successful leaders are dealing with the demands of our current world. From this discussion, a few perspectives will be shared, after which leading oneself as part of leadership in a VUCA environment will be discussed. The chapter will end by focusing on the relevance of leading oneself in 21st century environments and sharing some concluding thoughts.

---

8   Campbell, 2018: 2.
9   Amaladas & Byrne, 2018: 2.
10 Gruwez, 2017: 12.
11 Campbell, 2018: 149.
12 Van Zyl, 2013: 62.
13 Nel & Van Zyl, 2017: 13

CAPABILITIES OF MODERN WORLD LEADERS IN A VUCA WORLD

Emmanuel Macron

Emmanuel Jean-Michel Frederic Macron (born 21 December 1977) is a French politician who has been the President of France since May 2017.

Macron's ideology stands for cohesion and commonality. His decisive stance against all forms of nationalism and isolationism sets a good example and shows the right way forward. Macron believes that no state on its own can successfully meet the challenges of a globalised and VUCA world (e.g., dealing with the coronavirus pandemic). For Macron, the key to sovereignty lies in European cooperation and in a unified Europe that:

- ensures security in all its dimensions – in defence, in the fight against terrorism, and civil defence;
- reacts to the challenge of migration, with common protection of borders, a European asylum office and a common integration programme;
- focuses its foreign policy primarily on the Mediterranean region and a new partnership with Africa;
- champions sustainable developments in energy and environmental policies;
- does not simply acquiesce to the digital revolution, but takes the lead in shaping it; and
- in the Eurozone as the centre of Europe's economic strength, stabilises through national reforms, as well as through coordination of economic policies and a common budget.[14]

Macron realised that uncertainty and change would be part of his term as a leader and that he would have to adapt accordingly. Furthermore, he knows that he cannot accomplish goals on his own. He stated:

> "And that is exactly the goal I have set for myself: to try and encourage French people to change and to develop further. But that can only be done as a collective, with one another (including myself, who is willing to learn from mistakes). You have to bundle the strength of those who want to take that step."[15]

During the coronavirus pandemic, which is still raging at the time of writing this chapter, Macron continues to give direction and meaning in his country. He does

---

14 Momtaz, 2020: 3.

15 Ibid.

this by making, and explaining, his critical decisions, which are based on constantly evolving data on a virus which the world's leading scientists are still struggling to fully understand.[16]

Jacinda Ardern

Jacinda Kate Laurell Ardern (born 26 July 1980) is a New Zealand politician, who has been serving as the 40th prime minister of New Zealand since 26 October 2017.

Ardern stands for optimism, empathy, kindness, inclusion, approachability and collaboration in order to achieve a goal. On Friday 15 March 2019, 50 people were shot and killed during prayers at two mosques in central Christchurch. Ardern acted immediately by offering emotional and financial support to families of the victims, in their native languages. A week after the attack, the lunchtime call to prayer was broadcast nationally, followed by a two-minute silence. She also personally approached the families of the victims and empathised with them, using phrases like "they are us" when referring to the dead and wounded. Her focus was on being approachable, showing empathy, helping where she could and encouraging all citizens to do the same.[17]

Early in the coronavirus pandemic, Ardern asked the citizens of New Zealand to stay at home (giving direction) and explained why they should stay at home (giving meaning).[18]

Sophie Wilmes

Sophie Wilmes (born 15 January 1975) is a Belgian politician who currently serves as the prime minister of Belgium. She is the first female head of the government of Belgium.

Wilmes is regarded as a person with high emotional intelligence who is always looking beyond herself to improve lives in a transparent way. She has proven her transparency by regularly answering questions on the coronavirus and on how government is addressing the crisis.[19] She is sensitive to societal problems in the broadest sense: family life, work-life balance, gender equality, education, sports, and support for the sick and elderly. She believes in cohesion and the unity of her country and its different communities, and cherishes linguistic and cultural diversity, as well as the right to be respected. She advocates for a society where people can develop fully and freely. According to her, agility and adaptability amid unexpected events are highly valued attributes which can contribute to a successful nation.[20]

---

16 Momtaz, 2020: 3.
17 Wilson, 2020: 3.
18 Ibid.
19 Rankin, 2020: 2.
20 Rankin, 2020: 2.

Wilmes persuaded Belgian political parties to put aside differences in their fight against the coronavirus. She then announced the closure of schools, bars and restaurants, and banned weekend shopping, except for necessities such as food and medicine. She explained why she made this decision, giving meaning to her actions.[21]

PERSPECTIVE

From the above discussion of how three young, successful world leaders approach challenges, some observations can be made. It is clear that Macron believes in commonality and cohesion in his leadership approach. By being adaptable and considering the viewpoints and needs of all stakeholders, he believes his demands can be met. Jacinda Ardern also emphasises cohesion and commonality in her leadership approach, but focuses on being approachable, kind, empathetic and supportive in her aim to achieve cohesion and commonality. Similarly, Wilmes believes in commonality and cohesion among different communities, as well as cultural and linguistic groups, and advocates the practising of transparency, emotional intelligence, sensitivity and agility in order to reach goals. All three leaders attempt to give direction and meaning to their decisions.

Clearly, in the process of giving direction and meaning to decisions, commonality and cohesion should be fostered. This can only be achieved by accommodating the needs of people, which requires people to be inclusive, approachable, supportive, transparent, agile/adaptable to different needs, empathetic and sensitive. The aforementioned might indicate a humane-oriented leadership approach.

According to Graig and Snook[22], leaders can adapt to difficult changes by improving the human element in the way leadership is practised. In humane-oriented leadership the emphasis is on being supportive, considerate, empathetic, sensitive, compassionate and generous.[23] Van Zyl and Campbell[24] indicated that the first step in implementing a humane-oriented leadership approach is leading oneself. By leading oneself and focusing on self-awareness and self-influencing behaviour, leaders will be able to understand their behavioural preferences, manage their emotions, be able to adapt to the unexpected, and be keenly aware of the need to create and sustain interpersonal relations by means of support, sensitivity, transparency, good communication, consideration and generosity.[25]

---

21 Ibid.
22 Graig & Snook, 2014: 22.
23 Booysen, 2016: 365 in Veldsman & Johnson, 2016: 365.
24 Van Zyl & Campbell, 2019: 36.
25 Graig & Snook, 2014: 22.

Manz and Sims[26] argued that leaders should first be able to lead themselves before they can lead others. Leading oneself means, inter alia, knowing oneself, knowing one's strong and not-so-strong points, and developing oneself. Van Zyl and Campbell[27] contended that leading oneself is part of the self-influencing approach of leadership. Houghton and Yoho[28], as well as Van Zyl[29], called for modern leadership approaches to put greater emphasis on leading oneself and the self-influencing processes of leadership. Similarly, Amaladas and Byrne[30] argued that modern leaders should first know and influence themselves before they attempt to influence others. One way to influence ourselves is to transform inner blockages into peace and good relations.[31] Manz and Sims[32] added that true leadership comes mainly from within a person, not from outside.

LEADING ONESELF AS AN IMPORTANT ELEMENT OF LEADERSHIP IN A VUCA ENVIRONMENT

Self-influence approach to leadership

With the self-influence approach to leadership, the focus is on self-influencing processes rather than hierarchical control processes.[33] Self-observation, self-management, and relational observation/mastery are also important.[34] In the self-influence approach, the modelling of self-leadership behaviour is emphasised to enable subordinates to learn the behaviour.[35] In contrast to the directive leadership approach, where objectives are set for subordinates, participative objective setting is encouraged in the self-influencing approach. In other words, subordinates should establish and try to achieve their own objectives.[36]

According to the Canadian College of Health Leaders[37], the self-influencing approach to leadership recognises that leadership needs to be enacted on all organisational levels. Since leadership is no longer focused solely at the top of the

---

26 Manz & Sims, 2001: 4.
27 Van Zyl & Campbell, 2019: 38.
28 Houghton & Yoho, 2006: 68.
29 Van Zyl, 2016: 92.
30 Amaladas & Byrne, 2018: 213.
31 Ibid.
32 Manz & Sims, 2001: 4.
33 Van Zyl & Campbell, 2019: 34.
34 Houghton & Yoho, 2006: 69; Van Zyl, 2016: 91.
35 Elloy, 2004: 122.
36 Van Zyl, 2013: 67.
37 Canadian College of Health Leaders, 2010: 6.

organisation, it becomes imperative to hold management at all levels accountable for the development of employees. This ensures leadership bench strength and creates a culture of growth and development that is more holistic and less hierarchical.[38]

The self-influence approach to leadership involves high levels of commitment, independent behaviour, and creativity and empowerment.[39] According to Manz and Sims[40], the outcomes of the self-influencing approach to leadership include: high long-term performance, short-term confusion/frustration, high follower self-confidence, high follower development, very high flexibility, high innovation, the ability to work in the absence of a leader, and improved teamwork.

Leaders with high emotional awareness tend to have a greater sense of self-worth and capabilities.[41] They take the time to quietly reflect rather than to act impulsively. They strive to understand their emotional reactions and trigger points, continuously monitor their emotional states, and leverage positive feelings to drive their motivation and actions.

LEADING ONESELF AS AN IMPORTANT BUILDING BLOCK OF THE SELF-INFLUENCING APPROACH TO LEADERSHIP

The starting point of the self-influencing approach to leadership is leading oneself.[42] To lead oneself is to focus on self-awareness and self-management. Self-awareness includes competencies such as awareness, accurate self-assessment, and self-confidence, whereas self-management includes self-control, transparency, adaptability, optimism, and resilience.[43]

Van Zyl and Campbell[44] described self-awareness as a focus on one's assumptions, values, principles, strengths, and limitations and on how this awareness contributes to peacefulness. Thus, before people can attain or maintain good interpersonal relations, they must first know and experience peace within themselves. Self-awareness requires one to listen effectively to internal dialogue through introspection and defeating non-productive emotions and attitudes. Self-awareness also helps us to observe our responses to activities and work relationships, to determine which activities are motivating, and to focus on improving our weaknesses.[45]

---

38 Canadian College of Health Leaders, 2010: 7.

39 Van Zyl, 2013: 62, 66.

40 Manz & Sims, 2001: 47.

41 Canadian College of Health Leaders, 2010: 6.

42 Livermore, 2010: 18.

43 Goleman, 1995: 13.

44 Van Zyl & Campbell, 2019: 23.

45 Ibid.

Once an individual has reached a reasonable level of self-awareness, it is only natural to move forward and deepen peace leadership practices, thoughts, attitudes and behaviours to the point of mastery (self-management). At this point, one's level of self-awareness might be high enough to know the way forward to self-management.[46]

According to Verwey, Miriam and Mooney[47], leaders who can lead themselves are emotionally intelligent. Those leaders probably:

- monitor their moods through self-awareness;
- change themselves for the better through self-management;
- understand their impact through empathy; and
- act in ways that boost others' moods through relationship management.

OTHER THEORIES CONTRIBUTING TO THE CONCEPT OF LEADING ONESELF

Self-control theory[48]

People practise self-control when they engage in behaviours designed to counteract or override a predominant response (e.g., behavioural tendencies, an emotion, or a motivation).[49] Practising self-control means that people modify their response tendencies in a way that suppresses one goal in order to pursue another goal that is considered to be more valuable long term.[50] Self-control might rely on methods that are used for self-regulation[51], and may also be associated with transparency, resilience, and self-goalsetting.[52] On the other hand, self-control can be related to uncertainty. For instance, emotional self-control can help to manage feelings of uncertainty by shining light on future goals.[53]

Self-management theory[54]

Self-management theory provides a set of strategies for managing the behaviour intended to reduce deviations from existing standards determined by higher-level

---

46 Van Zyl & Campbell, 2019: 24.

47 Verwey, Minaar & Mooney, 2016 in Veldsman & Johnson, 2016: 356.

48 Kerr & Jermier, 1978: 18.

49 Akwa-Nde, 2015: 44.

50 Ibid.

51 McCullough & Willoughby, 2009: 73.

52 Joosten, Van Dijke, Van Hiel & De Cremer, 2014: 7.

53 Akwa-Nde, 2015: 44.

54 Kerr & Jermier, 1978: 378.

controls.[55] This entails the practice of choosing a less attractive option which might lead to a more desirable behaviour from among alternatives.[56] Self-management may be associated with effectiveness, problem solving, flexibility, calmness, reliability, as well as fairness and self-determination.[57] Self-management may counteract the challenges in a complex and uncertain world by helping the individual to solve problems and create calmness, etc.[58]

Self-regulation theory[59]

Self-regulation theory states that human behaviour is regulated by triggers in the environment, which monitor performance to reduce the discrepancy between actual performance levels and goals.[60] According to Van Zyl[61], individuals who believe in their own abilities anticipate probable consequences of prospective actions. They set objectives and make an effort to gain desired outcomes. In general, self-regulation allows individuals to be motivated and guides their actions in an anticipatory way.[62] Self-regulation theory may be associated with autonomy, empathy, self-efficacy, and self-control.[63] Self-regulation as a component of emotional intelligence may help people regulate their feelings in times of uncertainty and fear.[64]

Intrinsic motivation theory[65]

Intrinsic motivation theory suggests that individuals have the potential to harness motivational forces within themselves by performing activities that they can enjoy. Intrinsic motivation leads to an increase in feelings of competence, self-determination, self-esteem, self-enhancement, purpose, stillness, and calmness.[66] This view implies that satisfaction is obtained from having an opportunity to act with purpose, increased feelings of competence, and self-determination.[67] The intrinsic motivation which relates to a person's internal values could be helpful in uncertain and complex situations.

---

55 Mokuoane, 2014: 64.

56 Ibid.

57 Neck & Manz, 2010: 12.

58 Ibid.

59 Carver & Scheier, 1981: 22.

60 Mokuoane, 2014: 64.

61 Van Zyl, 2009: 24.

62 Neck & Manz, 2010: 12.

63 Neck & Manz, 2010: 12.

64 Ibid.

65 Deci & Ryan, 1985: 28.

66 Houghton & Neck, 2006: 675.

67 Ibid.

These values could give certainty and direction towards achieving positive results.[68]

Social cognitive theory[69]

Social cognitive theory claims that the self-referent thoughts of individuals mediate between their knowledge and actions.[70] Bandura[71] stated that human functioning is a consequence of the interaction between the environment, individuals and behaviour. That is, human behaviour is not only influenced by knowledge, skills and abilities, but also by beliefs that individuals have about their abilities and the outcome of their efforts based on their analyses of environment, individuals and behaviour.[72] Social cognitive theory involves four elements, namely observational learning, outcome expectation, self-efficacy, and goal setting, of which self-efficacy is the most central.[73] Self-efficacy can influence strategies like goal setting, positive thought patterns, determination, and flexibility.[74] Positive thought patterns, clear goalsetting, and determination to succeed are crucial in navigating uncertain and complex environments.

Self-leadership theory[75]

Self-leadership occurs when teams and individuals perceive a situation and choose to behave in a way that aligns their actions with standards. These standards will also monitor their activities and cognitions to encourage the desired behaviour to assess how the behaviour influences the situation.[76] Typical self-leadership strategies include self-observation, self-reward, self-punishment, management of cues, natural reward strategies, and constructive thought patterns (e.g., positive self-talk and visualising successful performance outcomes).[77] Self-leadership may be an effective strategy in uncertain and complex environments due to its correlation with positive and constructive thinking, feelings, and actions.[78]

---

68 Ibid.
69 Bandura, 1991: 249.
70 Mokuoane, 2014: 64.
71 Bandura, 1991: 249.
72 Houghton & Neck, 2006: 673.
73 Petrie, 2014: 12.
74 Ibid.
75 Manz, 1986: 12.
76 Akwa-Nde, 2015: 44.
77 Ibid.
78 Ibid.

A FEW EXAMPLES OF LEADING ONESELF SKILLS IN VUCA ENVIRONMENTS

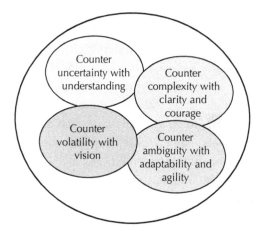

Figure 1.1: Examples of leading oneself skills in VUCA environments

Figure 1.1 provides examples of how VUCA environments can be countered by leading oneself skills, such as adaptability/agility, understanding, clarity and setting a clear vision.

Countering uncertainty with understanding

To create an organisational vision, strategic leaders must understand the uncertainty that derives from the unfamiliar tasks and unanticipated consequences associated with rapid technological change. This is particularly relevant to organisational initiatives in a VUCA environment. Bolman and Deal[79] argued that understanding how to strategically navigate within an uncertain, unpredictable, and chaotic environment is a required skill for future leaders. Strategic leaders need to understand the challenges which organisational leaders face in managing multiple projects with uncertain outcomes in a fast-paced environment. To countering an uncertain and unpredictable environment, leaders need to understand the critical role of fostering and managing strategic interconnective networks, not only up, down, and across organisational units, but also among key external stakeholders. The reason is that strategic and organisational leaders need insight into their organisation's dynamic capabilities to meta-strategically leverage its strengths and minimise its weaknesses. This enables the strategic leader to gain a competitive advantage within an uncertain and rapidly changing environment.[80]

---

79 Bolman & Deal, 2008.

80 Ibid.

In essence, strategic leaders need to understand the complexities of, and ways in which to manage, organisational problems in an unpredictable environment.

Countering complexity with clarity and courage

During an organisational crisis, it is often difficult, amid the globalisation of technological innovation, to try to disentangle the stream of interconnections and interdependencies into a singular decision-making pathway. Obolensky[81] defined "complexity" as "many interconnecting parts each affecting each other in an open interactive and iterative process which cannot be controlled or fully predicted." Mendenhall, Osland, Bird, Oddou, Maznevski, Stevens and Stahl[82] noted that "interdependencies generate complexity in that global leaders must be able to attend to, and manage, more complex systems of human and technological interaction compared to domestic leaders." Given the complexity of managing an organisational crisis, leaders bring order to chaos by not only creating clarity of purpose, but also by clearly articulating a tangible vision down to the lowest organisational level. No matter the level within the organisation, the greater the uncertainty, the greater the complexity for its leaders to navigate through the chaos. Thus, individuals in environments with high uncertainty and complexity need leaders with high emotional intelligence to help them stay calm and focused, and help them operate with courage and clarity.

According to Obolensky[83], "clarity means that everyone in the organisation understands the overall big-picture strategy and how they fit within it." Given the rapid changes from uncontrollable events, leaders can no longer afford to casually disseminate information in the organisation. Political, economic, and academic leaders must have clarity of purpose when disseminating information from executive leadership to the lowest-level employee. For a company to survive and thrive in an uncertain and complex environment, a strategic leader needs organisational units with followers to not only navigate through the chaos with clarity of purpose, but to have the courage to go against conventional wisdom and adapt quickly to changes.[84]

Leading globalised organisations is complicated and complex. Leadership scholar-practitioners recently recognised that traditional leadership strategies might no longer apply and that new leadership approaches are required to resolve complex organisational challenges. Moreover, conventional wisdom in applying emergent leadership approaches might not be highly endorsed by senior organisational leaders. It is imperative that emergent leadership methods be a mixture of change management strategies not only aligned with business strategies and measure of performance, but

---

81 Obolensky, 2010: 1.

82 Mendenhall, Osland, Bird, Oddou, Maznevski, Stevens & Stahl, 2018: 21.

83 Obolensky, 2010: 30.

84 Kok & Van den Heuvel, 2019: 33; Mendenhall et al., 2018.

also supported by servant leadership strategies. Organisations that lack clarity and strategic alignment frequently become disjointed and need leaders with the courage to disregard organisational politics and think outside the box.[85] In essence, breaking through the complexity dilemma requires courageous leaders with clarity of purpose and transparent communication, rather than leaders who create doubt and are led by their ego. Leaders need to make decisions based on clarity as opposed to certainty.

Countering ambiguity with adaptability and agility

Scholars like Kok and Van den Heuvel[86] have noted that ambiguity is an inherent by-product of a VUCA atmosphere. Adaptive and agile leaders are change agents in a VUCA environment. The leaders of institutions and organisations are flexible, agile, and adaptive in times of uncertainty and ambiguity when there are no clear solutions to organisational challenges. Jordaan[87] stated that "for organizations to survive and thrive in this environment, they need to become more 'agile' or adaptive." During times of organisational chaos, an adaptive or agile leader can rapidly disentangle, anticipate, and isolate the core problem, while strategising innovative approaches towards accomplishing institutional and organisational outcomes. According to Heifetz, Grashow and Linsky[88], "adaptive leadership is the practice of mobilizing people to tackle tough challenges and thrive." In addition, in a fluid environment, an adaptive leader understands that decisional actions frequently do not produce certainty and predictability.[89] For this reason, adaptive leaders need to not only think beyond the status quo, but must accept not knowing the right questions to ask or the answers to solve organisational problems. Moreover, effective agile leaders give up situational control, develop trust-building relationships, and push information and decision making down to the lowest level of the organisation. Heifetz et al.[90] argued that in the new global environment in which we interact with each other, we must focus on the need to embrace uncertainty rather than maintain tight control; focus on the need for adaptiveness over efficiency; focus on the need to collaborate and share ideas rather than to keep secrets; and lastly focus on the need for new tools and maps to help visualise the terrain we are attempting to navigate.

---

85 Ibid.
86 Kok & Van den Heuvel, 2019: 33.
87 Jordaan, 2019: 59.
88 Heifetz, Grashow & Linsky, 2009: 2.
89 Ibid.
90 Heifetz et al., 2009.

The seminal book by Bill Joiner and Stephen Josephs[91], *Leadership Agility*, presents the Agile Leadership Model. The model has three levels and serves as a framework for leaders to navigate through ambiguous situations. Joiner and Josephs[92] viewed the expert level as more of a tactical level, which focuses on task completion and measure of performance. The achiever level of an agile leader focuses on implementing a strategy with the aim to bring the vision into reality. Finally, the catalyst level of an agile leader sets the organisational vision and capacity building, pushes information down the organisation to provide direction, and generates ideas and opportunities to maximise competitive advantage. In this model, each level plays a role in disentangling and bringing clarity to interdependencies, in making meaning in order to bring about change, and in creating an adaptive environment which can thrive amid chaos. In other words, creating a transparent operational environment is key for adaptive leaders to find ways to cope with the ambiguity associated with changing circumstances.

THE RELEVANCE OF LEADING ONESELF IN THE 21ST CENTURY

Future leadership developments should pay more attention to improving the quality and availability of humanness in general. Jacinda Ardern (New Zealand), Emmanuel Macron (France) and Sophie Wilmes (Belgium) all aimed to improve the quality and availability of humanness in their dealing with the coronavirus pandemic. All three leaders tried to be empathetic, sensitive, inclusive, approachable, supportive, transparent, and agile/adaptable to different needs. The aforementioned might indicate a humane-oriented leadership approach.

The concept of humanness should, therefore, be emphasised more in future leadership thinking. Self-influencing behaviour and leading oneself are important concepts in the improvement and implementation of humanness in communities and organisations. Leading oneself will help leaders to be more effective, which, in turn, will help them to lead others. Alomair[93] claimed that leading oneself facilitates the leader's engagement and interaction with others (leading to humanness).

Manz and Sims[94] pointed out that those who can lead themselves should demonstrate this to others. Even if unintentional, this modelling behaviour will help other people to lead themselves as well.

Lipman-Blumen[95] argued that, by leading oneself first, one is in a better position to help lead others. She stated that we are living in a connective era (where everyone

---

91 Joiner & Josephs, 2006.

92 Ibid.

93 Alomair, 2016: 229.

94 Manz & Sims, 2001: 47.

95 Lipman-Blumen, 2011: 6.

and everything is inevitably connected), making inclusion and connection inevitable. Without leaders who can lead themselves and lead with others, the integration of opposing forces (e.g., diverse groups, people and nations) will not be realised.[96]

CONCLUDING REMARKS

It is clear from this chapter that leading oneself is the starting point for leaders to attain positive results. For any leadership effort to start successfully, one needs to come from a place of leading oneself, and from that place, one can lead others to be effective.

Albert Einstein said, "The world is a dangerous place, not because of those who do evil, but because of those who look on and do nothing."[97] Accepting the challenge to create and implement the self-influencing approach to leadership will contribute to leading oneself first before trying to lead with others. By accepting this challenge, leaders might discover that they have met their human need for meaning and significance, which Victor E. Frankl[98] referred to in *Man's Search for Meaning*.

Maxwell[99] put it as follows: "The bottom line is that the smallest crowd you will ever lead is you – but it is the most important one. If you do that well, then you will earn the right to lead others and even bigger crowds."

---

96 Ibid.

97 Lipman-Blumen, 2011: 6.

98 Victor E Frankl, 1946; 1984.

99 Maxwell, 2008: 2.

PART TWO

LEADING ONESELF IN
THE PRIVATE SECTOR

CHAPTER 3

CONFLICT WISDOM: THE ABILITY TO CHANGE THE FRAME

Barney Jordaan

ABSTRACT

This chapter explores the concept of conflict wisdom as an aspect of self-leadership and a critical competency for organisational agility. Agility (or adaptiveness) is required for organisations to succeed in an uncertain and volatile social, economic and political environment. Developing employees' conflict wisdom will not only benefit organisations and their employees directly, but can also contribute to the promotion of peaceful resolution of conflicts more generally. However, handling conflict effectively and sustainably needs more than just skills training. More than anything else, it requires the development of a different conflict frame or mindset because, as the saying goes, if we change the way we look at things, the things we look at also change. Some suggestions are proposed for how individuals can develop such a new frame and the role of business in this regard.

INTRODUCTION

The focus of this chapter is on how a business' investment in improving its employees' "conflict wisdom"[1] can deliver pay-offs far beyond the individual and the organisation. Conflict wisdom refers to: (i) having an understanding of conflict, its antecedents and acquiring productive conflict skills and behaviours; (ii) awareness of one's own conflict frame or mindset and the effect that has on how one deals with a conflict; (iii) awareness of one's own preferred conflict handling style while developing the ability to apply different styles depending on the context; and (iv) being equipped with conflict handling skills.

Conflict wisdom is not merely an individual leadership capability, but also a valuable asset for organisations operating in a volatile, uncertain, complex and

---

1   Leathes, 2009.

ambiguous (VUCA) environment. The ability to act cooperatively with others, and to express diverse ideas, positions, opinions, and feelings directly and in a non-violent manner, is essential for the success of agile business strategies.[2] First, the VUCA context requires organisations to quickly and constantly adapt to a rapidly changing operating environment. Team members need to be able to deal quickly, efficiently and constructively with differences that inevitably arise in situations of increased interdependence. In traditional, formal organisations, differences in opinions can be a source for displays of power and interpersonal conflicts, whereas in agile environments they should serve as a source for individual as well as team creativity and innovation.[3]

Second, the ability to deal with differences efficiently promotes effective coordinated effort and integrated solutions that, in turn, help teams perform better, especially in situations of uncertainty.[4,5] Third, conflict handling skills are empowering as they help individuals navigate their way through their conflicts and disputes outside of the work environment as well.[6] Finally, if these skills are embedded in an organisation and the behaviours of its employees, they become 'exportable' and can play an important role in helping to promote a peaceful and amicable resolution of conflicts and disputes beyond the organisation.[7]

This chapter begins with a brief overview of the impact of the contemporary turbulent (or 'VUCA') operating environment on business, and how businesses turn to 'agility' to try and meet the challenges implicit in this environment. Pol Polman, a past CEO of Unilever, is highlighted as an example of a successful and admired leader, for whom the role of business in addressing conflict drivers internally and in the broader operating environment were key pillars of his leadership during his tenure at the company. Polman's views on the role of business in society and leadership provide an example of how businesses can achieve financial success while developing leadership capabilities in their employees and contributing to a more peaceful and sustainable world.

This is followed by an explanation of the importance of effective conflict-handling as a critical element of organisational agility, as well as team and personal effectiveness. While training in general leadership strategies can enable employees to exercise more initiative in taking on the responsibility to lead others, training on topics such as conflict handling and how to effectively work with others is needed for developing shared leadership capabilities.[8]

---

2   Van den Broeck & Jordaan, 2018.

3   Ibid.

4   Alpe, Backman & Isaacs, 2000.

5   Elgoibar, Euwema & Munduate, 2016.

6   Tjosvold, 2008.

7   Spreitzer, 2007.

8   Pearce & Manz, 2005.

One's conflict frame (perception or thought pattern) is a key factor in developing 'conflict wisdom'. Our general inability as a species to engage others constructively when confronted by conflict requires more than just a new skill set. It requires first and foremost a fundamental change in how we see conflict. If we see conflict as a threat, fight or flight responses will come naturally to us. Yet, if we are able to see the opportunity as conflict – conflict as a potential resource – our approach to it is likely to change because the goal is no longer to get rid of conflict through confrontation or withdrawal, but to find a resolution. Some practical suggestions are made about how this could be achieved.

THE 'VUCA' ENVIRONMENT

"Traditionally, managers have been equated with ship captains, peering through a telescope deep into the future, setting a long-term vision, and proceeding steadily as she goes. In the new normal, however, managers must proceed through an impenetrable fog that obscures any view of the future."[9]

An organisational culture and leadership model that promoted the formalisation of policies and procedures, specialisation and hierarchical decision-making was well suited to the demands of a manufacturing economy. It allowed executives to understand the (fairly predictable) business environment and make decisions based on information that was not necessarily important to lower-level employees, to whom delineated functions within the organisation were assigned.[10, 11]

The contemporary business environment, on the other hand, is characterised by increasing levels of complexity, turbulence and uncertainty. The speed of technological development and the proliferation of disruptive new businesses poses particular problems for organisations that continue to operate in a hierarchical, formalised and siloed manner; whereas the new environment requires speedy decisions in the midst of uncertainty and information overload, these organisations' decision making processes tend to be slow and cumbersome, information is closely guarded, and internal competition for access to resources is not only present but sometimes actively encouraged.

For organisations to survive and also thrive in this environment, they need to become more 'agile' or 'adaptive'.[12, 13, 14] A 2009 survey conducted by *The Economist's* Intelligence Unit found organisational agility to be a core differentiator for businesses in

---

9   Sull, 2010: 9.

10 Van den Broeck & Jordaan, 2018.

11 Jordaan, 2019.

12 Doz & Kosonen, 2008.

13 Reeves & Daimler, 2011.

14 Rigby, Sutherland & Takeuchi, 2016.

the rapidly changing business environment and critical for business success. The report refers to a Massachusetts Institute of Technology study that suggests that agile firms grow revenue 37% faster and generate 30% higher profits than non-agile companies.

The need for greater agility causes many companies to move toward more organic and decentralised organisational forms.[15] Through the decentralisation of power, authority and decision-making responsibilities to the lowest possible level (commensurate with employees' capabilities), organisations try to find the flexibility and rapid response capabilities (agility) necessary to remain competitive, especially in high-tech or service-oriented industries.

According to Holsapple and Li[16], agility is the result of integrating alertness to internal and environmental changes (recognising opportunities and challenges) with a capability to use resources in responding (proactively or reactively) to such changes, all in a timely, flexible, affordable, relevant manner: "The alertness dimension highlights agility as an opportunity-seeking capability from both external and internal vantage points, while the response capability dimension emphasizes agility in terms of change-enabling capabilities, which are embedded in organizational processes. Although distinct, the two dimensions of the agility construct are complementary."[17]

Yet structural change and strategic adjustment alone are not sufficient to either meet the challenges of the turbulent environment or benefit from the opportunities they provide. Internal barriers tend to stall agile change efforts, e.g., slow decision-making, conflicting departmental goals and priorities, risk-averse cultures, and lack of access to information because of people operating in often competing silos. The successful implementation of agility is dependent on more than just the implementation of agile strategies and flatter structures – it also requires the ability to collaborate across levels and hierarchies and handle the conflicts that inevitably arise when cross-silo collaboration and team-based decision-making is required.[18]

Organisational leaders will find an increasing need to depend on individual employees across hierarchies to share the responsibility for leading themselves and others, rather than relying on traditional, hierarchical forms of leadership.[19] Therefore, despite the challenges posed by the VUCA environment, it is also creating unprecedented opportunities for employees at all levels to develop greater self-awareness through skills acquisition, and to be given greater responsibility for their job tasks and work behaviours (self-management).

---

15 Houghton, Neck & Many, 2003.
16 Holsapple & Li, 2008.
17 Holsapple & Li, 2008: 6.
18 Van den Broeck & Jordaan, 2018.
19 Houghton, Neck & Many, 2003.

SPOTLIGHT: POL POLMAN

Holding out particular leaders or businesses as exemplary is always a risk because one – even relatively minor – corporate or personal scandal can put paid to the public relations efforts that often accompany the accolades heaped on business leaders. An internet search did not reveal any personal scandals clinging to Pol Polman, CEO of Unilever (the world's third-largest consumer goods producer) for ten years until his retirement in January 2019. While the end of his tenure was marred by a dispute with shareholders over an unsuccessful attempt to shift the Anglo-Dutch company's main headquarters to the Netherlands, he has been widely praised as an ethical leader who empowered employees to lead themselves, and who positioned the company to drive profits and sustainability in an ethical manner.

Polman strongly promoted the philosophy that people achieve more when you don't tell them what to do, but rather allow them to accept responsibility for how they do their work, as well as how they make decisions and overcome their differences. Particularly in a VUCA environment, prescriptive frameworks don't work. Instead, people need to be given the courage and permission to lead themselves. Asked what his definition of leadership is, Polman stated:[20]

> *"I don't have a personal leadership definition, because, as I said, there are different styles of leadership. But actually, everybody is a leader, as far as I'm concerned. And my definition of leadership is very simple: if you positively influence someone, you are a leader. And I think the main thing is that people can be themselves. And I do it by a strong, as I said, inner compass and guidance. That is more important than anything else."*

In a later interview[21], he stated:

> *"It's clear that you need leadership skills that are focused on things like adaptability, resilience [and] systemic thinking. First, you have to be a normal human being. If you don't understand yourself, you're no good at understanding what your strengths and weaknesses are … For us, the standard is to spend a lot of time on the standards of leadership that we expect from people: being authentic, having high levels of integrity, a deeper sense of the common good. We would say it's simply putting the interests of others ahead of your own, and wanting to make an impact in the world."*

---

20 McKinsey, 2009.

21 CMI, 2015.

Polman also held firm beliefs about the role business can play in promoting peaceful co-existence in society. For him, leadership within companies can be a possible driver of peace-building activities in volatile environments.[22] For his efforts in that regard, he was named one of the winners of the Oslo Business for Peace Award by the Business for Peace Foundation (BPF) in 2015.[23] The BPF gives its annual awards to business leaders who promote peace within their organisations and communities. They represent the "ethical leadership" qualities of peace promotion and are chosen from among public nominations by a panel of Nobel Prize winners in Economics and Peace. They are not social entrepreneurs: the idea is not to solve conflict as a social problem through a business solution, but instead to harness the power of regular business activity, e.g., supply chain management, to solve underlying conflict drivers.

THE THEORETICAL FRAMEWORK

Broadly, self-leadership describes "a self-influence process through which people can and do achieve the self-direction and self-motivation necessary to perform their tasks and work."[24] Self-leadership encompasses a set of three complementary cognitive and behavioural strategies which impact subsequent outcomes[25, 26]: behaviour-focused strategies (self-observation, self-goal setting, self-motivation, positive self-feedback and reward, and self-coaching); reward-focused strategies (about positive perceptions and experiences associated with tasks to be accomplished which augment a sense of capability, competency and self-control); and constructive thought pattern strategies, which affect people's emotional and behavioural states and reactions.[27] The focus of thought pattern strategies is on identifying and replacing dysfunctional beliefs and assumptions, and practicing mental imagery, positive self-talk, and using positive scripts in place of ineffective ones.[28, 29] This aspect is particularly important in the context of the submission below, i.e. that "mindset change" will need to accompany efforts to improve employees' conflict handling skills.

Self-leadership is important for establishing a collaborative, decentralised workplace environment.[30] Conflicts are a normal feature of organisational life[31], thus the ability to handle conflict effectively is a key interpersonal – and thus self-

---

22 Katsos & Fort, 2016.

23 Ibid.

24 Houghton & Neck, 2002, p. 672

25 Neck & Manz, 1999.

26 Carmeli Meitar & Weisberg, 2006.

27 Neck & Manz, 1992.

28 Carmeli, Meitar & Weisberg, 2006.

29 D'Intino et al., 2007.

30 Browning, 2018.

31 Tsjovold, 2008.

leadership – skill.[32] If mastered, it can serve multiple purposes, i.e., it can contribute to improved interpersonal relations and decision-making, as well as higher levels of team performance[33], and it is essential for organisational agility.[34] Providing employees with conflict handling skills can also produce benefits beyond the organisation by empowering employees to engage more effectively with conflict in their personal lives[35], while potentially also contributing to the peaceful resolution of conflicts in society.[36, 37]

Self-leadership can be developed in different ways, e.g., formally designated leaders can lead by example in developing and reinforcing self-leadership behaviours. As in the case of Polman, organisational reward systems can be adapted to reward self-leading initiative and teamwork and not merely conformity; and training can be provided on topics such as conflict handling, communication, conducting meetings, persuasion skills, relationship orientation, and how to effectively work with others.[38, 39]

HANDLING CONFLICT PRODUCTIVELY

The term 'conflict' is notoriously difficult to define.[40] Here it is used in the generic sense as defined by, among others, Anstey[41], i.e., it occurs when the parties involved believe that their aspirations cannot be achieved simultaneously, or perceive that there is a divergence in their values, needs or interests.[42, 43, 44]

Conflict is a daily reality in organisations.[45] It is also dynamic; as parties attempt to manage conflict, its nature can change as issues are resolved and new ones emerge.[46] It is inherently emotional[47, 48] and 'contagious' – it can quickly escalate to the point of

---

32 Houghton, Neck & Many, 2003.

33 Zhang, Cao & Tjosvold, 2001.

34 Van den Broeck & Jordaan, 2018.

35 Spreitzer, 2007.

36 Rima, 2000.

37 Spreitzer, 2007.

38 Pearce & Manz, 2005.

39 Van Saane, 2019.

40 Schmidt & Kochan, 1972.

41 Anstey, 1991: 4.

42 Thomas, 1992.

43 Weingart et al., 2015.

44 Cronin & Bezrukova, 2019.

45 Eisenhardt, Kahwajy & Bourgeois, 1997.

46 Cronin & Bezrukova, 2019.

47 Barki & Hartwick, 2004.

48 Cronin & Bezrukova, 2019.

becoming dysfunctional.[49, 50] Conflict also tends to be multi-dimensional, i.e., it consists of both relationship and task-based elements.[51] In teams it may occur at multiple levels, including the dyadic level or the intra-team level.[52] The ability to handle conflict productively is necessary for people to do their jobs effectively.[53, 54] Behavioural skills associated with conflict handling (which include creativity, emotional intelligence, negotiation, coordination with others, active listening and complex problem-solving) have also been recognised by the WEF[55] as among the top skills required for the so-called fourth industrial revolution.

In traditional, hierarchical organisations, employees are typically expected to use formalised processes to inform their managers and supervisors about conflicts, and then to abide by the outcome decided on by management. By contrast, groups that rely on cooperative and co-creation approaches to do their jobs must be skilled in resolving problems and conflicts themselves, thereby contributing to the organisation in terms of innovation and relationship building.[56] Leaders and employees do not allow frustrations to brew; they manage their conflicts to develop quality relationships.[57] Quality relationships promote constructive conflict handling, which promotes increased employee involvement and performance.[58, 59] A 2003 UK survey of top management teams found that the more productive ones treated conflicts as opportunities for collaboration to achieve the best solution for the organisation as a whole. Conversely, when a separate research team studied a group of business failures arising from highly unsuccessful strategic decisions, they found a remarkably consistent pattern of stifled debate, with negative opinions or adverse information discounted as unhelpful.[60]

Conflict can help improve decision-making by challenging conventional thinking and forging new solutions. Through open conflict, employees can learn to combine and integrate their ideas to solve problems and strengthen their relationships.[61, 62] Discussing opposing views gives teams the confidence to take calculated risks.[63] Even

---

49 Eisenhardt, Kahwajy & Bourgeois, 1997.
50 Jehn et al., 2019.
51 Ibid.
52 Ibid.
53 Tjosvold, 2008.
54 Elgoibar, Euwema & Munduate, 2016.
55 WEF Report, 2018.
56 Tjosvold, 2008.
57 Ibid.
58 Ibid.
59 Tjosvold & Yu, 2009.
60 Quoted in Finkelstein, 2003.
61 Eisenhardt, Kahwajy & Bourgeois, 1997.
62 Tjosvold, 1998.
63 Tjosvold & Yu, 2009.

in a crisis, leaders are typically more effective when they seek out diverse views.[64] Rather than making tough decisions alone, effective leaders are oriented toward promoting the conditions and relationships for open-minded discussion of opposing views among colleagues and employees.

By helping employees to develop cooperative relationships and the skills to discuss diverse views open-mindedly, organisations are helping employees to develop important elements of self-leadership, i.e., shaping their ability to use conflict to probe problems, create innovative solutions, learn from their experiences, and enliven their relationships.[65]

There is also another, less obvious, benefit to be had – by developing the ability of their employees to act collaboratively when the situation requires and to resolve conflicts and disputes amicably wherever possible, there is also, potentially at least, a contribution made to empower employees to apply their conflict-handling abilities in the private sphere, and perhaps even society at large.[66]

For the benefits of conflict to materialise, however, skills training in conflict handling will not suffice. Given the deep-seated human tendency to see conflict as a threat, a new thought pattern or mindset about conflict must be developed at both the individual *and* organisational levels.[67]

MENTAL MODELS AND CONFLICT BEHAVIOURS

"The frames our minds create define – and confine – what we perceive to be possible. Every problem, every dilemma, every dead end we find ourselves facing in life, only appears unsolvable inside a particular frame or point of view."[68]

Mental models ('mindsets', 'frames', or 'thought patterns') form the basis of reasoning, decision making, and behaviour. They are deeply ingrained assumptions, generalisations, or even pictures and images that influence how we understand the world and how we take action.[69] They help us make sense of our world; they affect what we do and how we do it, where we direct our attention and energy, and what information we rely on.[70, 71] They determine the strategic approach we take to deal with problems or make decisions, which, in turn, influences the tactics and behaviours we

64 Tjosvold, 1984; 2008.

65 Tjosvold, 2008.

66 Milliken, Schipani, Bishara & Prado, 2015.

67 Coleman, 2018.

68 Zander & Zander, 2000.

69 Senge, 1990.

70 Van Boven & Thompson, 2003.

71 Pfeffer, 2005.

employ in pursuit of a solution. Ultimately, they determine the quality of the outcomes we achieve.[72, 73, 74, 75, 76]

While mental models have to be highly dynamic to adapt to continually changing circumstances[77], abandoning established mental models and adopting different ones can be very difficult. As Koestler[78] stated:

> *"Of all forms of mental activity, the most difficult to induce... is the art of handling the same bundle of data as before, by placing them in a new system of relations with one another by giving them a different framework, all of which virtually means putting on a different kind of thinking-cap for the moment. It is easy to teach anybody a new fact... but it needs light from heaven above to enable a teacher to break the old framework in which the student is accustomed to seeing."*

It has been said that as a species, we are not naturally gifted with the ability to handle conflict constructively because we have innate aggression that programmes us to win – and in winning we want to see others lose.[79, 80] Within this ingrained thought pattern, conflict is regarded as a predominantly negative phenomenon, thus triggering a typical fight, flight or freeze response when it arises.[81]

To change how we perceive and engage with conflict, a fundamental shift in our perceptions about it is therefore needed, apart from developing appropriate skill sets to handle it more productively. Fortunately, we do have the ability to 'change the frame' – to alter our negative perceptions of conflict.[82] As Victor Frankl put it so eloquently: "(E)verything can be taken from a man (sic) but one thing: the last of the human freedoms – to choose one's attitude in any given set of circumstances, to choose one's way."[83] This ability to intentionally influence one's thinking, feeling and actions to achieve set objectives is the essence of self-leadership.[84]

---

72 Seligman, 1991.
73 Van Boven & Thompson, 2003.
74 Armor & Taylor, 2003.
75 Carmeli, Meitar & Weisberg, 2006.
76 Dweck, 2007.
77 Van Boven & Thompson, 2003.
78 Koestler, 1972: 235.
79 Nicholson, 2003.
80 Randolph, 2010.
81 Nicholson, 2003.
82 Dweck & Ehrlinger, 2006.
83 Victor Frankl, 1992: 72.
84 Bryant & Kazan, 2012.

THE REALITY: HOW TO CHANGE CONFLICT FRAMES AT THE LEVEL OF THE INDIVIDUAL

While learning new skills could be challenging, it's the unlearning – getting rid of constricting and often well-established thought patterns – that can be the hardest to do.[85] Changing what people do is easier than changing what they think, since mindsets and assumptions are often deeply embedded beyond conscious thought. It involves questioning peoples' most basic assumptions and then confronting them with the impact of their thought patterns.[86, 87] Changing the way people think about situations is the most powerful and useful way to ultimately change behaviour, and thereby affect organisational results.[88]

The discipline of changing one's frame starts with self-reflection, learning to discover our own 'internal pictures' of the situations we face, and then bringing them to the surface and rigorously scrutinising them.[89]

Several techniques can be used to transform dysfunctional thoughts about conflict into functional ones. Senge[90], for example, referred to 'learningful conversations' where people expose their thinking and make that thinking open to the influence of others. Employees – and individuals generally – can also alter their negative self-talk about conflict into a more positive type of self-talk, thus substituting non-rational beliefs with more rational ones.[91, 92, 93] Mental imagery, e.g. imagining conflict as an oyster that produces a pearl when irritated by a grain of sand, can help to imagine a more positive result emanating from a conflict experience, thus strengthening their confidence in their abilities to deal with the real situation.[94]

Another example is to require someone who struggles with conflict to word their own, simple (preferably one line) definition of conflict that is completely positive. For example: 'Conflict is an opportunity to grow'; 'Conflict can create positive energy'; 'Conflict can promote understanding and perspective taking'. By making one's definition visible (e.g., as a screen saver or simply a notice on their desk or a wall), the brain, because of its neuro-plasticity, can be stimulated through exercises like these to develop fresh neural pathways that convey a different understanding of the conflict.[95, 96]

---

85 Bonchek, 2016.

86 Reger et al., 1994.

87 Jones et al., 2011.

88 Pfeffer, 2005.

89 Prussia, Anderson & Manz, 1998.

90 Senge, 1990.

91 Seligman, 1991.

92 Prussia, Anderson & Manz, 1998.

93 Carmeli Meitar & Weisberg, 2006.

94 Prussia, Anderson & Manz, 1998.

95 Draganski et al., 2004.

96 Dweck & Ehrlinger, 2006.

AT THE CORPORATE LEVEL

In his discussion on conflict management processes, Swanepoel[97] offered a useful distinction between 'conflict negative' and 'conflict positive' organisations. Conflict negative organisations tend to see conflicts as unnecessary, destructive and to be avoided. There is little understanding that, if understood and managed properly, the conflict could be an organisational asset or resource. This approach not only deprives an organisation of the potential benefits of conflict, but also of opportunities for improved decision-making and risk management.

In conflict positive organisations, however, there is an understanding that conflict is an integral part of organisational life and that unmanaged or poorly managed conflicts can be costly, both in terms of relationships and efficiency. The culture in this type of organisation allows for the expression of diverse opinions and liberal information exchange. The understanding is that conflict can mean the reconciliation of opposing tensions that can be directed into workable solutions and improved decision-making.

Companies that design their initiatives to support desired shifts in mindsets and behaviours see the most successful transformations.[98] Yet, as stated earlier, mental models are not easily altered. According to Reger et al.,[99] the optimal situation for change occurs when the gap between current and ideal is large enough to create the stress necessary for people to desire change, but the dissimilarities are not so great that the ideal is perceived to be unattainable. In such a situation, employees not only see the need for change, but also believe it can be accomplished.

Barker[100], however, warned that new thought patterns will not become fully operable until all parts of the system have been changed and aligned with the new way of thinking. Therefore, organisations need to create an environment where it becomes easier and more natural for employees to engage with differences in constructive ways, and to do so as soon as conflicts register themselves. Conflict wisdom – or what Coleman[101] referred to as conflict 'intelligence' and 'systemic wisdom' – needs to be promoted and conflict handling skills need to be developed. Process options for the resolution of conflicts, with a focus on an amicable inter-party resolution before resorting to managerial intervention, also need to be put in place.[102, 103, 104] Process options range from encouraging dialogue between protagonists to facilitated interactions guided by peers or team leaders.

---

97 Swanepoel, 1999.
98 McKinsey & Co, 2015.
99 Reger et al., 1994.
100 Barker, 1989.
101 Coleman, 2018.
102 Leathes, 2009.
103 Jordaan & Cillie, 2018.
104 Jordaan, 2019.

CONCLUDING REMARKS

This chapter examined conflict handling skills as a critical subset of self-leadership skills, and described the role that such skills can play in developing organisational agility in the current turbulent business environment. Moving from directive styles of leadership to more transformative forms of leadership that encourage self-leadership requires a change in assumptions about what leadership is about on the part of leaders themselves and those that they lead. To transform conflict from something regarded as necessarily negative and damaging to organisations equally requires a mindset shift, and perhaps even more so given our biological tendency to fight, flee or freeze when conflict arises. Merely teaching skills for handling conflict, whether on their own or as part of a learning journey towards improved self-leadership, will not suffice if we want to truly embed them and empower those who use them to become not only truly conflict wise, but also serve as potential catalysts for change outside their organisations.

The following words of Mary Parker Follett seem apposite in the current context:[105]

> "Our 'opponents' are our co-creators, for they have something to give which we have not. The basis of all cooperative activity is integrated diversity... What people often mean by getting rid of conflict is getting rid of diversity, and it is of the utmost importance that these should not be considered the same. We may wish to abolish conflict, but we cannot get rid of diversity. We must face life as it is and understand that diversity is its most essential feature... Fear of difference is the dread of life itself. It is possible to conceive conflict as not necessarily a wasteful outbreak of incompatibilities, but a normal process by which socially valuable differences register themselves for the enrichment of all concerned."

---

105 Quoted in Cloke & Goldsmith, 2011.

CHAPTER 4

LEADERSHIP BY SOCRATES:
SELF-CARE IN DIFFICULT AND
UNPREDICTABLE TIMES

Barbara Schellhammer

ABSTRACT

This chapter looks into the potential of the Socratic notion of "self-care" for leadership practices in VUCA environments. It does so by first utilising the example of Robert Bosch, a successful as well as a mindful entrepreneur, in difficult and unpredictable times. Secondly, it outlines some theoretical cornerstones of self-care exercises, drawing from the interpretation of Foucault and other philosophers of our time. The potential outcome of Socrates' plea for self-care becomes obvious when one looks at its capacity to help people tackle their inner turmoil in VUCA situations to deal with them in a calm and receptive manner. Applying the concept to staff training in the growing business of elderly care in Germany serves as an example. The chapter thus recommends that leaders turn around and face the VUCA environment in themselves, instead of mainly focusing on fixing the world around them.

INTRODUCTION

The leading oneself components of self-care are, first of all, *getting to know oneself*, including unwanted and hidden shadow-parts. As a form of "diagnosis", this is the prerequisite to find the right *self-care* (self-cure) exercises (*cura sui*). Here, leaders are asked to face and encounter the many voices in themselves, particularly when they experience inner chaos. It is absolutely crucial in volatile, uncertain, complex and ambiguous (VUCA) environments (for instance in the Covid-19 pandemic), to respond with a calm and mindful spirit instead of reacting out of a state of inner confusion. The most difficult part of self-care is engagement with unconscious and repressed parts that are prone to come out in moments of great uncertainty, volatility and ambiguity. The more a person ventures out to meet their shadow, the stronger his or her "alienability" gets – a prerequisite for leaders in VUCA times.

Chapter 4 highlights the importance of ancient Greek philosophy when it comes to the ability to lead oneself. Here, it particularly draws from Socrates, who considered the continuous practice of "self-care" as an ethical imperative. Since this famous forefather of Western philosophy was not involved in the business and private sector environments, it seems helpful to look at an example of a well-known entrepreneur, inventor and industrialist who lived through times of great upheaval and hardship: Robert Bosch. Having been drawn into both horrific world wars of the 20th century, he was truly a businessman in an "era of extremes", as is highlighted in a new biography.[1] With a sensitive and calm, yet assertive and undeviating, spirit, he was able to maneuver his huge and globally operating company through highly unpredictable, unstable and uncertain times. "I would rather lose money than trust", was one of his guiding principles when communicating with customers and employees.[2] Similar to Socrates, he knew that he would always have to live with his conscience and that it would be solely *his* responsibility to face the consequences of his actions.[3] He was acutely aware of the fact that he could not get away from what he was experiencing within himself. Although he grew up in Swabia, Germany, and did not talk much about his inner life in public[4], his attentive presence and discerning judgement reflected a lifelong practice of "self-care."

This chapter starts by highlighting some characteristics and activities of Robert Bosch as examples of leading oneself principles in complex and precarious times. Ensuing it presents some theoretical cornerstones of the Socratic notion of *epimeleia heautou* (self-care), drawing from philosophers like Michel Foucault, Hannah Arendt, Michail Bachtin and Gernot Böhme.

It then examines the practical reality of the philosophy of self-care, relating it to 21st century circumstances, i.e., the personal and social tensions that people experience through disruptive as well as alarming developments (e.g., mass migration and the loss of cultural stability, the recurring rise of nationalistic tendencies, fundamentalism, and political instabilities), particularly focusing on the business of elderly care. Here, possible answers to the question of whether "chaos is a gift" or an unbearable burden, will materialise. The chapter ends with a few recommendations and lessons learned from the philosophy of self-care for the practice of leading oneself as a peace leader, as well as some concluding remarks.

---

1   Theiner, 2017.
2   Bosch, 1957: 9.
3   Theiner, 2017: 35.
4   Bosch, 1957: 7.

Robert Bosch – Entrepreneur in an Era of Extremes

Robert Bosch was born in 1861 in Albeck, a village close to Ulm in southern Germany, as the 11th of 12 children. Back then infant mortality was still high and crop failures made life hard for people in rural areas. Bosch describes his parents as warm-hearted, loving, humorous and patient, who would always have food for people in need. From early on, the young Bosch was introduced to the civic values of self-development, empirical and critical observation of societal interactions, the exploratory approach towards the natural environment, open communication, responsibility and equality, productivity and accomplishment, immediacy, as well as the tempering of emotions.[5] In short, he grew into a culture of reflective self-leadership that enabled him to ask critical questions and to withstand radical tendencies as well as political propaganda by remaining truthful to himself and intellectually independent. Bosch learned to value democratic principles and to empower people instead of falling into authoritarian and patriarchal habits.

Following his school years and practical trades education, he spent several years in diverse companies in Germany, the United States, and the United Kingdom, continuously searching for alternative and unconventional ways to live. He tried to nurture a creative and free spirit, laying the foundation for his keen interest in nature, homeopathy and reform movements. To have natural light and fresh air in his manufacturing halls was just one expression of his longing to promote healthy alternatives in society.[6] Bosch always sought to cultivate a climate of mindfulness and care, which for him meant to enter a process of self-cultivation. "I don't owe my success to my knowledge, but rather to my character", he explained.[7]

For someone who was born into a peaceful society, it is hard to imagine what it must have been like to endure the horror of two world wars and the unstable and unpredictable time in-between. Without question, Bosch lived through volatile, uncertain, complex and ambiguous times, and he experienced this tension and turmoil not just as the chief executive officer of a fast-growing, international enterprise and as a politically engaged citizen, but also as a private person. Although the VUCA world we experience today looks different, what people experienced within themselves at that time was driven by similar emotions – a high level of anxiety and insecurity, and feelings of distress, despair and vulnerability.

As an entrepreneur, father and husband, and as somebody who always felt responsible for "his people", the rapid increase of change in a volatile and even hostile environment raised the level of uncertainty to an almost unbearable level. For Bosch, dealing with both the world around him and his intrapersonal experiences

---

5   Theiner, 2017: 17.

6   Theiner, 2017: 29.

7   Bosch, 1957: 11.

belonged together: "Be human and honor human dignity" became his life motto as a "entrepreneurial socialist"[8] – a combination which reflects the positive tension relationship that he promoted throughout his lifetime aiming at the development of a just society. He admitted that "it was not easy to keep the right middle ground between the entrepreneur who has to maintain himself and the social businessman."[9] Being drawn into this uncomfortable middle ground, he disliked every form of complacent and egocentric ignorance that takes life as it comes without trying to make things better.

He continuously asked himself who he was, trying to find his place. In 1886, he finally decided to establish a company in Stuttgart. From the very beginning, his employees earned a higher-than-average income, were involved in decision-making processes, had the most productive working environments, and were even encouraged to sing or engage in other creative activities. "We should get used to seeing our fellow men not as our inferiors or even our enemies", Bosch[10] stated. "Each of us, whether he stands lower or higher or right or left is a human being and as such, he longs for certain goals in his life, which originate in his identity."

Bosch was known for his quick temper; he had a strong reaction if he disliked something and worked hard to control himself. At the same time, he demonstrated the integrity that earned him respect, granting him natural authority over his employees. In the midst of the political disarray of 1918, Bosch tried to sketch out what could be seen as a personal account of his business philosophy. It became clear that he built his success on empowering his workers by giving them responsibility and fostering an atmosphere of critical thought. The latter gained its most obvious expression in the company journal "Bosch-Zünder" (Bosch-Detonator), which sought to establish a culture of transparency and debate about topics concerning the firm, political questions and leadership styles by utilising modern principles of adult education.[11]

For an entrepreneur like Bosch, the beginning of the First World War meant first and foremost… chaos. International business partnerships that had been established over a long time and with great effort, broke. Railway tracks were solely reserved for the armed forces, thus the transportation of goods became close to impossible. "As far as we know of the atmosphere and the feelings of entrepreneurs back then", Theiner[12] wrote, "there was no excitement or enthusiasm, but rather a deep sense of uncertainty and insecurity." People called for careful restraint. At the same time, there were desperate complaints about the lack of coal and the inability to ship goods. Approximately 82% of Bosch's business came from contracts with costumers who

---

8   Bosch, 1957: 22.
9   Bosch, 1957: 57.
10 Bosch, 1957: 22.
11 Theiner, 2017: 198.
12 Theiner, 2017: 99.

suddenly were enemies, and 6% from costumers who came from so-called "neutral" countries, to which deliveries were prohibited.[13] Just over half (52%) of his workers in German plants were conscripted. However, Bosch had the "advantage" that his company could adjust to produce "war-relevant" material, a fact that secured its survival.

Yet he experienced massive inner conflict. The VUCA environment he lived through had a profound moral dimension: He felt deeply regretful about his ability to prosper while others lost their lives, and thus decided to donate the profits he made as a military equipment supplier towards peace building and to minimise suffering. But even that became extremely difficult and complex because things happened suddenly without the ability to plan and prepare ahead. For example, in 1914, around 500 German and French wounded soldiers arrived in Stuttgart after the combat of Mulhouse. Without any hesitation, Bosch decided to use his brand-new factory halls in Feuerbach to establish a provisional hospital – there was no time to think, he had to act immediately.

The more brutal the war got, the more forcefully Bosch worked for ways to keep the door open for dialogue among the enemies. For him, this dialogue had to rest on processes of personal reflection, not on prescribed directives.[14] Peace had to come from the inside out to last. Bosch's striving for peace peaked with his efforts to bring about reconciliation between Germany and France as an important milestone of intercultural diplomacy (Völkerverständigung).

After the war, Bosch's company faced an extremely difficult situation. Again, he had to readjust. There was no longer a need for military equipment, and his American plant, including all of its highly successful patents, was dispossessed. Fiercely, he tried to find opportunities to enter the market with new products. Due to his ability to quickly diversify his array of offerings, he was able to revive his foreign operations. He was also driven by a profound motivation to foster peace among old enemies by working against deeply rooted feelings of distrust and hostility.

In 1932, Bosch turned 71. After Hitler seized power, his company resisted flying the Nazi flag at their buildings and they did not lay off workers for "racial reasons." On the contrary, they established an auxiliary operation to protect Jews and other endangered groups of people.[15] It was very hard to know who one could trust and life became extremely dangerous – particularly for people who resisted the fascist propaganda. Bosch's family feared that he could be deported to a concentration camp. Their attempt to bring him out of the country failed – he wanted to stay.

Although he dealt with several severe health issues, he tried to stay slim, physically fit and mentally active. Soon he became one of the key patrons of the civil and military

---

13 Theiner, 2017: 101.

14 Theiner, 2017: 138.

15 Theiner, 2017: 313.

resistance against the Nazi regime, and encouraged all of his employees to help Jews and other politically oppressed people "at all costs."[16] Bosch died in 1942 as a passionate advocate for tolerance – in reverence for life, he respected the dignity of every human person, even of his opponents. With his incorruptible anti-hegemonial plea for solidary civilisation as one global community, he stayed uncomfortable and obstreperous until the very end.

The Socratic notion of Self-Care – Theoretical Cornerstones

Socrates' notion of "self-care" can be seen in what Robert Bosch was capable of doing in challenging and erratic times. By reading Socrates' dialogue with Alcibiades, a good-looking student of his who had "one of the most enterprising families in the city"[17], we get a first impression of what this "caring" may entail. Socrates approached the cocky young man because he sought to enter politics aiming at governing others. Socrates warned him that he would have to deal with two types of opponents: internal rivals in the city of Athens and the city's enemies, and added that his arrogance had hindered him thus far from seeing that he was not well enough equipped to face both.

Therefore, Socrates demanded: "Obey the Delphic principle to know yourself" (Alcibiades I, 124a).[18] During an ensuing conversation about the question of what it would take to rule the city *well*, Alcibiades realised that "the city is well governed when harmony reigns among its citizens" (Alcibiades I, 126c).[19] Socrates then asked Alcibiades what this "harmony" may look like or how it can be achieved, but the young man is not able to answer and desperately starts to realise his own ignorance: "I no longer know what I am saying. Truly, it may well be that I have lived for a long time in a state of shameful ignorance without even being aware of it" (Alcibiades I, 127d).[20] Socrates comforts him by saying that it is not too late to take care of himself, considering the exercise of *epimeleia heautou* as the precondition to leading others. "It is not authority, nor power that you need to long for in order to rule the city well", Socrates states, "but justice and temperance" (Alcibiades I, 134c)[21], which can only be achieved by working on oneself and aiming at a congruent state of self-leadership. Foucault[22] later noted that "taking care of oneself is to care about justice."

As with the Socratic approach, the "Bosch-Zünder" sought to work against indifference by educating people through dialogue and debate – in their daily lives,

---

16 Theiner. 2017: 371.
17 Foucault, 2005: 32.
18 Platon, 2002.
19 Platon, 2002.
20 Platon, 2002.
21 Platon, 2002.
22 Foucault, 2005: 72.

during work, on the street and at home. It was Bosch's incentive for his employees to care for themselves, to think for themselves, and to actively engage as citizens through conversation. Education should not sustain people only economically, but also aid them politically to recognise heresy or "fake news."[23] Socrates' approach was to jolt them into waking up, to empower them to speak out against unjust and discriminatory conditions, to get involved in politics, and to change things for the better.[24] Both Socrates and Bosch were motivated by the awareness that they had to live with their conscience. Arendt[25] explicated this by saying that even if nobody sees you, you should not kill because you cannot want to live with a murderer for the rest of your life; "I have to get along with myself."[26]

Socrates was well aware of the necessity to practice governing ourselves, even if this can be a daunting task – especially when we become aware of shameful thoughts, unruly emotions, bodily reactions and things we did not know about ourselves. He knew that this honest encounter with oneself is essential to become considerate and able to respond to volatile environments instead of falling into reactive patterns. Böhme[27] argued that with his plea to care for oneself, Socrates intended to establish an intrapersonal "ruling authority through self-reflection." In his famous Apology (29d-e),[28] Socrates warned the citizens of Athens: "Aren't you ashamed to care for the acquisition of wealth, reputation and honor, when you neither care nor take thought for wisdom and truth and the perfection of your soul?"

Yet, the question that arises here is, what exactly does his plea to "perfect" one's soul involve, or how do we go about establishing a mindful, self-reflective authority within ourselves? In Arendt's work on Socrates[29] we find some helpful clues. At one point she argues that it is characteristic for "bad people" to suffer internal conflicts and that they try to escape from themselves because "their soul is up in arms against itself."[30] She explains that Socrates stressed that it is a key criterion for truthful dialogue is to speak with *one* voice, instead of claiming contradictory views.[31] In Socrates' words: "I should rather choose to have my lyre, or some chorus that I might provide for the public out of tune and discordant, or to have any number of people disagreeing with me and contradicting me, than that I should have internal discord and contradiction in my single self."[32] In other words: taking care of oneself means to create peace

---

23 Bosch, 1957: 57.

24 Arendt, 1998: 172.

25 Arendt, 2016: 27.

26 Arendt, 2016: 57.

27 Böhme, 2002: 53.

28 Arendt, 1998; 2016.

29 Arendt, 1998; 2016.

30 Arendt, 1998: 188.

31 Arendt, 2016: 55.

32 Gorgias, 482b-c.

within oneself, to deal with inner differences and to become a whole "single self." For Socrates, this was the personal condition of a leader to govern well.

With this in mind, one may ask whether chaos is a gift. With Socrates, I would argue that it can be a gift for creative development if we are able to keep a curious distance from our inner life without being drawn into or carried away by chaotic situations. However, this ability rests on our willingness to genuinely face the polyphonic "chaos" within ourselves. This also entails encountering uncomfortable shadow parts, which we would much rather try to ignore. Yet volatile, uncertain and ambiguous environments tend to trigger exactly these darker areas of our self that we have learned to suppress. In Bachtin's work on Dostoevsky we see that speaking with one voice cannot mean to overpower unwanted parts of ourselves in favour of a homogeneous whole. Rather, we ought to value the plurality of independent and unmerged voices within us.[33] Contrary to Arendt, he argued that a person can never be identical to herself[34], because she will never be able to eliminate a certain amount of disorder within herself. However, by learning how to deal with it, we will become mindful and yet firm in our encounters with unpredictable and confusing situations. This may be what Bosch[35] referred to when he spoke about "having character" as the basis to engage with his customers, his family and himself.

Interestingly enough, Bachtin also referred to Socrates leading his interlocutors into trembling paradoxes in which they were forced to uncover deeper layers of their identity.[36] This is extremely important for peace leaders in complex and uncertain times. Getting to know oneself does not mean to only engage with parts of me that I know and like, but rather with those parts that are alien and thus uncomfortable or even upsetting. It is not surprising that Socrates explains that we have to get to know ourselves *first*, before we can take care of us.[37] Here we get an idea of what Plato means when he argues that philosophy is a form of therapy seeking to heal inner conflicts – a notion that also strongly influenced Hellenistic ethics, because inner conflicts often lead to conflicts on the outside as they infect interpersonal relationships.[38, 39, 40] For a pertinent and thus successful as well as sustainable therapy (the practice of self-care), we have to have an accurate diagnosis (knowledge of self).

Nevertheless, current business and private sector environments often rely on rather superficial "therapeutic measures", which encounter global challenges on the surface without looking at the deeper levels of human experiences. The following

33 Bachtin, 1985: 27.
34 Bachtin, 1985: 67.
35 Bosch, 1957: 56.
36 Bachtin, 1985: 124.
37 Alcibiades I, 129a.
38 Nussbaum, 1994.
39 Foucault, 2015: 75.
40 Mall & Peikert, 2017.

section emphasises the practical relevance of the philosophy of self-care. To make it as concrete as possible, it will focus on the booming business of elder care in Germany. The relevance of Socratic approaches for today's circumstances becomes obvious through articles like one in *The Guardian* (2010), with the title "Socrates – a man of our times", and recent book publications like *Management by Sokrates*[41], *Socratic Management Techniques for the Modern Leader*[42], as well as a book that deals with the importance of Socratic thinking for conflict coaching practices.[43]

Self-Care Practices in Today's Reality of Business and Private sector Environments – particularly in the Area of Elder Care in Germany

Europe is currently undergoing a profound demographic alteration that has led to great uncertainties and tension. Over the last decades, fewer children were born than during their parents' generation, which means that the proportion of older people is rapidly growing. The aging population in Germany is one of the fastest-growing in the industrialised world. The increased costs will lead to an unpredictable fiscal situation, because public budgets have been deteriorating significantly in recent years[44], giving rise to several new businesses in the private sector of elder care. Young people, mostly from Eastern Europe as well as refugees from around the world, are being hired to take care of the elderly in Germany. These developments have led to volatile, uncertain, complex and ambiguous environments – a breeding ground for conflict on several levels.

For this reason, several big cities in Germany have been investing in programmes called *Interkulturelle Öffnung* (Intercultural Opening) in nursing homes for the elderly, with hopes of encountering negative tension and fostering healthy relationships in culturally diverse working environments.[45] Part of the organisational development initiative is to teach intercultural competencies and to train managers and staff in diversity and conflict management. However, these offerings often aim at controlling the otherness of the other, instead of learning how to deal with people's anxiety and discomfort in intercultural encounters. Socrates would consider this to be a rather "thin" approach to dealing with complex and uncertain circumstances. It is not enough to teach people *about* the "cultures" they work with, instead they should be prepared to adequately deal with an alien, and thus uncomfortable, behaviour by learning how to lead their inner self in stressful situations.

---

41 Wisniewski & Niehaus, 2016.

42 Daniels, 2018.

43 Schellhammer, 2019.

44 Hamm, Seitz & Werding, 2008.

45 Griese & Marburger, 2012.

In a trainer-manual for the *Münchenstift GmbH*, the largest elderly care agency in Munich, one can find a very practical and playful exercise called "The Inner Team"[46], which rests on the philosophy of self-care. This model seems to work for people from multiple cultural backgrounds.[47] It relies on the Socratic premise that one can be with oneself as one can be with others, and that both kinds of relationships are interconnected.[48] Thus, to become "alien-able" and to gain some form of inner versatility, people have to develop their "inner team" to practice speaking with one voice without silencing inner parts we tend to dislike or repress, but rather to include them into a balanced whole. The workshops usually start by asking the participants for concrete situations in which they were engaged in a conflict related to cultural differences. They are invited to explore their inner dialogues by becoming aware of what they were experiencing within themselves. Often, they begin by expressing rather vague and ambiguous feelings before deciphering individual inner voices that gridlocked them into inner conflict. There is, for example, the inner team member, "Ms. Tolerant", who wants to acknowledge and accept other people's behaviours, although it makes her work conditions more difficult. Thus "Ms. Tolerant" is in conflict with "Ms. Effective", who is time constrained due to the increasing workload of growing numbers of old people. The inner team model seeks to develop a comprehensive response, considering the diversity of a team with varying personality traits and cultural backgrounds on the one hand, and the need to work efficiently on the other.

In the context of the booming business of elder care within increasingly complex and unsteady environments, it is clear that an honest encounter with oneself helps to prevent the alarming illnesses of our time: depression, burnout and multiple personality disorder. Instead of prescribing tools and techniques, peace leadership should aim at creating calmness in our hearts and minds – a precondition for harmony and stability amid social turmoil and intercultural agitations.

RECOMMENDATIONS

In an article on the concept of the self and its transformation, Welsch[49] argued that the growing external plurality in recent years led to a process of intrapersonal pluralisation. It is not enough to fight against complex, diverse and ambiguous circumstances, therefore – we have to cultivate our ability to respond to the overwhelming feeling of an unstable and capricious self. As per Laing[50], it seems wise and recommendable that we do not focus on trying to fix seemingly unfitting behaviour, but rather explore

---

46 Schulz von Thun, 2003.

47 Schellhammer, 2018.

48 Arendt, 1998: 187.

49 Welsch, 1991: 352.

50 Laing, 1977.

the *experience* that led to this behaviour. Peace leadership thus means to help people work towards their inner peace instead of merely seeking to fix the world around us. This is easier said than done because we cannot rely on recipes anymore. Instead, we have to be willing to expose ourselves to what Laing[51] called an "inter-experience", to "your behavior and my behavior *as I experience it* and your behavior and my behavior *as you experience it.*"

This approach comes very close to the well-known *elicitive model* of conflict resolution by Lederach.[52] "[It] starts from the vantage point that training is an opportunity aimed primarily at discovery, creation, and solidification of models that emerge from the resources present in a particular setting and respond to needs in that context."[53] What Lederach describes here strongly reminds us of the Socratic method of *maieutics,* i.e., asking questions to give birth to ideas and underlying presuppositions like a midwife, instead of presenting ready-made solutions or prescriptive models. It does not come as a surprise that this method has been successfully adapted to psychotherapy[54] and peace building to deal with the fluid realities of a globalising world – realities that also transform how conflicts occur and how they evolve.[55]

What we currently observe in politics with the growing phenomena of nationalistic tendencies, the building of walls against refugees and the increase of a "we first mentality", goes hand-in-hand with the self foreclosing otherness by withdrawing into totalitarian concepts of identity. The Israeli psychologist Bar-On[56] aptly described a "monolithic identity" in opposition to the alleged hostile 'other'. He argued that the deconstruction and reconstruction of monolithic identities require an inner process of reflection and forgiveness. If the monolithic identity starts to crumble and people learn to address the bits and pieces within themselves, they find ways to the other.

Self-care practices can help to develop a polyphonic self that rests on means of "inner democracy"[57, 58] – a practice that is necessary to become global citizens in an increasingly complex world. Hermans et al.[59] argued that "a democratically organized self functions as a micro-society giving space to free expression and development of opposing, and contradicting I-positions with mutual dialogical relations from which they may learn in the service of their further development." Straub[60] also stated that it is inevitable to relate concepts of identity to concepts of democracy, as these presuppose

---

51 Laing, 1977: 13.
52 Lederach, 1995.
53 Lederach, 1995: 55.
54 Stavemann, 2015.
55 Dietrich, 2017.
56 Bar-On, 2001.
57 Hermans et al., 2017.
58 Straub, 2012.
59 Hermans et al., 2017: 523.
60 Straub, 2012: 66.

and need each other. Both establish normative principles against the backdrop of totalitarianism. Personal identity, as well as democratic societies, lie in a field of tension between the extremes of fragmentation on the one end and absolutism on the other. Very often one extreme leads to the other; people who are afraid of losing their cultural identity fight others whom they blame for their situation.

A key task for peace leaders in VUCA times is enabling people to live in the tension between self-assurance and openness towards otherness. This will require the ability to see through negative behaviour into the realm of inner turmoil, the fear of self-loss, transgenerational trauma and religious as well as cultural homelessness. People have to be able to stay calm in situations that are emotionally charged. This ability rests on their continuous practice of self-care, a curious and elicitive dialogue with oneself – especially with those parts we try to hide and exclude. Thus, we ought to continue our search for suitable theories and culturally sensitive methods in psychological schools and diverse cultural settings that help people to engage with the unknown other in self to test these approaches for the development of principles for self-leadership (e.g., psychodrama, shadow work, narrative conflict-coaching, philosophical counseling, neurological findings, and indigenous knowledge). Having said that, it is crucial to stress that processes of self-leadership never happen in isolation and away from societal realities and thus particular patterns of hegemonial power. It would be naïve to shift the burden of social transformation solely on the self. As per Socrates, it is clear that the development of inner democracy has to go hand-in-hand with political initiatives aimed at a just and harmonious society.

CONCLUDING REMARKS

In times of growing insecurities and anxieties, the need for self-leadership principles is acute. This move away from the notion of "fixing the world" towards caring for oneself – or to *be* the change one wants to see happening – is not new. Socrates knew that peace leadership has to come from the inside out, to have what it takes to rule the *polis* well, thus this book receives favourable back-up from the forefather of Western thought. The example of Robert Bosch gives us a glimpse into leading oneself practices in dangerous and ambiguous times. We can draw from some great and very creative methods (like the "Inner Team") that build on this philosophical wisdom and make it concrete and applicable. It will be our task to encourage people to expose themselves to "inter-experiences", and to care for themselves for the sake of their well-being, as well as for the development of healthy and just communities.

CHAPTER 5

HUMANNESS IN THE BUSINESS AND PRIVATE SECTORS

Erich P. Schellhammer

ABSTRACT

This chapter examines the humanistic leadership approach taken by the entrepreneur Oskar Schindler, who initially greatly benefitted from a VUCA environment when he established himself as a successful businessperson in Poland shortly after Nazi Germany had defeated that country. Poland suffered an incredibly cruel occupation from 1939 to 1945, and Schindler became increasingly disgusted by the terror of the SS and the suffering of Jews. In the process, he focused on the humanistic core of leadership that in the end trumped everything else, including lucrative profits. There are leadership lessons to be learned from Oskar Schindler that can be extrapolated to other volatile, uncertain, complex and ambiguous environments. This chapter consequently explores those tenets of leadership theory that support humanism at their core, including philosophical and political formulations of the primacy of human dignity as well as the role of empathy as an intrinsic human feature compelling people to take care of the other. This call can be denied, however, and there are many deplorable leadership examples of this. There are also numerous present day models available, some of which are highlighted at the conclusion of the chapter.

INTRODUCTION

This chapter identifies a core value, namely basic humanity, that usually is, and certainly should be, a universal condition and guidance for business and private sector endeavours in volatile, uncertain, complex and ambiguous (VUCA) environments. This chapter intends to demonstrate that, despite complicated situations, there is a core sense of humanness, which in most cases unconsciously constitute the foundation of the self leading a business or playing a leadership role in the private sector.

The case study used for this chapter is Oskar Schindler, a Sudeten German from Moravia, who benefitted from the VUCA environment in Poland after the German occupation in 1939 by leasing a formerly Jewish enamelware factory which he operated under the name *Deutsche Emalwarenfabrik (Emalia)*.[1] He also was involved in other business ventures. He used the connections he had established through his secret agent work in Czechoslovakia and Poland before both countries were occupied by Germany to secure valuable contracts for his business, initially for enamel cookware for the Wehrmacht (the German army under Hitler), and towards the end of the war for artillery shells.[2]

On the latter, he did not deliver the artillery shells because the circumstances had changed, creating a different VUCA environment where the objective, for Schindler and other conscientious Germans, had shifted from focusing on selfish interests, such as one's career or earning money, to saving lives.[3] The case, though necessarily dramatised, is well known through the Steven Spielberg film, *Schindler's List*. Schindler, maybe contrary to the impression of the film, was a man who could be called morally challenged in many ways. He was a spy for a very dubious cause, an alcoholic and a womaniser, and cultivated the company, if not a friendship[4], with evil men such as Amon Göth, who was detested for his excesses even by the Holocaust system of horror.[5,6] Despite these human shortcomings, Schindler has been rightfully immortalised and honoured for his decision to create a human response to a VUCA environment that made human life worthless and dispensable. With increasing determination, he worked to save Jews from almost certain death and created somewhat human-worthy conditions for his workers.[7]

What compelled Schindler in the extremely volatile, uncertain, complex and ambiguous times of World War II in Poland to do something most unusual compared to what most of his peers considered "acceptable"? It seems that he opened himself to an inner voice that told him that certain violations of human dignity are incompatible with our intrinsic sense and understanding of humanity, and that he listened and acted upon that voice.

This chapter explores those features that were conditional for Schindler's action to safeguard Jews; features that are honourable and should be guiding motifs for the self in a business environment or the private sector. Primarily it is empathy. With few exceptions, such as is the case with psychopaths, humans are empathetic and are deeply moved by the suffering of others. It is a feature of our basic humanity.

1   Roberts, 2000.
2   Ibid.
3   Ibid.
4   Crowe, 2004: 279.
5   Roberts, 2000.
6   Crowe, 2004: 318.
7   Roberts, 2000.

However, there are also helpful conceptualisations, such as the principle of human dignity, that are guiding voices for individuals and that are presented before venturing into the physiological nature of empathy.

Manifold theories/models support the leadership quality of honouring our basic humanity. The chapter focuses on the least contested and the most acceptable ones, not disregarding other motifs for humanly adequate behaviour as they are found, for example, in most religious traditions. In philosophy, humanistic assumptions are made in the field of ethics, whereas the discourse on human dignity seems to be the closest in explaining the leadership quality of humanism. The best known advocates of this position are Immanuel Kant[8] with his deontology, as well as representatives of being-with ethics, most prominently presented by Buber's *I and Thou*[9] and Levinas' appeal to endless *love towards the unknown face*.[10]

There is physiological evidence for empathy and basic humanism. Neuroscientists have identified the amygdala as the centre for empathy and have shown that it influences our reasoning.[11] Further, it is a desirable feature of our being that can be made stronger. Again, many authors scientifically argue for this, hence the chapter will focus on the findings of Damasio.[12]

The leadership theories that are the best candidates for translating the finding that humanism and empathy should guide a leader are authentic leadership[13] and servant leadership.[14] A basic sense of humanism seems to be the *sine qua non*, or the foundation, for all leadership. Authentic leadership aligns a leader's actions around her *"true north"*, i.e., her values. Acknowledging the findings in this chapter, this implies that there is a part of authentic leadership in all forms of leadership. Empathy drives servant leadership and thus this form of leadership is equally evident in all humanistic leadership approaches.

Moreover, peace has been now connected to the sustainable development goals of the international community[15], most of which express the tenets of human dignity, i.e., our basic humanism that is inalienable although it can be grossly violated. Consequently, business and private sector leaders are called upon their responsibility to align their self with a humanistic leadership and a peace leadership style which provides a safe harbour in VUCA environments.[16]

---

8   Kant, 1991.
9   Buber, 1970.
10 Levinas, 1999.
11 Damasio, 2010.
12 Damasio, 2010.
13 George & Sims, 2007.
14 Greenleaf, 1977.
15 General Assembly, 2015.
16 International Organization for Standardization, 2017.

This chapter concludes with modern day expressions of this basic humanism in leadership. There are many examples of humanistic acts of leaders, which are not even necessarily altruistic. They should not be dishonoured when the chapter only explores two case studies, i.e., Bill Gates and Warren Buffett, and their promise to spend a significant portion of their fortune to better the lives of the less fortunate.

OSKAR SCHINDLER AND THE HOLOCAUST

Oskar Schindler was born in 1908 in Zwittau. He was a member of the generation that experienced extreme changes to their lifeworlds numerous times until long after World War II. These changes were substantial and had extreme consequences for individuals, i.e., they lived in volatile times. These times were also characterised by uncertainty, including threats to their lives as well as a highly unpredictable future. Changes were driven by determinants that were unpredictable and embedded in complex systems, and characterised by events that were ambiguous because they were interpreted in many, often incompatible, ways.

Schindler is a good example of this generation. He grew up in the Austrian Hungarian Empire, which was dissolved after World War I, rendering the Schindlers and other ethnic Germans a national minority within the newly created Czechoslovakia. The country's first president, the highly educated Tomáš Garrigue Masaryk (who served from 1918 until his retirement in 1935), was able to maintain good relationships between the different constituents of Czechoslovakia, and is credited with creating the strongest democracy in central Europe.[17] Despite these golden times for the *Sudeten* (as the German minority in Czechoslovakia was called) and other minorities, such as the Jews, in Czechoslovakia, the proverbial dark clouds of war started to gather.

The Great Depression (1929-1933) put an end to the prosperity that Czechoslovakia had enjoyed after World War I.[18] Schindler's father's company struggled and went bankrupt in 1935.[19] Schindler, who worked in his father's company until 1929, was then employed until 1936 in the sales department of the Mährischen Elektrotechnischen AG, serving the Sudeten areas in Czechoslovakia.[20] In 1933, Hitler came to power in Germany and seduced many Germans with his charisma and his promise to serve German interests. From 1936 to 1939, Schindler was on the payroll of the *Abwehr*, the German military intelligence service, spying in Czechoslovakia and Poland.[21]

Schindler's service coincided with highly volatile times in Czechoslovakia, where the Sudetendeutsche were used as part of Hitler's expansionist foreign politics.

---

17 Walzel, Polak & Solar, 1960.

18 Pryor, 1979.

19 Roberts, 2000: 17.

20 Stuttgarter Zeitung, 1999: 12.

21 Ibid.

This deeply divided the country and brought Czechoslovakia to the brink of war in 1938. This was averted by the (in)famous Munich Agreement of September 30, 1938, when France and Great Britain agreed to the annexation by Germany of a large part of Czechoslovakia where three million Sudetendeutsche lived.[22] Soon afterward, Schindler became a member of Hitler's party, the National Socialist German Worker's Party[23], although he was less interested in party politics than in partying.[24] On March 15, 1939, the *Wehrmacht* invaded the rest of Czechoslovakia and the country was divided into the Protectorate of Bohemia and Moravia and Slovakia, fundamentally changing the lifeworld of its citizens.

Finally, France and Great Britain rebelled against Hitler's unimpeded aggression and declared war on Germany on September 3, 1939, after the Wehrmacht had attacked Poland. Within three weeks, Poland was occupied by Germany, the Soviet Union and Slovakia.[25] Poland was partly annexed by Germany and the Soviet Union (with Slovakia being allowed to re-annex "lost" territories). A third part became the General Governorate for the Occupied Polish Region, and its inhabitants (except for ethnic Germans) were declared by the German Supreme Court to be stateless[26], that is, to be without rights, with devastating consequences, particularly for Jews.

Schindler was aware of the opportunities this situation presented to Germans who, by their mere citizenship, were privileged in the General Governorate. He quickly chose Krakow after a first visit on Abwehr business in October 1939, renting an apartment in November which he visited weekly.[27] Being an excellent networker, often supported by liberal alcohol consumption and generous gifts, he soon established a friendship with Leopold Pfefferberg, a master in black market dealings[28], which became essential for his objectives during the war.

Schindler was advised by Itzhak Stern, who he got to know through a colleague in the Abwehr, Sepp Aue. Aue administered a formerly Jewish business that was, as with all Jewish property, appropriated by the German government.[29] Based on Stern's advice, Schindler leased an enamelware factory, previously owned by a Jewish consortium, that had gone bankrupt earlier in the year.[30] Backed by Jewish investors, including the former owner Abraham Bankier, the lease was formalised in January 1940. Schindler eventually bought the company in June 1942.[31] Bankier managed the

---

22 Encyclopaedia Britannica, (n.d.).

23 Crowe, 2004: 46-47.

24 Roberts, 2000: 15.

25 Majer, 2003.

26 Ibid.

27 Crowe, 2004: 87.

28 Crowe, 2004: 88-91.

29 Crowe, 2004: 100.

30 Crowe, 2004:111.

31 Crowe, 2004:109.

new company, now called *Deutsche Emailwarenfabrik* (DEF or Emalia). The company was successful in securing supply orders of enamel cookware for the *Wehrmacht* and proved to be highly profitable.[32]

Initially Schindler hired Jewish workers because they were cheaper than Polish workers, however the extremely violent and inhumane actions of the *Schutzstaffel* (SS) through its *Sicherheitsdienst* (the intelligence agency of the SS and the Nazi party) and its *Einsatzgruppen* (death squads) against the Jews[33] soon appalled Schindler, who endeavoured to create humane conditions for his Jewish workers.

Keneally's book[34], upon which Spielberg's movie, *Schindler's List*, was based, gives a glimpse of the unbelievable cruelty and hardship suffered by millions of Jews in Poland. All this was by premeditated design, which was formalised during the Wannsee Conference on January 20, 1942, which stipulated the *Endlösung* (Final Solution).[35] The Final Solution mustered precious resources in an attempt to bring about the annihilation of all European Jews. This involved[36], among many other murderous actions, the industrial killing through Zyklon B, a cyanide-based pesticide.[37]

Schindler did not approve of the actions of the SS, and although he was initially mainly interested in conducting business, he gradually shifted his emphasis to saving Jews. Mietek Pemper, contrary to the Spielberg version, dates the shift in emphasis to June 1942, when Schindler witnessed the cruelty of gathering and transporting Jews from the Krakow ghetto to the extermination camp Belzec.[38] Schindler, being rather different to most other industrialists in his use of Jewish slave labour, developed a passion to save as many Jews as he could, ultimately spending a fortune on bribes to get access to his workers by building a camp next to his factory; on food from the black market to provide basic but sufficient meals; on moving 1,200 workers from Poland to Moravia at the end of the war when the Red Army's advance forced the abandonment of business in Poland;[39] and on safeguarding his Jews through bribes from the end of the war SS excesses.[40]

Schindler, with his workers, listened to Winston Churchill on May 8th, 1945 as he announced the end of the war. The seemingly endless nightmare had come to an end.[41] Schindler advised his workers to be prudent and refrain from revenge acts, and to let formal justice instead reign to bring the culprits of the atrocities against Jews to

---

32 Crowe, 2004:136.
33 McNab, 2009: 113, 123-124.
34 Keneally, 1982.
35 Longerich, 2010.
36 Longerich, 2010: 309-310.
37 Longerich, 2010: 281-282.
38 Stuttgarter Zeitung, 1999: 37.
39 Keneally, 1982.
40 Roberts, 1996: 78.
41 Roberts, 1996: 83.

their just deserts. Little did he know that he would depend for the rest of his life on donations from his Schindler Jews, as he was not able to find success in business or find employment ever again.

THE CORE OF LEADERSHIP

VUCA environments present the greatest challenge for leaders because they are, by their very nature, unpredictable and defiant of pre-meditated action plans. They also hold the promise of revealing lessons for leaders that should be extrapolated as general leadership guidelines. Various leadership theories are assessed in the coming sections to ascertain their robustness in VUCA environments and their ability to ensure the protection of basic humanity. The protection of basic humanity, regardless of possible justifications/excuses allowing for transgressions, is taken as a non-negotiable premise, a quasi common-sense agreement, although more sophisticated philosophical arguments will be explored.

The murder of individuals just because they were Jewish was a crime that cannot be justified or excused. This is not negotiable, despite legal constructs such as declaring them stateless and thus without rights attempted to do so. Thus perpetrators cannot use the argument that they were just following orders. This was a core issue at the trial of Adolf Eichmann in Jerusalem.[42] The legal positivist H.L.A. Hart made a compelling case for this in his distinction of categorising law into primary rules and secondary rules, where primary rules comprise defined rules of human conduct. Primary rules also entail, as a core expression of natural law, indisputable human principles, such as the prohibition to murder, that must not be ratified as laws.[43]

How does this premise fit leadership theory and practice? And what is the extent of this premise: does it relate solely to the sanctity of life or does it go beyond that? The first question requires an exploration of leadership theory, as well as an analysis regarding whether there is a way to interpret leadership theories that includes obeyance to basic humanness in leadership practice that is more robust than the inherent morality of a leader. The latter, as is well known in history, cannot be assumed in leaders, as has been fairly indisputably demonstrated by leaders such as Hitler, who have little, if any, credibility as moral agents. The second question follows this exploration and introduces models that more clearly define what basic humanness should incorporate.

---

42 Arendt, 1963.

43 Hart, 1961.

THE ETHIC COMPONENT IN LEADERSHIP THEORY AND PRACTICE

Northouse, in his widely used and respected textbook on leadership theory and practice[44], mused on various definitions of leadership. He stated that:

> "...there are almost as many different definitions of leadership as there are people who have tried to define it. It is much like the words democracy, love, and peace. Although each of us intuitively knows what we mean by such words, the words can have different meanings for different people."

Still, Northouse extrapolated common elements from the myriad of leadership theories and practices. He found that leadership is a process that involves influence, happens in groups and has common goals.[45] His definition of leadership was that: "Leadership is a process whereby an individual influences a group of individuals to achieve a common goal."[46]

Applying this to the case study, Schindler used many methods to run a factory with the help of his mainly Jewish workers, who in various capacities managed to create the necessary output to fill the orders that Schindler managed to procure through his connections with the Wehrmacht. For influencing individuals he used different processes, such as convincing skilled personnel, such as Stern and Bankier, to administer operations. He also maintained a committed workforce by creating relatively favourable working conditions. He employed his social skills and tolerance of alcohol consumption to maintain good relationships with the SS to ensure that he could use Jews as a labour force, whose labour was far less expensive than that of Poles or Germans.[47] He also used his connections to influence the Wehrmacht to give him lucrative orders for kitchenware and utensils (and later for shells, which he refused to manufacture because of their deadly effects and because his priorities had changed). His dealings often needed to be greased by black market goods that Schindler managed to get with Pfefferberg's help.

The common goal of those involved was to run a factory, yet the motivations for this common goal were different. Schindler initially wished to use the situation to get rich, and as a nice side effect, avoid service in the Wehrmacht and live a grand lifestyle with the associated luxuries that certainly helped him charm women. During the war, this motivation changed and his focus became more and more on saving lives, although this did not impede his lifestyle much.

---

44 Northouse, 2016: 2.

45 Northouse, 2016: 6.

46 Ibid.

47 Roberts, 2000: 29.

The motivation for the SS is harder to establish because of a mindset that is difficult to fathom, that is, that all the ills of humanity are the responsibility of Jews. Their constraint in killing Schindler's workers was due to the importance of his products for the war effort, the illusion of his friendship with Amon Göth, and greed fueled by the generous bribes that Schindler handed out. The motivation of Schindler's workers is easier to establish. They knew that they were given an extension on life through their work permits.

This exploration of the common goal in the case study demonstrates that a common goal is multi-layered, and often depends on the motivation of a leader and their followers. There is more to it, however. Common goals can be as manifold as the human imagination and the circumstances allow for. Still, there seems to be a core – a kind of foundation – for all different common goals. Surely even essential elements of human dignity, such as the sanctity of life, can be violated, and certainly justifications or excuses can be developed for this purpose.[48] However, cases such as Himmler's (leader of the SS) justification of the Holocaust as "a difficult task for the love of our people"[49] goes against common sense, which is defined by the Oxford English Dictionary as:

> "2. ordinary, normal, or average understanding. (Without this a man is foolish or insane) 1535. B. Good sound practical sense; general sagacity 1726. C. A thing approved by common sense 1803. 3. The general sense of mankind, or of a community 1596. 4. Philos. The faculty of primary truths 1758."[50]

In what follows it will be argued that all human endeavours, and thus all leadership, need to follow an "ordinary, normal, or average understanding"[51] to be legitimate. Moreover, this general sense will be identified as the primacy of human dignity for leadership. This then constitutes the true north for leadership in the confusion that is often the result of volatile, uncertain, complex and ambiguous environments.

THE TRUE NORTH OF HUMAN DIGNITY

Common sense, as defined above, is unfortunately not as common as it should be. History is littered with stories of when the basic needs of individuals were denied by others. The morbid attraction to the horrors of war, genocide and all kinds of human suffering afflicted by individuals upon other human beings is married with the disapproval of such actions. Still, the Four Horsemen of the Apocalypse reign

---

48 Facing History and Ourselves, 1943.

49 Facing History and Ourselves, 1943.

50 Oxford University Press, 1973.

51 Ibid.

supreme, despite all the well-meaning efforts to constrain their reach. Common sense is frequently overruled – often, as Himmler horrifically showed, with an appeal to high ideals such as love for your country and your people.

Common sense

Common sense, as the primacy of human dignity, requires robustness that arms itself against its many challenges. By itself, it does not necessarily contain an appeal to human dignity. This is obvious studying the roots of common sense in Stoic thought. The best-known source for this is Marcus Aurelius' self-guidance as the leader of the Roman Empire, which is set out in the *Meditations*.[52] Although the *Meditations* contain valuable leadership lessons often distilled from other great leaders, they are not explicit regarding the necessary foundation of basic humanity for leadership.

Thus, the most common definitions of human dignity and the reasons for them will be visited here. This exploration is limited to the most important Western philosophical works on human dignity and to the latest findings in neuroscience about empathy, which gives common sense a biological foundation. The latter explains why people intuitively sense that human suffering is wrong and why most religious traditions and philosophical orientations agree on common sense as the mandate to take care of each other.

Enlightenment guides for human dignity

In Western philosophy, human dignity was addressed as a principle of humanism during the age of the Enlightenment. Giovanni Pico Dell Mirandola described human dignity as the God-given free will of humans[53]:

> "But upon man, at the moment of his creation, God bestowed seeds pregnant with all possibilities, the germs of every form of life. Whichever of these a man shall cultivate, the same will mature and bear fruit in him. If vegetative, he will become a plant; if sensual, he will become brutish; if rational, he will reveal himself a heavenly being; if intellectual, he will be an angel and the son of God."

Building on this historical precedence, Immanuel Kant developed the concept of human dignity (he called it the worth or value of human beings), which is predominantly credited as the foundation of our present-day understanding of human dignity. The clearest formulation can be found in his *Groundwork for the Metaphysics of Morals*.[54]

---

52 Aurelius, 2013.

53 Pico Dell Mirandola, 1956: 8-9.

54 Kant, 2017.

In Chapter 1, Kant based the philosophical development of morality on *gemeine Menschenvernunft*, a term that is appropriately translated as common sense.[55]

From this, he distilled from reason *a priori* principles[56], which he formulated as categorical imperatives.[57] For Kant, a categorical imperative must be based on "something whose *existence in itself* has absolute value, something which as *an end in itself* could support determinate laws."[58] This *something* is a human being, a person, in contrast to a thing.[59] Whereas a thing can be used as a means to an end, persons are categorically only an end in themselves and should never be treated as a means to an end.[60] The universality of law[61] derives its legitimacy from the practical imperative to act in such a way as to treat humanity, whether in your person or in that of anyone else, always as an end and never merely as a means.[62]

Kant coupled the universality of law with a corresponding duty to follow it. This part of Kant's philosophy gained popularity in Germany, culminating in the perverse justification, such as brought forward by Eichmann during his trial in Jerusalem, that the Holocaust can be legitimised by German law or SS policies. This is a violation of Kant's concept of the universality of law that must be guided by human dignity.

20th century developments for human dignity

After World War II, Kant's demand for human dignity to be considered the highest goal for humanity gained traction, probably in light of the atrocities and the general denial of this inherent right of every human being during the war. On December 10, 1948, the General Assembly of the United Nations proclaimed the Universal Declaration of Human Rights.[63] The Declaration in the Preamble refers to "barbarous acts which have outraged the conscience of mankind"[64] as a justification for proclaiming in its first Article:

> *"All human beings are born free and equal in dignity and rights. They are endowed with reason and consciousness and should act towards one another in a spirit of brotherhood."*

---

55 Kant, 2017: 13.

56 Kant, 2017: 17.

57 Kant, 2017: 17-19.

58 Kant, 2017: 28.

59 Ibid.

60 Ibid.

61 Kant, 2017: 24.

62 Kant, 2017: 29.

63 United Nations, 1948.

64 United Nations, 1948.

Although agreed upon by the majority of the world's nations, the implementation of this imperative lacked, and still does not have, the commitment based on duty that Kant prescribed. A notable exception is Germany which has been the main perpetrator of human rights abuses during Nazi rule from 1939 to 1945. Human dignity became the supreme principle of German law expressed in Article 1 of the Grundgesetz (Basic Law), the 1949 German constitution for West Germany, which became the legal framework for Germany on October 3, 1990.

HUMAN DIGNITY AND VUCA ENVIRONMENTS

It is difficult to derive rules of conduct from the demand to always treat human beings as an end in itself (Kant's categorical imperative). Individuals are embedded in their personal and cultural existences that create a predominant web of meaning within their frameworks of what is deemed ethical. Moreover, organisations and states are driven by a *realpolitik* that is not oriented on higher principles, such as human dignity.

Still, there are valuable guidelines for human decency. One of these is Martin Buber's (1970) recommendation to distinguish between the mindset that sees another human being as a *Thou* that is distinct from the mindset of seeing another as similar to disposable things, which he calls the mindset of the *It*. This principle was further developed by Emanuel Levinas,[65] who in response to the uniqueness of the person displayed by the *alterity of the face*, demanded "infinite responsibility for the other" because *"the right of man, absolutely and originally*, takes on meaning only in the other, as the right of the other man."[66]

These classical philosophical models for basic humanness guiding human thought and action, and by inference for leadership, reflect common sense for most of us, and might be dismissed as a self-evident platitude. However, these models are appealing in VUCA environments when the self-evident is no longer obvious. For example, Schindler proved to be the exception when he heard the call of human dignity in occupied Poland, although it is not known whether he was guided by philosophical considerations or other motivations, such as his Catholic upbringing.

Still, Schindler knew what the call of human dignity was and responded to it by risking his life and spending his fortune. From October 1944 to May 1945, Schindler spent 1,325,000 Reichsmark, a huge amount of money at that time, which contrary to Keneally's claim and the film that portrayed him, left Schindler with little money at the end of the war.[67]

Although Schindler's basic humanness is laudable, it is more difficult to accept its full meaning, that is, the need to apply it to all human beings, even evil men such as

---

65 Levinas, 1999: 128.

66 Levinas, 1999: 127.

67 Crowe, 2004: 455, 456.

Amon Göth, who, among other unbelievable atrocities, was known to shoot prisoners from the balcony of his villa. As hard as it is, even those men have dignity and need to be treated accordingly. Levinas, who himself spent the war in a German prisoner of war camp, confirms that men such as Klaus Barbie (a SS leader who is known as "The Butcher of Lyon" for his cruelty against Jews and members of the French resistance) deserve a fair trial with the presumption of innocence and the right to a defence.[68] Schindler also felt this call of human dignity by emphasising humanness and justice in his final address to his workers on May 8, 1945, reminding everyone that retribution should only be done "by those people who will be authorized to do so."[69] It is an appeal that would be hard to accept having experienced extreme cruelty, as it was when a Jewish Soviet soldier officially liberated Schindler's 'camp'.[70] Under his supervision, a questionable trial sentenced *Kapo* Willi, who, on the same day, was "hanged with thin wire from the factory's pipes."[71]

21ST CENTURY GOAL POSTS FOR HUMANNESS AS A GUIDING LEADERSHIP PRINCIPLE

The philosophical specifications for basic humanness, aka human dignity, described above are still operational through our collective consciousness and represented through common sense. However, the high ideals of the Enlightenment are no longer popular, or, for most, they do not even know anymore. Our times have developed a different *Zeitgeist*, where classical philosophy has lost its attraction or, to a certain degree, its credibility. The Holocaust cast the greatest doubt on Enlightenment thought: if all the efforts in thought cannot prevent something like an organised genocide, what good can Enlightenment be? This is ironic because it provided the Nazi ideology with its anti-rational biases an unwarranted victory.[72] Regardless, philosophy has lost its guiding role in human thought and action. Humanness is now generally justified by reference to allegedly more scientific evidence. These are findings on empathy as an essential part of our human response to the other that is now confirmed through neuroscience.

---

68 Levinas, 1998: 231.
69 Crowe, 2004: 453.
70 Crowe, 2004: 458.
71 Ibid.
72 Fackenheim, 2003.

Empathy and the human mind

"The Age of Reason is being eclipsed by the Age of Empathy", claimed Rifkin.[73] The phrase stands for a shift in our view of human nature, departing from an understanding of the Self as being "aggressive, materialistic, utilitarian, and self-interested."[74] The new vision of human beings is as *homo empathicus*.[75] Rifkin justified this claim according to his interpretation of human history and economic development. There are other equally enjoyable analyses, such as those expressed in Beck and Cowan's *Spiral Dynamics*[76], Wilber's *Integral Vision*, Gergen's *Relational Being*[77], or, in leadership, Lipman-Blumen's *Connective Leadership*[78], which all assert that the Self is constituted through relationships that require care for the other and is driven by empathy.

Research in neuroscience has also established that empathy and compassion are a natural function of our brains.[79] Suffering or a violation of a moral code triggers activation of the ventromedial prefrontal cortex[80] that informs other regions of the brain, such as the amygdala, to produce a multi-layered response involving emotions, such as disgust.[81] Most importantly, the emotion of disgust is the result of "the perception of morally reprehensible actions"[82] that is usually accompanied by the emotion of contempt.

The mechanism that triggers emotions is universal, that is, it is part of the human genome.[83] Still, the stimuli that are needed to invoke this mechanism are different for different people.[84] They depend on individual experiences or the cultural environment.[85] The mind can be trained to select causative stimuli[86] or to suppress an emotional response.[87] Thus, a set of emotions, namely "compassion, embarrassment, shame, guilt, contempt, jealousy, envy, pride and admiration"[88] are generic to humanity. Although these emotions might be invoked under rather different circumstances depending on the individual.

---

73 Rifkin, 2009: 3.
74 Rifkin, 2009: 1.
75 Rifkin, 2009: 2.
76 Beck & Cowan, 2006.
77 Wilber, 2009.
78 Lipman-Blumen, 1996.
79 Damasio, 2010: 119.
80 Damasio, 2010: 2019.
81 Damasio, 2010: 124-125.
82 Damasio, 2010: 125.
83 Damasio, 2010: 132.
84 Ibid.
85 Damasio, 2010: 132-133.
86 Damasio, 2010:133.
87 Damasio, 2010: 134.
88 Ibid.

Individual and cultural diversity is built on the ability of human beings to prioritise certain values, habits, and customs in contrast to others. This constitutes an admirable feature of humanity and is now acknowledged and protected by the world community through the UNESCO Universal Declaration on Cultural Diversity.

However, it is also generally acknowledged that individuals with highly developed compassion for others constitute healthy societies.[89] Knowing this should compel people and cultures to develop individual and social norms that reflect a high level of compassion for others, which can be achieved through education[90] and sensitising individuals to the *face of the other*.[91] It also can be approximated by following a programme to develop an empathic society, such as was modeled by Rifkin.[92] Multiple different approaches depend on a specific culture and its history, e.g., frequent reminders of the Holocaust prompt the German nation to stay on course to actualise human dignity as an overriding societal value.

CONCRETISATIONS OF HUMANNESS: THE INTERNATIONAL COMMUNITY AND PHILANTHROPY

In the 21st century, the international community has, through various United Nations Declarations, expressed its commitment to the goal of human dignity. The most remarkable agreements are the *Declaration and Programme of Action on a Culture of Peace* (1999) and *Transforming our World: The 2030 Agenda for Sustainable Development* (2015), which express an international commitment to positive peace that is founded on human dignity. The *Agenda for Sustainable Development* (2015) expresses the commitment of nations to work towards a world where peace and sustainable development go hand-in-hand (Preamble). It contains 17 goals and 169 targets, which are intended to erase poverty and provide for quality education, equality, sustainable production and consumption, peace, justice, and strong institutions, etc. It is a promising development and there is progress towards fulfilling these goals.[93] Still, the Sustainable Development Goals Tracker[94] shows that a lot still needs to be done.

The call of empathy is also noticeable in many other ways, confirming that it is truly common sense. It expresses itself in everyday civility and small acts of kindness. It also is heard and acted upon by the very wealthy, including Bill and Melinda Gates and

---

89 Damasio, 2010: 135.

90 Ibid.

91 Levinas, 1999.

92 Rifkin, year.

93 SDG Tracker, 2018.

94 Ibid.

Warren Buffet, who started the Giving Pledge campaign.[95] The signatories to Giving Pledge are the super-rich of the world, who have promised to give half of their wealth to philanthropic purposes. The campaign now has 204 pledgers from 23 countries, who donate to a variety of causes such as "poverty alleviation, disaster relief, global health, education, and medical research."[96]

CONCLUDING REMARKS

Schindler stands out as a business leader who did not forget his moral compass during volatile, uncertain, complex and ambiguous times. There are others who, as business leaders, prioritised the dignity of others over monetary gain. However, the years of Schindler's Emalia operations are also full of examples of companies that did not mitigate the fate of slave labourers and who continued to be successful after World War 2, such as Bayer, Hugo Boss, Siemens, etc.

Still, Schindler set an example that has been followed by many other business leaders. It has also found expression in leadership theory, most noticeably in the models of servant leadership and authentic leadership. Moreover, many businesses now organise operations according to international standards that show a clear commitment to the UN's sustainable development goals.[97]

Volatile, uncertain, complex and ambiguous environments tend to make people act upon their instincts and their emotions instead of using their rational abilities.[98] Thus it is important to be mindful of role models, such as Schindler, who remind us that we must abide by what is naturally a human tendency, that is, to be empathetic. It requires more, however, to actualise human dignity! For example, we are called upon to take responsibility for the other by being mindful as business leaders; as citizens in our right to vote; in our obligation, if needed, to challenge those in power in case they stray from their commitment towards creating a better world for all; and as human beings, to extend our kindness towards the other as a necessary condition of human dignity.

---

95 The Giving Pledge, 2019.
96 The Giving Pledge, 2019.
97 International Organization for Standardization, 2017.
98 Kahneman, 2011.

CHAPTER 6

PERSPECTIVES ON STILLNESS FOR A VUCA WORLD

Adrienne Castellon

ABSTRACT

Part of wisdom traditions for thousands of years, stillness is nonetheless germaine for the modern leader. Those who engage in times of daily stillness find they see the world more clearly, think more creatively, experience less stress, improve relationships and increase their ability to discern ethical decisions. Cultivating the discipline of daily times of stillness is a recommended practice to manage a noisy world characterised by volatility, uncertainly, complexity and ambiguity.

INTRODUCTION

It was one of the hardest things I've ever done and yet the impact was undeniably profound. In a very hot August 2019 I participated with close to 200 other participants in a four-day silent meditation retreat. For me, the retreat was an effort to foster an appropriate disposition in the face of my professional VUCA (volatile, uncertain, complex and ambiguous) environment. Not long before, I had been promoted at work and desired time to recalibrate. I am part of my academic department's own VUCA as it transitions in organisational structure and seeks to extend its influence to India, China, Africa and the Middle East. Exciting as the venture is, establishing learning centres in these varied contexts is indeed proving to be volatile, uncertain, complex and ambiguous. In contrast, the stillness I experienced at the retreat amidst the stunning landscape of the Pacific Northwest's mountains, sea and sky invited me to ponder and assess my role. In retrospect, I realise the significant impact of stillness during those four days. A seemingly small yet profound insight I gleaned was related to the fact that the clock in the large meeting room was not working and if we were tempted to ask the time we were told 'the time is now'! I have taken this lesson with me to encourage me to work on being truly present and avoiding worry over things that have not yet happened. This is an example of how the meaning of the retreat followed the lived experience, which is similar to how stillness often works in the lives of practitioners. The stillness helped me reflectively prepare for a launch into the unknown and I left with a quiet confidence and motivation to engage the good work ahead – work that brings out the best in those who do it and aims to bring lasting benefits to others.

Naturally, there are also figures in the private sector who incorporate stillness into their lives to help them stay well and able to effectively engage their roles. Peter Song is an example of a businessperson who did just that. In Canada, leaders in healthcare have jurisdiction over private facilities during the COVID-19 pandemic, and Theresa Tam and Bonnie Henry are two particularly strong examples of healthcare leaders described as "the calm, science-driven voices of reason as the COVID-19 pandemic threatens to sicken Canadians."[1] These and other diverse international examples in the private domain will be explored in this chapter.

This chapter explores stillness as a disruptive and important innovation for the busy professional in a VUCA environment. It begins by offering an example of a businessperson who incorporates stillness in his professional life. The example sheds light on the discipline of stillness and how the development of a contemplative mind can serve the professional and the organisation. Next, stillness is defined and a brief outline of its connection to leadership provided. Following this conceptual and theoretical base, persuasive benefits are given for leaders to create stillness in their own lives. The chapter concludes with suggested methods for incorporating stillness and identifies challenges as well as potential solutions for those interested in incorporating stillness as part of leading self and others in a VUCA world.

AN ILLUSTRATION OF INCORPORATING STILLNESS

Peter Ng Kok Song is an example of a businessperson who incorporates stillness in his professional life. Song was Chief Investment Officer of the Government of Singapore Investment Corporation from 2007 until his retirement in 2013. Now he is a member of the board of several public and private companies, as well as a respected speaker about the power of meditation. From a VUCA perspective, in a 2018 interview[2] Song noted the complexity of problems and challenges experienced in the industry from the perspective of China, saying:

> "A change that has taken place in the last five years is that the problems and the challenges have grown bigger. I mean for example the level of debt to GDP has climbed because China requires a lot of credit creation to finance its growth

---

1 Picard, 2020.
2 Song, 2018.

but the debt has now reached a level of two hundred and sixty percent of GDP. With that has created more constraints on how you can continue to manage the growth of the economy. There have been more problems in the area of shadow banking and so that carries a financial risk which means that they have to act in a timely fashion to prevent this crisis from getting out of hand and then finally in the area of managing the foreign exchange market the stock market compared to 2015 when the stock market fell and the uncertainty in the foreign exchange market caused loss of market confidence."

Song describes how the discipline of stillness and the development of a contemplative mind serves professionals and organisations faced with such complexity. He has practiced stillness for over 30 years and reports that over time he has benefitted by becoming less distracted and more calm, focused and peaceful. Describing his radically simple practice, he adds that it is demanding and not easy to follow the discipline. Each morning and evening he sets aside 25 minutes to sit still, spine upright and repeat a word or mantra.[3] Song's practice is grounded in the Christian contemplative tradition, drawing in particular from the teaching of the Benedictine monk John Main. He has noted that: "Meditation is a universal spiritual practice to be found in all the major world religions, and many people actually practice meditation in a secular context outside institutional religion."[4]

Song attributes his practice of meditation and stillness to helping direct his focus away from self to the other. To incorporate stillness in professional life is not to focus solely on one's individual life or role in the organisation, but to reclaim a greater sense of meaning and connection with the whole. Two consequences of excessive individualism during times of stillness are a skewed sense of reality and a disproportionate emphasis on self-fulfillment to the detriment of the common good. Freeman[5] warned against mistaking excessive self-analysis for true interiority, however. This assertion was supported by contemporary Canadian philosopher, Charles Taylor, on the limits of individualism: "to shut out demands emanating beyond the self is precisely to suppress the conditions of significance, and hence to court trivialization."[6] In contrast, Song experiences greater 'otherness' and a path to significance and meaning through the practice of stillness.

In addition to having a renewed focus on the significant and connection with the whole or common good, Song attributes to his practice of stillness the benefit of cultivating increased clarity of mind and objectivity. He says he has better judgment due to increased emotional awareness and focus. This benefit of more clarity enables

---

3   Berkley Center for Religion, Peace and World Affairs at Georgetown University, 2011.

4   Meditatio, 2012: 3.

5   Freeman, 2015.

6   Taylor, 1991: 40.

him to simplify the complicated to essentials while recognising uncertainty. It also helps him powerfully during conflict since he is better able to disagree thoughtfully without getting anxious. Song asserts that practicing stillness has helped his overall wellness by harmonising his emotions, intellect, body, personal and professional life. He concludes: "If you want to be a leader, this is an essential skill that you have to learn – meditation."[7] Furthermore, the experience that stillness increases personal and professional wellness, particularly emotional awareness and clarity, is supported by research.[8, 9, 10, 11, 12]

THEORY

Ryan Holiday, contemporary thinker and writer on ancient philosophy and its place in everyday life, asserts that many philosophies of the ancient world believed that stillness was necessary for leaders to think, be creative, write and make decisions.[13] He defines stillness as: "to be steady while the world spins around you. To act without frenzy. To hear only what needs to be heard. To possess quietude – exterior and interior – on command." In addition, an extensive literature base asserts that stillness cultivates the following dispositions: attentiveness, silence, resting, non-judgment, non-reactiveness, empathic perception, willingness to embrace discomfort and difficulty and openness to new insights.[14, 15, 16, 17, 18, 19, 20, 21, 22, 23, 24] A large body of research supports the diverse benefits of mindfulness and, by extension, stillness. A meta-analysis of 18,000 articles identified 47 randomised, controlled trials that supported the positive effects of

---

7 Freeman, 2019.

8 DeWees, 2019.

9 Freeman, 2015; 2019.

10 Holiday, 2019.

11 Meditatio, 2012.

12 Ying Gao, 2018.

13 Holiday, 1991: 40.

14 DeWees, 2019.

15 Freeman, 2015; 2019.

16 Friedland, 2016.

17 Goyal et al., 2014.

18 Heider, 2015.

19 Holiday, 2019.

20 Meditatio, 2012.

21 Rakoczy, 2006.

22 Tan, 2019.

23 Warneka, 2008.

24 Ying Gao, 2018.

mindfulness.[25] Specific to the private sector, several studies indicate the feasibility and effectiveness of stillness-related activities with the particular effect of increasing resilience and collaboration.[26, 27, 28]

The importance of stillness in leadership was anticipated in China more than 2,500 years ago by Laozi when he wrote:

> "The leader who is centred and grounded can work with erratic people and critical group situations without harm. Being centred means having the ability to recover one's balance, even in the midst of action."[29]

Stillness, mindfulness and meditation have been practiced in many of the wisdom traditions, including Hinduism, Daoism, Buddhism, Christianity, Islam and Judaism.[30, 31, 32, 33, 34, 35] Now, mindfulness has gone mainstream and is very much part of the secular world.

Centuries after Laozi, prolific author and prominent Oxford professor Evelyn Underhill[36] promoted stillness as the foundation of social action. In reference to stillness she asserted:

> "It increase[s] the efficiency, wisdom and steadfastness of persons that will help them to enter, more completely than ever before, into the life of the group to which they belong...to handle the world of things, and remake it, or at least some little bit of it."[37]

It wasn't until many years later that researchers became interested in why stillness has these and other effects, however.

Researcher, author and consultant Deborah Rowland wrote on the importance of mindful leadership, saying that "the inner state of leaders critically influences successful

25 Goyal et al., 2014.
26 Montero-Marin, Kuyken, Gasión, Barceló-Soler, Rojas, Manrique, Esteben & García Campayo, 2020.
27 Reitz, Waller, Chaskalson, Olivier & Rupprecht, 2020.
28 Randerson, 2020.
29 Heider, 2015: 51.
30 Anālayo, 2019.
31 Freeman, 2019.
32 Friedland, 2016.
33 Heyes, 2019.
34 Tan, 2019.
35 Warneka, 2008.
36 Underhill, 1857-1941.
37 Rakoczy, 2006: 106.

change."[38] She argued that stillness enables more effective action when we lead from our whole selves. Rowland's research spanned five continents and examined both the outer and inner practices of leaders as related to change efforts. Sixty-five senior leaders across multiple industries participated in the qualitative narrative inquiry, with the findings revealing that it was the inner state of a leader that made the most difference to change outcomes. Rowland identified four inner capacities that can be honed through building stillness into our routines. The first inner capacity refers to the ability to stay non-judgmentally present and not be distracted. The second is the capacity to consciously choose how to respond to experience, and not impulsively react to it. The third is an empathic capacity to be able to tune into systemic dynamics, while the fourth is a capacity to acknowledge discomfort and difficulty as being necessary for change and transition – an integrating skill. Rowland's research highlights four competencies that are enhanced through the discipline of cultivating stillness: noticing, choosing, perceiving and integrating.

In the midst of the COVID-19 pandemic, Canadians are benefitting greatly from the extraordinary leadership, empathic capacity, calm, measured and informative voices of Canadian health officers Theresa Tam and Bonnie Henry. Both leaders demonstrate the ability to acknowledge fear without perpetuating it, an integrating skill that recognises discomforting reactions to information shared. Asked how she maintains work-life balance and eases the stress of leading her province's health and safety response, Henry answered that she practices yoga. These health care servants are examples representing a large body of research that supports the diverse benefits of mindfulness and stillness.

PRACTICAL REALITY

Stillness is relevant for 21st century leaders. Leaders, indeed many individuals, seek purpose and significance, yet are faced with insecurities, rejection, failures and shame, which can render them immobilised or otherwise inhibited in their authentic contribution to the greater whole of the organisation. Stillness is considered an antidote to these negative realities which are so often a part of organisational life.[39, 40]

Leaders in a globally competitive world are regularly stretched to the limit, which often results in negative consequences. The most common consequence is that busyness limits our thresholds of patience; increases distractibility, preoccupation or fixation; and threatens our ability to be fully present. In turn, a reduced ability to be present negatively impacts our recognition of others' needs and restricts our grasp of the challenges and complexities they face. This can result in less empathy and

---

38 Rowland, 2017: 88.

39 Freeman, 2019.

40 Holiday, 2019.

compassion, and may additionally pose a challenge to our capacity for fairmindedness.

Integrating stillness into the rhythm of professional life can lead to clarity about oneself in the presenting reality, more critical analysis in uncertain and ambiguous situations, as well as nudge us towards a course of action that is grounded not only in the intellect or affectation, but in a more embodied, living wisdom. Ying Gao asserted that:

> *"When a leader repeatedly cultivates a state of stillness and a new level of awareness, his or her physical, mental, emotional and spiritual capacities develop accordingly. These capacities, in turn, support a more agile, creative, compassionate, collaborative and ethical leadership behavior."*[41]

A leader's ability to create and nurture a healthy atmosphere in the workplace is enhanced by their practice of stillness. Ying Gao's narrative inquiry identified the following organisational benefits: more respect, collegiality, collaboration, openness, willingness to listen and empathise; and a safe atmosphere free from fear, suspicion, backstabbing and hostility.

In addition to increased leadership capacity, there are persuasive health benefits for leaders who create stillness in their lives. Neuroscientific evidence supports practitioners' testimonies that stillness promotes physical and emotional health. Meditation is good for the cardiovascular system, heart, blood pressure and the immune system, and it reduces stress.[42, 43, 44, 45] Duke Medical School's Imke Kirste found that silence is associated with the development of new cells in the hippocampus, the key brain region associated with learning and memory.[46] During the practice of meditation the prefrontal cortex lights up and after a six week period of regular meditation, the brain's 'grey matter' becomes thicker than in a control group.[47, 48]

Regardless of the evidence supporting the positive effects of stillness, mindfulness and meditation, many leaders remain insufficiently convinced of the point of making lifestyle changes, and rather continue to live and work at a frenetic pace. Admittedly, resisting what's good for us is not uncommon. One compelling example of this is a study by Viswanathan et al.[49] which identified that 20% to 30% of medication prescriptions

---

41 Gao, 2018: 118.
42 Freeman, 2019.
43 Pascoe, Thompson & Ski, 2020.
44 Allen et al., 2017.
45 Strait et al., 2020.
46 Kirste et al., 2013.
47 Lazar et al., 2005.
48 Saleem & Samudrala, 2017.
49 Viswanathan et al., 2012.

are never filled, and that approximately 50% of medications for chronic disease are not taken as prescribed. We know that taking our medication is necessary and good for us, yet many choose not to. The same is true in other areas like exercise and nutrition. Knowing the research base that stillness can help us flourish and "become a more resilient, compassionate, productive, inspiring and conscious leader who leads from within",[50] leaders are advised to figure out ways to apply practices of stillness in their lives.

RECOMMENDATIONS

Harvard Business Review authors Talbot-Zorn and Marz[51] wrote a blog entitled, "The busier you are, the more you need quiet time." There are many ways to incorporate stillness, such as looking at or making art, yoga, meditation, prayer, listening to or creating music, walking in nature, journaling or reading. Additional investment may be required for media fasts or meditation retreats; Holiday[52] dedicated an entire chapter to limiting your inputs. During a busy workday, taking even five minutes of quiet time can clear your head for more perceptive and creative engagement. Some use a chime, a singing bowl or a phone timer. It doesn't much matter since the discipline cannot be reduced to a technique; it's different for each person. I recall during the meditation retreat that my rhythmic breathing had a sleep-inducing effect. It took discipline to stay alert and fully engage the work of meditation, but I slowly got better by paying more attention to my posture and attuning my focus rather than allowing my thoughts to go everywhere.

During times of stillness, Benefiel[53] suggests we might reflect on these or similar questions:
- What is driving me?
- What is driving us as an organisation?
- What part of my leadership is ego?
- What part is desire for self-perpetuation?
- What will help me/our organisation see blind spots?

After a stressful incident involving judgment, criticism, rejection or loss, Holiday[54] suggests an appraise-reappraise method inclusive of the following prompts during a time of stillness:

---

50 Friedland, 2016: 355.
51 Talbot-Zorn & Marz, 2017.
52 Holiday, 2019.
53 Benefiel, 2019.
54 Holiday, 2019: 164, 218.

- What happened? What am I feeling? What am I thinking?
- Can I be absolutely sure that the way I am seeing the situation is really true?
- How can I view this situation differently so that it causes me less stress or self-doubt?
- In this challenging situation, what is it that I'm here to learn?
- How can I better connect with this person?
- How can I express myself?
- How can I best serve?

There are certainly challenges with incorporating stillness. Finding time, lack of understanding or suspicion of others may prevent us from even starting, while distractions and competing demands may make it hard to continue. The best advice from practitioners and authorities alike seems to be to keep with it, return to the practice, savour it and be gentle with yourself. Off-beat advice that will at least bring a smile to our efforts comes from Ron Rolheiser, an Oblate priest, who exhorted us to "Fear not, you are inadequate!" The implication, of course, being to keep trying and not give up.[55] It is helpful to recall that we are indeed 'works in progress'. As the German theologian Karl Rahner reminds us: "In the torment of the insufficiency of everything attainable, we ultimately learn that in this life there is no finished symphony."[56]

CONCLUDING REMARKS

The experience of stillness has the benefits of increased attentiveness and detachment, while at the same time nurturing connectedness to a bigger picture and deeper meaning. This can be illustrated by Saint-Exupery's desert experience. In December 1935, Antoine de Saint-Exupery, author of *The Little Prince*, crashed in the desert. In his story of survival in *Wind, Sand and Stars*[57], he speaks of the virtues of attentiveness, detachment and single-mindedness:

> "He remained stubbornly indifferent to the panic, pain, and despair which preyed on his mind. Learning to be fiercely attentive, he learned also to ignore everything unnecessary, everything unrelated to the primary task of staying alive."[58]

Stillness has the effect of fostering a dispassionate approach to life, not suggestive of an uncaring disinterest, but rather the ordering of one's desires by paying attention to what matters and letting go of the rest. T.S. Eliot, in his poem, *Ash Wednesday*, prayed for

---

55 Rolheiser, 2019.

56 Rolheiser, 1994.

57 Saint-Exupery, 2000.

58 Lane, 1998: 186.

both: "Teach us to care and not to care."[59] In this sense, stillness serves as a corrective lens; a way to discover a balance between attentiveness and detachment, and thereby gain clarity about what to attend to and how to conduct oneself.

Stillness is also an antidote for stress and reactive behaviour in leaders, as medical doctor Daniel Friedland[60] admonishes:

> "Leaders who are unaware and/or ill-equipped to deal with their reactions to stress and self-doubt are predisposed to act from a reactive mindset, especially in VUCA environments. These leaders are prone to act from a place of personal power and self-interest, rather than the common good, where financial interests hold sway over core values, social interests, and the delivery of quality and value. All of these can erode a sense of meaning and purpose and increase the risk of burnout within a culture."

To counteract this erosion of meaning and risk of burnout, Victor Frankl's often-quoted phrase captures the conscious choice we all have: "Between stimulus and response there is a space. In that space is our power to choose our response. In our response lies our growth and our freedom."[61] Stillness can help us make this choice. Canada's longest serving Supreme Court Chief Justice, Beverley McLachlin, is an example of someone who, through long hours pouring over judgments and files, cultivated a disposition of stillness. She chose the stillness of solitary preparatory work as it enabled her to think more deeply and effectively. Even when faced with charged debates, McLachlin "did not wear her heart on her sleeve. Cool, methodical logic was her domain."[62]

The development of leadership studies points to a deeper appreciation of the interiority of the leader in which the personal growth, ongoing transformation, emotional wellbeing and resilience of the leader are seen as key elements of leadership excellence.[63, 64, 65, 66, 67, 68]

---

59 Eliot, 1971: 61.
60 Friedland, 2016.
61 Frankl et al., 2015.
62 Fine, 2019.
63 Benefiel, 2019.
64 Blanchard & Broadwell, 2018.
65 Fry & Kriger, 2009.
66 Gao, 2018.
67 George, 2003; 2010.
68 Walumbwa, Hartnell & Oke, 2010.

PART THREE

LEADING ONESELF IN THE ACADEMIC SECTOR

CHAPTER 7

RESILIENCE AND AGILITY IN ZIMBABWEAN HIGHER EDUCATION

Martha Harunavamwe

ABSTRACT

Zimbabwe's higher education faces challenges related to sustaining the education system in an ambiguous and fast-paced world with limited resources; leaders are overwhelmed and unable to keep up with the constant changes. This chapter assesses the influence of resilience and agility on responding to the VUCA environment posed by both the global economy and the Zimbabwe higher education system. Reflections based on research by Professor Kurasha and various literature suggest that to navigate through the VUCA environment, institutional leaders need to be agile and resilient. Although agility assists to map new ways, leaders need resilience to counter the difficult situations associated with change. Different methods of enhancing resilience and agility should be offered to institutional leaders; such efforts may focus on adaptability training and on approaches that encourage positive coping, positive thinking and behavioural control. These may include coaching, mindfulness, self-regulation and cognitive behavioural techniques.

INTRODUCTION

We live in a world that is driven by relentless challenges, issues and dilemmas. These factors are driving change and uncertainty in higher education; one has to decide whether to sink or swim. Zimbabwean institutions are facing dramatic changes at an accelerated rate, and the symptoms highlight the beginning of a new era. Universities in Zimbabwe face a real threat of becoming archaic institutions that offer irrelevant programmes to future graduates. With the economic hardships of the country, it has become very difficult to adjust to the so-called Fourth Industrial Revolution (4IR), which is ushering in a business environment that embeds the use of technology to disrupt and challenge conventional thinking and practices.[1]

---

1   Lucas, 2012.

The confounding of issues and the chaos that surrounds the universities are depressing. The 'new normal' operating environment is characterised by a lack of predictability, a hazy reality, and mixed meanings of conditions.[2] Zimbabwe is a fast-paced, increasingly unstable and rapidly changing world, coupled with a serious lack of resources as well as a dying economy. The chapter begins with an outline of the situation in the Zimbabwe Higher Education (ZHE) system, the volatility of the environment, as well as the uncertain and ambiguous nature of the future of university graduates. The chapter will then provide a detailed description of how Professor Kurasha applied the principles of lead-self to address some of these challenges. Two theories – Personal Resiliency and the Theory of Agility are applied to describe the successful adjustments made by Professor Kurasha in response to uncertainty and ambiguity of the Higher education in Zimbabwe. The chapter will end with a section addressing future directions and recommendations based on theories as well as the trends in the literature.

BACKGROUND: ZIMBABWE'S HIGHER EDUCATION

The education system of Zimbabwe was once reputed to be the best in Africa. Education was perhaps the greatest achievement of the Mugabe government's early years; it expanded at a spectacular rate from one institution at independence to 10 state and six private universities by 2013.[3] However, authoritarian rule and economic mismanagement inflicted heavy damage on the country and impacted negatively on the education system. Zimbabwean universities started to struggle with ways of providing quality education under massification against a background of limited and dwindling government funding.[4] The student enrolment at universities is believed to be over 55,000, and universities are overcrowded and poorly equipped.

The expansion of the university education system has brought about several challenges, such as a compromised quality assurance system, limited funding, poor infrastructure, low staff morale and a subsequent brain drain, and lack of support for staff development programmes.[5] Hyperinflation erupted from 2006 to 2008, forcing several academics to abandon their jobs and emigrate to seek other ways of survival. An estimated 20,000 academics left the country, with the lack of hands-on skills and good academics resulting in the production of graduates who are ill-prepared for work

---

2   Botha, 2017.

3   Uzhenyu, 2017.

4   Mutenga, 2012.

5   Madzimure, 2016.

in any industry.[6] This was followed by high student dropout rates due to uncertainty, financial constraints and economic hardships.[7]

The situation was worsened when the government withdrew funding for the post-secondary sector and reduced its grants and loans system for students.[8] This underfunding has resulted in archaic technological equipment in the universities, amongst other issues.[9] Some institutions responded by increasing student intake as a revenue-generating scheme, as well as doubling tuition fees, which led to the inability of many students to afford their fees. For the few who remained in the system, the infrastructure such as accommodation and textbooks became a major challenge, students' residents were overcrowded, and the conditions were even worse in the off-campus hovels where most students ended up residing.[10] In addition to that, most of the textbooks in the libraries were obsolete, damaged or outdated. Lecture rooms were unexpectedly taken over by other classes, which was confusing for the students, and there was little room to study at the crowded library. The computer/student ratio at the universities became unmanageable and the internet unbearably slow.[11]

While Zimbabwe's higher education is struggling with basic issues relating to libraries, textbooks, computers and accommodation, the global world is expanding at a very fast pace, and no matter how hard the economy is struggling, universities are expected to remain competitive. There is an increasingly rapid transformation in the higher education sector across the globe[12], which is seen across many dimensions, including the purpose of education, the content to be taught, technological change, pedagogy and methodologies to be used. To shape the future and ensure that graduates are equipped with suitable skills and knowledge, institutions of higher learning need to foster innovation and creativity to meet the demands of the Fourth Industrial Revolution.[13] The issue is whether Zimbabwe's higher education will be competitive internationally and adjust to the new developments and demands while the country is experiencing a wide range of domestic challenges and economic crises. Will the academics in higher education be able to speedily respond and equip their graduates with the requisite skills while operating under limited resources? Will the products from these poorly equipped universities meet the competency profiles required by modern industries? What used to be traditional methods of imparting knowledge and skills to students are rapidly evolving; the common brick and mortar institutions associated with modern education are now disrupted and complemented by new technologies,

---

6   Chimbganda, 2015.
7   York, 2018.
8   Ibid.
9   Uzhenyu, 2017.
10 Chimbganda, 2015.
11 York, 2018.
12 Garwe, 2015.
13 Rodney-Gumede, 2019.

while the academics are also trying to figure out the way forward.[14]

The higher education (HE) system in Zimbabwe is expected to continuously tap into the disruptive innovations initiated by new technologies. Academics need to constantly integrate new technologies into their teaching and learning to maintain high standards. To be able to respond, curricula at institutions of higher education should become dynamic, responsive and adaptable, i.e. constant changes are necessary to keep pace.[15] Universities are under increasing pressure to redesign curricula and the content of modules within those curricula. However, considering the economic hardships in Zimbabwe, there is a serious lack of resources and skills to facilitate the necessary innovations. This has cast a shadow of uncertainty for both the students and the academics.[16] Students are pondering their future lives after graduation, including whether they have adequate skills to compete in the global labour market. Academics and the management of institutions are also struggling to re-think and redesign the system to match international standards, global demands and infrastructural requirements.[17]

While society expects higher education to be a leader in sustainable socio-economic growth, its institutions are deteriorating and struggling to adjust to the new changes. Massification, a lack of resources, slow adjustment to technological changes and a lack of skilled academics are some of the major challenges being experienced by most universities. These challenges affect both academics and students, who look to the leaders of the institutions for solutions.

HIGHER EDUCATION IN ZIMBABWE: A VUCA ENVIRONMENT?

There is no doubt that the pace of technological change is faster today than ever before. The future has become uncertain for potential graduates; the World Economic Forum[18] estimates that nearly 50% of subject knowledge acquired during the first year of a four-year technical degree will be outdated by the time a student graduates. Relevant drivers for future success include a flexible working environment, mobile internet, cloud computing, big data, the Internet-of-Things (IoT), a sharing economy, robotics, artificial intelligence, and automation. These factors will revolutionise the working environment of the future[19] and have posed a threat to human knowledge and skills. Bhalla, Dyrcks and Strack[20] stated that a tidal wave of change is coming that will soon make the

---

14 Uzhenyu, 2017.

15 Chimbganda, 2015.

16 Uzhenyu, 2017.

17 Chimbganda, 2015.

18 WEF, 2016.

19 Ibid.

20 Bhalla, Dyrcks & Strack, 2017.

way we work almost unrecognisable to today's business leaders. In an age of rapidly evolving technologies, business models, demographics, and even workplace attitudes, change is not only constant but also exponential in its pace and scope. Several factors have led to Zimbabwe's higher education being seen as a volatile, uncertain, complex and ambiguous environment due to issues such as the paradigm shift, international influence, perceptions of poor quality education, future employment uncertainties and rapid technological advancement, coupled with economic hardships. These are explained in detail below.

Rapid technological advancement: a source of volatility and uncertainty

Zimbabwe's higher education is facing an uncertain future as it experiences an industrial (digital) revolution, which requires some time for adjustment. Technologists describe staggering upheaval – even a possible dystopian future, with the possibility of millions of professions being lost to automation and artificial intelligence. This has the potential to cause great chaos and uncertainty for both students and academics.[21] It seems as if no new jobs will be created anytime soon to push the situation through the technological disruption positively. An explosion in free online learning means that the knowledge once imparted to a lucky few has been released to anyone with a smartphone or laptop.[22] Some of those directly influencing HE are massive open online courses (MOOCs), open educational resources (OERs), new learning styles, and mounting financial and sustainability pressures on both institution leaders and academics. Technology seems to be pushing humans, rather than the other way round.[23]

Future employment uncertainty

Recent developments in the knowledge-driven, post-industrial economy have radically affected university students' prospects for entering and completing successful careers. Careers in accounting, banking and finance have recently become unstable, with several banks retrenching almost a quarter of their employees.[24] Technological advances have shifted the frontier between work tasks performed by employees and those performed by digitisation, which has led to the restructuring of financial organisations as well as a redefinition of work activities. In addition, uncertainty has been breeding because, over the last 20 years, traditional careers with lifelong security and opportunities for financial success, have been systematically replaced by a contract with workers who

---

21 Pandor, 2019: 2.

22 Lucas, 2012.

23 Ibid.

24 Mhlanga, 2017.

maintain their employability. The gig economy has replaced permanent employment.[25] Owing to the disruptions and changes in the processes and systems in organisations, college degrees no longer assure graduates of marketable knowledge and skills, and thus traditional career advice yields limited results in a VUCA environment.[26] The students see a bleak future full of sporadic layoffs, endless efforts to upgrade their job skills, and perpetually recombining work teams of insiders and outsourcers. Continuous corporate rightsizing will dictate a portfolio career strategy. This new consensus has far-reaching implications for higher education in general, and academic advising in particular.[27] In addition, witnessing the huge number of graduates who have left university but are still struggling to secure decent employment has thrown a dark cloud of uncertainty over many students. The unemployment rate in Zimbabwe was recorded at 92% by the end of 2018.[28]

Paradigm shift: Ambiguity

The previous HE model of lecturing, cramming and examinations seems to be fading away, posing challenges for academics who need to redesign their curricula.[29] An integration between technology (the use of online facilities as well as software) and its applications to assist humans in their work and personal environments has to take centre stage.[30] Information access, social change and the decades-long trend of ever-increasing costs have left higher education with a lot of unanswered questions, multiple challenges and unbearable uncertainty.

Pressure from international influence: Ambiguity

The internationalisation of HE and student mobility are now the order of the day in a world that has become a global village owing to access to technology. Due to international influence, higher education systems in countries such as South Africa and Botswana have been undergoing fundamental reforms, in response to the trend of globalisation as well as to meet the ever-changing expectations of knowledge-based societies.[31] Particularly, in Zimbabwe, membership of international organisations such as the Commonwealth, the United Nations and its specialized agencies like the United Nations Educational, Scientific and Cultural Organisation (UNESCO),

---

25 Pandor, 2019.

26 Bhalla et al., 2017.

27 Lucas, 2012.

28 York, 2018.

29 Lucas, 2012.

30 Pandor, 2019.

31 Garwe, 2015.

the United Nations Children's Fund (UNICEF), the United Nations Population Fund Activities (UNFPA) and African Unity (African Union), has influenced great changes in curricula.[32] Programmes such as HIV/AIDS Education, Environmental Science Education, Culture of Peace, and Population Education, have been introduced. As such, several universities are now functioning based on the demands of donors who are influencing the government to institute curricula reforms. Globalisation is also increasing pressure on tertiary institutions to move towards the use of new information and communication technologies (ICTs) to widen access to their programmes.[33] However, given the economic situation of Zimbabwe, it has been a big challenge for HE institutions to adjust to the changes.

Perceptions of poor quality education: Uncertainty

The universities lack formal quality structures to meet the basic requirements for global competitiveness. As highlighted above, the institutions have very limited resources, which makes it very difficult to be competitive. These present uncertainties to students in terms of whether their degree certificates are accredited or not. A study conducted by the local industry suggests that most degree programmes are theory-based, thus graduates fail to create employment and come up with their own inventions or have to respond to changing industrial demands.[34] This lack of hands-on skills and good academics has resulted in the production of graduates who are ill-prepared for work in the organisations.[35] A Presidential Commission of Inquiry into Education and Training in 1999 detected a disconnect between Zimbabwe's university curriculum and national development. The Higher Education aims to align its education system to countries such as China and the United States, where universities are think tanks that are key to socio-economic development.

LEADING ONESELF THROUGH RESILIENCE IN A VUCA WORLD: PROFESSOR PRIMROSE KURASHA

Given the rapid change and uncertainty experienced in HE, the most valuable assets that academics are left with are what make them human, i.e. "learnability and resilience", or the ability to adjust and the will and capacity to learn.[36] This ability is called "learning agility", and is made up of nine facets of behaviour, which include flexibility, speed, experimenting, collaborating, information gathering, feedback-seeking, self-efficacy,

---

32 Chimbganda, 2015.

33 Garwe, 2015.

34 Ibid.

35 Chimbganda, 2015.

36 Burke, 2017.

adaptability and reflecting. The primary goal for learning has now become creating learning agility. Academics and institutional leaders need self-directedness and agency to face volatility, uncertainty, complexity and ambiguity in HE.[37] The VUCA world does not present problems that have predictable solutions; there is a need to cultivate resilience, flexible thinking, reflectiveness, and the skills to approach challenges as they come. This chapter, therefore, focuses on the application of the Theory of Personal Resilience and the VUCA Prime Theory with special reference to agility.

The adjustments to the abovementioned challenges have not been so easy considering that Zimbabwean institutions are building their future on very fragile financial ground. A funding crisis has created a shortfall that the universities' brightest brains are struggling to solve. Institutions' costs are rising, owing to pricey investments in technology, academics' salaries and mounting administrative costs.[38] However, in the middle of all these challenges, a true leader sees an opportunity and the dire need to be more competitive. Professor Primrose Kurasha, who was the Vice-Chancellor for Zimbabwe Open University, realised that the internationalisation of HE and student mobility have become the order of the day in a global village, owing to rapid technological change. She indicated that to survive, leaders need to be innovative and constantly develop new strategies to leverage these developing challenges and opportunities.[39] Professor Kurasha's agility helped her to realise that Open Distance Learning (ODL) was the best way in which to attain a university education. This strategy, she believed, would compete better with the MOOCs offered globally by top tier universities. ODL was a measure in response to world demands which strategically support the never-ending, 24/7 nature of today's learning that extends beyond the classroom.[40] ODL had to be moved from the periphery to the centre of university life in order to cater to the chaos associated with a lack of time to attend classes, a lack of resources and poor infrastructure.

Professor Kurasha's leadership was characterised by vision, understanding, clarity and agility – the "flips" to the VUCA model. Because she had a vision, obstacles did not deter her – no matter how big or small. Her first point of departure was understanding that higher education is not steady, secure, simple or clear. She declared that to share knowledge to the universe, open distance learning (ODL) a roadmap. She designed her vision based on this new paradigm. Where there was a growing paucity of classroom facilities to offer university education to the growing number of would-be students in the country, Professor Kurasha noted that ODL could offer an excellent education without worrying about classroom space and university infrastructure.[41]

---

37 Meyer, 2016.
38 Burke, 2017.
39 ZOU, 2014.
40 Kurasha, 2015.
41 Ibid.

Professor Kurasha, with her agile ideas, started to advocate for open distance learning as a solution to the chaotic, turbulent and rapidly changing world of HE. It was through her astute leadership and innovative management that the Zimbabwe Open University promoted a revolution in education that aimed at promoting ODL.[42] She was a force to be reckoned with and not easily intimidated. She was highly resilient and self-driven, and managed to clear, level and reshape the contours around formal education with the single aim of providing everyone with an education. She had a clear vision and was the mother of ODL in Zimbabwe, in Africa, and the world. Professor Kurasha is credited with setting up the first University Quality Assurance Directorate in Zimbabwe in 2007, which subsequently led her to be appointed to the Advisory Board of the Harmonisation of African Higher Education Quality Assurance and Accreditation (HAQAA).[43] She believed that sharing of information would change the world. Professor Kurasha touched many lives; her commitment was to mobilise member institutions and African countries and governments towards entrenching ODL as a reputable, functional and sustainable educational system across the whole of the African continent.[44] In addition, she adjusted to the ever-changing demands on HE by overhauling university and college curricula, and aligning them with the modern job market and broad economic growth fundamentals. To manage this effectively and shield herself during the turbulent times, resilience and agility were the two weapons that sustained her.[45]

Professor Kurasha could identify and analyse a problem from various perspectives, and emphasised that the solution is to develop a problem-solving mind-set and build future-oriented capabilities.[46] She noted that to be effective in a turbulent environment, leaders must learn to look and listen beyond their functional areas of expertise and lead with vision. She communicated with other academics, formulated teams and collaborated with other universities that had practiced ODL[47], which helped her to be aware of uncertainties; she believed that clarifying problems helps to counter complexity. Professor Kurasha was very involved in the deliberative process of making sense of the chaos that was taking place in the HE field. She was capable of scrutinising all the trivial details associated with the chaos, which enabled her to make more informed business decisions. Most of all Professor Kurasha was agile, thus she could counter ambiguity easily; she could communicate across the university and quickly apply solutions.[48] Vision, understanding, clarity and agility are intertwined elements that helped her to persist through the challenges she was exposed to.

---

42 ZOU, 2014.
43 Kurasha, 2015.
44 ZOU, 2014.
45 Kurasha, 2015.
46 Ibid.
47 ZOU, 2014.
48 Kinsinger & Walch, 2012.

THE THEORY OF PERSONAL RESILIENCE

The above discussion indicates the importance of resilience in managing chaos and complexity. Resilience is defined as a process that consists of positive adaptations when facing significant hardship or adversity.[49] Adult personal resilience is a multi-faceted construct that includes a person's determination and ability to endure, adapt, and recover from adversity. The theory indicates that resilience is made up of four components: determination, endurance, adaptability, and recuperability.[50] These four components can be improved in an individual through self-awareness and self-efficacy. They can also be developed through increasing openness to learn, by turning perceived obstacles into challenges, as well as by focusing on self-care, self-compassion, and wellness.[51] Professor Kurasha faced both economic hardships and a turbulent environment, but she could bounce back from setbacks and overcome adversities; she managed to cope well with high levels of ongoing change and constant pressure.

Professor Kurasha also managed to discard the old ineffectual habits of Zimbabwe's HE that were dysfunctional and maladaptive to new methods of learning (ODL). Her ability to withstand and recover quickly from difficult conditions and still gather ideas to move forward indicate that endurance and innovativeness are key to success when leading in a VUCA environment.

On the side of the students, the VUCA environment requires leaders to redirect the attention of students to push back from the constant digital distractions and practice mindfulness to ensure healthy progress – both emotionally and intellectually. A world that is full of technological distractions presents too much ambiguity and complexity for students. Resilience, coupled with mindfulness, can be viewed as a tool with which students can handle the complexities of an ever-changing world. Institutional leaders in the Zimbabwean higher education environment need to teach students to be mindful, resilient and self-lead, which can be achieved by leading by example. Since life at university has become volatile, leaders need to offer steady and consistent guidance as solid role models. To cater for uncertainty, nurturing resilience and focus will surely combat an ambiguous society. Due to the complexity of life, leaders should equip students to practice mindfulness in order to be able to concentrate on one simple goal, rather than multi-task all the time. Finally, to deal with ambiguity, it is the role of leaders to assist students to clarify what they want in life and direct their efforts accordingly. It is important to emphasise that the winners of tomorrow will deal proactively with chaos; they will look at chaos per se as a source of opportunity, not as a problem to get around. In an environment where economic hardships and a lack

---

49 Zauszniewski, Bekhet & Suresky, 2010.

50 Britt, Shen, Sinclair, Grossman & Klieger, 2016.

51 Kotzé & Nel, 2013.

of resources also play a role, resilience on its own may not be adequate to navigate the VUCA environment; it needs to be coupled with agility. Professor Kurasha applied both agility and resilience to adjust to the challenges in the Zimbabwe HE system. The above section provided a discussion on resilience; the subsequent section will address agility from the perspective of the VUCA Prime Theory.

AGILITY

According to Professor Kurasha, "surviving and prospering in these turbulent situations will be possible if institutions have the essential capabilities to recognise and understand their changing environments and respond in a proper way to every unexpected change." This speaks to an agility which is referred to as the ability to handle constant change as well as threats and opportunities presented by the environment.[52] In the higher education context, agility has been put forward as a possible solution to compete in today's dynamic environment.[53] The key characteristics of agility are versatility, flexibility and responsiveness to the changing environment. With the call for institutions to be more responsive to the global economy and the changing nature of work demands, a strategy such as agility that is based on speed can provide a sustainable competitive advantage.[54] A good example is that, in response to the 4IR, the top-tier universities in the world have adopted an explicit multi-disciplinary approach by including modules related to the liberal arts. Consistent with that, several South African universities have recently followed suit, introducing degrees that integrate fields such as Economics, Psychology, Technology and Politics to promote integrated, critical and solution-based thinking. In addition to that, 60% of learning is now taking place online.[55]

The view that through the process of rapid response, agility could achieve a competitive advantage was supported by Meyer.[56] Agility facilitates responsiveness through innovation and quality, which comes from the implementation of an agile strategy. Agility is focused on rapid responsiveness and mastering market turbulence, and requires specific capabilities, some of which were displayed by Professor Kurasha. If institutions refuse to change, the world will die a slow death.[57] Rodney-Gumede[58] emphasised that the skills and experiences that were important only three years ago have begun, and will continue to, shift from being industry-specific to being transformable and centred on what he referred to as the 4Cs: collaboration, communication,

---

52 Sharifi & Zhang, 1999.
53 Crocitto & Youssef, 2003.
54 Meyer, 2016.
55 Gray, 2016.
56 Meyer, 2016.
57 Brown, 2012.
58 Rodney-Gumede, 2019.

creativity, and critical hinking. This was supported by Gray[59], who stated that "35% of the skills considered important today will change as the fourth Industrial Revolution (4IR) will have brought us advanced technologies." Ten crucial skills for the future of jobs due to the 4IR include complex problem-solving, critical thinking, creativity, people management, coordination with others, emotional intelligence, judgmental decision-making, service orientation, negotiation and cognitive flexibility. All of this will influence curricula change, but to be able to adjust to all this turbulence, leaders in institutions of higher learning need to be both agile and resilient.

Agility can be corroborated by the Contingency Theory, which claims that there is no best way to organise a corporation, lead a company or make decisions. Instead, the optimal course of action is contingent upon the internal and external situation. Thus, drawing from Brown[60], a contingent leader is more agile and effectively applies their style of leadership to the right situation. Collinson[61] noted that the success of an organisation in an uncertain environment largely depends on how leaders view the situation. The author[62] was of the view that when operating in a VUCA environment, there is no one 'best way' or approach to leading or doing things, as different situations call for different approaches to handling, leading and solving arising issues; leaders just need to be more flexible and respond rapidly to the changing environment. Leading an institution of higher learning which embraces anomalies or challenges now and then requires 'adaptable' and 'situational' approaches.

The VUCA Prime Theory, provides counteractive methods to deal with each VUCA element. The theory clearly indicates that, when the environment is volatile, leaders need to identify a clear vision. When the vision is clear leaders take control of actions, regardless of what is going on in the environment. When experiencing uncertainty, which is a major challenge in institutions of higher learning, one needs to seek understanding. Uncertainty is fed by a lack of understanding; when individuals seek understanding through previous experiences as well as from others, uncertainty is suppressed. Complexity is reduced by clarity and ambiguity yields agility.[63] Below is an illustration of the VUCA Prime Theory and how it counteracts VUCA environments.

---

59 Gray, 2016.
60 Brown, 2012.
61 Collinson, 2011.
62 Ibid.
63 Crocitto & Youssef, 2003.

VUCA
Volatile
Uncertainty
Complexity
Ambiguity

VUCA Prime
Vision
understanding
Clarity

Agility
*Lack of the prime
result in VUCA*

Figure 7.1: The VUCA Prime Theory (Source: Author's own)

Professor Kurasha[64] noted that leading today's students often feels like being in a new country with old maps that don't work. Understanding and connecting with this new generation can be frustrating and draining, which is coupled with the complex environment in which institutions are operating. We need new strategies on how to march off our old maps and create new ones that fit in with the new generation and the chaos. Although agility assists us to map new ways, we need resilience to counter the difficult situations associated with change. Resilient individuals possess some of the dynamic sets of skills utilised when facing a difficult situation, encompassing a range of thoughts such as positive outlook, and the capacity to bounce back after a challenging situation.[65] This enables resilient and agile leaders to navigate through chaos and complexity.

RECOMMENDATIONS

From the above discussion, two sets of recommendations can be drawn: one regarding the way forward for the Zimbabwean education system (through agility), and one on how leading self can be used to influence leaders in institutions of higher learning as a way to counter chaos and complexity. It is clearly stated in the literature that, to be able to navigate through the VUCA environment, institutional leaders need to be agile and resilient.

---

64 Kurasha, 2015.
65 Simpson & Jones, 2012.

Recommendation 1: Improving the resilience of leaders

Considering that resilience was one of the lead-self factors that was successfully applied by Professor Kurasha in Zimbabwe's Higher Education sector, improving resilience among leaders in institutions of higher learning may be critical as a way to assist them to navigate the VUCA environment. This is consistent with Crane[66], who noted that resilience can be enhanced among leaders for better results. Different methods of enhancing resilience should be explored and administered to institutional leaders; such efforts, according to Ivtzan, Lomas, Hefferon and Worth[67], may focus on approaches that encourage positive coping, positive thinking and behavioural control. These may include coaching, mindfulness, self-regulation and cognitive behavioural techniques.

Coaching

Coaching can improve both resilience and agility, thus it can be used as a way to equip leaders operating in chaotic and complex environments. Coaching facilitates learning, growth and reflection in the pursuit of goals. As individuals work through the self-regulation cycle towards their goals, they come across hurdles and challenges to overcome (negative self-talk, self-defeating behaviours, staying focused on one's goal over time).[68, 69] Overcoming these challenges is argued to improve an individual's self-confidence and consequently, they become more resilient.[70] Leaders in higher education are exposed to challenging conditions, which is why they need a recipe on how to overcome these hurdles. Providing them with practical coaching may assist them to bounce back after encountering major challenges.

Mindfulness and compassion-based practices

Other techniques that may be used to develop resilience among leaders in institutions of higher learning are mindfulness and compassion-based practices.[71] These approaches improve social-emotional skills and wellbeing, and in the long run improve an individual's ability to develop and maintain a well-managed work environment.[72] Given the complexity and chaotic environment presented by higher education, developing

---

66 Crane, 2017.

67 Ivtzan, Lomas, Hefferon & Worth, 2016.

68 Bachkirova, Jackson, Gannon, Iordanou & Myers, 2017.

69 Grant & Gelety, 2009.

70 Ibid.

71 Crane, 2017.

72 Ibid.

resilience through mindfulness may assist leaders to be more focused and work towards achieving specific sets of goals. Reb[73] claimed that certain practices may be applied, including enabling individuals to recognise and slow down automatic and typical reactions; to respond more effectively to complex or difficult situations; to see situations more clearly; and to become more creative and achieve balance and resilience.

Self-regulation of stress responses

The higher education environment in Zimbabwe is characterised by stress and uncertainty, thus leaders need strategic ways of responding to this environment. Crane[74] suggested that self-regulation skills can be used to handle stress and eventually develop resilience; these skills enable individuals to self regulate their mental, emotional and physical systems.[75] Overall, the self-regulation of stress response approaches involve helping individuals identify personal reactions to stress and teach them ways of positive coping that counter the negative effects.[76, 77]

Cognitive behavioural techniques

Ivtzan et al.[78] suggested that cognitive behavioural techniques that stem from cognitive behavioural therapy (CBT) may be employed to develop resilience. The main idea behind CBT is that learning to evaluate thinking patterns realistically and adaptively influences how individuals respond emotionally and behaviourally.[79] Some of the cognitive behavioural techniques for resilience include attentional training, energy management, relaxation training, imagery and self-talk.[80] These may help individuals to enhance their resilience, and in turn enable them to better manage the VUCA environment presented by higher education.

Recommendation 2: Improving the agility of leaders to impact transformation in the education system

Agility has been proven to be one of the key characteristics of successful leadership. Being agile means being quick; responding and acting swiftly in line with changes.

---

73 Reb, Narayanan & Ho, 2015.
74 Crane, 2017.
75 Crane, 2017.
76 Ibid.
77 Ivtzan et al., 2016.
78 Ibid.
79 Crane, 2017.
80 Ibid.

The intentional development of agility competencies through flexibility, an emphasis on personal strengths and speed in adaptability may thus assist in navigating a VUCA environment. This builds capacity and confidence, which in turn assists leaders to be more effective in ambiguous environments.[81] In line with agility in the context of HE in Zimbabwe, the following can be recommended to tackle the challenges experienced by most universities:

- From a reputational point of view, the HE system in Zimbabwe must transform and create a perception that it offers degree programmes that are current and relevant to future graduates entering the 4IR. The literature indicated that a shadow of doubt has been cast on Zimbabwe's HE system, and most companies no longer have confidence in the products of the university. It is time for leaders to re-build confidence in the labour market by revamping the curriculum to meet the new job demands. This simply calls for adaptability of both leaders and the system at large.
- Another major challenge causing chaos in Zimbabwe HE is the lack of resources. Realising that resources are limited, the reality is that the universities in Zimbabwe cannot compete directly with top-tier universities across the world. They can, however, compete against other African universities if they differentiate themselves through agile and adaptive methods, which may include the following:
  ◦ Offer programmes related to the 4IR, specifically through a blended approach to teaching and learning.
  ◦ Identify a niche competitive advantage within the African context, in terms of research expertise and local economic development initiatives.
  ◦ Identify teaching and research-based strengths and areas of specialisation intrinsic to Africa that differentiate the universities globally.
  ◦ Aggressively market 4IR related programmes on national (and international) news and social media platforms, including reputable newspapers and Business/Management/Leadership/Economics/Finance magazines. This should also include social and business networks such as LinkedIn, ZipRecruiter, Indeed, CareerBuilder and Facebook.

A complete change in the current business model adopted by many universities is recommended, but this can only be achieved with help of an adaptive and agile leader. There is a strong need to be proactive and responsive, as opposed to reactive. This implies that universities need to become more responsive (and even predictive or pre-emptive) to the dynamics of change, and more importantly, become more agile to address the changing environment as new developments arise (or are imminent). There is also a serious need for technology-driven approaches in higher education. The universities need to make a conscious decision to adapt to the challenges posed by technology, globalisation and competitors. Above that, these universities should

---

81 Meyer, 2016.

constantly interact with industry and public sector role players. All this can be enabled by leaders who are well equipped to navigate the VUCA environment through resilience and agility.

CONCLUDING REMARKS

In conclusion, as the custodians of disseminating knowledge, universities need to be at the forefront of equipping societies for the rigours of technological change and the 4IR. Given the socio-economic imbalances inherent to the Zimbabwean economy, a failure to adjust and manage change will have severe implications on the wellbeing of students, and exacerbate the problem from one of being unemployed to one of being unemployable. If Zimbabwean universities do not adapt, they run the risk of losing relevance in the broader higher education environment. As much as the country is suffering economically, with resilient leadership coupled with high adaptive behaviour, the universities can survive the turbulence of a VUCA environment imposed by globalisation and technology.

CHAPTER 8

OPTIMISM AND ADAPTABILITY WITHIN THE SOUTH AFRICAN HIGHER EDUCATION SECTOR

Daphne Pillay

ABSTRACT

The South African higher education sector remains in a state of transition. This necessitates a constant reappraisal of higher education in the country as the forces outlined in the VUCA model slowly permeate the abstruse environment of academia. It is expected that such a tumultuous environment will require strong elements of leading one's self as change and transition become the norm. This chapter aims to contextualise the South African higher education sector as a VUCA environment by referring to a specific example, i.e. #feesmustfall. The relevance of lead-self components as useful tools that can be used to manoeuvre through the turbulent South African higher education environment is emphasised, with particular emphasis on optimism and adaptability. The chapter concludes with a discussion on a theory of optimism and adaptability, and offers recommendations for theoretical and practical applications within higher education institutions.

INTRODUCTION

In the fluid context of the 21st century education environment, higher education is continually confronted with uncertainties that affect daily operations. These uncertainties are brought about by globalisation, the use of contemporary technologies and VUCA, which symbolises the chaotic, turbulent, and rapidly changing education environment.[1] While this highly volatile environment has become the norm in global higher education, the South African higher education environment must deal with its context-specific challenges. Some of these challenges are minute, often resulting from institutional factors such as changes in institutional policy, strategy and management. Other challenges are a result of externally motivated factors such as political,

---

1   Korsakova, 2019.

economic, technological, environmental and legislative changes. These external factors are more pronounced and have had a significant impact on the functioning of South African tertiary institutions. Penprase[2] stated that even without considering the specific influences on the education system, the higher education sector is one of the most rapidly changing sectors of society.

In the context of a post-colonial and post-apartheid South Africa, significant political, economic and legislative changes are influencing the South African higher education system.[3] These changes have resulted in higher education becoming increasingly complex, uncertain and turbulent. As a result, change is an ongoing characteristic of South African higher education institutions.[4] Changes in the size and shape of higher education, the character of student distributions, and changes in university management and governance, all add to the volatility of the higher education sector in South Africa.[5] Amidst these changes there are specific events that stand out due to their significant impact on the South African higher education system. Probably the most significant recent event was the contentious #feesmustfall movement. This student-led protest movement began in mid-October 2015 in response to an increase in tuition fees across South African universities.[6] The repercussions of the movement had devastating effects on the interpersonal relationships between universities and students, student learning and the academic calendar. These negative effects resulted in the South African higher education system entering a state of disequilibrium and symbolised a turning point for higher education in the country.[7] The uncertainty and complexity of the situation made it difficult for all involved parties to direct their cognitions and behaviours in ways that were inclusive and free from disparity. This ability, otherwise referred to as lead-self, was a concept that was integral to ensuring appropriate individual management during the tumultuous period of #feesmustfall, and will be further explored in this chapter.

SETTING THE SCENE: THE CONTEXT OF HIGHER EDUCATION IN SOUTH AFRICA

According to Jansen[8], the prominent role of students and student organisations within higher education institutions has for a long time been accepted as one of the most distinguishing features in South African higher education. However, with the emergence

---

2   Penprase, 2018.

3   Jansen, 2004.

4   Ibid.

5   Ibid.

6   Kgatle, 2018.

7   Ibid.

8   Jansen, 2004.

of the democratic dispensation post-1994, the focus of these student organisations began to gradually evolve. Jansen[9] asserted that during the apartheid regime, the focus of student organisations revolved around protests against an unlawful government system. However, since the emergence of the new democratic government, a newfound focus of student protests emphasises demands for easier access to higher education via lower fees, the decolonisation of the education system, financial assistance for disadvantaged students, and relief from personal debt to the institutions. Badat[10] asserted that the movement towards transformation in higher education post-1994 embodies paradoxes which serve two primary purposes. Firstly, it heightens the prevalence of social and political dilemmas by emphasising the prevailing inequality to educational access, and secondly, it gives rise to the types of radical change initiatives characterised through the #feesmustfall campaigns.

Introducing the VUCA environment: #feesmustfall in South African universities

The #feesmustfall movement can be likened to the metaphor of a "boiling pot." Mavunga[11] stated that students' disgruntlement with several areas of contention in the South African higher education system had been boiling under the surface for a long time. With the areas of discontent increasing in the higher education sector, the initial demand for easier access to higher education slowly began to evolve, and the movement progressed from demands for financial assistance and no fee increases to a call for government and tertiary institutions to eliminate tuition fees.[12] According to Kgatle[13], in 2015, the protest against fee increases for the 2016 academic year ended when the South African government announced that the protesters' demands would be met. While the unrest settled for a short period, protests resumed in 2016 when the South African Minister of Higher Education announced that there would be fee increases capped at 8% for the 2017 academic year.[14] However, institutions were given the freedom to decide by how much their tuition would increase.[15] Protests started at the University of the Witwatersrand and soon spread to the University of Cape Town and Rhodes University, before rapidly spreading to other universities across the country. According to Mavunga[16], while the protests were initially a reaction

9   Jansen, 2004.

10 Badat, 2010.

11 Mavunga, 2019.

12 Ibid.

13 Kgatle, 2018.

14 Ibid.

15 ENCA, 2016.

16 Mavunga, 2019.

to the proposed tuition fee increases, the agenda soon broadened in scope to highlight discontent with several other areas. The students were also protesting against the poor treatment of workers in support services such as cleaners, gardeners and security guards in universities. Furthermore, students began to call for the decolonisation of South African universities.[17] This emphasised the removal of any school of thought which regards anything non-European and non-white as inferior. The growing irritation and dissatisfaction amongst protesting students with how the South African government was addressing these concerns resulted in a series of protests, which spread rapidly across several higher education institutions in South Africa.

The inherent nature of the #feesmustfall protests were intense and characterised by damage to institutional property and the loss of valuable teaching time, placing universities under immense pressure as they began to engage in the damage control process. Mutekwe[18] provided further detail into the nature of these protests by stating that the majority of the uprisings resulted in burnt buildings and vehicles at several universities. Additionally, due to the unpredictable nature of the protest action, universities across the country were forced to initiate total campus shut-downs, which led to the suspension of all learning activities until student demands were addressed.[19] The after effects of these protests were significant, and had substantial financial implications as universities had to escalate security on campus and cater for students who did not have access to learning material.[20] Additionally, academic staff in universities were placed under immense pressure as they needed to work swiftly to assist students to meet revised deadlines for exams and graduation dates, and to complete the module syllabi in the limited amount of time that was left in the academic year.

The unpredictable nature of protest action during #feesmustfall: Volatility

The unannounced eruption of protest action during the #feesmustfall movement created an environment characterised by a high degree of volatility. According to Sullivan[21], volatility indicates a sudden unpredictable and extreme change, which in most cases occurs for the worst. The volatile nature of the higher education system during protest actions signified something greater than student dissatisfaction, however; it signified the unpredictability of future trends. Postma[22] stated that protest action is boundless

---

17 Naicker, 2016.

18 Mutekwe, 2017

19 Le Grange, 2016.

20 Kamga, 2019.

21 Sullivan, 2012.

22 Postma, 2016.

and unpredictable because it activates a chain reaction that cannot be controlled or predetermined. While there was a general awareness that students were disgruntled with the exorbitant cost of higher education, the first upsurge of student protests about #feesmustfall was unanticipated and presented itself at a time that created maximum impact, i.e. before the final examinations at the end of the academic year. Furthermore, at the apparent conclusion of the protest in December 2015, the entire higher education system was left in a state of turbulence, not knowing when to expect the next wave of protests. A consistent theme that appeared from the wide media coverage of the movement was the public's experience of the event as highly volatile and unpredictable. Both civil society and management and staff within South African universities shared the same sentiments, which echoed the fact that the situation was extremely volatile.[23] Although government and higher education institutions had managed to demobilise the students for a short period, there was still the risk of protest action erupting when least expected.[24] Bennett and Lemoine[25] stated that volatile environments are characterised by the availability of information in a situation that is understandable, but where change is frequent and sometimes unpredictable. This was indeed the case with the #feesmustfall movement, as according to Kgatle[26], during the protest the students changed their demands from simply protesting against a fee hike to protesting for a fee-free higher education for all, a decolonised education system, and better conditions of employment for outsourced staff. The emerging demands of the protesters occurred frequently with no prior warning. Additionally, the response of the protesters to the government's delay in meeting their demands for a fee-free decolonised education system was unpredictable, with short periods of calm followed by sudden and unannounced periods of protest action.[27]

Student protestors' need for concrete answers during #feesmustfall: Uncertainty

A defining characteristic of the #feesmustfall movement was the disruption of the established way of functioning regarding student learning and university processes. This disruption resulted in uncertainty, as the higher education system was left in a state of transition with a lack of clarity about the present situation and future outcomes. Langa, Ndelu, Edwin and Vilakazi[28] stated that the high degree of confusion and lack of clarity during the #feesmustfall movement was to a large extent due to the shifting

---

23 Madia, 2016.

24 Ibid.

25 Lemoine, 2014.

26 Kgatle, 2018.

27 Ibid.

28 Langa, Ndelu, Edwin & Vilakazi, 2017.

of accountability between stakeholders. The protesters maintained their stance that education is a right that all students are entitled to, and therefore it should not be treated as a commodity, while university management argued that satisfying this need was not possible as there were insufficient annual subsidies from the South African government.[29] In return, the South African government argued that while it acknowledged the demands of the students, they were still awaiting the findings of the Commission of Inquiry into Higher Education and Training to provide feedback on the feasibility and affordability of free higher education in South Africa. According to Langa et al.[30], the uncertainty surrounding the possibility of free education was compounded by the fact that while government had given an undertaking to provide universities with additional funding, there were conflicting reports about whether this obligation had been met or not. The lack of concrete solutions fuelled the frustrations of students and had a significant impact on the teaching and support staff within the universities, as there was still no direction or certainty regarding a way forward and what to expect in the year to come.[31]

The multifaceted nature of decolonising the education system: Complexity

Bennett and Lemoine[32] defined a complex environment as one that consists of many interconnected parts and variables. While the primary focus of the #feesmustfall movement was around fee-free education, protesters soon voiced their demands for a decolonised education system, which in itself comprised various complex issues. According to Bennett and Lemoine[33], while some information is available in a complex environment, the volume and nature of the available information is too overwhelming to process. The demand for a decolonised education system comprises several multi-faceted areas that must be considered. De Carvalho and Florez-Florez[34] asserted that the demands for a decolonised education curriculum cannot be fulfilled unless the concept of decolonisation is examined within the specific cultural context in which it is expected to occur. The authors added that decolonising the higher education curriculum requires both students and academics to analyse and remove any values, norms, practices and thinking that regard anything non-European and non-white as

---

29 Langa et al., 2017.
30 Ibid.
31 Mutekwe, 2017.
32 Bennett & Lemoine, 2014.
33 Lemoine, 2014.
34 De Carvalho & Florez-Florez, 2014.

inferior; a task which has several intricate aspects to consider.[35] According to Mutekwe[36], whilst the act of decolonising the education system appears to be easily achievable, the concept in practice is characterised by a high level of complexity, as decolonisation involves more than simply amending module content, but involves redesigning content to decolonise attitudes, values, and world views. Therefore, it is argued that the demand for a decolonised education system extends far beyond changing curriculum, but involves the intricate and complex task of first informing and broadening existing attitudes, values and worldviews to embrace schools of thought and philosophies that are non-western and non-white, and to begin using these thoughts to extend teaching philosophies. While the very act of analysing and removing Eurocentric values, norms and attitudes is multi-faceted, within the South African environment decolonisation is also tied to the complex issues of justice, restitution, and transformation that must also be dealt with.[37] Within the African context, the narrative of decolonisation symbolises the depth of the reaction against the influence of racist imperial colonists, who for many years were responsible for the dehumanisation of black Africans on the continent.[38] Therefore, it goes without saying that addressing the decolonisation of the education system warrants addressing aspects of justice, restoration and transformation, which made the #feesmustfall movement truly complex.

Conflicting approaches by student protesters: Ambiguity

According to Sullivan[39], an ambiguous situation occurs when information is incomplete, contradictory or too inaccurate for individuals to draw clear conclusions. Additionally, ambiguity represents the inability to accurately conceptualise threats and opportunities before they become lethal due to inadequate information.[40] Ambiguity during the #feesmustfall movement stemmed from the violent nature of the protests. While students shared a common agenda regarding the decolonisation of the education system and fee-free education, it quickly became apparent that there was a proportion of students and university staff who strongly disapproved of how protesters went about furthering their agenda, i.e. through the use of violence.[41] The disapproval of violence demonstrated that despite being confronted by the same form of adversity, when spurred by the power of individual agency, some of the students began to differ in the manner in which they interpreted the situations around them.[42] Based on the

---

35 Ibid.

36 Mutekwe, 2017.

37 Ndlovu-Gatsheni, 2014.

38 Ibid.

39 Sullivan, 2012.

40 Kail, 2010.

41 Mavunga, 2019.

42 Ibid.

differences in opinion between groups of students regarding the use of violence as a tool for resolving conflict, the #feesmustfall movement became characterised by internal contradictions and ambiguities.[43] The volatile, uncertain, complex and ambiguous nature of #feesmustfall heightened the need for self-leadership, especially since the implications of certain actions would have far-reaching effects on various stakeholders.

Spotlight example of lead self during #feesmustfall: Professor Adam Habib

"I thought #FeesMustFall was a progressive struggle. I think, as a demand, [it was] absolutely a legitimate demand. Where I differed with the 'Fallers' [students] was around the tactics, strategies and how they played out."
–Adam Habib[44]

While several examples of lead-self were demonstrated during the #feesmustfall movement, a prominent figure and one that featured extensively in the media coverage of the movement was Adam Mahomed Habib. Adam Habib was a South African professor of political geography and the Vice-Chancellor and Principal of the University of the Witwatersrand (Wits) in Johannesburg, South Africa.[45] His prominence during the #feesmustfall saga placed him in the spotlight as a self-leader who possessed the ability to reflect on how the decisions taken would affect all involved parties. This characteristic reflects the actions of an individual who was aware of, and actively managed, his thoughts, emotions, and behaviours, which is consistent with self-leadership. In his book entitled *Rebels and Rage: Reflecting on #feesmustfall*, Professor Habib speaks about his personal experiences and involvement during the student protests that hit South Africa's higher education institutions from late 2015.[46] Leadership literature [47, 48] concurs on the notion that the best leaders must lead themselves first before leading others. While Professor Habib was often looked at as a leader who was responsible for the leadership of students, staff and university management, during the protest action his journey required strong elements of self-leadership, which influenced how he dealt with the situation. In interviews conducted with Professor Habib, he stated that many of the decisions he had taken as vice-chancellor during the time of the protests were "difficult" ones that had to be made.[49] While Professor Habib supported the call for

43 Mavunga, 2019.

44 Ngqakamba, 2019.

45 Ngqakamba, 2019.

46 Ibid.

47 Bryant & Kazan, 2012.

48 Kolzow, 2014.

49 Ngqakamba, 2019.

greater access to education and the decolonisation of the curriculum, he was clear on the notion of not relinquishing the power to determine how such goals would be achieved to a small group.[50] Conceding to this would have led to the marginalisation the majority, and by making decisions that took into account the needs of both the protesting and non-protesting staff and students, Professor Habib employed a leadership strategy that required both self-awareness and the management of personal feelings and thoughts, thus displaying characteristics of a self-leader.

Lead-self components emerging from the spotlight example

The Emotional Competency Model introduced by Goleman[51] focuses on emotional intelligence as a crucial competency needed for leading one's self. According to Ackley[52], emotional intelligence enables the self-leader to successfully recognise and manage his/her own emotions and subsequently manage the emotions of others. Goleman[53] stated that there are essentially four quadrants of emotional intelligence: self-awareness, self-management, social awareness and relationship management. Both adaptability and optimism are competencies found within the self-management quadrant.[54] The section below focuses on adaptability and optimism as components of lead-self that were evident in the spotlight example of Professor Adam Habib.

According to Spencer and Spencer[55], self-leaders display flexibility in receiving new information, which promotes letting go of old assumptions. This allows for easy adaptation to new environments. The volatility of the higher education sector during the #feesmustfall movement required constant adaptive responses, as the environment was in a permanent state of transition. By being adaptable, the self-leader can anticipate unexpected change and respond effectively. This was especially needed during the #feesmustfall movement, given the ambiguity that characterised the higher education environment because of changes in the curriculum and unexpected violent outbursts by protesters. According to Sanaghan[56], the volatile nature of the higher education employment sector will continue to be characterised by ambiguity and complexity, with no fast, fixed solutions. This requires university management to become self-leaders and adapt – especially during times of uncertainty. Weatherspoon-Robinson[57] stated that a key factor that differentiates effective self-leaders from ineffective self-leaders is the ability to refrain from dwelling on what is unfair about the situation,

---

50 Morell, 2019.
51 Goleman, 1995.
52 Ackley, 2016.
53 Goleman, 1995.
54 Ibid.
55 Spencer & Spencer, 1993.
56 Sanaghan, 2016.
57 Robinson, 2013.

and instead being resourceful in dealing with challenges in original ways. Amidst the call for a total campus shutdown by protestors, Professor Habib stated that he had a responsibility to ensure that the needs of all students and staff were considered.[58] He added that the majority of students and staff had indicated, through a poll, that they wanted to complete the academic year.[59] Through publicly indicating that the needs of all students were considered during the decision making processes regarding #feesmustfall, Professor Habib applied a flexible leadership style consistent with adaptability.

In addition to being adaptable, self-leaders display the psychological strength of optimism.[60] Optimism is a key ingredient of leading oneself as it can determine one's reaction to unfavourable events or circumstances. In an environment characterised by volatility, uncertainty, complexity and ambiguity, being optimistic is crucial as it allows for survival despite the negative circumstances that surround an individual. Goleman[61] stated that self-leaders are steadfast in their belief that an unfavourable situation will improve, while still adopting a realistic perspective of the current state of affairs. According to Goleman[62], optimism plays a role in effective decision making, especially in high-pressure situations. The author added that adopting an optimistic approach significantly affects the decision making capabilities and effectiveness of a leader. Therefore, optimism is seen as a key aspect for self-leaders, especially in less than suitable environments. Despite the bleak future at the time of #feesmustfall, Professor Habib remained optimistic that the future of South African education would improve. In his book, he addressed how the demands for unrestricted access to education and the decolonisation of the education system can be achieved through a practically workable solution.[63] Professor Habib maintained that there is a strong hope that demands for fee-free education might still be possible, more especially in a manner that does not infringe on the rights of parties involved. In his book, he dedicates a chapter to show how this could be something that could work while showing how the existing models are flawed.[64] He also demonstrated that through a series of analyses, these models can be fixed. His actions demonstrated that he maintained an optimistic view of the situation, which allowed him to persuade others that things would improve.

---

58 Ngqakamba, 2019.
59 Ibid.
60 Goleman, 1995.
61 Ibid.
62 Ibid.
63 Saunders, 2019.
64 Saunders, 2019.

Theory of adaptability and optimism

The self-regulation theory[65] can be used as a broad theoretical framework to understand how human behaviour can be regulated to adapt to VUCA environments. The process of self-regulation refers to the practice of personal management that involves directing one's own cognitions, behaviours and emotions to reach certain goals or adapt to changes in the environment.[66] Ackerman[67] asserted that self-regulation aims allow the individual to construct new thought processes and ways of cognitive processing that allow for more flexibility when selecting emotional and behavioural responses. Thus, through the regulation of cognitions, behaviours and emotional strategies, self-regulation allows for greater adaptability to events within the environment. In explaining the link between the theory of self-regulation and adaptability, Baumeister and Vohs[68] stated that regulation in any form implies change or adaptability, especially adapting thoughts, behaviours and emotions to ensure that they are in line with some standard or expectation. Thus, through self-regulation, the individual displays adaptability in a VUCA environment. According to Goleman[69], when a person engages in self-regulation, the goal is to control their emotions and impulses and thereby adapt to changing circumstances. By adapting to threats in the immediate environment, the self-leader can manage how they respond to less than optimal circumstances.

By elaborating on the processes through which behavioural and cognitive strategies are regulated, the self-regulation theory can also be used to explain how self-leaders remain optimistic in VUCA environments. According to Samoilov and Goldfried[70], early cognitive theories maintain that emotion is a product of a cognitive interpretation of either external or internal stimuli. This implies that cognition works to influence emotions, which ultimately determines behavioural responses. Therefore, through inferring that the regulation of cognitive processes in turn affects emotional responses, self-regulation theory explains why some people are optimistic compared to others. Individuals who are able to shift/regulate their perspectives can transform negative thoughts and emotions into positive ones, which makes them feel more optimistic about the future. Bergland[71] offered support for this argument by adding that self-regulators possess the capacity to regulate negative thoughts and emotions, and as a result are more likely to remain optimistic in adverse environments. Through actively regulating their emotions, the self-leader can view situations with a positive outlook,

---

65 Bandura, 1991.

66 Artuch-Gaurde et al., 2017.

67 Ackerman, 2020.

68 Baumeister & Vohs, 2007.

69 Goleman, 1995.

70 Samoilov & Goldfried, 2000.

71 Bergland, 2016.

which places them in a better position to deal with environmental threats. According to D'Intino, Goldsby, Houghton and Neck[72], individuals who have a positive outlook are usually more effective in leading themselves. Therefore, by regulating their emotions and mood states, an individual can manage their outlook on life and remain optimistic even in the face of adversity.

Practical reality and recommendations

The role of self-regulation in facilitating both adaptability and optimism places the self-regulation theory as a crucial and relevant aspect of self-leadership, especially in the 21st century work environment, which is characterised by a high degree of volatility, uncertainty, complexity and ambiguity. According to Orejarena, Zambrano and Carvajal[73], through emphasising cognitive and emotional regulation and mental flexibility, which facilitates both an optimistic worldview and adaptive behavioural responses, self-regulation allows individuals to deal with uncertainty in a realistic way and has great relevance for adapting to the different changes in a VUCA environment. Self-leaders can increase their ability to adapt to, and remain optimistic in, VUCA environments through a range of practical strategies.

Strategies to improve Adaptability

Cognitive flexibility and receptiveness

Two key concepts which determine adaptability are cognitive flexibility and being receptive to incoming information.[74] An individual who is cognitively flexible can keep an open mind and is able to adapt effectively to changes in the environment. Likewise, an individual who is receptive can respond to uncertain environments with a positive attitude and a willingness to learn new ways to adapt to the environment. Therefore, attempts to increase adaptability should focus on increasing cognitive flexibility and receptiveness. This can be done through cognitive techniques such as mindfulness training or through more structured approaches such as cognitive flexibility training.[75] Cognitive flexibility training emphasises a series of activities designed to target three primary domains, i.e. reasoning, working memory and attention. Through maintaining flexible thought processes, the individual is able to easily adapt to environments that involve sudden and abrupt change.[76]

---

72 D'Intino, Goldsby, Houghton & Neck, 2007.
73 Orejarena, Zambrano & Carvajal, 2019.
74 Stenger, 2017.
75 Buitenweg, van der Ven, Prinssen, Murrel & Ridderinkhof, 2017.
76 Ibid.

Mindfulness Training

Mindfulness emphasises living in the present by being aware of, and paying attention to, present experience in a transparent and accepting manner.[77] By being mindful, the self-leader becomes aware of self-defeating thoughts, emotions and behaviours, and can then engage in the process of regulating these thoughts. This regulation assists in adapting to changes in the environment and maintaining a positive outlook. Self-leaders who are aware of their emotions and how to respond to them can manage distressing feelings and remain calm in stressful environments, which is essential for adaptability. According to Jamieson and Tuckey[78], mindfulness training increases an individual's ability to be mindful, which allows them to be more focused on the present moment. This focus allows them to notice both external events and internal reactions to those events, allowing them to appropriately adapt their cognitive and behavioural responses.

Strategies to improve Optimism

Optimism Interventions

Researchers in positive psychology[79] claim that optimism can change over time if the external environment changes. Given the significant and frequent changes that are present in VUCA environments, it is imperative that self-leaders engage in continuous attempts to increase optimism. Optimism interventions[80] can assist in enhancing a positive life outlook through setting realistic expectations. These interventions are designed to focus on strengths, achievements and positive aspects of the individual's life. Techniques such as imagination are used to assist participants to understand how positive they are about life events, which allows them to identify negative feelings and deal with them effectively.[81]

Cognitive Behavioural Therapy (CBT)

According to Padesky and Mooney[82], CBT is a therapeutic model that focuses on changing unhelpful cognitive distortions and behaviours and improving emotional

---

77 Brown & Ryan, 2003.
78 Jamieson & Tuckey, 2017.
79 Prati & Pietrantoni, 2009.
80 Malouff & Schutte, 2017.
81 King, 2001.
82 Padesky & Mooney, 2012.

113

regulation. Authors in optimism[83, 84] state that a more direct way of boosting optimism is for the individual to notice and be aware of negative thought patterns. Through assisting the individual to understand the root of maladaptive and distorted thought patterns and replacing them with constructive thought patterns, CBT interventions have been successful in increasing gratitude, optimism and resilience.[85] Since constructive thought patterns consist of the construction and maintenance of functional thinking patterns, therapists can work with self-leaders to facilitate positive self-talk (i.e. what people covertly tell themselves), and teach self-leaders strategies on how to identify and replace negative and destructive self-talk with more positive internal dialogues.[86] These positive strategies increase feelings of self-worth which contribute to optimism.

CONCLUDING REMARKS

This contribution explored the role of adaptability and optimism as crucial resources of leading oneself in VUCA environments. The future of higher education will be characterised by a vast and dynamic landscape that will be influenced by abundant drivers of change. In such a changing environment, the ability to self-lead will become increasingly important, and leaders will need to be fully aware of how the VUCA environment affects their thoughts, emotions, and behaviours so that they can adapt and remain optimistic in the face of change. University management and staff members alike will be expected to successfully navigate through the tumultuous higher education environment, but to do this they must be equipped with the crucial competencies of adaptability and optimism.

---

83 Seligman, 2006.

84 Sugay, 2020.

85 Ibid.

86 Manz & Neck, 2004.

CHAPTER 9

BASIC PSYCHOLOGICAL NEED SATISFACTION AT THE UNIVERSITY OF NAMIBIA (UNAM)

Wesley Pieters

ABSTRACT

Organisations are constantly evolving and adapting to the demands of the job market and the workplace. Employees are required to make regular adjustments and at times meet new demands without the needed resources. Leadership within an organisation can be one of these resources that mitigate the challenges within a constant changing and demanding work environment. Leading oneself skills may assist employees during turbulent times at work. Basic psychological need satisfaction emphasises the importance of satisfying the needs of autonomy, relatedness and competence in order for human beings to grow and flourish in life and other domains of life (work). By applying the principles of basic psychological needs and self-awareness, leading self can help employees cope well during difficult times, continue to develop, and flourish. It is recommended to include employees in decision-making processes, fostering healthy relationships amongst staff members, and maintaining a healthy work-life balance.

INTRODUCTION

In 2017, the University of Namibia (UNAM) celebrated its 25th year of existence. At that time, the university accommodated students from 43 different countries around the world, had a student population of 24,759, and had graduated 37,085 students across a variety of disciplines. Despite this, over the years UNAM has lost many renowned academics to industry or other tertiary institutions within and outside Namibia. Losing these scarce and valuable resources makes success unpredictable and the future uncertain. Many changes need to be made within the constraints of limited finances, reduced funding from government, fewer tuition fees, an increasing salary burden, and a growth in many operational costs.

This chapter is based on an interview conducted (italicised in chapter) with a respected and prominent leader, Dr. Manfred Janik, Head of Department; Human Sciences at the University of Namibia. Dr. Janik has served on numerous decision-making bodies and has extensive experience as a leader working in diverse contexts. This chapter will start by discussing some of the leading oneself skills of Dr. Janik and explore if the UNAM environment can be regarded as a VUCA environment (Volatile, Uncertain, Complex and Ambiguous). The chapter discusses some of the abilities and skills (self-awareness, autonomy, relatedness, competence) used by Dr. Janik to function in the environment of UNAM. To conclude, this chapter integrates information from the interview and the basic psychological needs theory to discuss leading oneself, the practical realities and VUCA environments, and makes recommendations to develop and thrive as a leader within academia.

LEADING ONESELF QUALITIES

Tell us a bit about your journey as an academic and leader?

Teaching has always been part of my blood. I taught as a life skills teacher at a high school and that is where I discovered my passion for psychology. I furthered my studies in psychology and later opened a private practice as a Clinical psychologist. During my years in private practice, I yearned for education and academia. I started teaching as a part-time lecturer at UNAM and in 2008 I joined the department on a full-time basis. I enjoy teaching, creating knowledge and research, even if it is a literature review. I do not get much time for research anymore. In 2016 I was elected as Head of Department and this put my plans and passions for research on hold for a while. The role is more administrative but I think it is also an important part of this stage in my life and personal development. I have dedicated five years to this leadership role.

Considering the different dimensions of leading oneself; self-awareness which is the ability to have awareness and accurate self-assessment, do you possess this quality?

I try to strive towards it. We are complex beings and may be clouded in our own subjectivity. The process of having self-awareness and being accurate needs to be complemented or supported by information from the environment. At times my private thoughts need to be evaluated against what I see from the external environment, trying to be as self-aware as possible. I think what is important is to know about self-awareness and to never seize to scrutinise about the self.

116

Based on self-awareness, accurate self-assessment and self-confidence; which one do you regard as the most important?

I would say self-awareness. If you don't know yourself and what your strong or weak points are, you are likely to struggle on different levels. If I have issues with self-confidence, I can work on it because I know about it. When I am bullied in my role, I know why it's happening and why I'm allowing it. The self-assessment is also important but if you are self-aware, you are already self-assessing.

Would you say that your relationships and the ability to nurture these relationships is what help your work as a leader?

Yes. What I see is the need for leaders to be the ones washing the feet of followers, being the first to pick up trash in the classroom and not to expect people lower than you to do the "dirty work." Be mindful of what your roles expect of you as well, not becoming distracted from other equally important duties (competence). Being open and helpful towards people allows the relationship to grow. People tend to confide in you, you get to know them better and this ultimately helps the working relationship (relatedness, competence).

VUCA ENVIRONMENTS

A VUCA environment is characterised by an environment that is Volatile (unpredictable; things change suddenly), Uncertain (unclear or unknown), Complex (many different interrelated parts; diverse components), and Ambiguous (open to interpretation; being understood in different ways).[1] The UNAM environment was evaluated against these characteristics by posing certain questions to Dr. Janik.

The first part of a VUCA environment is characterised by a volatile environment that's unpredictable where things change suddenly or extremely. Do you think this is characteristic of the UNAM environment?

That is my experience at times, especially being afraid to open e-mails the next day to find communications about changes or new requirements. Changes related to the management of UNAM do not cause significant unrest. These changes are manageable with the needed motivation for the changes. In the faculty and department, the environment is mostly stable. There is a lot of stability in terms of classes, work roles and flexibility.

---

1   De Wet, 2019.

It was noted by Carley that organisations change to either fit the environment or the task that needs to be performed.[2] Organisational change takes time and effort. Working in an environment that is volatile means constant changes and constant adaptation. Being reactive instead of proactive could also result in the organisation trying to catch up instead of thriving in a volatile environment with constant changes and expectations.

The second part of a VUCA environment deals with an uncertain environment where some information is unknown or definite, doubtful or being unclear about the present situation and future outcomes. Is this the reality for the UNAM environment?

The environment of UNAM is uncertain at times. Communication channels are not effective. There may be changes in work roles, procedures, duties without guidance or positive feedback. Inquiries are met with resistance and it is required to accept the decisions that have been made. Issues like ethical clearance of research projects; Information Communication Technology or systems and open communication between academic and administrative staff. There seems to be a big rift between academic and administrative staff. Decisions made amongst administrative staff are not always communicated to academic staff. Academic staff is only made aware of these changes once you apply for certain benefits or enquiry about procedures such as hiring a new part-time lecturer. A lack of communication and transparency makes the environment uncertain and difficult.

It was found that leaders are not communicating effectively and efficiently with followers. There is thus a need to identify the areas of communication that are unsatisfactory and improve on these, since leadership communication has an impact on shared vision, employee morale and organisational effectiveness.[3] Pincus and Rayfield[4] found that top management communication relates positively to employee job satisfaction. It was noted that perhaps employees may expect top management and supervisors to fulfil distinct communication needs. This emphasises the importance of communication and the need for communication – not only with immediate supervisors, but also with top management. On 14 August 2019, the Vice-Chancellor (VC) of UNAM addressed UNAM staff members from the main campus. The meeting was called an engagement session, however some staff questioned the top-down approach instead of a more democratic and inclusive approach to decision-making and planning (autonomy). A poorer relationship was reported between assertive communication, the quality of communication and employee-organisational

---

2   Carley, 2000.

3   Bornman & Puth, 2017.

4   Pincus & Rayfield, 1987.

relationship than when compared with responsive communication.[5] A responsive communicator is characterised by being empathic, a good listener, compassionate and understanding, while an assertive communicator is characterised by being goal-oriented, dominant, forceful and competitive.[6]

What is your view of free tertiary education?

At this stage with UNAM relying heavily on government and many students being funded by the Ministry of Higher Education, Training and Innovation, it is not possible at this stage. It remains a good dream to have but practically it is not financially viable. UNAM has huge financial challenges where some programs are discontinued or cannot function fully because of the reduced government subsidy. The government is a major contributor towards UNAM's budgetary needs and the rest is obtained from student fees which may also be indirectly coming from the government. The reduced funding and budget cuts put pressure on UNAM and ads to the uncertainty of the working environment.

Nakale[7] noted that the subsidy from the government fell short of the budgetary needs of UNAM for the 2019 financial year. It was reported that some students may not be able to sit for examinations since their tuition fees were not paid and they had not received a letter from the Namibian Student Financial Assistance Fund (NSFAF) due to a lack of funds.[8, 9] It seems that these challenges were continuing from 2017[10] when students had to rely on government loans and grants to further their studies from NSFAF, however in 2019, 12,000 applicants were rejected.[11]

The third aspect of a VUCA environment is related to a complex environment with multiple key decision factors, multiple different and connected parts. Is this the reality for UNAM?

Yes, with different personalities, visions, agendas and the directions that UNAM plans to take. There seems to be a lot of undercover politics that is not so in-your-face, where certain factions or camps may need something (in political terms) from you. Trying to remain neutral and as objective as possible makes the environment even more complex. People from the different camps may identify you as either being for or against them.

---

5   Men, 2015.

6   Ibid.

7   Nakale, 2019.

8   Hartman, 2019.

9   Shikololo, 2019.

10 Ileka, 2017.

11 Shikololo, 2019.

Negotiating your place within the organisation becomes difficult, especially if you don't want to join any of these camps.

As a leader, you need to be OK with the fact that followers may not always be cooperative, being OK with the different personalities, be OK that followers might have different agendas and not to take anything personally. Taking these differences and challenges personally will only affect you negatively.

You spoke about the rift between academic and administrative staff. How does this add to the complexity of the UNAM environment?

The rift does add to the complexity of the environment. The environment is becoming even more complex because the people that went on strike towards the end of 2018 were both academic and administrative staff. Previously, it seemed like some staff members preferred to keep this rift uptight, an "us" versus "them" feeling. During the strike, interacting with the colleagues from Human Resources, it felt like staff (academic and administrative) were standing together in the industrial action. This was a strange feeling. The feeling of solidarity and togetherness seems to have changed again. After the strike, it was business as usual, HR dictates what needs to happen, how many part-time lecturers may be employed...just fill in the forms (limited to no room for negotiations). All that the department need is for the students to learn and to have a lecturer to do teach them. It's difficult to have a relationship (with administration) where you can negotiate and communicate openly about the department's needs.

It was found that employees who experience relatedness, feelings of togetherness and good interactions amongst colleagues, experience lower levels of turnover intention.[12]

The last part of the VUCA environment includes an environment that's ambiguous. This means it may be open to different interpretations. Is this a reality at UNAM?

It's not always clear. Some policies at UNAM guide us to reach goals and objectives. However, even if you follow these guidelines, you are likely to be overruled by a higher office. For example; the rules are clear in terms of pass and fail grades. The seniors may intervene and question if you are going to hinder students from having more opportunities to pass, progress and graduate or follow the rule. The outcomes are different and applying the rules becomes open to different interpretations. The ambiguity also extends to management and the new vision for the institution. At management meetings staff members are reminded to stay true to the vision and mission of the institution and being a beacon of excellence. Considering the things that

---

12 Rothmann, Diedericks & Swart, 2013.

are not so excellent, I don't think we are that beacon of excellence anymore. It ties into with, where we are heading and what we are trying to achieve.

Based on what you are saying Dr. Janik, taking a different approach when applying the rules, accommodating students whilst "bending" the rules...and referring back to the VC opening remarks about the number of colleagues disciplined in 2018, how does this affect staff members and add to the levels of ambiguity?

It immediately creates panic and anxiety. If you follow the rule you should feel safe but once you start "bending" the rules you become uncertain and anxious because you don't know what is right and wrong anymore. Bending the rules, being pressured emotionally may indicate whether you are supportive or against a certain camp. Having a temperament that wants peace and trying to execute your job without emotional pressure, makes it difficult to navigate in this environment.

Procedural justice can be defined as the manner in which procedures and policies within an organisation are implemented fairly and equitably.[13] It was found by Pieters that procedural justice related positively to job satisfaction and employee engagement.[14]

LEADING ONESELF IN A VUCA ENVIRONMENT

Apart from improving of communication between academic and admin staff, what can be done to improve the managing of staff members at UNAM in a VUCA environment?

At UNAM the workloads need to be looked at. There are increased work expectations without the needed resources or compensation. We have a wellness centre for staff but the centre is not visible, no reports/documentation about what has been done for the well-being of staff or the services provided. As the psychology department, we play a key role in the knowledge about health and well-being but we are never approached about the way forward and what can be done to improve things. How functional and effective it is, needs to be explored.

---

13 Greenberg, 2011.

14 Pieters, 2018a.

Tertiary institutions are constantly trying to evolve and change with the times, but may fail to provide the needed resources and support or facilitate these changes.[15, 16] Constant increases in workload cause burnout and depression, and with the uncertainty comes anxiety.

You spoke about the rift between academic and administrative staff, what would you suggest to improve the working relationship?

First of all, let's acknowledge this divide and talk openly about it. Some colleagues prefer to remain ignorant about it even though we experience the impact on a regular basis. What is also important is for the management to deal with this divide openly. Communication channels should be cleared including from the side of the department. All of us need to start prioritising healthy interactions with each other (relatedness). It takes some time but change can happen and we all need to work towards a united institution.

You spoke about staff and management not being on the same page about the vision of UNAM. What can be done to clarify the vision and improve implementation amongst staff?

We need to talk more and openly (autonomy). We need to have meetings to discuss these challenges even if it may become uncomfortable at times. At times, open frank communication isn't always welcome. Many activities are not talked about enough but the implementation is required, almost like its being forced down your throat. This takes away from the autonomy and perceived competence of staff.

So you think we have the platforms to discuss these issues? Does the environment allow for open discussions about these challenges?

At this stage people don't feel safe to talk (lack of autonomy). We have been silence for too long. With silence and autocracy, people withdraw and focus on other things. At faculty meetings, there are colleagues that refuse to be silenced by the forceful implementation of other people's vision and that's why we don't have these meeting regularly enough. People don't want to have these uncomfortable conversations but it's something that we need to become comfortable with again and create an atmosphere where dialogue and conversations become normal again.

---

15 Rothmann & Jordaan, 2006.
16 Soltis, Agneessens, Sasovova & Labianca, 2013.

Dr. Janik, you spoke about the vision of the new VC and how this may add to the complexity of the UNAM environment. What do you think can be done to sooth these challenges?

Communication is vital.

Dhurup and Dubihlela[17] found that employees who experience role ambiguity tend to experience lower levels of job satisfaction. Employees who experience job satisfaction were also found to be healthier[18], and experience higher levels of work engagement and affective commitment.[19] Job satisfaction, work engagement and organisational commitment of influence how employees interact with customers. Customer satisfaction and loyalty is dependent on how the clients are treated.[20]

It would really help if top management can be transparent and inform the university community about where the institution is heading in terms of the restructuring, why the need to restructure and how (autonomy, relatedness). Once staff members understand the new vision and objectives, we can all work towards the common goal. If we need to become a more post-graduate institution, the plans also need to include how we plan to fund these research projects, attend conferences and how to move the research agenda forward. Having these expectations from management without clear documented rules makes role completion frustrating.

How is it possible that the HOD writes an email to management about issues related to your job (part-time lecturers' contracts) – issues that impact on the service delivery to clients (students) – and these emails are ignored with no consequences that follow; an innocent question that needs guidance or clarity (autonomy, relatedness)? I don't know if egos are at play, could it be that they believe that they have more power than others, or regard their rank as more superior than others…why should I answer to you? These issues make it difficult and impossible to deliver quality education to our students (competence). If lecturers are unable to get feedback from administration, the students suffer.

Are you saying that communication between mid-level management and senior management isn't open, even though you all form part of management?

Exactly!!! Take for example when you write an important email to the management of the examinations department, I can almost guarantee that you will not get a response (competence, relatedness). If you call their office phone, you are likely not to get

17 Dhurup & Dubihlela, 2013.

18 Ajala, 2013.

19 Brunetto, Teo, Shacklock & Farr-Wharton, 2012.

20 Bettencourt & Brown, 1997.

an answer. You need to walk over to their offices, make contact with an angry face; because you are disturbing them, and insist on getting an answer to your enquiries (autonomy, relatedness, competence). This takes a lot of energy and causes a certain level of frustration that at times you decide to not to inquire anymore.

How does this influence your workload and that of other staff members within the department?

It does affect our workload (competence). This seems to be not only my reality but also the reality of many of the other lecturers. The challenges faced with the examinations department and lack of support is also experienced by colleagues in other departments at UNAM (relatedness, competence).

Considering that UNAM operates in a VUCA environment, how do you function as a leader?

Constant analyses (self-awareness). I think a lot about what is happening at work, at the university, in my private life and how these worlds impact each other. Being part of management, you need to be clear about your goals and what is expected (competence). It definitely helps to have healthy relationships (relatedness). If a colleague is unhappy about a firm email or something, I need to be able to go to them and discuss how they feel, to nurture those relationships. We always need people (relatedness). Some people don't value the importance of nurturing relationships; it is uncommon. If you mend relationships or nurture a relationship, people become suspicious since they think you may ask for a favour.

Dr. Janik indicated that one of the key strategies for managing during these challenging times and a VUCA environment is to *"take some time-out, relax and nurture the self for emotional resource renewal."* Leisure affects the quality of work-life of employees[21]; when employees spend time relaxing and on leisure activities, they are able to experience their work more meaningfully, and have a higher level of well-being and performance at work.

---

21 Naude, Kruger & Saayman, 2012.

THEORY RELATED TO LEADERS' CHARACTERISTICS

Based on the characteristics and leadership style of Dr. Janik, it would seem that the Basic Psychological Need Satisfaction theory (BPNS) by Deci and Ryan[22] explains his leadership style best. The BPNS theory states that in order for people to improve their integrity and health, certain needs ought to be satisfied. BPNS is the key ingredient, which is characterised by the need for autonomy, relatedness and competence. Autonomy can be defined as the employees' choice in how to execute work-related duties or the psychological freedom to choose.[23] As explained by Dr. Janik, UNAM employees feel left out of the decision-making process and the manner in which certain decisions or policies are implemented, reducing the autonomy experienced by employees. Considering the current workforce, employees want to feel included and involved in decision-making. Working in academia, staff members are educated and believe that their views and opinions need to be considered instead of them being dictated to.

Relatedness is the feeling of togetherness or a sense of belonging.[24] *Relatedness was also regarded as vital and instrumental for the success of a leader and organisation. People spend most of their lives at work and working with colleagues where they don't necessarily work well together can negatively influence their overall levels of well-being as stated by Dr. Janik.*

Organisations need to ensure that grievance policies and procedures are put in place to relieve work conflict, and team building and conflict resolution activities need to be prioritised. When employees are functioning well and have good interpersonal relationships, they are likely to be willing to assist another colleague when in need, engage in organisational citizenship behaviour, and add to the overall productivity of the organisation.

If employees do not get the needed information or resources, they are less likely to feel competent in their jobs. Competence is regarded as employees' feelings of effectiveness and being capable of reaching their work goals.[25] Based on the abilities and skills of Dr. Janik, as well as his interactions and leadership approach, he facilitates an environment that supports the views of the BPNS theory, where employee's needs must be satisfied in order for them to flourish and thrive. Organisations must make the needed resources available to ensure that staff members are performing to the best of their abilities. If staff members experience challenges due to a lack of skills or abilities, organisations need to provide the needed training and development opportunities to

---

22 Deci & Ryan, 2000.

23 Verstuyf, Vansteenkiste, Soenens, Boone & Mouratidis, 2013.

24 Verstuyf et al., 2013.

25 Ibid.

enhance the overall effectiveness and competence of staff members. Investing in the training and development of staff enhances the likelihood that they will be successful, competent and healthy, i.e. their overall well-being will improve. Organisations need to understand that when investing in the competence (effectiveness) of employees, the organisation is investing in the future of the organisation. Ensuring that the staff perform to their utmost best, these staff members are likely to remain optimistic and productive instead of experiencing burnout, frustration and turnover intention. Pieters, Van Zyl and Nel[26] found that there is a positive relationship between autonomy, relatedness and competence and normative and affective commitment as well as work engagement (vigour, dedication, absorption), and a negative relationship with turnover intention[27] of academic staff at UNAM.

RECOMMENDATIONS

Based on the interview conducted, the literature reviewed, the practical reality at UNUM and the basic psychological needs satisfaction theory, the following recommendations are made. Even though it may seem like the authoritarian leadership style is the preferred leadership style in some African countries, it blocks creativity and people tend to leave such an organisation. It is thus recommended that leaders should learn the skills and abilities of peace leadership. It may sound more challenging, but can also be more beneficial to the leader, followers and the organisation.

By being self-aware, leaders come to know about the diversity within the organisation, the different kinds of people there, and how they all play a role in fulfilling the overall organisational goals. Practicing mindfulness, trying to remain in the moment, and not being too past or future oriented will result in competence.

It is also recommended that transparency is allowed when needed. Inform followers about the needed decisions, as well as how they can influence the outcomes or how they will impact on their working environment. Being adaptable and allowing employees into the decision-making process (autonomy) can ensure that they buy into the plan, structure the best possible plan, and work effectively towards achieving the plan. Inform followers about policies and procedures that require their input in advance in order to stimulate and encourage healthy dialogue amongst staff members (relatedness).

It was also highlighted that healthy relationships are fundamental to the success of an organisation and a leader (relatedness). As a leader, ensure that you treat people fairly and with the needed respect. Practicing organisational justice ensures that followers respect you as a leader, but also influence the job attitudes of followers positively. Nurture relationships – people need to be included, feel important and valued.

---

26 Pieters, Van Zyl & Nel, 2019.

27 Pieters, 2018b.

As a leader, self-care is important to ensure that you are able to effectively implement the characteristics of peace leadership (self-awareness). Ensure that you respect employees' boundaries when it comes to family time. As a leader, you should know when to say "no" – especially when you are not coping or the workload becomes too much or is beyond your scope of practice (competence; autonomy).

CONCLUDING REMARKS

If we remain hopeful, optimistic and genuine we should be on the right path. I wish we could lose our own agendas and stop with the backstabbing and work towards the goals and objectives of the institution. If we can be a united front, we can become the beacon of excellence and produce students that will be an example of that.

This chapter started by discussing the different characteristics of a VUCA environment. Based on the interview with Dr. Janik, it is clear that UNAM meets most of the characteristics of a VUCA environment. These challenges hinder the flourishing and thriving of UNAM as an academic institution. Working in a VUCA environment may cause staff members to experience ill-health and work stress.

Leadership roles are stressful and influence a leader's effectiveness. Exercising peace leadership may be challenging at times, however with certain key skills and competencies, the tasks of a leader become easier. This chapter concluded by discussing some of the suggestions for leaders to try and improve organisations, societies and the nation.

PART FOUR

LEADING ONESELF IN THE PUBLIC SECTOR

CHAPTER 10

SOUTH AFRICA'S SURVIVING VUCA ENVIRONMENTS

Liezel Lues

ABSTRACT

Of the South African presidents who have been in power since the advent of democracy in 1994, the terms of Nelson Mandela and Thabo Mbeki could be seen as the pinnacle of success of South African democracy. At the time, few people anticipated that they would be able to lead the country, in such a short period of time and amidst a VUCA environment, through a peaceful transition to a democratic dispensation. Unfortunately Zuma and his administration did not continue on this path. Self-interest became the driver of many of those in positions of authority during his term of office. The result has been unnecessary turbulence in South Africa, which has undermined the morale of the public as well as confidence in the state, and created a new VUCA environment. In this chapter, the importance of the lead-self narrative is told, followed by a discussion of the implications thereof for SA.

INTRODUCTION

Within a typical democratic dispensation such as South Africa (SA), the public sector environment refers to the respective spheres of government that govern the country. Within the public sector environment, there are usually institutions that make laws and ensure that order is maintained through clear policy and legislative rule. These public sector institutions reside under the legislative function of government. Having a legislative platform, the effective and efficient rendering of services to the citizens of the country relies greatly on administrators and political leaders to ensure that services are provided. The three South African spheres of government (national, provincial and local) typically provide for the country's main needs, i.e. safety, health, education, social welfare, and order. The execution of these functions is vested in the executive, and the executive institution(s) need to account for what they do, or do not do. Finally, courts and the rule of law are put in place to ensure that public sector officials, as well as citizens, account for their deeds, especially if they do not adhere to legislative rules. The legislature, executive and judiciary all adhere to common national legislative directives and the Constitution of the country. When there is a public sector where the administrators and political leaders do what is expected of them, when public sector institutions render effective and efficient services to the citizens of the country, and when a country has a responsible citizenry, one can expect a robust democracy to be the result.

However, for this to materialise, a leader (head of state, monarch, dictator, despot, etc.) in the 21st century needs to steer their country amid demanding circumstances such as food insecurity, political unrest, migration issues, unemployment, public service capacity challenges, divided societies, global warming[1], economic uncertainty, cultural and religious confrontations[2], and the more recent Covid-19 pandemic. The effect of these demanding circumstances is that government institutions today need to render more services due to aging populations, as well as provide innovative solutions due to the Fourth Industrial Revolution, with fewer resources at hand.[3]

This state of affairs has largely been intensified by volatile, uncertain, complex and ambiguous (VUCA) environments. A VUCA environment reflects a state of the external world, or external to the leader, community or nation, as much as it seems to reflect an internal frame of mind. The constant pressure to lead, while being uncertain about the outcomes of your decisions and even fearful of not being in control all the time, are some of the hallmarks of a VUCA world. A good way of thinking about this concept is to view it as the "new narrative" – the volatility, uncertainty, complexity, and ambiguity inherent in today's world.[4] Johanson[5] highlighted how it profoundly changes leadership, business, organisational endeavours and required thought structures. Hartley[6] stated that it creates "white-water conditions for leadership", i.e. "context and conditions change rapidly… where the purposes and processes of leadership are not necessarily shared or understood." The concept *volatile* refers to circumstances that change unpredictably, often suddenly[7] and for the worse. The recent unrest in the Middle East, and the resulting volatile environment, for example, caused many Syrian migrants to travel to Europe in search of safety, and in this regard placed an enormous responsibility on the statutory position of many European countries.[8] Such volatile circumstances usually create a state of *uncertainty*, where there is confusion and doubt

---

1   Hartley, 2018: 203.
2   Lues, 2016: 298.
3   Lues, 2019a: 157.
4   Bushe & Marshak, 2016.
5   Johanson, 2017.
6   Hartley, 2018: 204.
7   Hartley, 2018.
8   Lues, 2019a: 158.

about the present and future[9] well-being of a nation and its people. Linked to the aforementioned example of the huge influx of Syrian immigrants, in 2015 the European Union (EU) introduced the European Agenda on Migration, a statutory intervention to serve as a form of control and lessen the uncertainty. Functioning within volatile and uncertain environments makes it extremely difficult for leaders to predict the outcomes of their decisions, thus creating *complexity* in many ways. For example, it was a 2015 announcement by Angela Merkel that no refugees from Syria would be prevented from entering Germany that contributed to the complexity of the situation.[10] Her decision further created *ambiguity* for many Germans in that this unprecedented influx could pose economic, fiscal, political, socio-cultural and legal challenges.

Against this introduction, it unfortunately appears as if there is an increase in VUCA problems in the 21st century, and leaders often fail in their attempts to provide solutions to these demanding circumstances. Indeed, it appears as if leaders in the 21st century are actually contributing to VUCA environments. So-called "state-capture"[11] and the "Gangster State"[12] in South Africa, "make America Great Again" and "America First"[13], the Brexit no-deal option[14], "trade wars"[15], and "the deadly coronavirus"[16] are examples when leaders have not appeared to solve challenges, but to rather intensify them.

Seeing the political leader as vital in the outcomes of demanding circumstances, this chapter examines the leading self as a founding tenet of leadership in a VUCA public sector environment. The focus of this chapter is on the South African public sector and the implementation of lead self in public sector leaders in a VUCA environment.

This chapter introduces the case of SA and the transition that took place from an apartheid minority regime to a full accepted democratic dispensation in the early 1990s, and how this case study relates to a typical VUCA environment. Examples of the respective South African Presidents will be given and the theories supporting the mentioned leading oneself components will be highlighted, before the chapter concludes with some practical and theoretical recommendations.

---

9   Rimita, 2019: 39.

10 Lues, 2019a: 158.

11 Africa Growth Initiative, 2019.

12 Myburgh, 2019.

13 Winters, 2019.

14 Parker, 2019.

15 Churchill, Mai, Lee, Zhou & Tang, 2019.

16 Yang, Peng, Wang, Guan, Jiang, Xu, Sun & Chang, 2020.

BACKGROUND ON BECOMING A DEMOCRACY (SOUTH AFRICA)

Between 1994 and 2020, SA had five presidents, all of whom had to lead within a VUCA environment. All pledged to support peace and justice, as well as to promote accountable institutions to support peace and justice (similar to Sustainable Development Goal 16).[17]

In 1994 SA was in the midst of a VUCA environment, as it changed from an apartheid, minority regime to a democratic, majority rule dispensation. The situation in the country was extremely *volatile* during the time before the transition to democracy in 1994. The African National Congress (ANC), led by Nelson Mandela, made great strides both within the country and internationally to bring into focus the inhumane manner in which the apartheid regime ruled. The discussions and negotiations that took place during the transition period were clouded with volatile events. Protest actions and violent displays of power were ever-present, even among citizens. At the time, international sanctions weakened the South African economy, and international investors likewise did not want to venture into an environment where things could change unpredictably for the worse.[18] These *volatile* events could derail all the effort that was concomitant with the discussion and negotiations for a peaceful transition.

In the events before and after the first democratic elections in 1994, many South Africans from different ethnic groups experienced an immense feeling of uncertainty about the outcomes of this transition period. It was thus also an extraordinarily *uncertain* time, not only for ordinary South Africans, but also for neighbouring countries (Namibia, Botswana, Lesotho, and Zimbabwe) and foreign investors. The main reason for this uncertainty was that there was a deep distrust amongst political leaders and citizens as to what the future would hold for all South Africans. It was the most sensitive time in the history of the country; if anything was going to go wrong, this was the time for it.

A successful transition required political and public sector leaders to discuss and negotiate *complex* matters such as the official languages of the country, a new anthem and a new flag, amongst others. The complexity of the situation was due to the many different but connected matters that needed to be taken into account not only for a peaceful transition period, but also for the future of the country. The political leadership had to be sensitive not to create an antagonistic regulatory environment, but was also to a large extent reliant on the negotiation between two political parties (the ANC, under the leadership of Nelson Mandela, and the National Party, led by F.W. de Klerk), as well as the team of mediators behind the scenes who were responsible for the adoption of an un*ambiguous* interim and later final Constitution (1996). Chapter Two of the South African Constitution outlines the concepts of equality; human dignity; forced

---

17   United Nations, 2018.

18   Lues, 2019b.

labour; freedom of religion, expression and association; and access to information, courts, education and housing. The South African Constitution is known as one of the best in the world, and aims to mobilise people to get involved; create a representative, responsive democratic policymaking process; educate citizens to effectively participate in government affairs; and promote public leadership.

This section started by referring to the most recent five South African presidents. Table 1 depicts how each president respectively had to lead within a VUCA environment. Mandela focused on healing a deeply divided nation and led the country through a transition from an apartheid to a democratic dispensation. His successor, Mbeki, realised that the country needed to be reliant on much more than unity, and took on the difficult task of strengthening the South African economy following the sanctions and financial boycotts against the former apartheid regime. Zuma's administration unfortunately did not continue on this path, with the result being unnecessary turbulence in South Africa, undermined public morale and a lack of confidence in the state, which led to a new VUCA environment. For almost nine years it felt as if the work done by the former two presidents was broken down to the ground, and that South Africa might never achieve the status of developed countries. In 2018, Ramaphosa, a seasoned businessman, took office. The so-called VUCA environment left by the former president was clouded by service delivery protests, an erratic electricity supply, bankruptcy in South African Airways and several other state-owned enterprises, a downgrade to "junk status" by the credit-rating agencies[19], and the outbreak of the Coronavirus in SA. As per Table One, it appears as if SA has found itself moving from one VUCA situation to the next.

Table 10.1: South African VUCA environments

VOLATITLE	UNCERTAIN	COMPLEX	AMBIGUOUS
Pre-1994 apartheid era/post-1994 democracy			
Nelson Mandela (10 May 1994 to 14 June 1999)			
Reconcile and heal relationships, set a humane platform to move forward.			
Thabo Mbeki (16 June 1999 to 24 September 2008)			
Strengthen the economy, build partnerships.			
Jacob Zuma (9 May 2009 to 14 February 2018)			
Created a self-interest above everything and everyone.			
Cyril Ramaphosa (15 February 2018 to present)			
Fighting against corruption, aiming to restore the economy. Mobilising the fight against the Coronavirus.			

---

19 Simpson, 2020.

Leading oneself in a VUCA environment: Nelson Mandela and Thabo Mbeki

The focus of this section falls on the leading-self components of Mandela and Mbeki. The broad vision of the 1994 South African government was to build a united, non-racial, non-sexist and prosperous democracy to ensure a better life for all. Mandela, together with F.W. de Klerk, were the cornerstones of realising this peaceful transition from an apartheid regime to building a new patriotism and fostering the moral renewal of the society. This historical transition was largely initiated by de Klerk, for which he shared the 1993 Nobel Peace Prize with Mandela. However, it was Mandela who took the "long walk to freedom" and created a peaceful transition to democracy. Both of these statesmen offered their collective influence and experience to support peacebuilding, address major causes of human suffering, and promote the shared interests of humanity.[20] They promised to speak truth to power, raise the voices of the voiceless, and offer hope where there was despair.

Many people may find it difficult to comprehend how these two leaders overcame their bitterness and found the strength to forgive, making South Africans, as well as world leaders, believe in the power of a democratic dispensation. They both had an inner war to fight, similar to those that were taking place inside and outside South Africa's borders. In this instance, it was obvious that being a peace leader started with knowledge of themselves and developing the skill to lead themselves before attempting to lead the rest of the country. This ability requires a leader to reflect on the 'now' as well as the bigger picture, while not placing oneself before focusing on leading others. The South African success story could not be achieved if it were any other way round.

The ANC, under the leadership of Mandela, upheld four guiding principles: nation-building and reconciliation; reconstruction and transformation; National Democratic Revolution; and unity and solidarity.[21] Mandela's most significant initiative was probably[22] The Growth Employment and Redistribution economic policy. This economic strategy was aimed at, *inter alia*, enhancing human resource development and creating flexibility in the labour market. Employment was mainly created for those in the middle class through the Black Economic Empowerment program. Along with Mandela's capacity to unify people, these developments contributed to much-needed solidarity among South Africans. This attribute was also depicted in Mbeki when he extended an invitation for unity towards the whole of Africa. Backed by a well-managed but conservative fiscal policy, the government showed its commitment towards policy changes in favour of formerly excluded groups, and an acknowledgment

---

20 Anon, 2013.

21 Venter & Landsberg, 2011.

22 Department of Finance, 1996.

of the importance of basic needs satisfaction and democratic rights and processes.[23]

The sudden and overwhelming demands of communities for service delivery placed an enormous responsibility on the respective government departments and leaders. Several examples of these demands were addressed through strategic development projects, including: the Reconstruction and Development Housing project; the Commission on the Restitution of Land Rights; and the Truth and Reconciliation Commission. The Reconstruction and Development Housing project dealt with several social challenges, including the provision of housing, clean water, electricity, land and healthcare. The Commission on the Restitution of Land Rights assisted claimants to submitting their land claims, received and acknowledged all claims lodged, and advised claimants on the progress of their land claims. The Truth and Reconciliation Commission helped to heal the country and bring about a reconciliation of its people by uncovering the truth about human rights violations that had occurred during the period of apartheid. There was no question that the demands of the community did not always take into account the enormous personal sacrifices that Presidents Mandela and Mbeki had to make, however these sacrifices led to them developing their ability to endure tough challenges; become resilient; demonstrate humanity, compassion and reconciliation; and lead the country through VUCA periods.

Unfortunately, the legacy that was left by Mandela and Mbeki was short-lived, and from 2009 there was a noticeable decline in public confidence in the leadership of the country. Qualified audit reports, the mismanagement of taxes and public resources, nepotism, and inadequate service provision[24] are all examples of the maladministration that took place. These, coupled with inequality and a weakening economy, further fueled divides and violence, instigating a new VUCA environment. Political leaders, including traditional leaders and opposition parties, played a role in fueling protests. High unemployment rates (27% in 2019)[25] and a lack of opportunities were at the root of these protests, but the electricity and water crisis compounded the situation. Zuma created unnecessary turbulence during his term as President; it is anticipated that without drastic reform to the current economic, political and security systems, more than half of the population will remain unemployed, uneducated, poor and thus vulnerable to political manipulation and coercion, The inner strength and leadership characteristics and styles of the former South African statesmen, Mandela and Mbeki, was notably absent in Zuma.

---

23 Cloete, 1999.
24 Du Preez, 2014.
25 Statistics South Africa, 2019.

Leadership theories

Alongside literature on leadership traits, a rich debate on leadership styles and theories has developed that has been dominated by studies on organisational theory, industrial psychology, and management.[26] Nonetheless, other disciplines (politics, communication, psychology) have also contributed significantly, clearly making leadership, even in the public sector domain, a multidisciplinary concept. While general theories apply, there are also distinctive views about public sector leadership. The goal of creating public value and the importance of lawfulness and accountability take precedence.[27]

Acknowledging the influence and contribution of multidisciplinary theories, the following leadership theories became prominent during the presidential tenure of Mandela and Mbeki, i.e. Transformational-, Relationship- and Participative leadership.

In 1978, Burns introduced the transformational leadership style in his research on political leaders. Burns identified two types of leadership: (i) transactional, where a leader influences others by what they offer in exchange, i.e. the transaction; and (ii) transformational, where a leader connects with followers such that their level of motivation and morale is raised. Burns[28] hypothesised that transformational leadership is the result of the leadership style and abilities of a leader, who can convey a vision and guide the transformation. These abilities were notable in the leadership of Mandela, who realised that transformation needs to come from within, and that by leading by example, he could influence South Africans to believe it is possible to transform a deeply embedded apartheid regime into a democratic dispensation. Burns[29] added that a transformational leader needs to have an interpersonal relationship with others if they want to influence them to comply because they want to, not because they have to. Mandela succeeded in building these relationships with role players from abroad, members of his political party, as well as those from the opposition.

In achieving strong interpersonal relationships, Mandela succeeded in making what Covey[30] described as a move to a higher standard of leadership using an inside-out approach. This inside-out self-leadership approach is strongly reliant on the development of own values (such as human dignity, equality and freedom, which are enshrined in the South African Bill of Rights), as well as finding internal power. Burns[31] referred to these as end values that cannot be negotiated. In support, Blanchard[32] argued

---

26 Hartley, 2018.

27 University of Cambridge Institute for Sustainability Leadership, 2017.

28 Burns, 1978.

29 Ibid.

30 Covey, 1996.

31 Burns, 1978

32 Blanchard, 2007.

that the capacity to influence others to make an impact on the greater good should start with oneself (one must lead oneself before one can lead others). That should be followed by one-on-one leadership, then smaller teams, and then leadership within the broader community context[33], which places the focus on relationship theories. Again, both presidents relied on building strong and lasting relationships for future envisaged success.

Relationship theories focus on the connections formed between leaders and followers. Transformational leaders motivate and inspire people by helping group members see the importance and higher good of the task.[34] Leaders with this style often have high ethical and moral standards; this was typical of the style portrayed by Mandela as well as Mbeki (see Table 2). It is important to note that building relationships through negotiation was the winning strategy to implement the change that was envisaged. In essence, it is understood that Mandela and Mbeki (who were both part of the negotiation process before they were elected President) built these relationships because they had the inner strength to forgive injustices, a personal vision to reconcile people with different ideologies, and the ability to unite a strongly divided country. It is further relevant to this chapter to acknowledge their courage and ability to lead a country towards an unpredictable and unknown future (which could be seen as a VUCA environment), even for themselves. They dared to do just that, having strong relationships (national and international) to support them.

Table 10.2: Theory and practice

Ideology	Theories of leadership
Nelson Mandela (10 May 1994 to 14 June 1999)	
Reconcile and heal relationships, set a humane platform to move forward.	Transformational leadership Relationship leadership Participative leadership
Thabo Mbeki (16 June 1999 to 24 September 2008)	
Strengthen the economy, build partnerships	Relationship leadership Participative leadership

In support of building relationships, the participative leadership theories suggest that the ideal leadership style is one that takes the input of others into account. These leaders encourage participation and contributions from group members, and help

---

33 Blanchard, 2007.

34 Bushe & Marshak, 2016.

them to feel more relevant and committed to the decision-making process. It was as if Mandela and Mbeki realised that the most important component of leading in a VUCA environment was to be able to bring together the skills, values, beliefs and cultures of all the people in SA. Mbeki was able to assess the needs of his fellow South Africans, as well as the needs of all countries on the African continent, take stock of the situation, and encourage participation, especially from the African continent.

Practical reality

The charisma, caring, and dignity of Mandela was nowhere to be matched at the time of SA becoming a democracy in 1994. It was even felt that it was too good to be true – no human being could experience such suffering and inhumanity, yet still have a humane relationship with the people who were responsible for his and the majority of Black South Africans' oppression.[35] He succeeded in leading the country from an 'old state', through a transition state, to a new state. This transition also required South Africans to go through deep personal change, which many were willing to do because of the inner strength portrayed by their leader.

Since 1994, the concept of transformation has been the cornerstone of every initiative, project and strategy undertaken by the government, led by a flurry of legislative directives and policies. These policies, white papers, and legislative directives were introduced to redress imbalances, mostly in respect of race and gender. It felt as if the country was at peace and ready for the next phase of creating a sustainable democracy.

This next phase, moving forward in by creating a sustainable democracy, appeared to come naturally with the election of Mbeki (see Table 2), who was a strategist and an economist. His professional demeanor was welcomed at a time when South Africa's democracy needed to strengthen its economy. Mbeki was seen as negotiating for economic stability as well as a blooming financial future for the country. Typical of a transitional leader, he understood the dynamics within the micro and macro environments, and how to design effective processes to support sustainable growth.

During Mbeki's time in office, he focused on strengthening the institutions supporting the South African economy, which grew at an average rate of 4.5% per year.[36] The growth in the South African economy increased the demand for trained professionals such as medical practitioners and educationalists, but unfortunately failed to address unemployment amongst the unskilled masses. Mbeki created employment in the middle sectors of the economy, as well as a fast-growing black middle class with the implementation of Black Economic Empowerment. He further attracted the bulk of Africa's foreign direct investment through a well-established, integrated socio-economic development framework for Africa. Collaborative relationships, such as

---

35 Anon, 2013.

36 Duggan, 2014.

the New Partnership for Africa's Development, the African Union, the BRICS (Brazil, Russia, India, China, SA), are examples of Mbeki's ability to create economic ties.[37]

Maxwell's[38] pronouncement that, "Everything rises and falls on leadership" was reinforced by Ngambi[39], who stated that "[t]he success or failure of every nation is a true reflection of its leadership."

RECOMMENDATIONS

This section views public sector leadership in a political context, with a specific focus on delivering public value in a VUCA environment. There is a case to be made that in politics, political power and public accountability need to incorporate aspects such as negotiation, mediation and other relational skills, in addition to more general capabilities.[40] There is also an association between leading oneself, creating public value, and pursuing sustainable development.

Leadership for achieving sustainable development in SA seems to be rooted in a rapid process paradigm. Considering that the world is inherently inconsistent (fluctuation in economies), that multiple realities will emerge (outbreak of the Coronavirus), and that people will organise and adapt according to their environments (such as global warming), public sector leaders must be adaptive, flexible, self-renewing, resilient and willing to learn. The achievement of sustainable development and creating public value depends on clear leadership that supports the integration and adaptation of the global goals to the local content. Sustainability leadership, as described by Visser and Courtice[41], is geared towards bringing about profound change, whether in political and economic systems, business models and practices, or in the broad social contract with stakeholders and society.

The global challenges that a leader in the 21st century has to manage are, according to CISL[42], more complex than any other generation has had to face – it is truly a VUCA world.[43] According to the World Economic Forum's (WEF) *2019 Global Risks Report*, the categories of risks that world leaders need to manage can be identified as natural, technological, geopolitical, economic and societal. Although nature and environment are high on the agendas of most countries, the failure of countries to mitigate climate change has led to extreme weather and man-made environmental disasters. However, it appears that future drivers are technologies that are creating ways of living faster while simultaneously destroying old leadership ideologies.

---

37 Landsberg, 2007.

38 Maxwell, 1999: 134.

39 Ngambi, 2011: 5.

40 University of Cambridge Institute for Sustainability Leadership, 2017.

41 Visser & Courtice, 2017: 4.

42 University of Cambridge Institute for Sustainability Leadership, 2017.

43 Bushe & Marshak, 2016.

Technology not only sets the pace, but also outlines the actions to be taken by leaders. With concepts such as the Internet of Everything, the knowledge economy, smart cities, digital proficiency, and interruption free information technology, it appears overwhelming and an impossible task to lead in the 21st century. It has, therefore, becoming increasingly obvious that public sector leaders will have to undergo wholesale leadership renewal, which relies on a leader having a strong sense of his/her inner strength.

This inner strength will require leaders to show mental endurance, in other words, having the confidence to stretch their mental capacity to solve complex and new problems. Problems are seen as complex in the sense that leaders might have never before dealt with these emerging problems. A typical example would be to address the spread of the Coronavirus and the consequences thereof. If leaders experience anxiety in a VUCA environment they may inhibit themselves from moving forward.[44] Leaders need to not fear considering multiple solutions which might not work, or worry about solving problems on the first try, but must show mental elasticity to learn and try again.

Leadership in the 21st century further requires leaders to apply inner strength; they must dare, in layman's terms, to "think outside the box" and take a leap of faith in their creativeness. Although the focus of the Fourth Industrial Revolution (4IR) will be on managing data and connectivity, the human-technology interaction will require the skill of daring to lead in a VUCA environment.

As challenges faced by leaders in the 4IR spread across disciplines and borders, a leader needs to be comfortable with the fact that they cannot solve problems on their own. Having the ability to network, bring people from diverse disciplines on board, and facilitate problem-solving through pockets of excellence, will not be the exception but the norm (Rimita, 2019). A leader thus needs to invest diligently in advancing the human-technology relationship, while understanding that the human dimension will always get priority, not only now, but also into the future. Although several suggestions can be made regarding leading self in a VUCA environment, this discussion will concentrate on the last point, i.e. collaboration.

The so-called knowledge economy requires leaders to invest in human capital. Although the workforce is changing at a fast pace, it often still has to function within an older and less innovative public sector environment. The focus of leaders here is to create an environment and establish a culture that will enable public servants to render services required in a VUCA world; a leader will have to rely on prepared human resources to have a strong corps (also called the bench strength). In this regard, public service leaders cannot be content if they have not established a 21st century, values-driven public service; a trusted and capable administration; and responsive and adaptive citizenry.

---

44 Ibid.

CONCLUDING REMARKS

This chapter has focused on discussing the implementation of lead self in the SA public sector environment. The respective role players within this environment were identified (national, provincial and local government), as well as the institutions (legislative, executive and judiciary) that render effective and efficient services to the citizens of the country. However, the leader (head of state, monarch, dictator, despot, etc.) needs to lead. The VUCA environment, which includes natural resources, unemployment, public service capacity and economic uncertainty, to mention a few, was demarcated within the South African context. Against this discussion, it appears as if leaders in the 21st century often contribute to VUCA environments.

The chapter started with an introduction to the case of SA and the transition that took place from an apartheid minority regime to a full accepted democratic dispensation in the early 1990s. The leadership styles of Mandela and Mbeki were linked to the transformational-, relationship- and participative leadership theories.

The chapter concluded with a few practical and theoretical recommendations; the example of the spreading of the Coronavirus was used to illustrate this point. Although this chapter highlighted how important it is for a 21st century leader to trust their capacity, be fearless when innovative solutions are sought, and show confidence in offering new solutions to challenges that were never experienced before, these are not the only recommendations. Leaders around the world can announce emergency states, call for pandemic prevention, and put measures in place to manage a VUCA environment, however in these circumstances any success depends on the commitment of each citizen to show leadership and act responsibly.

CHAPTER 11

LEADING SELF IN SOUTH AFRICA'S VUCA LOCAL GOVERNMENT ENVIRONMENT

Maréve Biljohn

ABSTRACT

This chapter focuses on transformational leadership, with the aim of proposing how self-leadership could be applied by officials in South Africa's local government VUCA environment. Theories to lead self in respect of public sector VUCA environments, components of the Transformational Leadership and Transformational Social Innovation Theories, as well as leading-self qualities that best fit the 21st century public sector VUCA environment, are detailed. Significantly, this chapter recommends how officials in South Africa's local government volatile environments could apply self-leadership through the Transformational Leadership Theory, components of intellectual stimulation and individualised consideration, as well as the Transformational Social Innovation Theory of transformative change. The findings recommend that leading self in South Africa's Local Government VUCA environments requires a combination of intellectual stimulation, individualised consideration, and transformative change. An outcome of this chapter is that relational skills have become fundamental for LG officials when applying self-leadership to bring about transformative change in addressing recurring LG VUCA environments.

INTRODUCTION

Municipalities in the South African local government (LG) sphere are considered to be generally in distress.[1] This is attributed to political abuse of power and strife, the inability of a majority of municipalities to execute basic functions, poor infrastructure planning and maintenance, financial challenges, an increase in corruption, violent service delivery protests, and staff turbulence (Municipal Data and Intelligence[2]). The mentioned distress is also in part symptomatic of the challenges experienced by South

---

1   Reddy, 2018: 710.

2   Municipal IQ, 2020.

Africa's LG, which emanates from factors within their internal as well as their external environments.[3] As identified in *The State of LG in South Africa* by the Department of Cooperative Governance and Traditional Affairs (COGTA), these challenges relate to issues of governance, financial management, service delivery, and labour relations, which are inherent to the internal environment of the municipality.[4] Of significance regarding these challenges is their recurring nature, which has resulted in them being the focus of two LG reforms in South Africa, namely the 2009 Local Government Turnaround Strategy (LGTS) and the 2013 Back-to-Basics campaign. The latter's introduction seven years ago has, however, not yielded its intended impact. Similar to the failure of previous reforms such as the 1998 LG White Paper and the 2009 LGTS, Reddy[5] contended that this is a result of politicisation which stems from weak municipal leadership.

Against this background, this chapter starts with President Ramaphosa's leadership as an example of how components of transformational leadership are applied to respond to challenges in the LG environment. Leading-self qualities emerging from this example include the Transformational Leadership Theory (TLT) components of intellectual stimulation (IS) and individualised consideration (IC), as well as the Transformational Social Innovation Theory (TSIT) of transformative change. This example highlights the transformational leadership role of President Ramaphosa in South Africa's LG VUCA environment. The following section describes the components of the TLT and TSIT theories, as well as the leading-self qualities that best fit the 21st century public sector VUCA environment. In the next section, the practical reality is presented along with an argument regarding how to apply lead self in a VUCA environment. Subsequently, the Recommendations section presents practical and theoretical recommendations to leading self in a LG VUCA environment, while the Conclusion section summarises the chapter and draws conclusions.

RAMAPHOSA'S TRANSFORMATIONAL LEADERSHIP ROLE IN SOUTH AFRICA'S LOCAL GOVERNMENT VUCA ENVIRONMENT

Transformational leaders are celebrated for bringing about major positive changes. Transformational leadership focuses on what the leader accomplishes as opposed to their relationships with their team members or their characteristics.[6] Their roles can be achieved through, amongst other, (i) raising mindfulness amongst people; (ii)

---

3   Van der Waldt, Venter, Phutiagae, Nealer, Khalo & Vyas-Doorgapersad, 2018: 107.

4   Van der Waldt et al., 2018: 104.

5   Reddy, 2018: 718.

6   Dubrin, 2007: 83.

assisting people to adopt an attitude beyond self-interest; (iii) helping people search for self-fulfillment; (iv) providing and understanding regarding the need for change, (v) investing managers with a sense of urgency; (iv) committing to greatness; (vii) adopting a long-range perspective; (viii) building trust; and (ix) focusing resources where change is most needed.[7] A leader who had to adopt some of the mentioned transformational roles to address VUCA environments in South Africa's LG, where transformation is required towards building a capable and developmental South African state, is President Ramaphosa. The remainder of this section explicates the transformational leadership roles played by Ramaphosa to implore South African LG to achieve this capable and developmental state.

President Ramaphosa was not only a drafter of the first democratic South African Constitution, but was also the deputy chairperson of the National Planning Commission, which drafted the National Development Plan (NDP).[8, 9, 10] When he announced his vision for his Administration, Ramaphosa, who is a visionary, appealed to South African citizens and public sector officials, which includes LG, to share in this vision through the "new dawn" and "thuma mina (send me)" contexts.[11] With his "thuma mina" plea, Ramaphosa thus set the tone as a transformational leader for the country to adopt an attitude beyond self-interest. This attitude is likewise required of South African LG, which is fundamental to realising Ramaphosa's vision for a new dawn, as well as to implement strategies and targets of achieving a capable and developmental state according to the NDP.[12, 13] A capable and developmental state, as prioritised in Chapter 13 of the NDP, outlines, amongst others, making working in South African LG a career of choice. The plan is to strengthen LG[14]; since taking office, Ramaphosa's plans have inter alia, been targeted at interventions that provide leadership in this context.

When it comes to his vision for the country, Ramaphosa's focus areas for South African LG include service delivery, financial management, capacity and skills development, as well as partnership formation, as he described during his address to the SALGA National Members Assembly in 2018.[15] Concerning service delivery, the critical role of LG in driving investment promotion and attraction in the country through their service delivery legislative mandate is highlighted by Ramaphosa.[16] Reliable and consistent service delivery is therefore amongst the key areas where

---

7   Dubrin, 2007: 85-86.
8   The Presidency, 2012: 3.
9   Municipal IQ, 2018.
10 Mail & Guardian, 2020.
11 Ibid.
12 The Presidency, 2012: 9.
13 Ramaphosa, 2018.
14 The Presidency, 2012: 9.
15 Ramaphosa, 2018.
16 Ramaphosa, 2018.

LG needs to improve to make their locations more attractive to potential investors.[17] Concerning financial management, a priority is the better use of LG financial resources by focusing their budgets on rehabilitating and maintaining neglected infrastructure instead of building new infrastructure. Regarding LG skills and capacity, Ramaphosa suggested that the development of LG skills and capacity be driven internally by improving the existing skills base. Additionally, information and technology should be used to improve LG efficiency and effectiveness.[18] Linked to this is the attraction of suitably qualified incumbents and graduates based on standardised remuneration levels for all municipalities.[19] Regarding partnership formation, LG is encouraged to establish these with organised labour, civil society, and business to collaborate on the mobilising of resources and developing investment plans.[20]

The significance of the mentioned focus areas is that they address VUCA environments in the South African LG environment where transformation is required. However, despite the prioritisation of these VUCA environments through the pillars of the Back-to-Basics LG reform, namely "delivering basic services, putting people first, good governance, sound financial management, and building capabilities"[21], the VUCA environments of financial management, service delivery, and labour relations remains recurring challenges. Therefore, as a transformational leader, Ramaphosa's identification of these focus areas not only emphasises the importance of LGs in achieving a capable and developmental state, but also highlights the impetus for change in these VUCA environments. This is in keeping with the transformational leadership quality of providing an understanding of the need for change.[22] The leadership quality of focusing resources where change is needed most is also evident in Ramaphosa's strategy of encouraging sound financial management amidst a shortage of fiscal resources.[23] As such, adopting practical strategies to address funding and resource limitations is required to address a particular issue.[24] Added to this, Ramaphosa reminded LG of the importance of partnership formation in transforming these VUCA environments. That partnership formation should also form the basis on new developments that LG undertakes, partnership formation should also be used by LG to achieve their developmental LG mandate, and partnership formations should also be used by LG to execute their legislative mandate.[25]

---

17 Ibid.
18 Ibid.
19 Ibid.
20 Ibid.
21 Van der Waldt, et al., 2018: 106.
22 Dubrin, 2007: 85.
23 Dubrin, 2007: 86.
24 Ibid.
25 (Ramaphosa, 2018.

Whilst the formation of partnerships is inherent to the 1998 developmental LG vision, Ramaphosa has also demonstrated to South African LG that collaboration should be inherent to addressing challenges in LG VUCA environments. In his 2019 State of the Nation Address (SONA), Ramaphosa demonstrated this through his vision for a new smart-city. Subsequently, in his 2020 SONA, he reported that the development of the new smart-city is well underway in Lanseria, through a collaborative effort between the cities of Johannesburg, Lanseria and Madibeng, the Presidency, and the Gauteng and Northwest provincial governments.[26] Implementation of this new smart-city vision is coherent with the transformational leadership quality of adopting a long-range perspective to deal with a current issue, as well as encouraging LG to adopt a future orientation of how the municipal areas can be transformed.[27] President Ramaphosa not only explained to LG that it needs to take on a long-range perspective and see the bigger picture during his 2019 SONA, but added that it is achievable during his 2020 SONA. This is consistent with the transformational leadership quality of investing managers with a sense of urgency.[28] This quality is also prevalent in Ramaphosa's action to deliver on his vision of a new smart-city through a team that shares his vision and the changes that are necessary to achieve this vision within the framework of available and necessary resources.[29]

Against this background, this section concludes by describing the self-leadership qualities demonstrated by President Ramaphosa that are embedded in the TLT and TSIT. The first leading-self quality of Ramaphosa in this example is consistent with the TLT component of IS. President Ramaphosa's actions to demonstrate this quality includes LG establishing partnerships and sound working relationship. In this regard, the transformational role played by Ramaphosa required the honing of self-influence and harnessing the exploration of new frameworks and approaches to attracting investment to municipal areas through, amongst others, sustainable service delivery. Moreover, through the new smart-city, Ramaphosa has set an example of a leader who through IS applies innovative plans and strategies, which LG can follow by applying similar new innovative frameworks and approaches to address existing challenges and situations.[30]

The second leading-self quality in this example is the TLT component of IC. President Ramaphosa demonstrated through this quality that LG officials are expected to demonstrate the leading-self qualities of steering oneself and exercising self-influence towards addressing challenges of sustainable service delivery, investment promotion and attraction, financial management and labour relations. The third

---

26 Ramaphosa, 2020.

27 Dubrin, 2007: 86.

28 Dubrin, 2007: 85.

29 Ibid.

30 Dubrin, 2007: 86.

leading-self quality present in this example is transformative change in the TSIT, which highlights the need to build social relationships premised on purpose, and building interpersonal relations grounded in trust, collaboration and co-ownership. "To this extent, Ramaphosa demonstrated that LG, VUCA environments are not only a government problem and to establish partnerships, the leading-self quality of relational skills is fundamental to devising innovative solutions to enhance LG responsiveness (another leading-self quality) to challenges in the VUCA environments."

THEORIES TO LEAD SELF IN RESPECT OF PUBLIC SECTOR VUCA ENVIRONMENTS

Transformational Leadership Theory

According to the seminal work of Burns, the relationship-oriented styles of transformational leaders include being inspirational, charismatic and visionary.[31, 32, 33, 34] Over time, these styles were categorised into four components, namely idealised influence (II), inspirational motivation (IM), intellectual stimulation (IS) and individualised consideration (IC), all of which make a leader transformational.[35]

Transformational leaders exhibit behaviours that include communicating an appealing vision to followers, and as such convincing followers to act in the interest of the organisation as opposed to self-interest.[36, 37, 38] This implies that first an organisational vision and goals must be set, which are consistently communicated with followers, which motivate them through incentives such as inspiration, appeals for ethical and moral behaviour, and persuasion.[39] As visionaries, transformational leaders communicate values aimed at motivating and guiding team members.[40] This behaviour is also referred to as IM (inspirational motivation), which has as its key characteristics optimism and enthusiasm[41]; the leader aligns the values of their employees with the

---

31 Dilts, 1996.

32 Nanus, 1992.

33 House, 1976.

34 Javidan & Waldman, 2003.

35 McCkleskey, 2014: 120.

36 Dubrin, 2007: 86.

37 McCleskey, 2014: 120.

38 De Vries, 2016: 119.

39 Bass & Avolio, 1994.

40 Dubrin, 2007: 86.

41 McCleskey, 2014: 120.

organisation's vision, mission and ideology.[42, 43] Secondly, transformational leaders exhibit behaviours such as enhancing their followers' loyalty and pride, which is known as II (idealized influence).[44] II is also considered consistent with a leader's ability to influence followers charismatically to imitate the leader's behaviour.[45, 46] Thirdly, these leaders encourage employee participation through new work structures and inspire them to view the world from new perspectives, which is also referred to as IS (intellectual stimulation). Through IS, followers' ability to innovate is improved by a leader who applies new frameworks and approaches towards addressing existing challenges and situations.[47, 48] The success of IS depends on the openness of the leader to the criticism of followers, as well as their increased self-efficacy.[49, 50] Lastly, these leaders model behaviours that are pro-social through the component of IC (individualised consideration).[51, 52, 53, 54, 55, 56, 57] Through IC, the leader sees employees or followers as valuable assets that are inherent to the success and productivity of the organisation.[58] Concerned with team members' development, leaders provide supportive leadership by acknowledging the achievements of team members, providing positive feedback, and empowering members through participation in decision making.[59] The leader, therefore, provides learning opportunities, gives individual or personal attention to employees, and offers coaching and mentoring to assist followers to reach their full potential.[60, 61]

42 Sarros & Santora, 2001: 385 in Shokane et al., 2004: 2.

43 Stanz & Slabbert, 2004: 2.

44 McCleskey, 2014: 120.

45 Sarros & Santora, 2001: 387 in Shokane et al., 2004: 2.

46 Dubrin, 2007: 86.

47 Ibid.

48 Chawla & Lenka, 2018: 216.

49 Bass & Riggio, 2006.

50 McCleskey, 2014: 120.

51 Albrecht, 2005.

52 Bodla & Nawaz, 2010.

53 Leslie & Canwell, 2010.

54 Paarlberg & Lavigna, 2010.

55 Rainey, 2003.

56 Wright & Pandey, 2010.

57 McCleskey, 2014: 120.

58 Sarros & Santora, 2001: 385 in Shokane et al., 2004: 2.

59 Dubrin, 2007: 86.

60 McCleskey, 2014: 120.

61 De Vries, 2016: 119.

Transformative Social Innovation Theory

The theory of TSI, which is grounded in the concepts of social innovation (SI) and transformative change, is concerned with how SIs can contribute to achieving transformative change.[62] Within TSI, the concept of SI is defined as the establishment of new social relations that culminate into "new ways of doing, organizing, framing and knowing."[63, 64] These social relations can be between public sector officials and citizens, government and citizens, native inhabitants and refugees, or politicians and civil society organisations or stakeholders.[65] The nature of these social relations could be based on purpose as opposed to profit, on building interpersonal relations premised on trust instead of status, and on replacing hierarchical relations and competition with collaboration and co-ownership.[66]

The TSIT describes the concept of transformative change as challenging, replacing or altering the formal and/or informal institutions of an organisation.[67] Formal and informal institutions include the rules, norms, values, and conventions of the organisation that could either enable or hinder the development of social relations, as well as establish patterns of doing, organising, framing and knowing."[68, 69, 70] It is argued that whilst the achievement of transformative change encompasses institutional change, the latter is not necessarily transformative.[71] Hence, for public sector organisations and its officials to attain a transformative change in VUCA environments, SI is ideal to institutionalise changes in social relations that could challenge or replace dominant institutions.[72] Social innovation that is applied for transformative change could emerge as: (i) a set of ideas concerning what should change; (ii) principles and values that are required for such change; (iii) a narrative of required changes, and; (iv) ideas as to how the desired change could be achieved.[73] The process of institutionalising transformative change through SI could be met with challenges, including the marginalisation or adoption of dominant institutions and risks of capture.[74]

---

62 Strasser, Kraker & Kemp, 2019: 2.
63 Haxeltine, Pel, Dumitru, Kemp, Avelino, Jørgensen, Wittmayer, Kunze, Dorland & Baule, 2017.
64 Moulaert, MacCallum, Mehmood & Hamdouch, 2013.
65 Strasser et al., 2019: 3.
66 Ibid.
67 Ibid.
68 Lowndes & Roberts, 2013.
69 Cajaiba-Santana, 2014.
70 Haxeltine et al., 2017 in Strasser et al., 2019: 3
71 Strasser et al., 2019: 3.
72 Ibid.
73 Strasser et al., 2019: 4.
74 Ibid.

CASE OF SOUTH AFRICA'S LOCAL GOVERNMENT VUCA ENVIRONMENTS

Financial Management

The Consolidated General Report on LG audit outcomes of South Africa for the 2017-2018 financial year attribute the dire financial health in municipalities to accountability failures.[75] As such, almost a third of the municipalities were in a financially vulnerable position[76] due to a lack of accountability systems, corruption, fraud as well as municipal funds and assets that were misused.[77, 78] Accountability systems and financial management are inherent to the formal organisational institutions of the internal municipal internal environment. Arguably, the external environment also influences the extent to which sound financial management is exercised or corruption and fraud are perpetuated.

Sound financial management is influenced by, amongst others, the financial viability of a municipality, which is affected by internal and external factors. The latter include communities who are reluctant to pay service fees due to a culture of non-payment, a high number of indigents (3.6 million households) living in a municipal area who are unable to pay for municipal services, increasing aged debts, and not enforcing debt collection.[79, 80, 81] Factors such as a culture of non-payment and the inability of indigents to pay service fees are part of the external environment, whereas aging debt and a lack of debt collection emanate from the formal institutions in the internal municipal environment. At the end of the 2018/2019 financial year, municipalities were owed R36.6 billion by business and "other" stakeholders, R10.3 billion by government, and R118.6 billion from households.[82] All these factors impact municipalities' ability to remain efficient and responsive amidst the top-down pressures posed by the environment in which municipalities operate. Some top-down pressures include quality and sustainable service delivery to communities that can pay for services, as well as those community members classified as indigent who cannot pay for basic municipal services.-

---

75 Auditor-General SA, 2019.

76 Ibid.

77 Van der Waldt et al., 2018: 105.

78 Reddy, 2018: 71.

79 Van der Waldt et al., 2018: 104.

80 Auditor-General SA, 2019.

81 StatsSA, 2019.

82 BusinessDay, 2019.

Service delivery

Concerning service delivery, although municipalities are provided with municipal infrastructure grants, the latter are often misused.[83] To this extent, insufficient funds pose a threat to the elimination of infrastructure backlogs, of which the consequences are service delivery backlogs that may result in the non-achievement of the post-2015 sustainable development goals.[84] Municipalities' role concerning the sustainable development goals is premised on its service delivery mandate that contributes to enhancing development and the targets set by national government.[85] The misuse of the mentioned grants could be perpetuated by factors such as an organisational culture and norms of non-accountability, a lack of values and ethics, as well as non-compliance with the codes of conduct that constitute the underlying informal organisational institutions within the internal municipal environment. Additionally, informal organisational institutions have been affecting the ability of South African municipalities to fulfil their service delivery mandate and contribute to national priorities. Therefore, more formal institutions (accountability measures and consequence management through policies) may be required to address the misuse of grants and financial misconduct.

Measures that will ensure engagement between municipalities and communities, and in turn, ensure that the provisions of the Municipal Systems Act 32 of 2000 regarding community participation are complied with, became the focus of service delivery in the Back-to-Basics Campaign. Communities' participation in respect of legislative compliance should not merely be for compliance purposes, but should be prioritised as part of the formal (policies, plans, strategies) and informal (culture) institutions of the organisation. A lack of community participation has affected LG responsiveness to their service delivery needs.[86] In turn, this lack of responsiveness is reported as part of the contributory reasons for the service delivery protests experienced by municipalities since 2004.[87] Seven years since the 2013 Back-to-Basics campaign, 11 years since the 2009 LGTS, and 22 years since the 1998 White Paper on Developmental LG, community participation remains a challenge emanating from formal and informal institutions within internal municipal environments. Thus, the importance of community participation to achieve transformative and social change is seemingly underestimated, and in some respects ignored, by municipalities.

---

83 Van der Waldt et al., 2018: 105.

84 Ibid.

85 Reddy, 2018: 714.

86 Breakfast, 2019: 113.

87 Masiya, Davids & Mangai, 2019: 38.

Labour relations

Labour relations challenges pertain to developing capacities that set out to "build" strong processes and systems for the municipal administration[88], i.e. filling administrative positions with suitably qualified competent candidates and closely monitoring such appointments.[89] However, existing human resources management systems are not conducive for attracting skilled and qualified officials, moreover retaining qualified skilled personnel for achieving LGs' service delivery mandate.[90, 91] Retaining qualified and skilled personnel is part of the bottom-up pressures that municipalities might experience, and is of importance given the breadth and depth of knowledge of such officials to meaningfully contribute to a municipality's attainment of priorities in its integrated development plan.

High staff turnover, vacancies, and instability in key positions, as well as key officials who lack appropriate financial skills and competencies, remain a challenge.[92, 93, 94, 95] This is exacerbated by political interference in the recruitment and appointment processes of new officials[96], which results in the appointment of officials who are not suitably qualified for some vacancies. Further, the politicisation of municipalities has been detrimental to building a capable municipal administration and is blamed for dysfunctional administrations as well as administrative performance that is inferior.[97] Hence, the appointment of cadres in the absence of skills assessment is detrimental to: (i) service delivery; (ii) the achievement of the legislative and executive obligations and mandate of municipalities; and (iii) the ability of some municipalities to remain responsive to the needs and demands of communities and stakeholders within their external environment.[98, 99] The appointment of unqualified officials, together with officials' non-compliance with work obligations, is seemingly part of the underlying reason for some municipalities' poor performance.[100] Similar to misusing grants that are intended for eliminating service delivery backlogs, non-compliance with work obligations is not only part of the informal institutions of an organisation where such

---

88 Van der Waldt, 2018: 106.
89 Ibid.
90 Van der Waldt et al., 2018: 104.
91 Reddy, 2015: 335.
92 Auditor-General SA, 2019.
93 COGTA, 2009 cited in Ndevu, 2019: 6.
94 Reddy, 2015: 335.
95 Van der Waldt, 2018: 104.
96 Van der Waldt et al., 2018: 104.
97 COGTA, 2009 cited in Ndevu, 2019: 6.
98 Breakfast, 2019: 108.
99 Reddy, 2018: 718.
100 Waldt et al., 2018: 104.

a culture has been allowed to exist, but should be addressed through changes to both the formal and informal institutions of the organisation.

Against the background of the three imminent challenges that underscore the South African LG VUCA environment, these challenges are predominantly influenced by volatility (financial management, service delivery, labour relations), uncertainty (labour relations), and complexity (financial management). Consistent with the conceptualisation of volatility, all three of these imminent challenges have been recurring in the South African LG environment. Their reoccurrence can be associated with a lack of inadequate formal and informal organisational institutions (internal environment). Coherent with uncertainty, labour relations have become subject to politicisation, which is linked to dysfunctional administrations and inferior administrative performance.[101] Despite formal organisational institutions (policies and procedures) guiding the appointment processes of officials, these processes seem to be flouted by political interference. Concerning complexity, compounding factors internal and external to the organisation seem to contribute to the challenge of financial management. Convergent with the challenges regarding labour relations of existing formal organisational institutions that govern financial management, the latter is subject to increased corruption, fraud, misuse of funds and assets, poor financial management, as well as a lack of accountability and control systems, and recurrent poor audit outcomes.[102, 103]

RECOMMENDATIONS

The relationship between TLT and self-leadership for the 21st century

All four TLT components, namely II, IM, IS, and IC, seem relevant to exercising self-leadership. However, components of II and IM appeal more to the traditional leader-follower relationships with a focus on the leader, whereas the components of IS and IC makes leadership applicable to the "follower" as well. In light of this, the relationship between TLT and self-leadership could be defined in the TLT components of IS, which asserts criticism as well as increased self-efficacy from followers,[104, 105] and IC that renders employees as essential to organisational success and productivity.[106] This disposition is supported by the fact that self-leadership requires an individual to control their behaviour

101 COGTA, 2009 cited in Ndevu, 2019: 6.

102 Van der Waldt et al., 2018: 104-105.

103 Thornhill & Cloete, 2014: 94, 118 cited in Reddy, 2018: 718.

104 Bass & Riggio, 2006.

105 McCleskey, 2014: 120.

106 Sarros & Santora, 2001: 385 in Shokane et al., 2004: 2.

to influence and lead self by applying specific cognitive and behavioural strategies[107], which is facilitated through IS and IC. These TLT components are thus consistent with cultivating the process of self-influence during self-leadership, whereby an individual acquires self-direction and self-motivation that is required to perform.[108]

In the 21st century, the relevance of TLT for LG is predicated on adopting a learning mindset through IS (intellectual stimulation), which enhances one's self-influence in the work environment. Such self-influence, which is consistent with self-leadership[109], could be achieved by taking advantage of learning (formal or informal), mentoring, coaching and SI opportunities. These opportunities are considered essential for making an impact in achieving organisational success and productivity. More importantly, such opportunities empower officials to develop skill sets to convey the organisational vision and objectives with external stakeholders, and to persuade these stakeholders to buy into and contribute towards the attainment of these objectives and vision amidst top-down and bottom-up organisational pressures. Further, learning opportunities could contribute to capacitating officials to explore new frameworks and approaches to existing challenges emanating from service delivery, labour relations, and financial management.

The relationship between TSIT and self-leadership for the 21st century

The relationship between TSIT and self-leadership is underscored by the strategies that would be required of a public sector official to bring about transformative changes in addressing top-down and bottom-up organisational pressures, which in turn contribute to addressing societal challenges. These strategies could include managing your behaviour to meet set objectives and standards, setting and/or modifying standards, and undertaking the evaluation of standards,[110, 111] which is deemed important to achieve transformative change that is inherent to SI. Social innovation which is process-oriented (collaboration, networks, co-production) and goal-oriented (problem-solving)[112] makes it contingent upon public sector officials to initiate transformative change through self-leadership strategies such as: (i) addressing "what should be done"; (ii) understanding "why it should be done"; and (iii) "how to do it."[113] This highlights that the process of achieving transformative change, which is inherent to the TSIT, would include the mentioned strategies that are consistent with those employed during self-leadership.

---

107 Neck & Houghton, 2006: 270.

108 Manz, 1986 cited in Neck & Houghton, 2004: 271.

109 Ibid.

110 Pearce & Manz, 2005: 133.

111 Stewart & Courtright, 2011: 177.

112 Grimm, Fox, Baines & Albertson, 2013: 438.

113 Pearce & Manz, 2005: 133.

In the 21st century, the relevance of TSIT for self-leadership in LG is premised on the importance of network governance to address the challenges presented by volatile public sector top-down and bottom-up pressures from its internal and external environments. Social innovation, which is grounded in finding solutions to societal challenges through engaging and collaborating with various stakeholders to address such challenges[114, 115, 116, 117], is therefore seemingly consistent with network governance. Network governance involves cross-sectoral participation (citizens, non-governmental organisations, community-based organisations, public and private sector) in policy-making processes and public affairs.[118] As such, network governance has become essential to the ability of South African municipalities in the 21st century to deal with challenges of financial constraints, capacity constraints due to labour relations, and service delivery challenges. It is apparent from the mentioned recurring challenges that South African municipalities cannot address these through their own formal and informal institutions. For this reason, network governance requires LG officials to have and develop strong interpersonal relationships with external stakeholders, which Gentry et al. (2007, cited in Browning, 2018[119]) referred to as relational skills. Consistent with TSIT, these relational skills are fundamental to self-leadership for achieving transformative change in addressing challenges of financial constraints, labour relations, and service delivery through the formal and informal institutions of organisations.[120] Its focus on transformative change and relational skills thus make TSIT relevant for self-leadership in the 21st century.

CONCLUDING REMARKS

This chapter addressed the concept of leading self in South Africa's LG VUCA environments. This chapter started with the example of President Ramaphosa as a transformational leader. Leading-self qualities that emerged from this example included the TLT components of IS and IC, as well as the TSIT component of transformative change. In the next section, components of the TLT and TSIT theories and leading-self qualities that best fit the 21st century public sector VUCA environment were discussed. This section highlighted that the top-heavy traditional model of leadership, which persisted through the 20th and partly the 21st century[121] are no longer relevant, given

---

114 Sørensen & Torfing, 2011: 845.

115 Cipolla & Moura, 2012: 40.

116 OECD, 2014.

117 Hart, Jacobs, Ramoroka, Mangqalazah, Mhula, Ngwenya & Letty, 2014.

118 Bogason & Musso, 2006: 4.

119 Browning, 2018: 17.

120 Strasser et al, 2019: 3.

121 Pearce & Manz, 2005:132.

the challenges confronting public sector organisations amidst top-down and bottom-up pressures. This was followed by the Case of South Africa's LG VUCA environment (financial management, service delivery, labour relations). Whilst all three challenges were categorised as contributing to the volatile environments in municipalities, challenges of labour relations were also categorised as uncertain and financial management as part of the complex environments of municipalities. Subsequently, the Recommendations section outlined how self-leadership could be applied by LG officials in volatile environments through the TLT components of IS and IC. Further, it proposed how self-leadership could be applied by LG officials in volatile environments through the TSIT component of transformative change. From these recommendations, it was deduced that leading self in South Africa's LG VUCA environments requires a combination of IS, IC, and transformative change. These components of the TLT and the TSIT are consistent with the leading-self qualities present in the example of President Ramaphosa.

CHAPTER 12

A MODEL OF LEADING SELF IN VUCA ENVIRONMENTS

Ajay K. Jain

The ultimate measure of a man is not where he stands in moments of comfort and convenience, but where he stands at times of challenge and controversy.
—*Martin Luther King, Jr.*

ABSTRACT

This chapter proposes a model of leading self in VUCA environments that is grounded in psychological and sociological theories on self development and motivation. The chapter argues that most individuals do not explore the source of their "leadership potential" within a deeper self, but rather keep depending on support from the external environment to lead proactive change at their workplaces. The chapter presents a set of inhibitors and facilitators of leading self in VUCA environments, and suggests that one should be able to overcome environmental constraints in order to realise one's true leadership potential. Finally, the chapter concludes that "self" is a reservoir of energy which must be stimulated to nurture leadership in self.

INTRODUCTION

This chapter is aimed at investigating the sources of motivation for leaders who prefer to set a difficult goal and navigate their life through upheavals and adapt to various challenges. Leadership does not exist in isolation; rather it continuously interacts with the environment, i.e. individuals impact the environment and are impacted by their surroundings. Drawn from Conditioning Theory, Social Cognitive Theory, Positive Psychology, Existential Psychology and the Theory of Self-Concept, this chapter suggests the characteristics of a conditioned mind (preventing factors of leading self) and a de-conditioned mind (features of leading self), before suggesting four factors of sustained motivation in order to cope with VUCA environments.

Example

It may be argued that one's leadership potential can be realised while operating and working under the adverse conditions of life. For example, Gandhi fought against the British Empire in India, Mandela fought against the policy of apartheid in South Africa, and Martin Luther King Jr. fought against racism in the USA. A leadership journey begins in a highly chaotic environment with the aim of establishing justice and fairness, and to bring peace, harmony and integration to the organisation or society. Similar to Gandhi, Mandela and King Jr., the corporate world has several such examples where CEOs and MDs, despite personal and professional crises, stood tall and strong. A recent example of this is Rajat Gupta, who was the Managing Director of McKinsey & Company from 1994 to 2007. Gupta published his autobiography, *Mind without Fear*, based on his experiences in an American federal prison, which described how he was inspired by Hindu's holy book, *Srimad Bhagvad Gita*.

Rajat Gupta went to Harvard Business School for his MBA (1973) after graduating in 1971 from the Indian Institute of Technology in New Delhi. Immediately after his MBA, he joined McKinsey where he was hired and mentored by Ronnald "Ron" Daniel, a former managing director. Gupta began to rise through the ranks, first becoming head of the McKinsey office in Scandinavia in 1981, and then the head of the Chicago office in 1990 as a senior partner. In 1994, he was elected the firm's first Indian-born CEO of a multinational corporation. He was re-elected twice – in 1997 and 2000 (the maximum allowed term). During Gupta's time as head of McKinsey, the firm opened offices in 23 new countries and doubled its consultant base to 891 partners, increasing revenue 280% to $3.4 billion. The Indian School of Business in Hyderabad (ranked 28th in Financial Times Global MBA 2018 rankings[1]) was his brainchild. Gupta also served on several high-profile corporate boards as a director during his career, including Procter & Gamble, Goldman Sachs, Genpact and the Russian bank Sberbank. Gupta again became a senior partner of McKinsey in 2003 and senior partner emeritus in 2007.

Yet after enjoying huge success from 1973 to 2008, the US Securities and Exchange Commission filed an administrative civil complaint on 1st March 2009 against Gupta for insider trading with billionaire and Galleon Group hedge fund founder, Raj Rajaratnam. On October 26, 2010, the United States Attorney's Office filed criminal charges against Gupta. He was arrested in New York City by the FBI and pleaded not guilty when his jury trial began on May 22, 2012. On June 15, 2012, Gupta was found guilty on three counts of securities fraud and one count of conspiracy. He was found not guilty on two other securities fraud charges. On October 24, 2012, Gupta was sentenced to two years in prison for leaking boardroom secrets to Rajaratnam. His prison sentence began on June 17, 2014, and he was released from federal prison

---

1   List of Journals FT 50, journals used by the Financial Times to compile their lists of top Business Schools.

on January 5, 2016. In the wake of the scandal, McKinsey ended its professional relationship with Gupta and dropped him from its alumni database.

On March 2019, Gupta described his experience in his autobiography, *Mind without Fear*. In an interview with a newspaper, Gupta argued that "I was a big fish and easier target", and called himself a "political prisoner" during the time of the financial crisis in the USA. According to him, half of the jury members were crying after giving him sentence of two years. Media has put his book in the category of St Augustine's Confessions and Gandhi's The Story of My Experiments with Truth.

What makes Rajat Gupta a literary character for the ages, his life a parable for humanity's virtues and vices. And what of his legacy and what he says is. "If my legacy is, 'this guy was an insider trader' it doesn't matter. My legacy could also be 'he built two great institutions', or 'he took McKinsey global'. I am indifferent."

What kept him motivated to fight for his honour and respect were the lessons of Srimad Bhagvad Gita, which he learnt during the time of his imprisonment. He practiced the philosophy of Gita's Karma Yoga (doing the right actions without being attached to their results), which he learnt from his father, Ashwani Gupta. Gupta's father is well-known in Indian history, having served time in prison during India's fight for independence from the British. Ashwini Gupta contracted tuberculosis in prison, which eventually led to his early death while Rajat Gupta was still a teenager. Gupta wrote that, "In many ways our situations could not have been more different. He was jailed for a noble cause and a high-minded ideal; I was jailed for alleged personal gain, for a fabricated white-collar crime, and, at most, a careless mistake... Yet one of the lessons he taught me was that while we cannot always control what happens to us, we can control our attitude in response."[2]

The case of Rajat Gupta characterises the opening quotation from Martin Luther King Jr. I was fortunate to have him as my teacher at ISB Hyderabad in 2002 where I attended a course on leadership and transformation.

The concept of a VUCA world

To describe the business environment in which leaders have to operate, management thinkers have coined the acronym VUCA: V = Volatility (a rapid speed of change of environmental forces); U = Uncertainty (unpredictable events and outcomes in a situation); C = Complexity (the multiplicity of forces; the confounding of issues); and A = Ambiguity (the haziness of reality, the potential for misreads, and the mixed meanings of conditions; cause-and-effect confusion).[3] The notion of VUCA was introduced by the U.S. Army War College at the end of the Cold War[4] and gained popularity after

---

2   Business Insider, 2019.

3   Stiehm & Townsend, 2002.

4   Kinsinger & Walch, 2012.

the terrorist attacks of September 11, 2001. Subsequently, VUCA has been adopted by strategic business leaders to describe the chaotic, turbulent, and rapidly changing business environment that has become the "new normal."

1. *Volatile:* If you do not grow either as a person or a company, others may keep growing. A person has relatively better control over their own growth than others'. For example, During the 1980s, many Japanese companies became more successful than the existing market leaders in Europe and the USA, because of cost competitiveness.

2. *Uncertainty:* Past success does not guarantee your future success; any person, corporate or country can fall from the top. This happens to individuals in sport (e.g. tennis), team events (football), corporates (Philips and Xerox), and civilisations (India and Greece).

3. *Complexity:* Stakeholders are free to exercise their own choices; customers can chose a product, vendors can chose a company, politicians can frame their policies, and organisations can chose their alliances.

4. *Ambiguous:* A future market that does not exist yet can never be analysed. Although we make an effort to cope with the ambiguity of the future, we do not have data about future scenarios. Nobody knows whose efforts will lead to success and who will see failures in the future.

VUCA circumstances have the potential to change an individual's or a company's strength into a major weakness. Most successful individuals, teams, corporations or civilisations would not be able to survive if there were a sudden and unpredictable change in their environment.

A recent example is that of JIO (a subsidiary of Reliance) in the Indian telecoms sector. JIO has begun to dominate the traditional market players in India, e.g. Airtel and Vodafone. Even the most successful companies are not prepared to compete with a sudden change in their business environment; Airtel and Vodafone had been successful for many years, which made them complacent. Evidence suggests that the downfall of Xerox, Philips, Nokia and IBM was due to changes in their business environment, as their competitors started rising in the changed business environment. Why do some companies and individuals fall from the top while others rise from the bottom in a VUCA world?

Inhibitors of Leading Self: Theory of Conditioning

A question that management practitioners should ask themselves is: *"What stops a company from setting stretch goals or remaining successful in the VUCA environment?"* In order to explain the reasons for why companies fail to cope in a VUCA world, this paper uses the Theory of Conditioning[5] to develop its arguments. This Theory explains the development of human personality in terms of habit formations. Human personality is made up of 'reinforced experiences', which means that only those spontaneous and natural behaviours become the part of personality which receives 'enough reinforcements'. (Events that increase the likelihood of a behaviour occurring in the future are called reinforcers). Our attitudes are formed in response to our successes and failures in life. Two important responses to success and failures are described below:

1. A sense of comfort: A mindset of complacency in response to consistent success.

2. A sense of fear: A mindset of helplessness in response to consistent failures.

A sense of comfort (complacency)

Any successful individual or company, than less successful ones, is more likely to move into a comfort zone. Drawn from conditioning theory, a comfort zone is a state of human mind which results due to the formation of the learning plateau. When people join a workplace, they not only learn to perform, but they also learn tricks of the trade (shortcuts) to create positive impressions on their bosses to get benefits, e.g. a promotion or salary hike. Consequently, people stop excelling in their respective work areas due to a loss in their motivational processes and start adapting to the boss' expectations to achieve rewards and promotion. Their success is limited to their hierarchical growth, i.e. they do not increase their contribution and strengthen the organisation's sustainability. Such people learn to maximise their gains through minimum pain and effort, which becomes a major barrier to their competency development. Gradually, a sense of comfort leads to the development of complacency.

Complacent people ignore opportunities to make a contribution to their organisation, and companies ignore opportunities for innovation or market expansion due to complacency. Companies such as IBM, Philips, General Motors, Hindustan Motors, Xerox, Nokia and Blackberry were guilty of this, while Rajat Gupta faced a decline after becoming managing director of McKinsey. Success is not permanent phenomena, but rather a discontinuous process. The challenge for a leader or a company is how to overcome a sense of complacency and develop another growth curve.

---

5   Skinner, 1991.

A sense of fear (helplessness)

Fear is an unpleasant emotion caused by being aware of danger. The initial response of fear to an unpleasant stimulus leads to a situation of helplessness. In behavioural science, accustomed helplessness occurs when an animal is repeatedly subjected to an averse stimulus that it cannot escape. Eventually, the animal will stop trying to avoid the stimulus and behave as if it is utterly helpless to change the situation. Even when opportunities to escape are presented, this accustomed helplessness will prevent any action. This inaction leads people to overlook opportunities for relief or change. Similarly, such employees do not work hard and do not even try to think beyond the obvious because of deep rooted fears. They prefer to set goals which are within their limits and can be achieved comfortably, i.e. they are more likely to set obvious goals rather than challenging ones. The challenge is thus to overcome feelings of helplessness or performance inertia, and focus on continuing to put in an effort.

A real example of conditioning

In the game of cricket, a captain asks a bowler to propel the ball to a batsman. If the batsman hits three sixes on three consecutive balls, the bowler may start suffering from a sense of helplessness and the batsman may suffer from a sense of complacency. A team is always at risk of losing after winning or losing a couple of matches due to the effect of complacency or helplessness.

Empirical Study: Social Cognitive Theory

A qualitative research study was carried out to understand the source of leaders' motivation in private and public sector organisations in India. The purpose was to understand whether they are driven by external or internal sources of motivation. Managers were asked to think about a situation related to their motivation for bringing about a positive change in their workplace, and then answer the following research question: "What motivates you to lead a proactive change at your workplace?" The responses were collected from 150 managers in face-to-face interviews. These managers had a minimum of five years of work experience, and 65% were male and 35% were female.

Social Cognitive Theory[6] was used to analyse the qualitative data received from the interviews. According to the Triadic Reciprocal Causation Model, behaviour is result of interactions between personal factors (cognitive, affective and biological), external environmental factors and behavioural factors. This means that individual behaviour is driven by the external environment (positive work environment, salary, promotion,

---

6   Bandura, 1986.

appreciation etc.) and personal factors (self-satisfaction, learning and knowledge, ownership). These variables were categorised into personal and environmental factors. It was noted that only six responses fell under the category of personal factors, while 26 factors belonged to the category of external environment. This means that employees largely depend on the external environment for their motivation to lead proactive change at their workplace. In addition, the frequency count of 382 for environmental factors was significantly higher than 58 for personal factors.

In contrast to Conditioning Theory, Social Cognitive Theory suggests that a person has the capacity to influence the environment as the environment influences the individual. Conditioning theories use animals and children as subjects for their experimentation, thus they do not explain what motivates people to work under painful conditions and how they bring about transformation, e.g. Mahatma Gandhi, Nelson Mandela, Martin Luther King Jr. and Mother Teresa. Nor do they explain how Rajat Gupta faced the crisis in his life successfully. This chapter proposes a model for 'Leading-Self in VUCA Environments' based on the sources of personal motivation, and also outlines what the psychological attributes of a de-conditioned mind (a mind without comfort and fear) are.

Practical Reality: Positive Psychology

Psychological attributes of a de-conditioned mind: The basis of conditioned behaviour is a strong need for survival in our jobs. Because of this, we get involved in 'impression management' behaviour rather than focusing on 'performance management'. Alternatively, we 'chose to remain silent' rather than 'raising our voice'. Coping is necessary for one's survival, however it is not enough for the 'development of one's potential'. To continuously develop, one must possess the features of a de-conditioned mind. Grounded in the literature on positive psychology[7], the following four features of de-conditioned mind are proposed: (1) Risk-taking; (2) Learning to unlearn; (3) Simplicity; and (4) Optimism.

Risk-taking is any consciously or non-consciously controlled behaviour where there is a perceived uncertainty about its outcome, and/or about its possible benefits or costs for the physical, economic or psycho-social well-being of oneself or others. Risk-taking is a common feature of all great leaders, as one cannot set a difficult goal without taking risk. Whistle blowers take risks when raising their voices against unethical practices in an organisation.

Learning to unlearn is a psychological state which encourages people to learn new things from others or from their situations, rather than applying old solutions. As the futurist Alvin Toffler once wrote, "The illiterate of the 21st century will not be those who cannot read and write, but those who cannot learn, unlearn and relearn.

---

7   Csikszentmihalyi, 1990.

Alvin Toffler"[8] In opposition to Conditioning Theory, therefore, one must believe in unlearning and relearning for the sake of new learning in order to remain effective at coping with the uncertainty and ambiguity of the environment.

Simplicity refers to a down to earth attitude and to remain humble and straightforward in all situations. Simplicity can help to prevent the negative effects of money, status, power, praise and blame. The Indian scriptures (Srimad Bhagwat Gita) say that 'ego' (Ahamkaar) is the biggest evil within us as it stops us from seeing merit in others. In India, the practice of touching the feet of elders (Charan-Sparsh) was adopted to regulate a false ego. A recent example of this was when the film star, Rajinikanth, touched the feet of another film star, Amitabh Bacchan. The businessman, Narayana Murthy (co-founder of Infosys), has touched the feet of the Chairman of the Tata Group, Ratan Tata. Such people demonstrate the strength of simplicity in their behaviour.

Optimism is a mental attitude that reflects a belief or hope that the outcome of some specific endeavour or outcomes will, in general, be positive, favourable and desirable. It thus reflects a belief that future conditions will work out for the best. In contrast to the concept of learned helplessness, Seligman[9] popularised the concept of learned optimism through his 1990 book, Learned Optimism.

In my view, leaders like Gandhi, Mandela, King Jr. and Rajat Gupta demonstrate the qualities of risk-taking, learning to unlearn, simplicity and optimism to face the VUCA world.

Story 1: The following story about Lord Buddha explains the importance of the concepts of risk-taking, unlearning, simplicity and optimism.

This story is from when Buddha was in the process of becoming a saint. There was a time when he had almost given up after putting six to seven years of hard work in but failed to achieve his goal of self-knowledge and self-enlightenment. Then one day, he had a great personal experience which became a strong base for his future efforts.

Buddha was sitting under a tree near to a pond. He observed that a squirrel went into the water, came out of it and shook her body to dry it. The process continued, wherein she went in, came out and dried herself. She kept repeating this cycle. When Buddha tried to understand why the squirrel was doing this, he realised that her two little children had drowned in the pond and she wanted to dry up the entire pond to save them; she was trying to achieve an impossible goal where "failure" was guaranteed. On that day, Buddha realised that if she was not ready to give up, then he should continue to make an effort. Thereafter, he never looked back. He started his search for knowledge and later developed the Theory of the Middle Path, which argues that one must live a life in the centre, avoiding the extreme feelings of pleasure and pain or success and failure.

---

8   Toffler, (n.d.).

9   Selignman, 1990.

This story tells us about the power of risk-taking, simplicity, unlearning and optimism when trying to achieve something that nobody else has achieved. Buddha was a king who left his family and palace to find salvation. He failed several times but kept working hard and developed a new theory in the field of spirituality. A real example is a cricket match that took place between Australia and South Africa, which Australia lost after scoring 434 runs in a 50-over match. The South African team was optimistic and successfully surpassed this mammoth score; they unlearned the fact that nobody had done it before. Rajat Gupta also demonstrated these traits while reaching the top, as he did later when dealing with his crisis. In simple words, this is the concept of "Karma Yoga", wherein one makes consistent efforts to attain a goal without being attached to the results.

In contrast, those who suffer from a sense of comfort or a sense of fear are more likely to face depression or commit suicide. The billionaire coffee tycoon, VG Siddhartha, owner of Café Coffee Day (CCD), committed suicide by jumping into a river in July 2019, while Joy Arakkal, Managing Director of the Dubai-based Innova Group of Companies, committed suicide by jumping from the 14th floor in April 2020. Why do successful people suffer from depression or commit suicide when they face adversity? It is likely that they are unable to cope with the VUCA world and lack the ability to lead self, despite their successes. However, Rajat Gupta demonstrated his ability to lead self in a VUCA environment.

Facilitators of leading self: Existentialism and the Theory of Self-Concept

Having discussed the inhibitors and characteristics of "leading-self", the main challenge is how to move from a state of a conditioned mind to a state of de-conditioned mind. Successes and failures produce immediate effects and take us back to the conditioned mind. For example, the main challenge for the bowler in cricket is to unlearn their bad experiences and remain optimistic after being hit for three consecutive sixes, while for the batsman the challenge is how to maintain simplicity and take the required risk after scoring three consecutive sixes. Therefore, leaders need to learn and practice the sustainable sources of motivation, which create an unending desire for performance excellence. Drawn from psychological and philosophical approaches, this paper suggests the following four ways to lead self for sustained motivation under a VUCA environment: (1) meaning, (2) self-concept, (3) non-violence (Ahimsa); and (4) gratitude.

1. *Meaning or Purpose (The Theory of Existentialism):* The theory of existentialism was propounded by the Danish philosopher, Soren Kierkegaard (1813–55), and later popularised by Viktor Frankl (1905–97). Frankl had survived internment at the Nazi death camp and wrote personally about the events that shaped his beliefs.

Existential psychology is an approach to psychology that is based on the premise that people have free will and are participants rather than observers in their own lives, and people live for a meaning or purpose. Similar to Theory of Meaning, the Japanese have propagated the concept of *ikigai*, while Indian scripture (e.g. *Srimad Bhagvad Gita*) has promoted the concept of "Dharma" and Jainism suggests a concept of "Ahimsa" (non-violence). Lord Krishna told his disciple, Arjuna, to perform his "dharma" on the battlefield in order to establish peace, harmony and justice in society. *Gita* is the book that gave inner strength to Rajat Gupta to face his crisis successfully and live his life for a purpose; he wants to die a fighter.

A person who is driven by meaning or a purpose in life develops a strong belief system that helps them to convert negative thought patterns into positive ones. Such people take a larger or broader perspective in life, and are deeply rooted in the values of justice, fairness and peace. A leader's personal experiences play a critical role in deriving a meaning for their life. The idea of leading-self includes an ability to convert personal pain and suffering into a more pious and sacred goal, e.g. freedom, justice, harmony, serving the nation and peace for humanity.

Story 2: The following story of two poor girls from a slum area in Mumbai describes the concept of leading self in a VUCA environment to lead change.

In Dharavi (a slum area in Mumbai), a young mother who worked as a housemaid in the nearby houses lived with her two young daughters. Her husband was a drunkard and gambler who abused and beat her and took all her income. It was very difficult to her to nurture her daughters without any support from her husband.

After a few years, her husband died of cancer, so the young mother had to take full responsibility for her family. She worked very hard and provided her daughters with a good education and a decent life. As the time passed, the girls grew to marriageable age. When her elder daughter was around 25 years old, the mother asked her to marry as per Indian tradition, however the daughter refused. She told her mother that she would never marry, as she did not want to ruin her whole life as her mother's life was ruined by her father. She had developed a negative attitude towards all men and was afraid of marriage; her mother could not convince her despite all her efforts. After three years, when the younger daughter reached to marriageable age, her mother requested that at least she should marry. The younger daughter, after a little persuasion, agreed to marry. Her mother was pleasantly surprised. Curiously, she asked her daughter what she wanted from a marriage. The reason she shared explains the meaning of a meaningful life.

When this story is shared in training programmes for senior executives, they are asked why they thought she agreed to marry. The executives give the following reasons for her decision: (1) she wanted to make her mother happy; (2) she wanted to be a role model for her elder sister; (3) she wanted to support her mother and sister; and (4) she dared to take a risk and was ready to handle any man with courage and fearlessness.

Although these reasons are very convincing, she actually had a different thought process. She said, "I want to marry because I hope that God will bless me with a son, and before I die I shall make him learn to respect women in a way that my father never did." This story clearly explains the meaning of a meaningful life. The idea of leading self is related to pattern of thoughts in the difficult and challenging situations of life as Gandhi or Mandela or Rajat Gupta experienced. The difference between a leader and a non-leader is related to their ability to derive meaning from a crisis situation. Crises help us to realise the meaning of life; we should use them as opportunities. Other examples of this are Dasrath Manjhi, Mark Inglis and Arunima Sinha, who achieved great success despite their physical limitations

After the death of his wife, Dasrath Manjhi set himself a huge target of manually carving out a road through the Gahlour Mountain in the Gaya district of Bihar, India. Although, he was not a trained civil engineer, his belief was stronger than the mountain. He used a chisel and hammer and worked for 22 years to achieve his goal. After constructing the road, he said, "I am indifferent to any reward or punishment from the government." Mark Inglis, a mountaineer from New Zealand, had a dream to climb Mount Everest, despite the fact that he had lost both of his legs when he was trapped in an avalanche. It took him almost ten years of hard work and preparation to summit Everest, and led him to state that, "Now I realise the value of my legs."

Arunima Sinha climbed up Mount Everest with just one leg after being thrown from a train and spending the whole night on the railway track. Similarly, Rajat Gupta, who lost his father at an early age, graduated from two top institutions, was able to break the glass ceiling in order to become the first non-US-born CEO of McKinsey, and successfully faced a big crisis.

2. *Self-Concept:* Psychologists, sociologists and philosophers have argued that we need to seek an answer for two universal questions: "Who am I?" and "What is the purpose of my life?" According to Rosenberg[10], self-concept is "...the totality of an individual's thoughts and feelings having reference to himself as an object." Similar to Self-Concept Theory, the influential self-efficacy researcher Roy Baumeister[11] defined self-concept as, "the individual's belief about himself or herself, including the person's attributes and who and what the self is." In his Theory of the Looking-Glass Self, Cooley[12] opined that a person develops their self-concept by understanding the following: i) What I think about me; ii) What you think about me; iii) What I think about me based on the interaction of the

---

10 Rosenberg, 1979.

11 Baumeister, 1999.

12 Cooley, 1902.

previous two. The examples of self-concept can be as follows: i) I am a good teacher of Mathematics; ii) I am a good batsman and can chase any score; iii) I am a great doctor and can save lives; and iv) I am a good actor and can entertain people.

Individuals with a positive self-concept have a tendency to perform and excel in their lives without materialistic benefits because they enjoy the work that they do. A positive self-concept becomes a source of a sustained motivation, even under adverse conditions

Story 3: The following story of a farmer in ancient India emphasises the importance of a positive self-concept.

Many years ago, a highly respected soothsayer was living in a small village of India. One day, he informed the villagers that the village would not have any rain for the next seven years. People trusted him and started migrating from their village to those places where they could get food and shelter. Gradually the village emptied of people, however one farmer did not leave and kept on working as he always had. He ploughed his fields every day and two years passed without rain. During the third year, while he was ploughing, a cloud passed over his fields. The cloud was perplexed why the farmer was ploughing the fields when he knew that his village would not get any rain for seven years. Curiously, the cloud asked the farmer, "Why are you ploughing the field when you know that there will not be any rain for the next seven years?" The farmer replied politely, "I know this, but I am a farmer so I am practicing my farming skills to keep me healthy and the field ready to grow crops whenever it rains." After listening to the farmer, the cloud started thinking that he might also forget how to rain on the village after a gap of seven years, so decided to practice by showering on that day. Other clouds came along that did not have any idea of this conversation, so following the little cloud, they too poured rain over the entire village.

So the village which was not supposed to have any rain, received rain because of the sheer hard work (law of karma), faith and the positive beliefs of a farmer. When the villagers came to know about this, they returned to the village and started believing in hard work and karma. This is a law of "Karma Yoga" taught in Gita and practiced by Rajat Gupta during his imprisonment. He formed this self-concept by watching his father's struggle for India's freedom. Leaders differ from non-leaders in their self-concept. The idea of leading self is deeply rooted in the theories of self-concept.

3. *Non-violence (Ahimsa):* The idea of non-violence is deeply rooted in the Jain philosophy. Jainism is said to be the oldest organised religion of the world. It was started by Lord Rshabh Dev; the last Lord of Jainism was Lord Mahavira who was born in 599 BC. The fundamental philosophy of Jainism is the concept of

Anekantwad (non-absolutism). The idea of non-absolutism signifies the usefulness of multiple perspectives in order to understand a person or a situation in a holistic manner. Jainism believes that there is nothing absolutely right or wrong; everything is matter of relative perspective. For example, rain is good for a farmer but can be bad for a potter. Taking it further, Jainism argues that we can all survive on this earth without hurting another's life. The concept of non-violence (Ahimsa) is derived from the philosophy of non-absolutism. This means that one should not hurt the well-being of others (including any living organisms or plants) for the sake of one's own well-being; instead, we can all co-exist peacefully. Jainism, therefore, extolls the concept of 'live and let live'. The idea of non-violence is the antithesis to aggressive and violent behaviour. Gandhi used non-violence as a tool in the struggle against the British Empire.

Story 4: Lord Mahavira, 24th God (Tirthnkara, born in 599 BC) of Jainism, explains the meaning of Ahimsa (non-violence).

Lord Mahavira used to spend six to eight hours a day in meditation. One day, when he was in deep meditation sitting under a mango tree, some children came and started throwing stones on the tree to get the mangos. One of the stones hit Lord Mahavira because the children could not see him as he was on the other side of the tree. The children heard him crying; when they went to the other side of the tree, they realised their mistake and sought forgiveness. Lord Mahavira responded, "I am not crying because you hit me with a stone. Rather I feel sad that the tree might have been injured in the same way but it offered you mangos when you hit it with the stone and I could not offer you anything in return." Lord Mahavira had adopted the perspective of 'life' even in a tree, and was as empathic for it as we are for other human beings. Non-violence, therefore, is a state of mind which helps us relate to other living organisms, and helps us to deal with the negative experiences of life, e.g. the insulting or abusive behaviour of others.

Forgiveness is a state of mind which you can carry under any circumstances, as Gandhi did with the British. Similar experiences of forgiveness are also told about Mandela, who forgave his jailor in order to focus on bigger issues and the challenges facing South African society, rather than taking revenge on him or abusing his power. Gandhi also had no hatred for the British; rather he wanted to get freedom for India without hurting them. One cannot grow without forgiving those who cause misfortune to us.

4. *Gratitude:* Forgiveness helps you to save your energy, which would otherwise be consumed by negative feelings such as hatred and revenge. However, the virtue of gratitude makes a person thankful for everything they possess or receive from

others – whether a job or love. We develop a feeling of gratitude when someone does something good to us, and we feel indebted and wish to reciprocate through kind actions. Many people develop a philanthropic attitude and readily give back whatever they receive from society. In India, Azim Prem Ji (Wipro), Ratan Tata (Tata) and Naryanan Krishnamurthy (Infosys) are well known for their philanthropic initiatives, as are Bill Gates and Mark Zuckerberg. We notice that even animals show kindness, affection and loyalty to their owners in return for their kindness. However man still needs to learn and develop the virtue of gratitude.

Story 5: The following anecdote about the American President, Howard Taft, explains the meaning of gratitude.

Paderewski, a Polish pianist, used to perform concerts in America in 1874, from which he could earn almost $10,000. Once he gave a chance to a young man, allowing him to organising his show. The young man tried hard, but could not earn more than $3,000. When he offered the $3,000 to Paderewski, the pianist asked him how he would pay the rent for the auditorium. The young man replied that he would work harder, and apologised for not having been able to organise his show well. However, Paderewski asked the boy to keep all the money and said that he should pay the rent and do some business for himself.

During a major economic recession in 1905, the American President helped Poland to pay back their large debt. When the President was asked why he helped Poland he said, that I was under debt of a Polish who had shaped my life and helped in becoming what I am today. I owe my success to him. This was the 27th American President, Howard Taft.

Gratitude, therefore, not only brings two people closer to each other, but can also bring two organisations or countries together. Gratitude is the basis of both friendships and families. We have gratitude for our parents, teachers, bosses and organisations. Gratitude is an act of humility, which even animals demonstrate for their saviours or those who feed them. Gratitude can make people work collaboratively, so it can be a good basis for joint ventures, mergers, alliances and the transfer of technology.

Recommendation: A Model of Leading Self

As described above, the idea of leading self in a VUCA world is practiced by people with de-conditioned minds (characteristics: risk-taking, learning to unlearn, simplicity, optimism). This can be nurtured through several catalytic variables, including meaning, self-concept, non-violence, and gratitude. Leading self includes the ability to influence one's own cognitive, affective and behavioural processes in order to achieve a challenging goal or to navigate one's life through a difficult phase in the larger interest of society or an organisation. This chapter proposes that motivation is all about channeling one's energy in a particular direction to achieve the desired goals In our daily lives, we can get easily deviated from our goal-oriented behaviour due to negative feelings of hatred and jealousy at the workplace. We thus need to develop certain traits in ourselves that can help us to manage our goal-oriented behaviour over the years. In his autobiography, Rajat Gupta commented that one has to overcome one's fears to face adversities (a mind without fear). A model of leading self is presented in Figure 12.1:

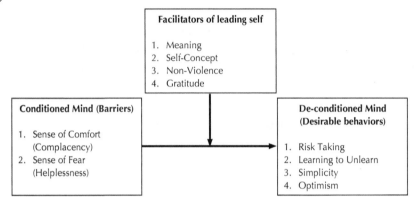

Figure 12.1: A proposed model of leading self

CONCLUDING REMARKS

Recognising leadership in self: A person demonstrates the virtue of leading-self when s/he is not driven by materialistic gains, and rather focuses on their contribution to a social unit. Such people accept both good and bad with equanimity. For example, Rajat Gupta and Dasrath Manjhi said that they were indifferent to any appreciation or criticism. The idea of leading self helps one to focus on performance excellence and apply consistent effort in any situation. Those who lead self are at peace with themselves and maintain calmness even under stressful conditions. They do not strive for any major transformation at the societal level; rather, the biggest transformation they bring about is at the level of self. They always show cool, calm and composed gestures. They rarely get excited or raise the level of their voice, and rarely express anger or irritation. They are committed to their tasks rather than their organisations. They focus on people's development and cultural change to help people to realise their true potential. They trust others, allow people to make mistakes, and extend their support to them. Such people become a source of inspiration for any transformation or change. The moment they achieve their goals of bringing positivity and happiness to one place, they move to another place for the same purpose. Most of the Indian religious and spiritual leaders, e.g. Lord Mahavira, Lord Buddha and Guru Nanak, brought about successful change in a very quiet manner, and they did not stay in one place. They all believed that leadership is a journey, not a destination; it is a process, not an outcome.

To conclude, people who demonstrate the concept of leading self have the following three characteristics: i) an ability to convert their painful experiences or sufferings into a meaningful purpose (Gandhi's insult in South Africa resulted in India's freedom); ii) they realise their personal strengths while facing a crisis (meaning, self-concept, forgiveness and gratitude); and iii) they regulate the negative emotions (lust, rage, greed, attachment, ego, jealousy) that can deviate them from achieving their purpose. People like Gandhi, Mandela and Gupta operated in VUCA environments. The model of 'leading self' prepares us to not only face, but also flourish in, such an environment. In my view, VUCA world is not a threat but rather an opportunity. Leadership grows in VUCA world, thus it should be welcomed rather perceived negatively. The term VUCA refers to an occurrence of unpredictable or uncontrollable negative events in life. None of us can avoid a VUCA environment, but we can choose to respond or cope in a constructive and meaningful manner to become a role model or inspiration for generations to come.

PART FIVE

LEADING ONESELF IN CONFLICT AND POST-CONFLICT ENVIRONMENTS

CHAPTER 13

CONFLICT RESOLUTION FOR PEACEBUILDING: LEADING ONESELF IN AN UNCERTAIN AND COMPLEX ENVIRONMENT

Andrew Campbell

ABSTRACT

As technology interconnects political, economic, human security, legal, and financial institutions, the resulting challenge is how to strategically lead events that are unpredictable and uncontrollable with unexpected consequences. In a rapidly changing volatile, complex, and uncertain global environment, leaders are exposed to many complex challenges in a technological environment, and what we know about leadership theory and development may no longer be effective.[1] Additionally, the effect of technology on relations between state and non-state actors has influenced geopolitical decisions regarding conflict and peace, and has outpaced the ability of peace organisations to contain spoilers in the aftermath of state discord. This chapter introduces a brief explanation of leadership challenges, a theoretical leadership framework, and the practical realities for leading oneself within a fluid, uncertain, and complex environment.

INTRODUCTION

In today's global environment, national leaders have the responsibility to protect and defend national instruments of power from internal and external threats. These threats of political and economic intimidation, structural and armed conflict, and other forms of systematic forms of violence, impact international peace and stability. With the expansion in the number and variety of ongoing conflicts, the need for examining peaceful ways of resolving conflicts has become more urgent now than ever. In order to understand conflict among nations, conflict management practitioners and theoreticians are now studying the field and disseminating results to aid the peace development practice. Globalisation and technological innovation are producing

---

1   Campbell, 2019.

a significant global international relations challenge. For example, the actions of a young man in Tanzania initiated the Arab Spring using a Facebook account. This action changed the political and socio-economic landscape across the geopolitical spectrum, impacting regional peace and security.

This event highlighted to political power brokers how the use of social media and other technological innovations can drive social change beyond domestic and international leaders' control. A significant challenge for peace development practitioners is posed in the following question: How does a nation-state leader influence the actions of another state leader or non-state actor to destabilise its institutions when they have no authority? Arguably, the actions by state and non-state leaders will stop conflict or promulgate peace. As a result, leaders within the international community are struggling to identify effective means to bring peace and stability in an ever-changing, fluid, complex, and uncertain environment.

As the emergence of technology interconnects political, economic, human security, legal, and financial institutions, the challenge is how to strategically lead events that are unpredictable and uncontrollable with unexpected consequences. In a rapidly changing volatile, complex, and uncertain global environment, leaders are exposed to many complex challenges in a technological environment, and what we know about leadership theory and development may no longer be effective.[2] More importantly, leadership researchers argue that there is a global, national, communal and tribal leadership deficit that is impacting international relations as well as peace and security among nations. Widening the aperture of traditional leadership frameworks by integrating the complexity of nation-building will necessitate a leadership paradigm shift. This is particularly so when mitigating and responding to socio-political, economic, ideological and religious discord in preventing a return to conflict.

As long as intrastate conflict, human rights violations, and economic deprivations persist, the need for capacity building mechanisms will require critical leadership from international, regional, and sub-regional actors to de-escalate the conflict. Non-state and state leaders are responsible for not only the initiation of conflict and its victim impact, but also conflict cessation. However, the effect of technology on relations between states and non-state actors has influenced geopolitical decisions surrounding conflict and peace, and they have outpaced the ability of peace organisations to contain spoilers in the aftermath of state discord.[3] Hence, leaders need the absorptive capacity to navigate the complex, uncertain, and ambiguous challenges of diplomacy, defense, and the development of confidence-building activities in a geopolitical context.[4]

This chapter proceeds as follows: the first section introduces a brief explanation of leadership challenges within an uncertain and complex environment. Additionally,

---

2   Campbell, 2019.

3   Brand-Jacobsen, Curran, Demarest, Annan, Wolter, Tanase, Tunney & Shiroka, 2018.

4   Campbell, 2019.

this section illustrates the challenges of leading oneself, which President Nelson Mandela encountered within a complex and uncertain setting that changed a nation. The second section introduces a theoretical leadership framework that conceptually underpins leading within a fluid, uncertain, and complex context. The third section presents the practical realities of leading oneself in an unpredictable environment. Finally, a brief discussion of applicational recommendations for leading in a complex and uncertain environment is provided.

VUCA ENVIRONMENT

Conflict management scholar-practitioners note that there is a myriad of complex challenges for intercommunal, local, and national leaders, as well as IGOs, NGOs, and CSOs that are facing the aftermath of conflict. Literature reveals that the challenge that domestic leaders have is in establishing the priority and sequence of events in the aftermath of conflict. For example, it is the importance of stability and reconstruction when holding perpetrators accountable for human rights violations, providing human security, or developing macro-economic packages for access to basic services and employment. Hence, as domestic leaders balance the competing internal and external demands of nation-building, the struggle of how to lead a united effort with key stakeholders toward stabilising a country requires unique leadership attributes. There is a strong case to be made that domestic leaders must create the climate for intercommunal leaders to facilitate conflict resolution activities, while simultaneously persuading and deterring spoilers from threatening human security protection measures and economic and infrastructure development. In the end, the complexity of peace development activities is fraught with uncertainty in the hypersensitive political, ideological, and socio-ethnic environment.

The barriers to effective nation-building consist of a mixture where political, diplomatic, economic, ethnocultural, and ideological tensions are unpredictable. Nevertheless, the root cause of conflict is situational dependent, requiring different planning factors and solution sets for stabilisation and reconstruction actions. The turbulence of leading a nation through change in a post-conflict environment is not only complex, but also fraught with uncertain risks and outcomes. To illustrate, the risk to post-conflict reconstruction efforts commonly stem from the volatility of spoilers initiating the resurgence of inter-ethnic and cultural tension. Economic obstacles often entail the proliferation of illicit weapons, the exploitation of natural resources, corruption, and the prohibited funding activities of ex-combatants, which frequently disrupt the delivery of basic humanitarian service and local infrastructure projects. Finally, the clash of cultures between ideological religious and ethnic groups brings a human dimension to peace development that is complex and frequently uncertain.

These hurdles to reconstitute a nation's instruments of power in the aftermath of conflict require leaders with the political will, courage, and personal strength to go against the grain, and shield their constituencies from the underlying reasons for violence. The distrust between the elite and elected officials is extremely high. According to Fukuyama[5], "public servants are no different from any other economic agent in seeking to maximize their interests. The behavior of public officials can be influenced by bribes, campaign contributions, the payoff to family members, or promises of future employment." In the end, stabilisation and reconstruction measures require elite and elected officials who do what is in the best interest of the country instead of engaging in power politics and self-interest.

Much of the literature points out that while domestic leaders shape the strategic environment in a post-conflict context, most practitioners believe intercommunal leaders facilitate the reintegration of ex-combatants back into the community, as well as reconcile socio-ethnic tensions.[6] Cohen and Insko[7] "suggest that groups entrenched in conflict may be made to cooperate if they are induced to think about the long-term consequences of their actions." That said, leading transformation change from state conflict to non-violence brings a state of turbulence and chaos, where leaders need the capability to strategically navigate unpredictable and rapid changes as situations unfold.

Leading the political, economic, security, and legal polarities from violence to non-violence requires unique tribal, communal, regional, and national leadership attributes to lead a nation toward transformational change. Research on political leadership in chaotic environments shows that many leaders are not only ill-equipped to deal with the complexity and unpredictability associated with disruptive situations, but they also do not have the necessary leadership skills to navigate the challenging terrain of nation-building. The capability of leaders to navigate complex and uncertain environments requires unique individual leadership attributes, such as a self-awareness of one's strengths and weaknesses when responding to complex and uncertain environments, the emotional agility to make sound decisions in a tense political context, and the compassion to serve others.[8]

Stein and Brooks[9] suggested that emotional intelligence components such as self-awareness, emotional self-regulation, empathy, motivation, and social skills can be developed through introspection and self-reflection. Leadership scholars argue that emotional intelligence components develop individual leadership attributes to manage and control the emotional regulation of one's behaviour and thoughts during rapid

---

5   Fukuyama, 2008: 49.

6   Campbell, 2019.

7   Cohen & Insko, 2008: 89.

8   Campbell, 2019.

9   Stein & Brooks, 2011.

changing, unpredictable, and complex settings.[10, 11] As a result, leaders influence more through who they are than through what they do. In the end, leaders cannot rise above the level of leading themselves.

For several decades, the South African government enacted a political and economic strategy that segregated the white minority and Indian and black majority constituents. The governance strategy called 'apartheid' created a massive racial disparity in education, basic services, and wealth. This resulted in socio-ethnic discord that weakened the state's institutional instruments of power, formed intercommunal antagonists, and limited political and socio-economic freedom. As human rights violations by the white minority reached a fever pitch, the unrestrained anger and unrest by the black majority made South Africa ungovernable.[12] The response to the large death toll of civilians and violent incidents by government forces became an inflection point in the struggle against apartheid, hence it is useful to briefly address the political interests between power elites and the relationships of non-state actors to prevent or resolve state conflict.

The African National Congress (ANC), one of the leading civil society organisations in South Africa, led by Nelson Mandela, advocated for systematic governance reform against apartheid. The ANC, with over 600 anti-apartheid civil society organisations, coalesced under the United Democratic Front (UDF) banner. Mandela[13] pointed out that while the white minority government employed militant threats, intimidation, and acts of violence to suppress the apartheid agenda, the black majority became a political force of civil resistance for transformational societal change. Additionally, the international community applied enormous pressure through economic sanctions and other mechanisms on the white minority government, aiming to address anti-apartheid issues and institute permanent reforms.[14] Over time, Mandela[15] pursued the replacement of armed resistance with non-violence and civil resistance to meet the apartheid strategic end state objective. This takes us to contextualising the leadership attributes of Nelson Mandela's capacity to unify people and organisations around transforming a nation from socio-ethnic violence to peace. A brief understanding of Mandela's leadership journey provides a glimpse into the challenges of leading oneself in uncertain political and complex chaotic situations.

---

10 Campbell, 2019.

11 Stein & Brooks, 2011.

12 Mandela & Langa, 2017.

13 Ibid.

14 Ibid.

15 Ibid.

APPLICATION

The literature on leadership indicates that developing the skills to lead oneself is a prerequisite ingredient in leading others within organisations. In the same vein, leadership research indicates that personal solitude and reflection is an effective tool in developing oneself as a leader. To illustrate the virtues of solitude for effective self-leadership, Mandela leveraged his time in solitary confinement to explore the emotional contemplation associated with both resolving complex problems and managing the unexpected during times of rapid change.[16] Personal reflection enables leaders to develop the clarity and conviction of purpose and moral courage to sustain them through adversity. Essentially, the key to leading oneself through complex barriers in a crisis necessitates an emotional awareness in order to control one's trigger points and the ripple effects from unpredictable events.[17]

Nelson Mandela and Mandla Langa, in Dare to Linger-The Presidential Years[18], noted that Mandela's personal leadership journey came from not only the time spent in incarceration, but also the solitary confinement. Mandela and Langa[19] commented that Mandela credited his solitary confinement as a time of introspection, reflection, and reframing the perspective of his life circumstances to lead with a mindset of clarity in vision, character development, and courage. Mandela and Langa[20] reiterated that the daily time Mandela spent in solitude enabled him to reflect on his emotional agility toward embracing change, respond with clarity in times of confusion, and develop the empathy to understand others' perspectives. In fact, developing emotional agility takes inner courage when dealing with resentment, the discipline of processing painful thoughts and feelings, and resolving emotions and thoughts. One could argue that the time in confinement forced Mandela to examine his fears, anger and insecurities, shifting painful emotions toward confidence, trust and forgiveness. In other words, the byproduct of a personal leadership journey produces leaders with the self-compassion and emotional agility to navigate the complexity of unexpected situations.

In Leading Yourself First: Inspiring Leadership Through Solitude, Kethledge and Erwin21 suggested that it is the internal process of honest self-reflection in isolation that brings "an insight, or even a broader vision, that brings mind and soul together in clear-eyed, inspired conviction and that kind of conviction is the foundation of leadership." The literature shows that during times of crisis, self-awareness, self-regulation and courage are foundational ingredients of leading oneself through periods of political chaos and uncertainty. Figure 13.1 shows two components within the emotional intelligence construct that undergird the principles of leading oneself. Campbell[22] noted that the foundational ingredients of leading oneself are self-awareness and self-regulation. Scholars argue that self-awareness leaders are those who know

---

21 Kethledge & Erwin, 2017: 4.

22 Campbell, 2019.

their strengths and limitations, and possess a deep understanding of the impact one's emotions and feelings have on others.[23] Additionally, scholars note that leaders with self-regulation can manage and control their emotional impulses.[24] An individual with self-awareness and self-regulation is best able to constructively navigate through the personal frustration that accompanies chaos in a complex and uncertain environment.

Figure 13.1: Leading Self, Others and Community[25]

"Leaders with high self-awareness know their capabilities and emotional trigger points when constructively responding to wicked problems succumbing toward political pressure in resolving key issues."[26] Goleman et al.[27] suggested that one of the best ways to increase one's self-awareness is through daily reflection; writing in a personal journal one's thoughts, emotions, and feelings of personal challenges. Another strategy is by understanding and identifying one's emotional trigger points through a process called introspection.[28, 29] Regulating one's emotional state is particularly important during stressful, chaotic, complex and uncontrollable events. Campbell[30] argued that, "the key to knowing others' emotional terrain is an intimate familiarity with your own. Personal transformation is at the heart of self-leadership." That said, leading oneself requires continuous intentional self-reflection and self-introspection to bridge the gap between who you are as a leader with who you want to be. All in all, developing the two foundational components of leading self fosters a climate of authentic leadership

---

23 Goleman, Kaplan, David & Eurich, 2019.

24 Goleman, Boyatzis, McKee & Finkestein, 2015.

25 Campbell, 2019.

26 Campbell, 2019.

27 Goleman et al., 2019.

28 Campbell, 2019.

29 Goleman et al., 2019.

30 Campbell, 2019: 61.

and empathy, which facilitates conflict resolution between parties, listening for common ground, and collaboration to reach a shared objective.

Much of the literature points out that while Mandela spent time strategically arranging ANC activities and covertly negotiating with government officials, most of his time was used to develop the components to leading self in a complex and unpredictable environment. In *Prison Letters of Nelson Mandela, Mandela and Venter*[31] showed that it was through the painful circumstances of incarceration that Mandela discovered his strengths and limitations, identified and accepted his failures and successes, and recognised the importance of being true to oneself – no matter the cost.[32] In *Conversations with Myself*, Mandela[33] states, "the cell is an ideal place to learn to know yourself, to search realistically and regularly the process of your mind and feelings." In fact, Mandela revealed that it was during periods of confinement when he learned the importance of understanding and controlling one's emotions. Writings by Mandela and Langa[34] show that:

> "...prison, a place of punishment, instead became a place where he was able to find himself. A place where he could think, indulging in the one thing that gave him a sense of self. And it was, of course, in prison that his vision for rebuilding South Africa into a new democratic nation was born."

Instead of ruminating as a victim filled with resentment about his circumstances, Mandela used the time to find positive aspects of imprisonment by internally reflecting on what kind of leader he wanted to be to effectively lead change in a politically complex and unpredictable environment.

The writings of Mandela are rich with examples that demonstrate the process of developing the qualities of leading oneself. By comparing several letters at the beginning, middle, and end of his incarceration, one discovers that Mandela read political and biographical books of leaders he admired, wrote letters to family and friends knowing the correspondence frequently did not reach the intended receiver, and journaled about personal struggles with prison treatment and feelings of confinement.[35] In a review of leadership research, scholars revealed that consistent personal reflection and journaling transforms the plasticity of the mind to think differently, builds emotional awareness, and develops humility and openness to build the skills of self-leadership.[36] Reflective journaling creates "a set of behaviors and is enacted in the leader's communication, building supporting networks, negotiation in

---

31 Mandela & Venter, 2018.
32 Mandela, 2010.
33 Ibid.
34 Mandela & Langa, 2017: 287.
35 Mandela & Venter, 2018.
36 Cseh, Davis & Khilji, 2013.

implementing change."[37] Thus, it is important to note that Mandela's letters expressed a sense of frustration with the difficulty of ending the government's policies of threats and repression against poor and marginalised people of colour. Notably, several letters revealed Mandela's concern regarding the political complexity, as well as uncertainty of his leadership ability to bring about meaningful change and transform the intercommunal social injustices.[38, 39] In fact, the personal letters of Nelson Mandela reveal that the introspective time journaling in prison provided an outlet to express and control his emotions during the heat of the moment with government officials when negotiating the complex issues of ending apartheid. Mandela credited his consistent introspection, reflection, reading and journaling with not only developing his self-awareness, resilience and emotional agility, but also the personal intelligence skills to lead with humility, grace, compassion and forgiveness, instead of retributive forms of leadership for intrapersonal transgressions.[40, 41]

Mandela applied the principles of leading oneself during periods of driving change within South Africa. The drive for transformational change requires a mindset change away from resentment and retribution against perpetrators for human rights violations, to rebuilding national institutions, confidence-building measures, and reconciliation. However, Mandela found it difficult to get past his frustration and anger, and to forgive himself for mistakes he made when working out complex problems with the ANC and government officials. Several of Mandela's letters credit reflecting, letter writing, and journaling with the time and space to internally resolve his anger against government officials, and forgive himself for the mistakes he made.[42, 43] Mandela recognised that resolving one's own demons through internal forgiveness and reconciliation is a key issue for any leader. For example, he demonstrated self-leadership during tense negotiations by displaying a conciliatory tone, despite broken promises of retaliation and betrayals by ANC and government officials.[44] Moreover, post-apartheid, there was a demand by people of colour for retribution against those perpetrators who had committed human rights violations. In the process of internally addressing his resentment and emotional triggers through both journaling and personal introspection, Mandela was able to forgive the wrongs done against him.[45] Mandela and Venter[46] revealed that:

---

37 Cseh et al., 2013: 493.
38 Mandela & Venter, 2018.
39 Mandela, 2010.
40 Mandela & Langa, 2017.
41 Mandela, 2010.
42 Ibid.
43 Mandela & Venter, 2018.
44 Mandela & Langa, 2017.
45 Campbell, 2019.
46 Mandela & Venter, 2018: 287.

> *"...one of the first acts of the representatives of the past involved the generals*
> *and leaders of the security services; one of them handed Mandela a file, which*
> *he said contained the names of highly placed people in the ANC who had been*
> *agents of the apartheid regime. Mandela scanned the file but handed it back to*
> *the source. His vision of a new society would not be hobbled by the past. He*
> *had told himself that this project would involve all people, friend and foe alike.*
> *There was neither time nor resources to waste on witch-hunts."*

In essence, Mandela demonstrated the leadership characteristics of humility, resilience, accountability and spirituality, which enabled him to lead South Africa in developing a national policy of forgiveness and reconciliation as a means to heal societal injustices.[47, 48, 49]

After spending 27 years in prison, Mandela provided leadership by coalescing differing political parties and ideologies, sharing leadership among socio-ethnic lines, bestowing values of resilience, and through forgiveness and reconciliation, unifying a country for future generations.[50] That said, Mandela recognised that leadership fundamentally started with himself. Over time, he understood the need to accept his internal trigger points and develop a better way of controlling and managing his emotions when dealing with unpredictable situations. Second, he learned that a key indicator of leading oneself is the ability to recognise that a leader is only responsible for those situations under her/his control. Third, through journaling and introspection, he was able to resolve his demons and be the kind of empathetic and servant leader he wanted to be to lead South Africa toward healing and restoration from apartheid. Overall, Mandela credits the discipline of daily journaling, reflection, and introspection as a critical ingredient in leading himself through the chaos of complex political situations with unpredictable outcomes.[51]

THEORETICAL DISCUSSION

This section presents a complexity leadership theoretical perspective of leading oneself in a complex and uncertain environment. Rimita[52], in *Leader Readiness in a Volatile, Uncertain, Complex and Ambiguous (VUCA) Business Environment*, posited that:
> *"...uncertainty is being unable to predict events and lacking clarity on what is*
> *happening in the business environment. The speed of change is the multitude*

---

47 Ferch, 2012.

48 Tutu, 2000.

49 Worthington, 2013.

50 Tutu, 2000.

51 Mandela, 2010.

52 Rimita, 2019: 38-39.

of players with often conflicting interests complicates the level of uncertainty experienced by leaders. Complexity refers to the many moving parts, their iterations, and the multiplicity of actors in any given situation causing chaos, confusion, and a lack of mastering the -intricacies to formulate cohesive responses."

As revealed by scholars, the argument is that the theoretical underpinning of leading self in a chaotic, complex, and unpredictable context resides within the complex leadership theory.[53, 54] Bakshi[55], in *Forward-Looking Manager in a VUCA World, suggested that the "complex leadership theory is a process through which leaders within organisational and societal entities emerge from an interconnective network across situational chaos and unpredictable events. Given rapid glocalised change, interconnective networks with signs of uncertainty and complexity are pervasive. The underlying driving forces within the political, economic, social, and security structures entail dynamic networks where governance relationships are hard to predict. Thus, complex leadership theory provides strategic and operational leaders with the theoretical blueprint to construct solutions when there is a lack of clarity, certainty and instability. Uncertainty is a consequence of complex, large and decentralised organisations, where explicit deterministic solutions are multi-faceted and dynamic."[56]*

The review of the complexity leadership literature reveals a framework that examines three separate but integrated leadership functions: enabling leadership, adaptive leadership, and administrative leadership.[57, 58, 59] Enabling leadership theoretically functions in three ways. First, the function works to manage the disentanglement of complex organisational conditions and uncertainty from an unpredictable environment. Second, the enabling leadership function is frequently self-organised, as well as socially organised. Moreover, these functions foster opportunities among local and grassroots actors to build powerful networks that not only create innovative strategies to address and effectively respond to an emerging concern, but also cultivate the conditions for interacting and adaptive agents to co-evolve.[60, 61] Finally, the function examines the emergence of a cause and effect to predict events in an unpredictable environment that rests within the domain of complexity leadership. Enabling leadership posits that amid organisational disruption, the process of disentanglement encompasses a

---

53 Cambel, 1993.
54 Mack, Khare, Kramer & Burgartz, 2016.
55 Bakshi, 2017.
56 Baltaci & Balci, 2017.
57 Ibid.
58 Rimita, 2019.
59 Uhl-Bien & Arena, 2017.
60 Rimita, 2019.
61 Siemans, Dawson & Eshleman, 2018.

cause and effect relationship with uncertain outcomes that influence the emergent dynamic interaction among key stakeholders.[62] With the changing political and social landscape, the complexity of social networks exposes the uncertainty of enabled structural elasticity and reveals that non-linear pattern-based leadership creates the conditions for exploring societal change.[63, 64] Enabling leadership balances adaptive leadership and administrative leadership functions.

The adaptive leadership function works within an emerging asymmetrical interaction and non-linear collaborative exchange among actors to create societal change.[65] Baltici and Balci[66] posited that, "adaptive leadership evolved from the necessity for managing overlapping needs, ideas and preferences of individual organizational members and groups, and aims to reach resonance in individual organizational members and groups." Adaptive leadership is about leaders creating innovative strategies toward innovation, experimentation and exploitation in efforts to build an organisation's adaptive capacity for significant systematic change. Tenets of adaptive leadership guide the understanding for organisational leaders to transition from the known or predictable to the unknown and unpredictable. Here, as knowledge creation fuels ideas for societal change, leaders in emerging complex and uncertain environments adapt by mobilising agents toward addressing and resolving organisational challenges to thrive.[67] Adaptive leaders create a sense of purpose, using their soft skills to influence and push tactical decisions at lower levels within the organisation. Just as different complex situations and uncertain events deliver organisational chaos, leaders adapt to situational disruptions by not only working across organisational boundaries and taking risks that challenge the status quo, but also by applying innovative ideas that resolve issues while mobilising organisational change with unpredictable outcomes. Effective leaders will adapt to the unknown and become comfortable with unpredictable outcomes amid political, socio-ethnic and security environments.

Lastly, the role of administrative leadership practices within the complex leadership theoretical context is to build a tailorable organisational vision that manages the chaos, uncertainty, and unpredictability from wicked problems. Administrative leadership functions mitigate frequent misperceptions and confusion by not only articulating a clear tangible vision down to the lowest organisational level, but also through exploiting formal and informal managerial roles that implement management processes, policies and procedures.[68] The theoretical complex leadership framework shows that a key

---

62   Rimita, 2019.

63   Baltaci & Balci, 2017.

64   Uhl-Bien & Arena, 2017.

65   Uhl-Bien & Arena, 2018.

66   Baltici & Balci, 2017: 44.

67   Heifetz, Grashow & Linskey, 2009.

68   Baltici & Balci, 2017; Mack et al., 2016.

function of administrative leadership is a focus on organisational alignment. This is seen where the vision, mission, organisational goals, and objectives line up with efficiency and effectiveness metrics in a fiscally constrained environment to accomplish organisational outcomes.[69] Thus, as strategic leaders create an organisational vision and engage in strategic planning, a lack of agile structure tasks means there is greater uncertainty and complexity. Individual organisational leader actions and activities need an in-depth understanding of more than organisational dynamic capabilities to navigate through the chaos.[70] Thus, no matter what level within the organisation encounters an uncertain and unpredictable environment, the need to understand the critical role of creating strategic connective networks is a function of administrative leadership. In essence, the implication of the current perspectives underpinning complexity leadership theoretical constructs is that organisational leaders must be action-centred guides during the unpredictable events from wicked challenges. In chaotic settings, organisational leaders must disentangle operational structures and navigate through an unpredictable ecosystem to move the organisation forward in a rapidly changing complex and uncertain environment.

PRACTICAL REALITY

In today's interconnected network and rapidly changing atmosphere, impacts and shapes enabling adaptive leadership and administrative leaderships practices both on within the local and global environment? To illustrate, local intercommunal tension caused by differing ideologies, long-held perceptions, and religious and political movements shapes interstate, intrastate, and non-state relations. As such, the power politics of political elites and ethnocultural groups frequently 'draw lines in the sand', thereby creating conflict. As a result, conflict in developing countries has heavy human, economic and social costs, and are a major cause of poverty and underdevelopment. While the conflict remains unaddressed or even intensifies, wars, poverty, and even genocide become natural consequences, which have a large toll on humanity. However, to solve major problems – such as economic depressions, diminishing resources, or violence between groups – the interplay among political leaders must disentangle and mitigate the complex political and socio-economic inequalities, as well as cultural and religious ideological tensions, to reduce private incentives to fight and bring people together toward understanding and reconciliation. In addition, perhaps the biggest challenges are disentangling the complex interdependent relationships of intrastate conflict, sequencing priorities without knowing their outcome, and managing the interconnective and cooperative relationships across the full spectrum of the peace

---

69 Baltici & Balci, 2017.

70 Uhl-Bein & Arena, 2017.

development approach. The *Joint Guidance Note on Integrated Recovery Planning*[71] noted that:

> "...post-conflict environments are characterized by high volatility. Needs may change (new population displacements, for example); priorities may change (a subsequent realization that a marginalized region or population segment poses a risk for peacebuilding if their needs are not addressed); national counterparts may change, with implications for their views on recovery priorities; reforms or capacity building may prove to be more difficult than originally envisaged, necessitating changes in timing; the composition of the donor or international support group may change; costs for reconstructing may change, due to security conditions or changes in possible sources of supply of material or services."

Nonetheless, during the last 50 years, the urgency for conflict resolution practices has increased as intercommunal actors, and national and international players have sought stability and peace across all levels of society. In a post-conflict context, the practice of conflict resolution is a complex leadership challenge as key stakeholders within the national and international community seek a peaceful solution to political, socio-economic, and ideological discord. Hence, the goal of leaders to bring about peace is to reconcile and spread the spirit of reconciliation across an entire people group. Three famous peace leaders from history who transformed a conflict state to stability were Nelson Mandela, Mahatma Gandhi, and Martin Luther King Jr.

The primary responsibility of a state leader is to protect their citizenry from emerging internal and external threats by non-state actors and violent extremist organisations. Within this context, leaders and policymakers need to strengthen the political and economic institutions of failed states, to prevent spoiler activities from destabilising the state and regional players, and to employ confidence-building tasks for long-term sustainable peace. Leaders like Mandela found it challenging to lead in an adaptive and dynamic environment[72]; as ANC leaders and their outliers responded to rapid political changes, the coordination of tasks with key stakeholders and centralised controls, they found it difficult to respond and adapt in an increasingly dynamic environment. In fact, during chaotic situations, a leader's world view that sees events not 'as they are' but 'as they should be' distorts the responsive activities in a fluid and unknown environment. To illustrate, in an unpredictable operational environment the strategic and operational leader must approach the existing operational context from a different set of lenses, based on the current context rather than shaping an environment based on past experience. In other words, leaders must accept their lack of control when managing chaos and outcomes based on past experience do not turn out as expected.

---

71 Joint Guidance Note on Integrated Recovery Planning, 2007.

72 Mandela & Langa, 2018.

In an unpredictable domain, the fluidity of information rapidly changes from moment to moment. Therefore, leaders need to assess and make strategic decisions based on the snapshot of available information at the time to protect their citizenry. As several practitioners and academics have noted, a key leadership challenge within an unpredictable context is that key stakeholders across the ecosystem demand attention and the implementation of special interests during chaotic, complex situations. As a result, the mandate to implement outlier interests frequently derails a decision-maker's ability, not only to clearly disentangle the critical operational nodes, but also to balance the structural rules with the flexibility to adapt and reflect on the variables in determining the best course of action. During chaos, what is most important for a leader is the ability to navigate and feel comfortable with the unknown, as well as making sense of what is going on before making a decision. According to Campbell[73], leaders are only effective when letting go of command and control; accepting accountability, risk-taking and failure is part of leading amid a fluid changing environment with unknown outcomes. Campbell[74] posited that leaders who understand and accept there is no way a decision can be absolutely 100% certain in a chaotic and unpredictable environment are gifts to organisations that seek to thrive in today's environment.

Within a post-apartheid context, Mandela, who yearned for inclusion whereby individuals are enabled to live in liberty to their fullest potential as well as free from the oppression of powers that seek to wield dominance, found a complex system of chaotic interconnective parts where outcomes were unpredictable and fluid.[75] The conceptual tenets of conflict resolution are not only complex, but also rely on the leader's ability to integrate national instruments of power to holistically transform the autocratic practices of the predecessor regime into a new democratic regime. Various analyses point out that conflict management literature has evolved to argue that pursuing a full agenda of governance reforms requires multi-tiered leadership across the full institutional architecture of the state. Interstate and intrastate conflict cripple a country's national instruments of power leading to a humanitarian crisis, human rights violations, and fundamental economic instability. Consequently, post-conflict states necessitate a catalyst leader who has the strategic foresight to dissect the complexity of interconnective parts and anticipate the unknown with clarity, as well as the agility to co-create the transformation of intractable conflicts into recovering state stability.[76]

Figure 13.2 depicts an overarching framework that illustrates the interconnective convergence of the political, economic, security, legal, and governance dimensions that leaders must address to restore national instruments of power in a post-conflict

---

73 Campbell, 2019.

74 Ibid.

75 Mandela, 2010.

76 Joiner & Josephs, 2007.

environment. *The Guiding Principles for Stabilization and Reconstruction*[77] provides a stabilisation and reconstruction comprehensive roadmap with five domains that intertwine interdependently, overlapping in creating formal governance architecture and processes. The sequence of competing domains cuts across multiple disciplines, as stabilisation and reconstruction "missions are messy and complex endeavors involving thousands, if not millions, of moving parts."[78] Mandela [79] noted that the societal expectation management of transforming violent actions from apartheid to peaceful means involves a public dialogue of not only the political will to hold perpetrators accountable for human rights violations, but to also address the root drivers of conflict in a secure environment. The Mandela and Venter[80] letters revealed how the actionable decisions made in one sector domain directly or indirectly impacted other domains. *The Guiding Principles for Stabilization and Reconstruction*[81] addresses domain interdependence, where "security requires the rule of law, essential services require governance, the rule of law is dependent on security, sustainable economies are dependent on the rule of law, ownership requires capacity, and meeting basic human needs require all of the above." Against this background, Mandela and Venter[82] describe how the delicate balance of delivering humanitarian assistance and the creation of employment opportunities hinged on strategic actions of disarmament, demobilisation, and reintegration, coupled with security sector reform within the safety and security domain. As a result, amid chaos, the leadership challenge within post-conflict environments is that leaders' actions frequently influence the outcomes in ways that cannot fully be forecasted. Importantly, nothing tests a leader's ability to lead more than navigating through chaos with unpredictable and unknown outcomes.

---

77 The Guiding Principles for Stabilization and Reconstruction, 2009.

78 Cole, 2009: 3-13.

79 Mandela, 2010.

80 Mandela & Venter, 2018.

81 The Guiding Principles for Stabilization and Reconstruction, 2009: 5-30.

82 Mandela & Venter, 2018.

Figure 13.2: Stabilisation and Reconstruction Framework

In practical reality, leadership challenges in a complex and uncertain environment go beyond the individual leader's capabilities. The true test of leadership is not illustrated during steady-state activities, but rather in times of organisational crisis and chaos. The argument in this chapter is that navigating organisational chaos requires a new kind of leader and leadership competencies. More importantly, complex organisational challenges require innovative leadership solutions. For that reason, leadership researchers are exploring innovative organisational and strategic leaders' methodologies and competencies in a rapidly changing complex, uncertain and ambiguous environment. Initially, the traditional leadership model where operational and strategic leaders primarily function around direct reports, command and control structures, and developing competency-based skills. Now, an innovative leadership methodology is emerging from traditional leadership frameworks to a leadership framework focused on mission-driven agility with cognitive readiness, and cross-functional collaboration across organisational lines. Consequently, it is imperative to note that in a fluid, complex, and uncertain context, effective operational leaders develop a culture of flexibility, adaptation, and discretion while remaining action-oriented. In essence, a leadership approach that executes stabilisation and reconstruction activities requires strategic decisions that are flexible, adaptable, and agile within a post-conflict environment.

Leadership researchers point out that with the emergence of uncertainty and complexity, most leadership practitioners suggest that new competencies are needed to succeed. Embedded within the Complexity Leadership and Uncertain Reduction Theory literature are two components that prepare leaders to understand the landscape in which they lead.[83, 84] The first component is strategic intelligence; to lead effectively in a complex and uncertain environment, there are two key competencies of strategic intelligence. The first key competency is strategic thinking, which synthesises complex challenges; questions the status quo; and identifies, defines, and develops planning actions for decision-makers.[85] The second key competency leverages the strategic thinking process, and develops the strategic planning that takes developmental action plans from the strategic thinking process and operationalising, in addition to implementing the directive action into achievable outcomes made by decision-makers.[86] It is a reality that often, by the time strategic plans are produced and ready for execution, the operational situation and variables have changed and the strategic plans are obsolete. For this reason, leaders who have the strategic mindset to see the big picture rapidly, sift out the non-essential and essential information with clarity, relinquish the need for control and predictability, and empower decision-makers at the tactical level, are a valuable organisational asset during times of chaos. The reason is that organisations need leaders who have the ability to disentangle the multiple threads and connect the dots when managing the unknown.

Leaders who are unable to strategically think through the disentanglement of complex issues and execute goals and objectives set forth within the strategic planning process are ineffective as organisational leaders in complex and uncertain environments.[87] It is important to note that the domain of strategic intelligence that provides a leader with the ability to identify emerging trends and patterns with clarity and accuracy has changed. Once reserved for senior leaders, strategic thinking, strategic planning and decision-making are now being pushed to the tactical level, where situational awareness of unexpected events is realised. In essence, strategic intelligence provides a conceptual framework of leading oneself during times of ambiguity and uncertainty.

The second component of strategic leadership is the 'people strategy'. The people strategy must encompass the mental, emotional and interpersonal readiness to lead in a complex, fluid, and uncertain environment. A great deal of research has confirmed that one of the most important components of managing in a complex and uncertain environment centres on building a people strategy with the vital skillsets to lead oneself with self-awareness and self-control in complex and unpredictable

---

83 Redmond, 2015.

84 Veldsman & Johnson, 2016.

85 Betz, 2016.

86 Ibid.

87 Mendenhall, Osland, Bird, Oddou, Stevens, Maznevski & Stahl, 2018.

environments.[88, 89] In practical terms, leaders are presiding over organisations that are complex, rapidly changing, ambiguous and unpredictable due to glocalised political and socio-economic disruption. Hence, organisations that create an enduring people strategy with the capacity to cope with complexity and unpredictability build individual leadership schemes based on character-based leadership development.[90] In the complex domain, leaders who have strength as a characteristic lead from their own point of view by being self-aware and transparent, setting high standards of moral and ethical conduct, and acting without impulse or hidden agenda. Character-based leadership means doing the right thing, despite the pressure to compromise your principles. For example, Mandela exhibited character-based leadership by not getting hooked on internal thoughts and feelings of retribution against his perpetrators; instead, by demonstrating forgiveness and reconciliation, he led others toward national healing and reconciliation. An argument can be made that developing character-based leadership, coupled with emotional and social intelligence, is a unique combination of the mental characteristics and behaviours needed to lead oneself during times of chaos. In other words, leading oneself through the practice of introspection, mindfulness, journalling, and self-solitude creates a character-based leadership schema that is essential for effective leadership and one of the most important assets one can have as a leader.

RECOMMENDATIONS

Leaders do not respond to uncertainty in the same way, however leaders who learn to manage unexpected disruptions amidst organisational chaos are an asset. While every organisational disruption may produce various complex and uncertain situational events, leaders must consistently display the following attributes to lead self in times of unpredictability and unknown factors: self-awareness, emotional self-control, decisiveness, integrity, strategic intelligence, and character-based leadership. The true test of leadership is found through the unforgiving pressure felt during times of organisational disruption, complexity and uncertainty, making leaders feel like the weight of the entire organisation is on their shoulders. It must be clear that that is what executive leaders sign up for when they take on leadership roles. For that reason, we propose the below recommendations to build a leader's self-leadership capacity in times of organisational chaos.

- Design, develop and execute a realistic notional organisational simulation and/or tabletop exercise that prepares current and emerging leaders to lead in volatile, complex, uncertain, and ambiguous events.

---

88 van Zyl & Campbell, 2019.

89 Kethledge & Erwin, 2017.

90 Ibid.

- In these simulations, the organisational leaders can practice navigating rapidly changing informational pathways in an uncertain operational environment that places their strategic intelligence, character-based leadership skills, and test decision-making skills under pressure. The aim is to develop the senior leadership skills required for managing complex multi-dimensional organisational challenges, such as crisis management, emotional intelligence, communication, collaborative decision-making, problem-solving, and team development. The ultimate objective of the simulation exercise is to identify not only the individual capability gaps of leading oneself, but to also develop the knowledge, skills, and attributes needed to prepare leader effectiveness in a complex and uncertain environment.

- Design and develop a talent management and leadership development strategic roadmap for leading oneself with character. Literature shows that leaders draw on a personal source of energy and cornerstone of strength to guide their choices and actions in meeting the challenges of a complex and uncertain environment.[91] The qualities of leading oneself with character, beliefs, and habits of thinking ground leaders who are striving to achieve organisational outcomes with a sense of purpose. The roadmap might include areas such as emotional and social intelligence, strategic intelligence, sensemaking, authenticity, psychological and social capital, shared leadership, and resilience. The aim of a talent management and leadership development strategic roadmap is to create a pipeline of effective leadership capability while simultaneously building an organisational leadership capability, which is crucial to any organisation.

CONCLUDING REMARKS

This chapter addressed the challenge of leading oneself within an uncertain and complex environment, as illustrated by the success and failures of President Nelson Mandela. Moreover, an emotional intelligence model offers practical ways to develop self-awareness and self-regulation components. Second, a brief discussion on complexity leadership with its enabling, administrative, and adaptive leadership frameworks provided a theoretical backdrop to leading oneself within a fluid, uncertain and complex context. Third, a discussion presented the practical realities of leading oneself through uncertainty and complexity during the stabilisation and reconstruction of a post-conflict environment through by building a people's strategy and character-based leadership skillset for strategic leaders. Finally, the design and development of a simulation exercise and talent development and leadership development strategy were presented to identify gaps and build individual leadership capacity in complex and uncertain environments.

---

91 Kethledge & Erwin, 2017.

CHAPTER 14

LIMINAL LEADERSHIP IN A VUCA WORLD

Randal Joy Thompson

ABSTRACT

This chapter explores the necessary qualities of leading oneself and others to peace in the liminal VUCA world of war in Iraq. The most appropriate qualities for leading oneself in this liminal VUCA situation include connection, courage, empathy, resilience, expanded consciousness, spiritual intelligence, and agility in the face of paradox. Liminal leadership is the most appropriate leadership approach in this situation because it provides a transformational process to facilitate the creation of a new, peaceful future and outlines the steps to achieve this. Liminal leaders in a VUCA war situation have a possible path to lead others to peace. This chapter offers an original approach to leading self and others in the liminal VUCA situation caused by war. It provides qualities one can practice in leading oneself and a leadership approach which one can follow and apply in such situations.

INTRODUCTION

Globalisation, together with the fall of the Berlin Wall, created a world characterised as volatile, uncertain, complex and ambiguous, namely "VUCA." No longer can the globe be carved into distinct categories as during the Cold War. Rather, divisions are blurred and constantly changing. Terrorism and the proliferation of local wars and conflicts have become the defining reality. In the world of international development, funding is largely channeled to countries to "democratise" them and address their internal security issues. As a consequence, international development professionals are increasingly working in conflict and post-conflict countries where local stakeholders are being, or have been, traumatised. Leading international development projects in such contexts rely on qualities of leading oneself not typically required in peaceful countries, including the ability to manoeuver in an extreme VUCA environment and the necessity to build peace from the bottom up.

This chapter discusses leading a foreign assistance project in Iraq during the war initiated by the United States of America (USA) in 2003, and proposes a model of leading oneself and others towards peace in a VUCA environment. The chapter identifies the key components of leading oneself such as connection, courage, empathy, resilience, expanded consciousness, spiritual intelligence, and agility in the face of paradox. Finally, the chapter proposes that liminal leadership is the most efficacious approach to lead an organisation or society in chaos toward a more hopeful future.

The chapter begins with an "Example" section, which describes the project case study and its VUCA features. The "leading oneself" qualities that emerged are highlighted and the challenges of leading oneself dissected. The "Theory" section details liminal leadership, i.e. the model that best fits the case study in the VUCA world. "Practical Reality" discusses in more detail the topic of this chapter in terms of leadership practice. The "Recommendations" section then presents practical and theoretical recommendations for leading self toward peace in a VUCA environment. Finally, the "Conclusion" summarises the chapter and draws conclusions.

EXAMPLE

Leading a monitoring, evaluation, and learning project in Iraq, funded by the United States Agency for International Development (USAID), highlighted the challenges of leading a temporary project organisation within an intense VUCA environment. The project's responsibilities included: 1) monitoring and evaluating the 25 USAID-funded projects in Iraq that were designed to rebuild the country and establish a peaceful democracy; 2) conducting assessments and studies of various challenges in Iraq to inform USAID regarding sectors they should invest in; 3) implementing training and capacity building of Iraqis to design, monitor, and evaluate their projects; and 4) building the management capacity of Iraqi ministries and non-governmental organisations. The project team included an American leader and two American and 12 Iraqi staff. The Iraqis included Sunnis, the Muslim sect of Saddam Hussein and his regime, Shias, the sect of his opposition, and Christians.

Conflict environments such as Iraq are VUCA environments, being volatile, uncertain, complex, and ambiguous. Leading international development projects in these environments is subject firstly to the volatility of war. *Volatility*, i.e. unpredictable fluctuations, magnitudes, rates, and effects of changes[1], manifests in: 1) issues of safety, including the risk that personnel and project beneficiaries can be killed or taken captive and/or the project office attacked; 2) the ability of the project to work in certain regions of the country; 3) the reality that the achievement of project objectives depends upon which government ultimately takes control; and 4) uncertainty of remaining in the country to continue the project, depending on security and political issues.

---

1   Bawany, 2018.

Uncertainty, closely related to volatility, includes the inability to predict the impact of factors that influence results and the tendency to rely on past behaviours to solve new challenges.[2] The social and political situation in Iraq changed almost daily. Since many Shiite leaders had been exiled in Iran, Iran eventually took control of the country, despite denials by the US and its coalition partners.[3] This situation caused a great deal of uncertainty regarding whether the government would be friendly toward the US and whether our project and other US projects would continue.

Complexity, the manifestation of multiple factors at play[4], caused confusion and the inability to clearly understand the situation in Iraq. The US miscalculated the receptiveness of Iraq to being transformed into a democratic outpost in the Middle East, and also misunderstood the culture and governance structure of the country. Iraq remained a tribal culture; tribal and religious interests superseded individual or societal interests, and political wrangling, assassinations, and corruption were still widely practiced. The transformation of Iraq into a peaceful democracy was subject to complex factors that could not be predicted nor controlled.

Ambiguity in such conflict situations stems from the confusion of not knowing the true meaning of what is happening as caused by the other VUCA factors.[5] The view of leaders is hazy.[6] Ambiguity is worsened by not being aware of all the actions that various individuals are taking behind the scenes that might have a major impact on the outcomes of other US-funded projects. Meaning-making is severely challenged in this environment. Paradox reigns in an ambiguous situation because it is often necessary to hold opposing approaches and beliefs simultaneously.

IMPORTANT FACTORS IN LEADING ONESELF

Leading teams in conflict countries involves helping to move a damaged and broken system toward peace and normalcy, and creating new systems and organisations that formalise more equalitarian and democratic processes. Conflict and post-conflict countries are trapped in liminal space; a space betwixt and between two socio-economic and political orders and between war and peace.[7, 8, 9] Liminal space is also VUCA since it is characterised by "limbo" and is hence paradoxical, ambiguous,uncertain, potentially

---

2   Ibid.

3   Arango, 2017.

4   Bawany, 2018.

5   Ibid.

6   Ibid.

7   Hawkins & Edwards, 2017.

8   Orton & Withrow, 2015.

9   Shaw Van-Buskirk, Lim & Leong, 2019.

volatile, and complex.[10]   Leaders in this space "must have a clear sense of self...a willingness to be challenged and changed...and to live with ambiguity, dissonance, and conflict."[11] Leading oneself qualities that are especially important in liminal VUCA environments include connection, courage, empathy, resilience, expanded consciousness, spiritual intelligence, and agility in the face of paradox. These qualities are equally important in liminal leaders.

The foundation of leading self in a conflict and liminal VUCA environment is the leader's intent and ability to build relationships of trust and authenticity, and to "connect" with their team or staff in the organisation. Global leadership scholar-practitioner Kathleen Curran's concept of global resonance is a useful model to employ to establish such relationships.[12] Global resonance is the mutual and subliminal non-cognitive connection between people that arises from: 1) sincere intent to connect; 2) respecting, honouring, and caring for each other; and 3) expecting brilliance from each other. Global resonance goes beyond the notion of cultural intelligence or cultural mindset, which tends to be based on knowledge and action rather than on "being" a leader, a state that reflects an emotional and even spiritual connection with others. Close relationships build trust, which is important in all contexts but supremely important in a conflict situation where team members often have to depend on each other for personal safety. Trust building depends on one's ability, integrity and benevolence.[13]

Through global resonance, individuals develop connections in common situations, interests, values, and objectives. The team is stabilised in a VUCA environment through connection and is more capable of enduring external shocks. Global resonance is an inside-out approach to leadership derived from one's inner sense of self vis-à-vis the world and the desire to shift the "I-You" relationship to a "We" relationship.

---

10 Shaw Van-Buskirk, et al., 2019.

11 Orton & Withrow, 2015: 41.

12 Curran, 2018.

13 Jordaan, 2019.

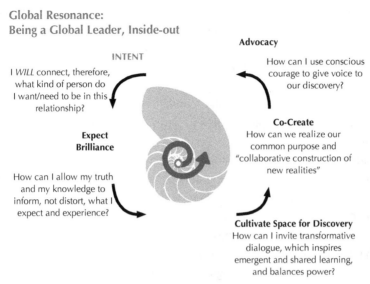

Figure 14.1: Leading from Inside-Out

Figure 14.2: "Being" a Global Leader

Close relationships serve to reduce volatility. They create the internal stability that allows the team to unite to achieve a common vision that they are intellectually, emotionally and spiritually committed to. Further, such "We" relationships "co-create" change toward peace and stability, and establish shared understanding and communal intelligence.[14] They also ensure that the transformation process is owned by the conflict or post-conflict country. Global resonance thus becomes the foundation of lead-self, lead-others and lead-community, which peace leadership scholars Van Zyl and Campbell[15] argued are the necessary phases for peace leadership.

---

14 Van Zyl & Campbell, 2019.

15 Ibid.

"Courage" is an essential component of leading oneself in a conflict VUCA environment because of the uncertainty of one's safety and the safety of one's team. Courage stems from strong values and faith that derives from knowing that one is strengthened by, and in the hands of, a higher power. In a conflict or post-conflict environment, courage derives from a deep-seated belief that peace is possible. It also results from the belief that there are viable options to resolve conflict resolution other than war. Courage stems from the faith that people can live in harmony and that a leader can contribute to human flourishing.

Courage manifests in empathising with staff who risk their lives coming to and leaving from work. "Empathy" is being able to experience a small part of the team's terror of being bombed and of having their world turned upside down, of losing loved ones, of an uncertain future, of having a new government that may discriminate against them, and so on. Courage also comes from "resilience"; having the ability to recover from a setback and occurrences such as nearby bombs, and from knowing that one will be able to move forward with even greater strength and commitment. Courage helps to deal with the uncertainty of a conflict or post-conflict situation, and hence serves as an antidote for the "U" in VUCA.

Openness to an "expanded consciousness" or expanded awareness is a critical leading oneself quality to deal with complexity in a VUCA world. Developmental psychologists, integral thinkers, and spiritual leaders agree that people's perceptions and experiences of the world and others traverse a development trajectory that is: 1) progressively broader and more focused on the world rather than the self; 2) pluralistic in the sense of understanding and accepting the veracity of multiple viewpoints; 3) increasingly compassionate and accepting of humanity; and 4) able to see the world in terms of complexity of systems.[16, 17, 18] Consciousness moves from centering on the self to ultimately centering on the cosmos.

Stages of consciousness are divided into egocentric, ethnocentric, world-centric, and cosmocentric, and are often assigned colours by integral thinkers.[19] To handle the complexity of the VUCA world, leaders need to be at least at the "world-centric" stage, but ideally at the "cosmocentric stage."[20, 21] World-centric leaders, who are characterised as post-modern, believe in communal harmony and equality, and seek inner peace and caring for others. They have tolerance for self and others based on their understanding of individual and cultural differences, and seek harmony and sustainability through bonding and participatory approaches.[22] Cosmocentric leaders

---

16 Beck & Cowen, 1996.

17 Kegan, 1982.

18 Wilbur, 2000.

19 Brown, 2006.

20 Beck & Cowen, 1996.

21 Brown, 2006.

22 Ibid.

understand "multiple interconnected systems of relationships and processes [and are] able to deal with conflicting needs and duties in constantly shifting contexts."[23] They can lead to reframing and reinterpreting situations based on principles. Higher levels of consciousness help leaders master two required competencies of leaders in VUCA environments, according to Turner.[24] These include "contextual thinking" and "decision-making processes." Contextual thinking allows leaders to understand the various contributions of individuals in the solution of complex problems. Successful decision-making requires taking all the perspectives in a complex problem into account when coming up with a solution.[25]

Most integral thinkers contend that disruptions, challenges, uncomfortable situations, and crises are required to move higher along the spectrum of levels of consciousness. The chaos of a VUCA world, especially as experienced in a conflict or post-conflict situation, potentially catalyses an expanded awareness, the ability to perceive and accept complexity, and the skills to understand it. Kegan and Lahey[26] argued that one can also move up the ladder of consciousness by changing the way one talks and makes meaning, often as a consequence of being confronted by oneself, by others, and by chaos. Living through conflict challenges how one makes meaning in the world and can broaden one's view of the world.

An expanded consciousness reflects "spiritual intelligence", which Vaughn[27] defined as "the ability to create meaning based on a deep understanding of existential questions and the awareness of and ability to use multiple levels of consciousness to solve problems."[28] Spirituality involves the continual search for meaning and is inextricably linked to ethical and moral behaviour "with a focus on sustainability and credibility, rooted in self-knowledge and in the desire for growth and development."[29] The experience of transcendence "may help one to cope with difficulties and to experience higher feelings of purpose and meaning."[30] Wigglesworth[31] operationalised spiritual intelligence as "the ability to behave with compassion and wisdom while maintaining inner and outer peace (equanimity) regardless of the circumstances."

Leading with spiritual intelligence requires continued spiritual practice. Nullens[32] pointed out that the practice of Ignatian spirituality and Otto Scharmer's *Theory U*[33]

---

23 Brown, 2006: 8.

24 Turner, 2018.

25 Ibid.

26 Kegan & Lahey, 2001.

27 Vaughn, 2002.

28 Nullens, 2019.

29 Nullens, 2019: n.p.

30 Van Zyl & Campbell, 2019: n.p.

31 Wigglesworth, 2011: 5.

32 Nullens, 2019.

33 Scharmer, 2016.

can help leaders become sensitive to interior movements or motions of the soul, such as "desires, feelings, thoughts, imaginings, emotions, repulsions, and attractions", and thereby become more open and mindful leaders in a VUCA world. Nullens emphasised that Ignatian principles create an awareness that the future is not in our hands[34], and argued that Scharmer's *Theory U*[35] carries leaders to a receptive inner space that requires them to be open to their inner voices of resistance that include judgment, cynicism and fear. Leaders then become receptive, good listeners, and ultimately humble. Spiritual practice may lead people "to focus more on human dignity and their relationship with the environment and society and lead them to focus less on themselves and more on society, the world, and the cosmos."[36]

In terms of leading oneself, then, leaders must be open to having their world views shaken and having their egos wounded by understanding that others' experiences of them may be different than their conceptions of self. They must self-reflect on their inner states and open up to be more receptive to input from others. Such disruptions can shift their mental models and facilitate their thinking to be collaborative rather than competitive.[37] Further, this disruption can also free leaders from being stuck in one mindset with certain cemented perspectives, into understanding many different perspectives. Hence, leaders become more agile and able to adapt to dramatically changing situations. Expanded consciousness is an antidote for the complexity in a VUCA world because leaders can perceive the world in terms of complex systems.

Another important facet of expanded consciousness is the agility to navigate paradoxes and to shift from "either/or" thinking to "both/and" thinking. Such thinking is necessary to effectively deal with VUCA ambiguity where meanings are not clear or changing. In a conflict or post-conflict situation, there often is no "right" or "wrong" side among the warring factions. All sides in the conflict have "their story" and their "justification" for battling. This is a fundamental paradox and leading in this environment requires that a leader hold this paradox in balance and keep the focus on the project's vision to rebuild a reconciled and peaceful democratic society. By balancing this paradox, the leader is making meaning in a post-conflict society and possibly aiding the resolution of differences by providing a commonly held vision. Leslie, Li, and Zhao[38] called this balancing "duality", which, like the Eastern notion of yin-yang, includes opposite elements that are partially conflicting and partially complementary.

---

34 Nullens, 2019.

35 Scharmer, 2016.

36 Van Zyl, 2019: n.p.

37 Kok & van den Heuvel, 2019.

38 Leslie, Li & Zhao, 2015.

Theory

Liminal leadership best encapsulates the transformational process that occurs in the self, the team or organisation, and the country during a conflict or post-conflict situation. Such leadership requires the same qualities of leading oneself as described above, namely connection, courage, empathy, resilience, expanded consciousness, spiritual intelligence and agility in the face of a paradox. These qualities are still required because liminal leadership requires leaders to form close personal and trustworthy relationships, and to facilitate a process to lead people from the darkness to a new positive future which they co-create. This certainly requires courage, empathy, resilience and agility. Expanded consciousness and spiritual intelligence help the leader see the bigger picture of possibilities. Leaders and their teams are operating in liminal spaces during and immediately following conflict. Such spaces are "transitional or transformative spaces...waiting areas between one point in time and space and the next." "Liminal" comes from the Latin root "limen", which means "threshold."[39] In liminal space, "our old world [is] left behind, while we are not yet sure of the new existence...[It is] a good space where genuine newness can begin...a sacred space where the old world can fall apart and a bigger world is revealed."[40] As Horvath, et al.[41] explained:

> *"Liminality captures in-between situations and conditions characterized by the dislocation of established structures, the reversal of hierarchies, and the uncertainty about the continuity of tradition and future outcomes....As a fundamental human experience, liminality transmits cultural practices, codes, rituals, and meanings in between aggregate structures and uncertain outcomes."*

The liminal space is generally marked by a ritual that formalises the transformation. Sadly, war has been a historically repeated "ritual" that has marked the transition from one state to an altered one.[42] Three stages characterise the liminal transition. First, there is a separation from the previous self and of the previous socio-political order. Second, there is the liminal space – the "limbo", the space in between, the space of possibilities – and third, there is the reincorporation with a more developed sense of self and/or a new socio-economic order.[43] The entire project team in a conflict or post-conflict environment, including the leader, is in a liminal space, and everyone is forced to undergo a liminal transformation.

---

39 Orton & Withrow, 2015.
40 Rohr, 1999
41 Horvath et al., 2015: n.p.
42 Smith, 1991.
43 Hawkins & Edwards, 2017.

The US invasion obliterated the previous socio-political order in Iraq and tore away the identities of the team in this project case study. Most of the team were Sunnis whose families were part of the elite in Saddam Hussein's regime. The invasion ousted them along with the Baathist party. The Shiites on the team also were included in the elite because of their education and relationship with the Sunnis. The team members were forced to decide whether they would create a new identity under Shia rule and stay in Iraq where they may no longer be in the elite, or leave the country. Most of them eventually left the country and emigrated to the US or Britain. The team traversed the process of recreating themselves, their identities, and their position in the "new Iraq" or in a foreign country where they would become "outsiders."

Expatriate leaders and members of a team in a conflict or post-conflict society also traverse a major personal transformation, which significantly impacts their leading oneself. Such a transformation generally broadens one's awareness about the world and builds compassion. Preconceptions about the conflict are shattered as one comes to know the victims. Victims' stories intertwine with the leader's own stories and their resonant relationships lead them to create new perceptions of each other and of the society they are working in. Preconceptions about ethnic and religious differences are often swept away.

Liminal Leadership

Liminal leading involves joining in a transformational process with the individuals trapped in the conflict.[44,45, 46] Although expatriates' and staff's transformations are different, their hopes for the transformation of the conflict situation into one of resolution and some sort of peace overlap. Liminal leadership, as well as peace, takes place between people and between organisations, nations, religions and institutions.[47] Liminal leading is hence relational and fits with the recent emphasis on leading as "interactive and reciprocal influencing processes...the symbiotic relationships between followers and leaders as a process of mutual influence."[48]

Such reciprocal and influencing processes force people to examine their mental models and attitudes, and ultimately to change their behaviour. Rituals are helpful in this process. In the project case study, the entire team "broke bread" together every Friday by ordering lunch from an Iraqi restaurant and enjoying the meal together, talking not about work, but our families and our hopes and dreams.

---

44 Hawkins & Edwards, 2017.

45 Orton & Withrow, 2015.

46 Shaw Van-Buskirk, Lim & Leong, 2019.

47 Bateson, 2017.

48 Joubert, 2019: n.p.

Liminal Leadership Within Organisational and Social Chaos

Organisational and social chaos is infused with conflict and dissonance. Organisation members often become:

> "'off-balance' and not completely in control of their thoughts and feelings... Dissonance can escalate to disruption, or crisis, where 'business as usual' becomes interrupted and frameworks for relationships or functions no longer apply in the disrupted state."[49]

The initial response of leaders in such a chaotic situation may be to try to return the organisation to the previous state in which stability and predictability existed. However, transformative liminal leaders employ the tension and uncertainty of the liminal space to stimulate creativity and to facilitate a highly collaborative process that seeks novel solutions and new futures. They "bring people together across boundaries" and enable "critical collective reflection that creates new ways forward."[50] Liminal leaders implement "VUCA prime", which is considered one of the antidotes to VUCA.[51] Through VUCA prime, volatility yields to "vision"; uncertainly becomes "understanding"; complexity leads to "clarity"; and ambiguity creates "agility."[52]

In addition, liminal leaders have the capabilities inherent in the LEAP approach, considered another antidote to VUCA.[53] LEAP stands for: 1) "liberal"- being open to new behaviours and opinions; 2) "exuberant" – bringing passion to the transformational process; 3) "agility" – helping to instill the new organisation with "with next-gen leadership competencies including cognitive readiness, critical thinking, and emotional and social intelligence";[54] and 4) fostering "partnership" – namely trustworthy relationships.[55]

Liminal leaders facilitate the group's move into an imaginative collective where participants: 1) introduce their different perspectives into the creative process; 2) critically review the aims and processes of the organisation or society in chaos; 3) introduce new perspectives into their view of the current organisation or society; 4) converse together to construct a new narrative; and 5) reflect on their identities and the identity of the future organisation or society. Together, they carve a route out of the liminal space by reorienting or reintegrating the organisation's or society's aim and

---

49 Orton & Withrow, 2015: 28.
50 Orton & Withrow, 2015: 23.
51 Mannherz, 2017.
52 Ibid.
53 Bawany, 2018.
54 Mannherz, 2017: n.p.
55 Mannherz, 2017.

values, and together co-create a more resilient organisation or society that can better cope with a VUCA environment.

Deep relation-building, trust, empowerment of all participants, and honest self-reflection are essential aspects of this process. Leaders often employ "symbols, stories, and rituals to create community" and stimulate creativity. They employ mindfulness to help participants focus on the present disruptive liminal space because that focus opens up future possibilities.[56] Finally, they promote creative problem-solving and collective intelligence to co-create the future from those possibilities.

Practical Reality

Liminal leadership and the leading oneself components of resonant relationships, courage, empathy, resilience, openness to an expanded consciousness, spiritual intelligence, and agility to navigate a paradox are relevant to leading in the 21st century, and are appropriate to leading in a VUCA environment, especially in a conflict or post-conflict situation. Globalisation, the transition to the Fourth Industrial Age, and the proliferation of civil and regional conflicts, have situated the world on the verge of a major transformation of the global order. In other words, the world is in societal liminal space. Bateson[57] argued that inter-systemic change in our inter-connected world is what is required now during what she called "a murky territory of alive in-betweenness." The implication of this inter-connectedness is the inextricable connection between lead-self, lead-others, and lead-community.[58]

RECOMMENDATIONS

Based on the aforementioned, the following recommendations are key to lead-self and lead-others in a conflict or post-conflict situation in a liminal VUCA environment:

- Leaders should look to a VUCA environment as a positive force for personal growth and an enhanced understanding of the complexities of the world, as well as a better-honed ability to help to bring about peace.
- Resonant relationships are necessary and are a prelude to effective leading oneself or leading others. Close relationships are the antidote to volatility and the foundation of the transformative process that accompanies a conflict or post-conflict situation.
- A transformative process opens the door to expanding consciousness and the ability to deal with complexity, to transcend differences to see common ground, and to imagine a unified global whole.

---

56 Shaw Van-Buskirk, et al., 2019: 653.

57 Bateson, 2017: 3.

58 Van Zyl & Campbell, 2019.

- Liminal space, although unsettling, opens the door for co-creating a better future, and liminal leadership can facilitate the process of realising that future.

CONCLUDING REMARKS

This chapter presented a case study of a project in Iraq during the conflict years that began with the US invasion in 2003 as an example of leading in a liminal VUCA environment. Leading oneself in such a VUCA environment must achieve some stability in the face of volatility; the way to do this is to form close, resonant and trustworthy relationships with one's team. Relationships are strengthened by having courage, empathy, and resilience. Courage and resilience help to manage the uncertainty in the environment. Having a clear vision based on solid values also serves as an antidote to uncertainty. A liminal VUCA environment challenges leaders to open themselves to expanded consciousness and broader world-centric awareness. Hence, this environment provides an opportunity for personal growth. Examining one's meaning-making can lead to changes in one's attitudes and behaviour; one can become more open and accepting and see oneself in connection with others and the world. Such a process merges with spiritual intelligence in which one's focus moves from the self to the higher reaches of the unknown. Leading oneself requires agility in a liminal VUCA environment and the ability to manage a paradox in a both/and manner. Moving to higher levels of consciousness and seeing the world through a complexity lens helps manage paradoxes in this way.

Liminal leadership views the "limbo" of being between war and peace as a space of creativity and possibilities to redesign ourselves, our future, our organisations, and our societies. Being aware that a liminal VUCA environment requires a transformation of ourselves and our relationships makes it apparent that this environment, rather than being alarming, provides fertile ground for a positive future for ourselves and the world.

CHAPTER 15

LEADING ONESELF IN A VUCA WORLD: LESSONS FROM THE FIELD OF RELIGIOUS LEADERSHIP

Jack Barentsen

ABSTRACT

The aspects of self-leadership discussed in this chapter include close listening to context, willingness to adapt one's leadership role, emotional regulation and self control, safe spaces for dialogue, honesty and transparency, optimism and resilience, sensitivity to social identity, and bridge-building skills.

These skills are evident in the three case studies presented, where religious leaders adapted to changing and uncertain environments, where the significance of religious identity is rather ambiguous, and when it can at times generate very volatile situations.

The case studies present how several religious leaders in very different contexts created innovative forms of religious communities that became strongly locally rooted while being shaped by conservative theological understandings. Each leader demonstrated a willingness to first listen to their constituencies in their context, to reshape their leader identity for fruitful collaboration, and to honestly engage in open dialogue to discover. The analysis of how they engaged their VUCA context pointed out that deep personal change, sensitivity to social, civic and religious identities at group and intergroup levels, and rootedness in personal spirituality, were demonstrably important aspects of their self-leadership – which merits further investigation and theoretical development.

INTRODUCTION: RELIGIOUS LEADERSHIP, SELF-LEADERSHIP AND THE VUCA WORLD

"Blessed are the peacemakers: for they shall be called sons of God."
–(Gospel of Matthew 5:9, Holy Bible: English Standard Version)

211

> *"Let all bitterness and wrath and anger and clamour and slander be put away from you, along with all malice. Be kind to one another, tenderhearted, forgiving one another, as God in Christ forgave you."*
> –(Paul's letter to the Ephesians 4:31-32, Holy Bible: English Standard Version).

Religion and peace seem contradictory terms in a world where terror and violence are often religiously inspired. In addition, the list of leadership abuses and scandals in the religious world (no less than elsewhere), suggests that religious leadership sometimes obscures the development of healthy self-leadership.

It can also be otherwise. For most of the world's population, their most treasured religious convictions focus on peace and reconciliation. This involves the intrapersonal – finding peace with oneself, and the interpersonal – living in peace with God and with others, including those of other religious convictions. For instance, the Christian tradition nurtures deeply rooted religious convictions about reconciliation, forgiveness, hospitality and respect, precisely for those who are 'other' who do not belong to 'our' community. Such convictions are embodied within the beliefs and practices of Christian faith communities, while their leaders are called to proclaim and embody these convictions as (imperfect) exemplars for and of the community. Inspiring religious leaders, such as Desmond Tutu and Martin Luther King Jr., have moved thousands to peaceful practices, inspired by deeply rooted religious convictions. Similar sentiments are manifested in Buddhism, which is broadly considered to be a peaceful religion, and in the example of Mahatma Gandhi in a Hindu environment, although Buddhism and Hinduism also have their moments and locations of violence. Religion, then, can be a strong source of inspiration and motivation for health self-leadership, which moves people towards reconciliation and peace.[1]

To address the urgent needs of peace leadership, this chapter focuses primarily on how religious leaders can contribute to healthy self-leadership, which in turn can be a source for reconciliation and peace-making, rather than for violence. Although religious leadership theoretically encompasses leaders of faith communities in all religions, it is impossible to do justice to this full spectrum in one book, much less in one chapter. The current focus is therefore limited to leadership in Christian faith communities, more specifically on Evangelical-Protestant communities in North-West Europe and North America.[2] The central question is, "How do Christian religious leaders demonstrate self-leadership in their response to the VUCA world, and how do they nurture self-leadership amongst the people they lead, empowering them to navigate this VUCA world?"

---

1   Kollontai, Yore & Kim, 2018.

2   Barentsen, 2016.

This chapter will first narrate the story of several religious leaders in their adaptation to the VUCA environment, with a special eye for aspects of self-leadership that they demonstrated. Further reflection on these stories will highlight the collaborative and interpretive leadership style that these leaders adopted, enabling their 'followers' to dialogue amidst diversity and to develop a relevant sense of religious identity. Next, the VUCA context within which religious leaders and their communities function is analysed, to demonstrate how strongly all dimensions of the VUCA context affect religious leaders; religious identity is complex, uncertain and ambiguous, and often suffers from very volatile situations. Finally, a number of recommendations are gleaned from this analysis, suggesting that deep personal change, safe spaces for open dialogue, a concern for relevant (religious) identity (at group and intergroup levels), as well as spirituality, are vital dimensions of self-leadership that these religious leaders ably demonstrate. The conclusion notes several of these aspects for further research and development of self-leadership.

Examples of religious self-leadership to a VUCA context

This chapter begins with three examples of self-leadership by innovative and adaptive Christian leaders in a quickly changing and uncertain environment. Each of them is unique and yet also paradigmatic for similar leaders. Their self-leadership is characterised by a willingness to learn from empirical observation through close observation and listening, a high degree of emotional regulation and intrinsic motivation, and a willingness to adapt to their context without losing their vision, integrity or identity. Other elements of self-leadership include optimism, resilience, transparency, openness for diversity and orientation towards collaboration.

The first story of a religious leader is about Rick Warren, the founder and pastor of what became the megachurch, Saddleback Church. Although Warren was a successful seminary student and received several offers for pastoring a church, he and his wife packed up everything and moved to Saddleback Valley in California, a place they had carefully researched by studying US census data. In 1980, they started their first meetings in a rented apartment, with no money and with a clear fundamentalist stance. About a decade and many facilities later, the church reached 10,000 members and continued to grow well beyond 20,000, spawning dozens of church plants in the meantime and developing a large international church network with over 40,000 churches. Warren's *Purpose-Driven Church* became a well-known church growth book among Christian pastors, and his *Purpose-Driven Life* was on the *New York Times* best-seller list for over two years.[3]

Warren deliberately kept his distance from denominational affairs within the Southern Baptist Convention in the 1980s, believing that authenticity and the personal

---

3   Warren, 1995; 2012.

search for the purpose would soon be more important than denominational loyalty and spirituality. He learned to focus on purpose in life and church from a long-term friendship with Peter Drucker, one of his mentors.

He also oriented himself very methodically to reaching unbelievers, refusing to simply pastor those already part of a particular church. He studied the social and cultural characteristics of the 'typical' dweller in Saddleback Valley, and labeled this person "Saddleback Sam." His efforts led him to design worship services where everything was geared to enable unbelievers to understand and participate, including his "preaching on purpose" method. He thus focused on growth and large-scale gatherings, realising that even in a highly individualised culture, people still flocked to collective gatherings such as concerts and festivals. As some commentators have stated, "The pastor needed to be a great entrepreneur because inside the nova effect growth mattered more than ever."[4] Warren's purpose-driven model of church was then personalised in the Christian life as a life aligned with God's purposes, which was a form of personal spirituality well suited for a highly individualised and authentic age.[5]

Warren's leadership became a model for followers. He focuses on his strengths and empowers others to serve in their unique way. He dresses like an average guy in Saddleback Valley, and sometimes preaches in a Hawaiian shirt and sandals, visibly showing that he is simply one of the guys. Unlike many celebrities, Warren did not up-scale his house or car when his books became bestsellers; he practices what he calls "reverse tithing", living off 10% of his income and giving away the rest, exemplifying a generous lifestyle. Remarkably, he also connects with famous music artists, dialogues with presidents from various parties, and manages to maintain both a pro-life and a pro-poverty perspective. His focus on non-churched people, on outsiders, is thus something that he lives out every day at all societal levels.

Warren demonstrates several self-leadership characteristics. His leadership is not primarily driven by the beliefs, values and norms he learned in seminary, although he identified and still identifies as a conservative evangelical (some would label him a fundamentalist). Instead, Warren demonstrates willingness and skill to learn from practical observations and empirical data, engaging in the circle of self-leadership (similar to Kolb's circle of learning) that some scholars find to be typical of self-leadership.[6]

Moreover, Warren is intrinsically motivated, for he started and continues to lead in ways that have little external or social support among his peers. He exercises a great deal of emotional regulation and self-management to lead people by design towards spiritual growth, putting their emotional and cognitive support ahead of his comforts. Warren can act independently with credibility and thus generates the willing

---

4   Lee & Sinitiere, 2009: 144.

5   See the chapters on Warren in Lee and Sinitiere, 2009:129–48; Root, 2019: 125–49.

6   Stewart, Courtright & Manz, 2011.

commitment of others to his style of church. The church and its leadership foster an atmosphere of creativity and innovation, while trust in the team and the church community is generally high.[7]

This brings us to the second story of religious leadership in a VUCA world, namely that of Nico Van Splunter, who started a new initiative in 2004 in Spangen, a formerly upper-class but now impoverished, degraded and completely de-churched neighborhood of Rotterdam, the Netherlands.[8] The median income is low and unemployment is high, with many people from non-Western backgrounds. Churches in the neighborhood had closed long ago, which was a concern for a nearby Protestant church whose people were white, middle class, and highly educated. The leadership realised that most people from Spangen would never set foot in their church, so they started a pioneering initiative to find a way of being church that would connect with Spangen's inhabitants.

In this neighborhood, van Splunter points out the construction container/office that now gathers children to play and borrow toys. Van Splunter had discovered that most of the neighborhood kids wandered the streets aimlessly, so the idea arose to offer them a place to play with toys and games they would never own. Elsewhere in Spangen, a schoolroom that functions as a daycare centre during the week is rearranged every Sunday to host 30 to 50 people – often entire families from a non-Western background – for worship. Van Splunter baptised half of them in the outside pool of the neighborhood playground. This small church is orthodox in conviction and very practical in its functioning: "…swimming lessons, language study, healthy meals, physical exercise, children's activities, affordable housing for young people", which were realised through the personal neighborhood network of this pastor.[9]

Van Splunter's leadership evidences various characteristics of self-leadership.[10] After his university education in theology, he served as a church planter in Amsterdam before coming to Rotterdam in 2010 (see his LinkedIn webpage).[11] Although connected with the IZB (Internal Mission Board) of the Protestant Church of the Netherlands, he is not denominationally oriented ("don't think *for* people what you think they need"), but engages in close listening to the people in the neighbourhood. Evaluating the many and varied answers to his frequent question, "What does this neighborhood need?", he discerned one common thread: belonging/connection, so he started a neighborhood BBQ (among other things). He manages himself and his leadership role in a way that adapts to the context, rather than operating from a pre-existing leadership framework.

---

7   Neck & Houghton, 2006.

8   Meijer, 2019; Geloven in Spangen, 2020.

9   Meijer, 2019.

10 Manz & Sims, 2001.

11 Nico Van Splunter LinkedIn webpage: https://www.linkedin.com/in/nico-van-splunter-98610713/?originalSubdomain=nl

Van Splunter also networks with people across a broad social and religious spectrum: the neighborhood policeman, the soccer club, a local government centre for youth and family, school board members and city officials, as well as with several church networks in the city. He moves with ease across religious and social boundaries to connect Spangen inhabitants and their needs with others and their resources. As Van Splunter lives and moves in this web of relationships, he models the bridge-building skills that are necessary in the fragile social fabric of Spangen.

Van Splunter also manifests a high degree of optimism and resilience. He transparently shares his doubts as he is frequently confronted with hopeless poverty, and observes the endless neighbourhood quarrels. Yet time and again, Van Splunter moves with confidence into another venture, such as a pop-up beauty salon in their neighborhood centre, complete with volunteer hairdressers and nail stylists, to reach into their community during the Christmas season. Time will tell if this activity bears repeating the next Christmas. Van Splunter isn't worried: he will not flog a dead horse, he drily comments – one of the lessons he has learned in pioneer ministry.[12]

The third story comes from two pastors in more traditional churches, drawn from interview research reported elsewhere.[13] In a medium size city in the Eastern US, a Baptist and a Presbyterian pastor, both around the age of 40, were hired by their church boards (with mostly people over age 50) to bring about change. The Presbyterian pastor framed this leadership challenge as in line with their tradition. His church was part of a respected centuries-old tradition, which was visibly enacted by their meeting in a historic downtown building. Continuity with the past was vital, yet innovation was necessary. The Baptist pastor framed his leadership challenge as a major break with tradition, ready to lead the church into new directions. This aligned him with the Baptist tradition, with its emphasis on revival and renewal. Here, the very act of leading change was a way of affirming one's connection with one's history. Innovation was vital, yet continuity with the past was also necessary. Interestingly, both pastors approached their task in leadership as a collaborative effort, respecting the fact that their church boards were older and more experienced than they, and that they lived in an environment where answers were no longer easily determined in a top-down leadership strategy.

Their example, too, demonstrates important marks of self-leadership. Both pastors have succeeded in adapting their leadership to the particular historical and theological values of the church that called them to lead. They framed their leadership differently and adaptively to fit that particular context, even though both were called to the similar challenge of initiating change. Both were consciously self-aware of their leadership role and how it would be perceived among their constituency. Also, both of these pastors were oriented more towards those outside than was typical for their predecessors.

---

12 Meijer, 2019.

13 Barentsen, 2015.

They were not focused exclusively on outsiders like Warren or Van Splunter, but they brought a new orientation in this direction to their leadership.

Their self-leadership models various qualities, such as close listening, resilience, transparency, openness to diversity and collaboration, in a way that is not unique to their religious context. These and other elements of self-leadership are highly relevant in various other contexts, such as in civil service, education, healthcare and the military.

Theoretical reflections on religious self-leadership

These three stories bring together quite different scenarios of religious leadership in a VUCA context. Together, they provide input for theoretical reflections about self-leadership in a VUCA environment.

The three stories demonstrate a deliberate shift in focus towards outsiders as part of their leadership focus. The leaders combined their innovative efforts to reach outsiders with a theologically conservative understanding of the gospel. Thus, these leaders adapted their leadership to devote new energies to external demands, both in their practice of including at least some outsiders and in rethinking their leadership theologically or ideologically. None of these leaders are strongly hierarchical, but act collaboratively to bring established and new worshippers together in a new sense of mission and belonging.

Yet their leadership practices are also very diverse. Warren serves the local white professionals in Silicon Valley, who are highly mobile change agents in their work; typically networked with professionals in other cities; and religious outsiders. Warren leads explicitly by his purpose-driven vision, drawing in thousands in their search for their life's purpose. The combination of this white professional context with a purpose-driven strategy enabled the growth of a mega-church with substantial international networks, yet based on local presence and connections.

Van Splunter also adopted a local approach, serving among under-resourced and (often) migrant populations in an impoverished, run-down city district, who were often estranged from church and religion. Although these people, too, might have international networks (i.e. their families in their native countries), such networks often serve to secure further access to Western resources for migrant families. Thus language and cultural learning, building a local basis for survival and inviting family members to migrate, and similar life tasks characterise these folks.[14] A new religious neighborhood community with such mixed people in a context of poverty has less potential to become a megachurch; its lack of resources limits mobility and large-scale organisations and buildings, while its international connections do not necessarily facilitate a worldwide network of partnership. Indeed, thousands of small, local communities are led by thousands of entrepreneurial religious leaders, mostly unknown outside of their own

---

14 Brugman, 2009.

urban or denominational circles. Van Splunter's leadership might be characterised as visionary, but only by working with and through people with great discernment, not by bringing a vision 'from the outside' and realising it with whoever shows up in support.

Finally, the two city pastors also demonstrated a local approach. They became part of an established church, yet hoped to bring change and renewed growth. These leaders collaborated with established local leaders to nurture new sensitivity to the local context. Slowly, a new vision began to take shape in the minds and discussion of the broader leadership in these churches.

These diverse stories of religious leadership illustrate that the social boundaries of religious communities decrease in clarity and value, and that as a result religious identity becomes fuzzy and contested. Consequently, religious leadership is no longer a matter of maintaining tradition and safeguarding community boundaries, a trend that has been signaled broadly in other types of organisations and their leadership.[15] A more collaborative and interpretive leadership style is required, enabling 'followers' to dialogue and find consensus amidst diversity, and to adapt or transform their socio-religious identity. This changes not only the religious identity of the community, but also the leader identity of the religious leader. Considering the studies on clergy role ambiguity and burnout,[16, 17] this indeed puts increasing stress on the religious leader and his or her leader identity, which is typically shaped and sustained by specific religious sources of meaning and identity.

A leadership theory that addresses the complexity and diversity of religious and other identities is the social identity model of leadership.[18] Social identity is a sense of belonging that is generated by a sense of affinity with a particular group identity. Leadership is then considered to derive from particular group dynamics, whereby some members are considered more "prototypical" than others with reference to group identity, so that such exemplary group members have greater influence and ability to lead the group. Moreover, social identity is a comparative phenomenon; identity is always shaped in comparison with other groups in a particular context. Religious leadership may be described as a form of identity leadership.[19, 20] The recommendations below will make use of this theory.

15 Barentsen, Kessler & van den Heuvel, 2018.
16 Faucett, Corwyn & Poling, 2013.
17 Tomic, Tomic & Evers, 2004.
18 Haslam, Reicher & Platow, 2011.
19 Carroll, 2011.
20 Barentsen, 2015; 2016.

Religious self-leadership as response to VUCA contexts

One of the reasons that religious leadership has grown to be more sensitive to self-leadership is the growing awareness of the complexity and volatility of Western societies, and the inability of older versions of more hierarchical forms of religious leadership to meet the needs of their constituencies while maintaining the vitality, relevance and growth of their communities in a VUCA world. Although this section focuses on the VUCA context of religious leadership, very similar issues play out in other societal sectors, such as in government and civil service.

Religious institutions face multiple challenges in the secular West. The increasing impact of a thorough-going individualism combines with the effect of social media on relationships to erode old-style collective religious identities based on geography and ideology. Both the village church and the city cathedral were once geographically rooted and ideologically defined. Such religious institutions were trusted, representing broadly accepted collective identities that offered social cohesion and security. However, the increasing autonomy of the individual (in the West), the ability to connect with others through social media based on individual preferences, and the availability of immense amounts of information, render such collective identities less valuable and significant in people's daily lives. The decline of religious institutions since the 1960s is therefore not an exclusive story of declining church membership; rather, this decline participates in the far broader societal Western trend of deinstitutionalisation.[21]

The Polish-British sociologist Zygmunt Bauman famously captured this development with his concept of liquid modernity. Indeed, modernism was largely a project of advancing the world by melting down the 'solids' of earlier societies, which often took the shape of dethroning tradition and "profaning the sacred."[22] Applying this to religious institutions, this liquefaction involves the shift from the cohesion provided by such religious institutions and their collective identities, to the ever-shifting demands of hyper-individualism, with "religious bricolage" as the climax to individual religious identity.[23] Even so, this individualism is deeply disciplined by the algorithms of modern tech giants whose data mining results in 'personalised advertising', which turns millions of unconnected individuals into fairly predictable 'swarms' that form new, albeit rather fleeting, economic collectivities.[24] This liquefaction is seen in the democratisation of information, now readily and everywhere available with the click of a button. It appears that people no longer flock to leaders because of their (presumed) access to privileged information or for access to certain social networks.

---

21 Ammerman, 2003.

22 Bauman, 2000:2–4.

23 Saroglou, 2006.

24 Westjohn, Singh & Magnusson, 2012.

Where institutions often brought a geographical or ideological sense of homogeneity and unity in relationships, institutional liquefaction leads to increasing diversity among especially city populations, and an increasing diversity of religious organisations, faith communities and much more.[25, 26]

In this highly dynamic, quickly changing and uncertain context, various types of religious communities, movements, networks and start-ups arise to fill the void left by religious institutions. Denominational networks now have to share their social and religious place with both new global religious networks[27] and innumerable local religious initiatives.[28] International initiatives may involve new networks of charismatic churches and their leaders,[29] but may also originate with more institutional religious forms, such as the city-to-city network originating with Redeemer Presbyterian Church in New York City.[30] Local initiatives are often labelled with terms like 'Fresh Expressions' or 'pioneer places'.[31] These are not new locations for traditional forms of church, but new forms of community often focused on particular local needs, where religion is a small or developing part of the community's identity. Finally, digital media facilitate the rise of new networks of religious leadership, such as The European Leadership Forum (euroleadership.org), the Forum of Christian Leaders (foclonline.org), and networks for church planters (icpnetwork.nl; m4europe.com).

These developments can be interpreted as religious leadership responses to the VUCA environment. The described complexity generates levels of religious ambiguity that exceed what previous generations had to cope with. Religious belonging is no longer institutionally anchored by geography and ideology. Instead, a wide variety of religious worldviews, experiences, rituals and practices compete for public attention.[32] These offerings are widely available through digital channels, but they also flood local bookshops, libraries and community centres. Many people pick and choose experiences and rituals along with pieces of worldview, to match their personal preferences, even if they would identify primarily with one particular faith community or religious tradition. However, that identification is no longer a barrier to participation in religious activities outside of that tradition. Where previous generations considered such multi-participation as contradictory with one's primary faith commitment, or even as a betrayal to one's faith community, newer generations have less difficulty combining various elements in their religious bricolage.[33] The nature of religious commitment

25 Vertovec, 2015.

26 Barentsen, Kessler & van den Heuvel, 2018.

27 Christerson & Flory, 2017.

28 Roxburgh, 2010.

29 Bangura, 2018.

30 Powell & James, 2019.

31 Goodhew, Roberts & Volland, 2012; Vellekoop, 2015.

32 Carrette & King, 2005.

33 Berghuijs, 2017; Cornille, 2010.

and the meaning of religious identity have become unclear, and the factors leading to religious commitment are difficult to determine.

In this complex and ambiguous environment, religious institutions, communities and organisations struggle to respond. Their religious claims often aimed to provide clarity of purpose and vision, generate a sense of stability and security, and foster strong motivation to mobilise people for a common cause. However, stability and security appear fleeting in today's VUCA world, and one can no longer easily predict what will motivate people and for what cause. Thus, religious belonging no longer generates the sense of certainty it once did, while the outcomes of religious involvement are uncertain and cannot easily be predicted.

Finally, volatility is an important but often underestimated factor in religious life. Public scandals over high-profile (and 'ordinary') religious leaders can erupt without notice, causing unexpected damage to religious leaders and the reputation of entire religious traditions. Concern over religiously motivated violence has, on occasion, led to drastic administrative measures to protect people against sectarian terrorism; for instance, several European nations generated lists of suspicious organisations that unexpectedly included many Christian denominations. Public sensitivities about sexual orientation and gay rights have occasionally led to explosive situations, with preachers or churches suddenly at the centre of public attention. Religious communities and movements pop up here and there, surprising established religious institutions that suddenly lose dozens of members to such newcomers.

The religious leaders whose stories were told in the examples cope with their VUCA environments by listening closely to their contexts and their people, by nurturing trust and openness in dialogue to move forward, and by collaborative leadership to discern the right balance between innovation and continuity. Their hope and resilience inspired others to stick together through enduring uncertainty and ambiguity without resorting to quick fixes and simplistic solutions. Through these aspects of self-leadership, they were able to shape or adapt the socio-religious identities of their faith communities in ways that were meaningful to their constituencies, as well as relevant for other sectors in society and public life in general.

Recommendations for self-leadership in a VUCA context

Navigating an uncertain and ambiguous environment presents significant challenges to religious leaders, who are often expected to use religious concepts and narratives to reduce uncertainty and ambiguity. This is not unlike many leaders in politics or government service, who provide leadership for multiple constituencies at a time of reduced institutional power and security. Current worldwide trends manifest various leaders who attempt to reduce ambiguity and enhance security by creating a polarising and often conflictual perspective on "us versus them." What recommendations for self-leadership are suggested by the religious leaders from the case studies that move instead towards reconciliation and peace?

First, organisational change does not simply require a few extra skills in change management or even conflict resolution; change starts within ourselves. Leading change involves a deep change in how one sees oneself and one's leadership in a rapidly changing context.[34] Each of the leaders from the case studies deliberately reconceived their own role as leader. They did not conform to existing patterns and expectations, sensing that a different type of leadership was necessary. And yet, they did not lose themselves in the complexity of their situations, nor did they lose touch with others on their teams. Instead, their openness, hope and transparency created an atmosphere where the leaders themselves, as well as their co-leaders, could change. Thus, organisational leadership and organisational change starts with reconceiving one's leader identity, which is a form of self-leadership, which is also where peace leadership begins.[35]

Second, the contexts within which these four religious leaders serve are marked by complexity and uncertainty. Frequently, many complex elements interact so that lines of cause and effect are no longer traceable; they are non-linear, non-predictable and non-stable. (Religious) leaders do not, and cannot, know the future. Hence, a key leadership task is to open spaces for dialogue in a context where both leaders and followers can be honest and transparent, because no one person is able to grasp the full complexity of the situation; there is room for doubt and uncertainty.[36] Within a context of open dialogue and trust, anxieties can be changed to healthy concerns that drive religious and social engagement in innovative ways. These features of self-leadership are also important building blocks for peace leadership.[37]

Third, religious leaders are identity leaders par excellence.[38] While companies and schools have particular social identities to serve their constituencies, religious communities are often more deeply invested in their allegiance to their religious identity; it is a treasured marker for how to live and express one's faith. Religious communities do not exist primarily to offer certain religious services (although they do), nor to cater to everyone's personal search for life's purpose (although they do so as well). They connect a diversity of people in particular expressions and practices of faith which are the foundation of their socio-religious identity. Many religious communities struggle with open boundaries, increasing diversity, one's sense of belonging, and new ways of religious meaning-making. Within forms of identity leadership, the (religious) leader often serves as a prototype or model for the community, embodying in his or her

---

34 Quinn, 1996.

35 van Zyl & Campbell, 2018.

36 Stanton, 2019.

37 McIntyre-Miller, 2016.

38 Hogg, Van Knippenberg & Rast, 2012a.

leadership the beliefs and practices of the community.[39, 40] At the core, the challenge for religious leaders, as for many other types of leaders, is to reshape the social and civic identities that are deeply challenged by a VUCA environment.[41]

Intergroup leadership is a feature of more recently developed forms of identity leadership.[42] This, too, is visible in the three leadership stories above. Warren and Van Splunter deliberately move beyond the boundaries of traditional religious identities to create new forms of community that may or may not fit with older models of religious identity. The Presbyterian and Baptist pastors start from within a traditional socio-religious identity, but innovate by adding activities and programmes that reach beyond traditional church boundaries. Such leaders are not simply concerned with the cohesion and identity of their religious community, but actively seek to connect it with outsiders in ways that are meaningful for all involved. Such intergroup leadership again involves a reconception of one's own role and identity as leader, and thus can be seen as an aspect of self-leadership.

Finally, a focus on spirituality is vital. Spirituality did not surface explicitly in the stories and the subsequent reflections, in part because the frame of self-leadership typically does not include leader or organisational spirituality as one of its considerations, yet there is now a steady stream of research on spiritual leadership (e.g. Fry, 2003; Barentsen, 2014; Allison, Kocher & Goethals, 2017). Self-leadership theory would benefit from taking on board some of the theory and concerns of spiritual leadership as defined within the broader discipline of leadership studies. Moreover, it is sometimes hard to observe leader spirituality directly in our three stories; it is often noticed indirectly in particular leader practices, although it could be directly investigated through interviews or by participation with these leaders in some of their personal spiritual practices. Hence, the spiritual aspect remained somewhat hidden in the arguments above. Yet, it is a vital aspect for religious leaders, whose hope and resilience are often grounded in particular spiritual practices of contemplation, Scripture reading, theological discernment and more. The willingness to adapt (or not) is often intimately connected to particular spiritual understandings and spiritual practices. Fortunately, spirituality has been recognised as a vital force in church renewal and pastoral leadership.[43, 44]

---

39 Barentsen, 2016.

40 Barentsen, Kessler & van den Heuvel, 2018.

41 Elliott, 2016.

42 Hogg Van Knippenberg & Rast, 2012b.

43 Hornikx, 2002.

44 Johnson & Dreitcer, 2001.

CONCLUDING REMARKS

The challenge of self-leadership for religious leaders

The VUCA world presents a formidable challenge to religious leadership, which is typically oriented towards sustaining religious life along the lines of traditional practices and beliefs, often within particular institutional forms. Although various religious leaders opt for fundamentalist strategies to resist these tendencies, which may at times lead to conflictual situations,[45] the case studies presented in this chapter demonstrate that other leadership strategies are more fruitful in leading towards reconciliation and peace. These case studies present some religious leaders who interacted with their VUCA environment by deep change in how they interpreted their own leadership role and identity, by opening themselves up to close listening and learning from their changing context, and by fostering open and honest dialogue so that uncertainties and doubts could be expressed and considered, even if resolution was not immediately possible.

For the future development of self-leadership, it seems evident that forms of innovation or entrepreneurial leadership should be considered for their potential in coping with a VUCA environment. But a VUCA world demands more than innovation, since it deeply challenges institutional, organisational and community identities at the group and individual, but especially intergroup, levels. Identity leadership, as developed within mainstream social identity theory, holds much promise in navigating groups through turbulent times in peaceful ways, while maintaining or adapting their social, civic and religious identities. In addition, the dimension of spirituality, as it is currently being investigated in theories of spiritual leadership, was suggested as a vital but hardly noticed dimension of self-leadership. Finally, the concept of leader identity and its development surfaced late in the above arguments, suggesting that it too may present a fruitful angle in the further investigation of self-leadership.

---

45 Herriot, 2007.

PART SIX

LOOKING AHEAD, OUTCOMES, RECOMMENDATIONS, AND CONCLUSIONS

CHAPTER 16

LOOKING AHEAD: STRATEGIC LEADING ONESELF SKILLS IN VUCA ENVIRONMENTS

Andrew Campbell

ABSTRACT

As the international environment increasingly becomes interconnected, the disruption from local, intercommunal, national and international events frequently drives instability and turbulence within the global operational environment. This turbulence impacts the full spectrum of daily life. In a world that is no longer predictable and stable, existing leadership frameworks and competencies need to be expanded with the capability to navigate chaos under stressful conditions. This chapter presents two sections: first, it examines the three layers of strategic leadership as leaders engage with the demands in a VUCA context. Second, a proposed innovative self-leadership framework with competencies and capabilities is presented to assist leaders in this new reality of leading in a chaotic and stressful environment.

INTRODUCTION

At the time of this writing, the spread of COVID-19 from Wuhan in China has caused political instability and economic disruption that is testing leaders' abilities to solve complex, wicked problems. The COVID-19 crisis is an unprecedented multi-disciplinary global and organisational leadership challenge that is not only hard to understand, but also chaotic. However, COVID-19 has revealed that leading wicked problems that are multi-dimensional, where actions in one domain drive consequences within another with unpredictable outcomes, are creating innovative ways of leading under stressful conditions.

The global pandemic shows that traditional leadership tools and frameworks that rely on predictability and certainty based on data analysis for strategic decisions are ineffective in a fluid and highly disruptive situation. For example, President Trump enacted targeted international travel restrictions and announced that COVID-19 would have a limited health and economic impact on United States. His actions and strategic messaging were based on predictive data analyses, yet shortly afterwards, as information changed along with national strategies on a daily basis. As policy makers create and announce on the management and treatment of COVID 19, the rapidly changing day-to-day information resulted in conflicting communication and distrust among leader's and general public. As a result, national health situation reached dangerous levels requiring personal quarantines and resulting in economic devastation. COVID 19 revealed the national, corporate, and academic leadership challenge of organizationally transforming and reshaping how to lead in this new terrain of uncertain, volatile, and complex environment. Overall, leaders have been unprepared and lack the complex problem-solving leadership capacity to strategically navigate within a volatile, uncertain, complex, and ambiguous operational environment handling.

As the international environment increasingly becomes interconnected, the disruption from local, intercommunal, national and international events frequently drive instability and turbulence within the global operational environment. This turbulence impacts the full spectrum of daily life. In a world that is no longer predictable and stable, existing leadership frameworks and competencies need to be expanded with the ability to navigate chaos under stressful conditions. This chapter presents two sections: first, it will examine the three layers of strategic leadership as leaders engage in the demands within a VUCA context. Second, a proposed innovative self-leadership framework with skills is presented to assist leaders in this new reality of leading in chaotic and stressful environments.

STRATEGIC LEADERSHIP

Much of the literature points out that while leading change in a crisis is complex and uncertain, most scholar-practitioners believe that strategic leadership principles provide the underpinning of leading within a VUCA context.[1] According to Tiefenbacher[2], "there is a great deal of research confirming that one of the most important components of managing VUCA is the strategy and strategic management." According to Hambert and Cannella[3], strategic leadership "focuses on the executives who have overall responsibility for an organization—their characteristics, what they do, how they do it, and particularly how they affect organizational outcomes." The scholars also identified three layers of strategic leadership in a VUCA world.

The first critical layer for strategic leadership in managing chaos and uncertainty is the leader's capacity for strategic foresight to scan the ecosystem for emerging issues and anticipate organisational disruptive events that may detract from desired outcomes. The challenge for leaders is to have the strategic foresight to anticipate

---

1   Fuchs, Messner & Sok, 2018.

2   Tiefenbacher, 2019.

3   Hambert, Finkelstein & Cannella, 2009: 5.

internal and/or external forces on the organisation, to calmly assess the situation with limited information, and to connect the dots to prevent unintended consequences.[4] That said, strategic foresight is an important leadership attribute in a VUCA context because without the ability to anticipate organisational threats and assess unpredictable incidents, leaders will blindly suggest actions and make ill-informed decisions. "Most organizations and leaders are poor at detecting ambiguous threats and opportunities on the periphery of their business."[5] Theorists suggest that strategic foresight "enable(s) leaders and managers to broaden their perceptions of what and how the future possibilities may unfold, as to identify and evaluate the strategic options for decision making and resource mobilization to achieve the medium to long term vision."[6]

The second critical layer is the leader's capacity to think strategically about complex problems and envision what can be accomplished within an evolving public or private setting.[7] The nature of strategic thinking is complex and multi-dimensional. *The Harvard Business Review Guide to Thinking Strategically*[8] points out that "strategic thinking is about analyzing opportunities and problems from a broad perspective and understanding the potential impact your actions might have on the future of your organization, your team, or your bottom line." Strategic thinking is defined as the glue that integrates operational systems and organisational initiatives together in one company.[9] According to Dufour and Steane[10], strategic thinking answers three fundamental questions: where are we now, where do we want to be and how will we get there? As leaders assess the environment beyond the operational patterns and reconceptualise organisational threats, strategic thinkers not only explore out-of-the-box approaches, but also exploit future opportunities to solve wicked problems. Therefore, strategic thinkers must proactively anticipate unpredictable scenarios as well as determine what actions impact organisational goals and objectives by understanding the complexity and interconnectivity within an ecosystem. More importantly, strategic thinking sets the stage for strategic foresight and strategic planning to navigate in complex and unpredictable settings.[11]

While strategically navigating across rapidly changing environments, leaders need not only the strategic foresight and strategic thinking capability to rise above the daily managerial processes and think long-term; they also need to plan strategically to operationalise the strategies created through the strategic thinking process.

---

4 Cheah, 2020.
5 Shoemaker, Krupp & Holwand, 2019: 10.
6 Cheah, 2020: 3.
7 Harvard Business Review, 2019.
8 Ibid.
9 Tavakoli & Lawton, 2005.
10 Dufour & Steane, 2014.
11 Chevallier, 2016.

Maleka[12] suggested that strategic planning is "used to set priorities, focus energy and resources, strengthen operations, ensure that employees and other stakeholders are working toward common goals, establish agreement around intended outcomes/ results, and assess and adjust the organization's direction in response to a changing environment."[13] In times of complexity and uncertainty, leaders must convey a sense of purpose, priorities and direction with clarity across organisational vertical and horizontal layers to mitigate chaos within a complex and uncertain environment. The purpose of strategic planning is to provide an organisational blueprint by aligning the company's vision, mission, goals and objectives, as well as the short- and long-term measures of effectiveness and measures of performance, as strategic and organisational leaders make decisions toward transforming organisational actions.

The question facing strategic leaders is how to proactively create and implement strategic plans in an increasingly complex and rapidly changing technological environment. To illustrate, strategic planning in the private sector needs an adaptive and flexible organisational structure and process to quickly respond to unexpected disruptive events. In the public sector, strategic planning is rigid and inhibits an organisation's ability to create innovative ideas or other alternatives as senior leaders develop strategic plans to move the organisation forward. Thus, the authority and responsibility rests with strategic leaders to formulate the strategic plan; it should not be delegated to organisational leaders. It is important to note that strategic planning is the most important function of senior leaders within a business, academic, and peace development organisation.

Amidst chaos, strategic leaders are frequently bombarded with rapidly changing and conflicting information. The more uncertain and unpredictable events are, the harder it is for policy makers to predict the outcomes. Therefore, leaders must have the cognitive complexity and flexibility to adapt to the unknown in the midst of not only chaos, but also crisis environments.[14] That said, the COVID-19 pandemic has caused socio-ethno-economic and political national and international chaos. The lethality of COVID-19 surprised global political, business, and academic leaders. Given their unpreparedness when responding to the health and economic crises, leaders have relied on predictive data modelling to determine response actions and forecast outcomes. As time progressed, the spread of COVID-19 challenged the use of predictive modelling as a decision tool and created confusion as the dynamics of COVID-19 changed from one day to the next. In chaos, prioritisation, impulse control, and trusting relationships are not only critical, but essential. Nevertheless, the rapidly changing and unpredictable indicators require leaders to have the courage to make good decisions, even if they are unpopular and divisive, and own the outcomes. To

---

12 Maleka, 2014.

13 Ibid.

14 Chevallier, 2016.

illustrate, against the predictive modelling and advice of leading experts, President Trump had the strategic foresight to close air travel from China and limit travel from Europe. Leaders are only as effective as the decisions they make in the midst of chaos. During chaotic times, leaders must balance decisions that minimise risks with social, financial, political, economic and environmental considerations to provide sustainable outcomes. In short, leaders must shift from being reactionary to proactive when responding during times of organisational and operational chaos.

STRATEGIC LEADERSHIP FRAMEWORK IN A VUCA WORLD

Today, our world is routinely in crisis mode. The chaos of COVID-19 presents a new disaster every week, plunging leaders considered top-notch performers under normal operations into a world of chaos and uncertainty. When it comes to leading under stressful conditions, leading oneself is quite different in a crisis than leading oneself in a time of normal conditions. Hence, as leaders seek certainty in an unpredictable context, the reliance on traditional strategic approaches frequently does not work. According to Kok and van den Heuvel, leaders have come "to realize that our old cognitive models do not fit this new world and what the new landscape demands of us."[15] Up to this point, leaders have been attempting to make strategic decisions in an unpredictable and complex environment using conventional leadership practices and decision-making processes. For that reason, to thrive in a VUCA context, organisational and strategic leaders need to unlearn long established patterns of leadership behaviours and engage with new emerging strategic leadership and management tools.[16, 17]

Figure 16.1 shows the basic leadership skills required to lead oneself in times of non-crisis. The list of skills reflects the belief that a set of competencies can be identified and are necessary to lead oneself. Therefore, Figure 16-1 presents a construct where leading oneself in a volatile, uncertain, complex, and ambiguous environment leverages not only conventional basic leadership skills such as trust building, decision making, and problem solving but also a set of critical additive needed core capabilities such as sensemaking, authenticity, and mindset to lead oneself during times of chaos. In VUCA situations, leaders are frequently ill-equipped to handle unpredictable conditions and are prone to making well-meaning yet disastrous decisions in the heat of the moment. In situations as fluid as the coronavirus outbreak, many leaders are naturally drawn to a more protective leadership mindset and behaviours. This may include defensiveness, denial, blaming others,

---

15 Kok & van den Heuvel, 2019.

16 Shoemaker et al., 2019.

17 Tiefenbacher, 2019.

and intransigence in the face of changing facts on the ground. However, basic essential skills such as critical thinking, collaboration, shared leadership, and authenticity are necessary as leaders navigate the unknown to counter volatility with visioning, uncertainty with understanding, complexity with clarity, and ambiguity with adaptability in the heat of the moment.

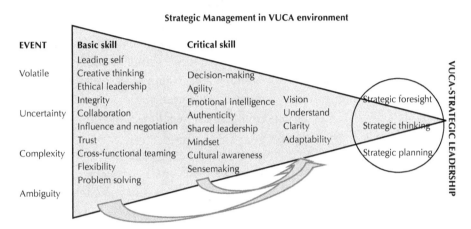

Strategic Management in VUCA environment

EVENT	Basic skill	Critical skill		
	Leading self			
Volatile	Creative thinking	Decision-making		
	Ethical leadership	Agility		
	Integrity	Emotional intelligence	Vision	Strategic foresight
Uncertainty	Collaboration	Authenticity	Understand	
	Influence and negotiation	Shared leadership	Clarity	Strategic thinking
	Trust	Mindset	Adaptability	
Complexity	Cross-functional teaming	Cultural awareness		Strategic planning
	Flexibility	Sensemaking		
	Problem solving			
Ambiguity				

VUCA-STRATEGIC LEADERSHIP

Figure 16.1 Strategic Leadership skills in VUCA Environments

The success or failure of self-leadership directly correlates to the development and depth of leading self with character. The basic skill of leading oneself rests on one's personal source of energy and individual strength to guide one's choices and actions in meeting wicked challenges associated with chaos situations. Leading oneself with integrity and a high set of ethical standards is an internalised set of values and beliefs. Thus, leading oneself demonstrates a willingness to accept the personal consequences of making difficult decisions, and establishes trust and credibility. More importantly, the leader's level of integrity lays the foundation to not only influence key individuals to gain cooperation from others, but also to negotiate and persuade others to find solutions to wicked problems during chaotic situations. The internal value of integrity in leading oneself fosters a climate where leaders influence and negotiate with others across conventional boundaries, while collaborating in constructive ways by addressing shared concerns and adapting to the turmoil of uncertainty. In other words, the basic leadership skills of problem solving, influence, negotiation, integrity and flexibility undergird leading oneself in times of adaptability, understanding the nuances of stressful conditions on decision-making, and embarking on a drive for clarity in the midst of confusion and in the heat of the moment.

During a crisis, the basic leadership skills undergird the critical skills through emotional intelligence, authenticity, and sensemaking in leading oneself. Emotional intelligence is important in leading oneself through self-awareness of the internal and external dialogues that a leader discusses within themselves and with others. Bass and Bass stated that emotional intelligence "is a state of mind."[18] The development of emotional intelligence components such as self-awareness, impulse control, and empathy will enhance the leadership-follower relationship through trust, the projection of self-confidence in one's decision making process, and authenticity – all necessary skills for leading oneself in chaos situations. Conversely, a lack of awareness of one's emotional triggers, such as frustration with rapidly changing information, fear of making the wrong decision, and loss of control of one's actions, can frequently derail the effectiveness of one's leadership capability under stressful conditions. Thus, an awareness and management of one's emotional triggers provide the relational capacity to calmly lead others in highly charged events. Essentially, the additive capability of emotionally intelligent leadership and authenticity sets the conditions for leaders to strategically navigate through the chaos.

In a crisis, much more than during normal operations, mature leaders with basic and critical leadership skills lay the foundation for strategic leaders to anticipate, manage and transform chaos into a stable conclusion. As a strategic leader develops the relational capacity to authentically lead from their personal core and convictions, leaders can calmly communicate complex ideas with clarity and adapt in a highly charged environment.[19] Mannherz[20] argued that a strategic leader "in a VUCA world seems to be an open-minded visionary with great communication skills, the ability to continuously scan his environments for potential opportunities and threats, and an empathic developer of teams and its individual team members."[21] That said, leaders who can think and act strategically understand the importance of identifying emerging trends and patterns, listening to and empowering others to think outside of the box, driving high levels of collaboration and accountability, and decentralising decision-making when navigating and adapting in the midst of chaos. In other words, the gift of leading oneself is having the inner strength of developing one's emotional intelligence to lead authentically with conviction and character-based leadership during times of chaos.

---

18 Bass & Bass, 2008: 1070.
19 Bawany, 2016.
20 Mannherz, 2017.
21 Ibid.

CONCLUDING REMARKS

This chapter addressed the challenges of leading oneself in an unpredictable and rapidly changing environment. The geo-political and socio-economic disruptions of COVID-19 illustrate the strategic leadership challenge of leading oneself and others through a VUCA environment; organisations that face VUCA situations like COVID-19 experience disruption and chaos in the personal and operational environments. Therefore, as organisations navigate through wicked challenges, the tenets of strategic foresight, strategic thinking and strategic planning provide the underpinning of strategic leadership within a VUCA context. A strategic leadership framework identified basic and critical leadership skills, such as strategic thinking, critical thinking, mindful focus, collaboration, empathy, problem solving, emotional intelligence and authenticity, that are critical benchmarks for all strategic leaders during a crisis. The gift is leading oneself in stressful and uncertain VUCA conditions with the inner resource of character-based leadership and authenticity.

CHAPTER 17

LEADING ONESELF IN UNCERTAIN AND COMPLEX ENVIRONMENTS: OUTCOMES, RECOMMENDATIONS AND CONCLUDING THOUGHTS

Ebben van Zyl

ABSTRACT

In a world that is no longer predictable and stable, new leadership frameworks and skills are required to help us navigate difficult circumstances. In this chapter the outcomes of the book (general leading oneself themes, as well as leading oneself skills per different environments), are discussed first. Secondly, general recommendations (indicating which of the already identified most prominent leading oneself skills can be applied to help the 21st century leader adapt to difficult demands) and specific recommendations are given. Lastly, concluding thoughts (indicating why chaos can indeed be considered as a gift), will be discussed.

INTRODUCTION

Kornelsen[1] claimed that leadership is typically influenced by three components, namely the leader, the follower, and the context. Currently, we are experiencing major challenges in both the general environment and the corporate world. At the time of writing, the coronavirus pandemic is having a very negative effect on the economic and political situation in most countries, making it very difficult for organisations to survive and thrive. Our environment can indeed be regarded as VUCA – volatile, uncertain, complex, and ambiguous. According to,[2] VUCA in plain language means: "Hey, it is absolutely crazy out there." The term describes the sense that, even with all our technological power, we are not in control, and the future is uncertain and complex.[3] For this reason, leadership, as well as the way we lead ourselves, becomes crucial in adapting to this new VUCA world.

---

1   Kornelsen, 2019.

2   Bennett & Lemoine, 2014.

3   Nullens, 2019.

This chapter will focus on three sections. First, the outcomes of the book (general leading oneself themes, as well as leading oneself skills per different environments) will be discussed. Secondly, general and specific recommendations are given, before the chapter ends with concluding thoughts.

OUTCOMES OF THE BOOK

General themes

The following leading oneself skills are emphasised in this book (Chapters 1-15) as skills which might help leaders, as well as non-leaders, to cope with VUCA situations (see Figure 17.1):

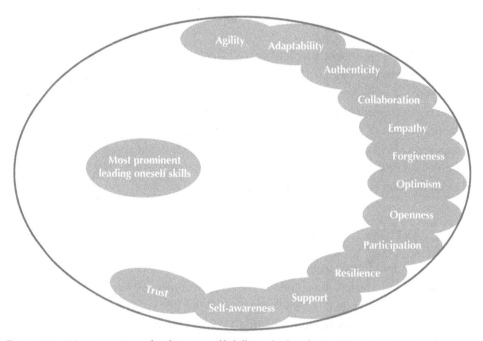

Figure 17.1: Most prominent leading oneself skills to deal with VUCA environments

From Figure 17.1, the following themes (leading oneself skills) can be identified as a way to deal with VUCA environments (also see Figure 17.2):

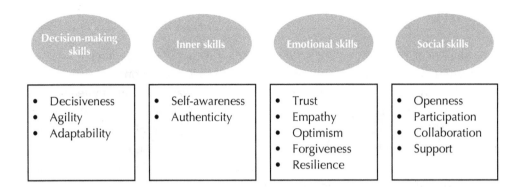

Figure 17.2: General themes based on the most prominent leading oneself skills for VUCA environments

Decision-making skills

Decision-making skills refer to one's proficiency in choosing between two or more alternatives.[4] In the context of VUCA environments, decisiveness, agility, and adaptability may help in dealing with complex situations.

Tsai Ing-wen, the president of Taiwan, demonstrated decisiveness by being among the first to respond to the coronavirus outbreak. At the first sign of the new disease in January 2020, she introduced 124 measures to block the spread without having to resort to a lockdown, which became the common response elsewhere in the world. Jacinda Ardern, the prime minister of New Zealand, was early to lock down, but provided clear explanations for the maximum level of alert under which she was putting the country. She imposed self-isolation on people entering New Zealand astonishingly early, when there were only six cases in the country, and banned foreigners from entering soon after. Decisiveness saved New Zealand from the storm.[5]

Zoom demonstrated agility by offering its platform for free to primary and secondary schools during the coronavirus pandemic. Stores around the world opened earlier than usual to allow safe shopping for senior citizens, and increased their delivery options for those who were homebound. The clothing industry helped to produce masks for governments to distribute among citizens. The leaders involved in these businesses and industries were clearly agile and adaptable, and made a huge contribution during difficult times.[6]

---

4   Veldsman & Johnson, 2016: 877.

5   Wittenberg-Cox, 2020: 2.

6   Wittenberg-Cox, 2020: 2.

Inner skills

Inner skills refer to a person's internal mind, soul, or nature.[7, 8] Being authentic and self-aware are such skills that will help one to deal with VUCA situations.

Nelson Mandela, having been jailed for 27 years, was self-aware by recognising and understanding his negative emotions and drives when he was elected president of South Africa in 1994. He was elected to be the president of all South Africans, including those who had sent him to jail, and he recognised the effect that negative feelings could have on reconciling the people of the country.9 In the process he also acted in an authentic manner; in other words, he was true and genuine to himself.[10]

Emotional skills

Emotional skills include the ability to recognise, express, and manage one's feelings and thoughts (Oxford Learners University Dictionary, 2020). Trust, empathy, optimism, resilience, and forgiveness can be regarded as emotional skills to apply when dealing with difficult VUCA situations.

Soon after the WHO declared the coronavirus pandemic, Angela Merkel, the chancellor of Germany, brought the severity of the situation to the citizens' attention, namely that the coronavirus was expected to infect up to 70% of the population. The relevant authorities showed enough trust in her to immediately start the process of widespread testing, avoiding the initial phases of denial, anger and disingenuousness, as was the case in many other countries.[11]

Jacinda Ardern showed empathy when she visited those affected by the murder of 50 people during prayers at two mosques in Christchurch on 15 March 2019. Wearing a black headscarf (hijab), she embraced and extended heartfelt condolences to families in mourning, and referred to the dead and wounded as "they are us." Ardern is an immensely popular and successful leader in New Zealand.[12] She also demonstrated optimism (being hopeful or confident about the future) by indicating that gun laws would be tightened, which was indeed implemented by the New Zealand parliament.[13]

Nelson Mandela demonstrated forgiveness by transforming himself from a political leader and freedom fighter to become the president of South Africa in 1994. He forgave those who had put him in jail in order to work towards a common goal, namely a non-

---

7   Oxford Learners University Dictionary, 2020: 33.

8   Veldsman & Johnson, 2016: 826.

9   Van Zyl & Campbell, 2019: 3.

10 Van Zyl & Campbell, 2019: 4.

11 Wittenberg-Cox, 2020: 2.

12 Moore, 2019: 1.

13 Moore, 2019: 1.

racial South Africa. In the process, he also demonstrated resilience by overcoming his experiences in jail and transforming into a successful leader of all citizens in South Africa.[14]

Social skills

Social skills refer to the proficiency in managing relationships and building networks.[15] The following social skills may help in dealing with VUCA demands: openness, participation, collaboration, and being supportive.

Franklin Delano Roosevelt was the American president from 4 March 1933 to 12 April 1945. He was known as a leader who demonstrated openness and was willing to listen, think and share. In this way, *inter alia*, he led the country through the Great Depression and World War 2. Roosevelt is the only American president who served more than two terms.[16]

Emmanuel Macron, the French president, is the youngest French head of state ever, and is considered to be one of Europe's most successful premiers. He believes that everyone should participate and collaborate in order for goals to be attained. He explained that: "No leader, especially not a president, can accomplish goals on his/her own. Goals can only be reached as a collective, with one another."[17]

Being supportive means providing encouragement or emotional help (Veldsman & Johnson, 2016: 194). As indicated before, Jacinda Ardern visited families who had lost loved ones in the shooting incident in New Zealand to encourage and support them in difficult times. Ardern can indeed be regarded as a supportive leader.[18]

Outcome per VUCA environment

The following leading oneself skills are emphasised in this book as guidelines to help leaders and non-leaders in different VUCA environments. (The leading oneself skills as indicated per environment/sector are the outcome of the different chapters of this book, yet this does not mean that some of the other leading oneself skills (see Figures 17.1 and 17.2) are not relevant in a specific environment).

---

14 Van Zyl & Campbell, 2019: 2.

15 Veldsman & Johnson, 2016: 351.

16 History.com, 2020.

17 Morse, 2017: 1.

18 Moore, 2019: 1.

Private sector

The following leading oneself skills were emphasised in the chapters on the private sector as guidelines according to which leaders and non-leaders can deal with VUCA demands: self-reflection, care for self, inner dialogue, calmness, basic humanness, conflict intelligence, empathy and stillness (mainly inner skills) also see Figure 17.2 and Table 17.1.

Internal dialogue (inner conversations) forms part of examining one's own character and actions, while self-reflection, inner dialogue and stillness mean to spend time with oneself. This should be done in a calm way in order to get the best results. Doing this means that we care about ourselves. Self-reflection and self-care may help us to act humanely towards others, to have empathy for others, and to handle conflict intelligently.

Due to the high and difficult demands placed on them, leaders and non-leaders in the private sector neglect themselves, which could be a reason why they often do not act humanely towards others (leading others should be from the inside out).[19]

Public sector

Participation and collaboration in formal and informal activities, good relationships (even if it means reconciling with those we had conflict with), and good communication skills (including the ability to influence others) are regarded as important leading oneself skills for leaders in public sector VUCA environments. Innovative ways of achieving this (e.g. team building) may help to achieve objectives in a meaningful way. These can be regarded as mainly social skills (also see Figure 17.1 and Table 17.1).

In some public sector environments, many rules and bureaucratic red tape are forced on employees, which may cause them to isolate themselves and to have poor interpersonal relations. Implementing the abovementioned may counteract these challenges.

Academic sector

Technology, new generational requirements, and the coronavirus pandemic have shaped a new normal for students and academics, requiring new and innovative ways of learning and assessment. To achieve this, online training and evaluation methods were introduced, for example. To stay positive, hopeful and competent in reaching their objectives, leaders and employees have to be aware of the situation (have knowledge about the situation) and be adaptable, agile and resilient. The abovementioned leading

---

19 Van Zyl & Campbell, 2019: 28.

oneself skills can be regarded as mainly decision-making skills (see Figure 17.2 and Table 17.1).

Conflict and post-conflict environments

In some conflict and post-conflict situations, difficult matters have to be dealt with, for instance, negotiating with people who have negative perceptions about you and what you believe in. World orders demand that leaders portray leading oneself skills to manage conflict and post-conflict situations, with the main focus being on the public good.

In these situations it is important that trust and openness are created and maintained among the parties involved. To achieve this, leading oneself skills are required, such as good listening skills, honesty, authenticity, transparency, self-regulating behaviour and self-awareness. Leading oneself skills like empathy, bridge-building, resilience and forgiveness may also help one to find solutions in demanding situations. The abovementioned leading oneself skills can be regarded as mainly emotional skills (also see Figure 17.2 and Table 17.1).

Table 17.1: Most prominent leading oneself skills per VUCA environment

	Outcomes per environment		Brief explanation of rationale
Private	• Self-reflection • Inner dialogue • Care for self • Calmness • Basic humanness	• Stillness • Conflict Intelligence • Empathy **Mainly inner skills**	Daily demands (personal, economic) cause business owners to fight for survival. As a consequence, they have neither time nor energy to focus on the self.
Public	• Participation • Relationships • Communication • Collaboration	• Influence • Reconciliation • Innovation • Meaning **Mainly social skills**	Political influences on business and bureaucratic strategies often cause departments to function in silos.
Academic	• Adaptability • Resilience • Optimism	• Hope • Agility • Awareness • Competency **Mainly decision-making skills**	Technology, new generational requirements, and the coronavirus pandemic have shaped a new normal for students and academics, demanding new and innovative ways of learning and assessment.

Outcomes per environment		Brief explanation of rationale
Conflict and post-conflict	• Self-awareness • Self-regulation • Good listening • Trust • Honesty • Empathy	• Authenticity • Transparency • Openness • Bridge-building • Forgiveness • Resilience **Mainly emotional skills**	World orders demand that leaders portray leading oneself skills to manage conflict and post-conflict situations with a focus on the public good.

RECOMMENDATIONS

Leading oneself skills to help the 21st century leader cope with demands

Leaders in the 21st century need to understand that the leadership skills of yesterday might not be relevant today (see Table 17.2). This will be discussed now with a focus on which prominent leading oneself skills (identified in this book) can help when dealing with demands.

Who is being led?

In the past, leaders' performance was measured based on individual success. Leadership performance was therefore defined by what leaders achieved as individuals, as well as what they could get out of their subordinates (direct reports). Today's leaders, however, are evaluated based on their performance as leaders of teams. Leaders today are managing agile teams, squads and tribes, which have to perform and innovate.[20]

As we have seen in this book, the most prominent leading oneself skills that help manage agile teams, squads and tribes to perform are collaboration, participation, influence and agility (see Table 17.2).

Framework of success

Yesterday's framework of "command and control" is outdated and should be replaced with "connect and collaborate." Today's leaders do not dictate; they guide and influence others by first connecting and then collaborating with them.[21]

---

20 Abelli, 2020.
21 Abelli, 2020.

As per this book, the most prominent leading oneself skills associated with good guidance and influence are collaboration, interpersonal relations, listening skills, influencing skills and awareness (see Table 17.2).

Critical task of leaders

The modern leader's most critical task is to create and empower teams, not to drive direction. There should be comfort in the contribution towards innovative ideas, shared purpose, experimentation, and an atmosphere of empowerment.[22]

The general leading oneself skills of trust, authenticity, openness and critical decision-making may contribute towards the empowerment of teams, while showing support and empathy may further help to create and empower teams.

Leaders' core competencies

The core competency of yesterday's leader was centred in execution. In the modern business context, the pace is fast, technology-enabled, and ever changing. The modern leader's core competency, therefore, is innovation. Leaders are the focal point for driving innovation. They must spot trends relating to emerging technologies, identify customer-driven opportunities, transform the business accordingly, and release new products and services.[23] The leading oneself skills of agility and decisiveness may contribute towards being an innovative leader.

What needs to be developed?

Previously, leadership development focused on developing the skills of leaders. However, leaders today should possess better capabilities for collaborative leadership in uncertain and complex situations. Leaders should develop mindsets that expect complex and fluid relationships as part of ever-changing business conditions.[24]

Leading oneself skills like collaboration, agility, adaptability, awareness and resilience may help to achieve the abovementioned.

The way leaders reach across and into organisations

Modern organisations have moved to flatter organisational structures, with cross-functional teams becoming the norm. Consequently, more employees are assuming leadership responsibilities across the organisation. Thus, to be successful, leaders

---

22 Abelli, 2020.

23 Abelli, 2020.

24 Abelli, 2020.

should reach out to all leadership levels of the organisation.[25]

Leading oneself skills like openness, trust, participation and collaboration could help leaders reach out to all levels in the organisation.

Table 17.2: Adapted leadership and leading oneself skills (yesterday vs. today)[26]

Yesterday	What has changed?	Today	Leading oneself skills
• Direct reports • Silo leader	**Who is being led?**	• Mission driven • Agile team • Innovation	• Collaboration • Participation • Influence • Agility
• Command and control	**Framework of Success**	• Interconnection • Collaboration	• Collaboration • Relations • Listening • Influence • Awareness
• Driving direction	**Critical tasks of leaders**	• Create and empower teams • Innovative ideas • Shared purpose • Experimentation	• Trust • Authenticity • Decision-making • Empathy • Openness
• Execution	**Leader core competency**	• Emerging technologies • Identify customer- driven opportunities • Transform business • Release new products/services	• Decisiveness • Innovation • Agility
• Skillsets	**What needs to be developed**	• Mindsets • Strategic foresight • Changing business conditions • Cultural awareness	• Resilience • Collaboration • Adaptability • Agility • Awareness

25 Abelli, 2020.

26 Abelli, 2020.

Yesterday	What has changed?	Today	Leading oneself skills
• Limited	**Reach into the organisation**	• Democratisation • Participation • Cross functional teams	• Participation • Collaboration • Trust • Openness

Specific recommendations

1. Leaders and non-leaders should be aware of the most prominent leading oneself skills identified in this book (see Figure 17.1), which can be used in most VUCA environments. In particular, they should be aware of the most prominent leading oneself themes (see Figure 17.2), as well as which themes they are lacking or can develop in order to handle difficult demands.

2. Although all the leading oneself skills should be regarded as important (see Figures 17.1 and 17.2), leaders and non-leaders should be aware of what leading oneself skills are indicated per environment (see Table 17.1). Developing those skills will help them to counter VUCA situations.

3. Strategic leadership and planning will help leaders who are navigating the unknown. The tenets of strategic foresight, strategic thinking and strategic planning (see Chapter 16), provide the underpinning of strategic leadership within a VUCA context. A strategic leadership framework (see Chapter 16) identifies the basic and critical leadership (and leading oneself) skills such as strategic thinking, critical thinking, agility, collaboration, trust, empathy, problem solving, emotional intelligence and authenticity, which are the critical benchmarks for all strategic thinking during a crisis.

4. Whether or not you are an emerging leader, first-level supervisor, middle-level or top- level manager, make sure you know which of your leading oneself skills can be developed in order to handle difficult demands. Consult someone you admire for his/her leadership qualities to help you identify those skills that should be developed. Although all the skills indicated in Figures 17.1 and 17.2 can be regarded as important in VUCA situations, decision-making skills in particular will enable us to think and understand quickly, to make well-informed and timely decisions, and to act accordingly. This will improve our ability to adapt easily to new situations.

CONCLUDING REMARKS

Following the title of the book, *Chaos is a gift? Leading oneself in uncertain and complex environments*, the question can indeed be asked: Is chaos a gift? Chaos can be regarded as a gift if VUCA environments can be dealt with effectively (leading, *inter alia*, to innovation, better teamwork, better interpersonal relations and better performance). The results and recommendations of this book may help to achieve that.

Jok Church[27] put it as follows: "Chaos does not mean total disorder. Chaos means a multiplicity of possibilities. Chaos is from the ancient Greek words that means a thing that is birthed from the void. Chaos creates the opening for new possibilities."

---

27 Church (n.d.).

LIST OF REFERENCES

Chapter 1 References

Cashman, G. 2014. *What Causes War and Introduction to Theories of International Conflict?* Lanham, MD: Rowman & Littlefield Publishers.

Codreanu, A. 2016. *A VUCA action framework for a VUCA environment: Leadership challenges and solutions.* Available from: http://researchgate.net/publication/316967836 (Accessed 24 April 2020).

Davis, R. 2011. *We need more mature leaders.* Available from: https://hbr.org/2011/10/we-need-more-mature-leaders (Accessed 24 April 2020).

Galacgac, J. & Singh, A. 2016. *Implications of chaos theory in management science.* Available from: http://www.cmsim.org/images/1Proceedings_CHAOS2015_G-H-249-336.pdf (Accessed 24 April 2020).

Glover, J., Jones, G. & Freidman, H. 2002. *Adaptive leadership: When change is not good enough (Part one).* Available from: https://www.questia.com/library/journal/1P3-122974061/adaptive-leadership-when-change-is-not-enough-part (Accessed 24 April 2020).

Heifetz, R., Grashow, A. & Linsky, M. 2009. *Leadership in a (permanent) crisis.* Available from: http://heller.brandeis.edu/executive-education/massmed-2014/january-2014/Jon/605FLeadership-in-Permanent-Crisis.pdf (Accessed 24 April 2020).

Heifetz, R. & Lindsky, M. 2011. *Becoming an adaptive leader.* Available from: https://thecrg.org/resources/becoming-an-adaptive-leader-based-on-the-work-of-ronald-heifetz-and-marty-linsky (Accessed 24 April 2020).

Ikenberry, G.J. 1996. The future of international leadership. *Political Science Quarterly, 111*(3), p. 396–387.

Kok, J. & ven den Heuvel, S.C. 2019. *Leading in a VUCA World: Integrating leadership, discernment and spirituality.* Cham, Switzerland: Springer.

Kolenda, C.D. 2001. What is leadership? Some classical ideas. In C.D. Kolenda. 2001. *Leadership: The Warrior's Art.* Carlisle, PA: Army War College Foundation Press, p3.

Kotter, J. 2012. *Leading change.* Cambridge, MA: Harvard Business Review Press.
leadership. Carol Stream, IL: Tyndal House Publishers.

Landsberg, M. 2016. *Mastering coaching: Practical insights for developing high performance.* London: Penguin Random House, p 236.

Lichtenstein, B.B. & Plowman, D.A. 2009. The leadership of emergence: A complex systems leadership theory of emergence at successive organizational levels. *The Leadership Quarterly, 20*(4): 617-630.

Mendenhall, M.E., Osland, J.S., Bird, A., Oddou, G.R., Maznevski, M.L., Stevens, M.J. & Stahl, G.K. 2018. *Global leadership: Research, practice, and development.* New York: Routledge.

Obolensky, N. 2010. *Complex adaptive leadership: Embracing paradox and uncertainty.* Burlington, VA: Gower Publishing.

Pearse, C. 2018. *5 Reasons Why Leadership Is in Crisis.* Available from: https://www.forbes.com/sites/chrispearse/2018/11/07/5-reasons-why-leadership-is-in-crisis/#6c2a5773aca4 (Accessed 24 April 2020).

Raymont, J. & Smith, J. 2011. *MisLeadership: Prevalence, causes, and consequences.* Burlington, VT: Ashgate Publishing.

Smith, M.A. 2012. *Why leadership sucks: The fundamentals of level 5 leadership and servant.* Wisconsin, US: Kompelling Publishing.

Spero, J.E. & Hart, J.A. 2003. *The politics of international economic relations*. Belmont, CA: Thomson and Wadsworth.

Steeffen, S., Trevenna, S. & Rappaport, S. 2018. *Evolving Leadership for Collective Wellbeing: Lessons implementing the United Nations Sustainable Development Goals*. Bringley, UK: Emerald Group Publishing.

Uhl-Bien, M., Marion, R. & McKleavy, J. 2008. *Complexity leadership: Part I conceptual foundations*. Charlotte, NC: Information Age Publishing.

Van Zyl, E. & Campbell, A. 2019. *Peace leadership: Self-transformation to peace*. Bryanston: KR Publishing.

Veldsman, T.H. & Johnson, A.J. 2016. *Leadership: Perspectives from the front line*. Bryanston: KR Publishing.

Weick, K.E. & Sutcliffe, K.M. 2015. *Managing the unexpected: Sustained performance in a complex world*. Hoboken, NJ: John Wiley and Sons.

Chapter 2: References

Akwa-Nde, A. 2015. *The effect of self-leadership and locus of control on work stress amongst managers in the financial services sector.* Unpublished master's dissertation, University of the Free State, Bloemfontein.

Alomair, M.O. 2016. Peace leadership for youth leaders: A literature review. *International Journal of Public Leadership*, *12*(3): 227-238.

Amaladas, S. & Byrne, S. 2018. *Peace leadership. The quest for connectedness*. London: Routledge.

Bandura, A. 1991. Social cognitive theory of self-regulation. *Organisational behaviour and decision making processes, 50*(9): 248-287.

Bolman, L.G. & Deal, T.E. 2008. *Reframing organizations: Artistry, choice, and leadership* (4th ed.). San Francisco, CA: Jossey-Bass.

Campbell, A. 2018. *Global leadership initiatives for conflict resolution and peacebuilding*. Hershey, USA: IGI Global.

Canadian College of Health Leaders. 2010. *Lead self: The root of the matter*. Ottawa, Canada: Canadian Health Leadership Network.

Carver, C.S. & Scheier, M.F. 1981. *Attention and self-regulation*. New York: Springer.

Deci, E.L. & Ryan, R.M. 1985. *Intrinsic motivation and self-determination in human behaviour*. London: Thompson.

Elloy, D.F. 2004. The influence of super leaders behaviours on organisational commitment, job satisfaction and organisation self-esteem in a self-managed work team. *Leadership and Organisational Development Journal*, *26*(2): 120-126.

Goleman, D. 1995. *Emotional intelligence: Why it can matter more than IQ*. New York: Bantam Books.

Graig, N. & Snook, S. 2014. From purpose to impact: Figure out your passion and put it into work. *Harvard Business Review*, *92*(5): 105-111.

Gruwez, E. 2017. *VUCA world: A quick summary*. Available from: https://www.tothepointatwork. com/article/vuca-world/ (Accessed 12 November 2018).

Heifetz, R., Grashow, A. & Linsky, M. 2009. Leadership in a (permanent) crisis. *Harvard Review*, 1-9. Available from: http://heller.brandeis.edu/executive-education/massmed-2014/january-2014/Jon/605FLeadership-in-Permanent-Crisis.pdf (Accessed: 12 November 2018).

Houghton, J.D. & Neck, C.P. 2006. Self-leadership in teams. *Journal of Organisational Behaviour*, *17*: 672-691.

Houghton, J.D. & Yoho, S.K. 2006. Toward a contingency model of leadership and psychological empowerment: When should self-leadership be encouraged? *Journal of Leadership and Organisational Studies*, *11*(94): 65-84.

Joiner, B. & Josephs, S. 2006. *Leadership agility*. New York, NY: Jossey-Bass.

Joosten, A., Van Dijke, M., Van Hiel, A. & De Cremer, D. 2014. Being in control may make you lose control: The role of self-regulation in unethical behaviour. *Journal of Business Ethics*, *121*: 1-14.

Jordaan, B. 2019. Leading organizations in turbulent times: Toward a different mental model. In J. Kok & S.C. van den Heuvel (Eds.). *Leading in a VUCA World: Integrating leadership, discernment and spirituality* (pp. 12-14). Cham, Switzerland: Springer.

Kerr, S. & Jermier, J.M. 1978. Substitutes for leadership: Their meaning and measurement. *Organisational Behaviour and Human performance*, *22*: 375-403.

Kok, J. & Van den Heuvel, S.C. 2019. *Leading in a VUCA world: Integrating leadership, discernment and spirituality*. Cham, Switzerland: Springer.

Ledbetter, B. 2012. Dialectics of leadership for peace: Towards a model of resistance. *Journal of Leadership, Accountability and Ethics*, *9*(5): 11-24.

Lipman-Blumen, J. 2011. *Peace and prosperity: Make it happen*. Paper presented at the International Leadership Association 12th Annual Meeting, London.

Livermore, D. 2010. *Leading with cultural intelligence. The real secret to success*. New York: American Management Association.

Lues, L. 2016. The dynamic and changing work environment, In E.J. van der Westhuizen (Ed.). *Human resource management in government: A South African perspective on theories, politics and processes* (pp. 38-48). Cape Town: Juta and Company.

Lues, L. 2019. Peace leadership in the public and private sectors, In E. van Zyl & A. Campbell (Eds.). *Peace leadership. Self-transformation to peace* (pp. 153-168). Randburg: KR Publishing.

Manz, C.C. & Sims, H. 2001. *The new super leadership: Leading others to lead themselves*. San Francisco: Berrett-Koehler Publishers.

Manz, C.C. 1986. Self-leadership: toward and expanded theory of self-influence processes in organisations. *Academy of Management Review*, *11*: 585-600.

Maxwell, J.C. 2008. *Leadership gold: Lessons I have learned from a lifetime of learning*. Nashville, Thomas Nelson Publishers.

McCullough, M.E. & Willoughby, L.B. 2009. Religion, self-regulation and self-control: Associations, explanations and implications. *American Psychological Association*, *135*(1): 69-93.

Mendenhall, M.E., Osland, J.S., Bird, A., Oddou, G.R., Maznevski, M.L., Stevens, M.J. & Stahl, G.K. 2018. *Global leadership: Research, practice, and development* (2nd ed.). New York, NY: Routledge.

Mokuoane, M.L. 2014. *The effect of work stress and emotional intelligence on self-leadership amongst nurses in leadership positions in the Ministry of Health and Social Welfare in Lesotho*. Master's dissertation, University of the Free State, Bloemfontein.

Momtaz, R. 2020. *Inside Macron's coronavirus war*. Available from: https://wwwpolitico.com/ (Accessed 14 April 2020).

Neck, C.P. & Manz, C.C. 2010. *Mastering self-leadership: Empowering yourself for personal excellence*. Upper Saddle River, Prentice Hall.

Nel, P. & Van Zyl, E.S. 2019. Assessing the psychometric properties of the Experience of Work and Life Circumstances Questionnaire. *African Journal of Psychology, 18*(2): 12-15.

Nel, P. & Van Zyl, E.S. 2019. Assessing the psychometric properties of the Experience of

Obolensky, N. 2010. *Complex adaptive leadership: Embracing paradox and uncertainty.* Burlington, VA: Gower Publishing.

Petrie, N. 2014. *Future trends in leadership development.* White paper: Centre for Creative Leadership. Colorado Springs: Colorado.

Rankin, N. 2020. *Belgium hands power to caretaker Prime Minister to fight Covid-19.* Available from: https://wwwthe guardian.com/ (Accessed 14 April 2020).

Van Zyl, E.S. & Campbell, A.H. 2019. *Peace leadership: Self-transformation to peace.* Johannesburg: KR Publishers.

Van Zyl, E.S. 2009. *Leadership in the African context.* Cape Town: Juta.

Van Zyl, E.S. 2013. Self-leadership and happiness within the African context. *Journal of Psychology, 4*(2): 59-66.

Van Zyl, E.S. 2016. *Leadership in the African context* (2nd ed). Cape Town: Juta.

Veldsman, T.H. & Johnson, A.J. 2016. *Leadership in context: Perspectives from the frontline.* Johannesburg: KR Publishers.

Wilson, E. 2020. *Three reasons why Jacinda Ardern's corona virus response has been a masterclass in crisis leadership.* Available from: https://wwwthecommonwealth.com/ (Accessed 14 April 2020).

Zupan, M. 2010. An economic perspective on leadership. In N. Nofia & R. Khurana (Eds.). *Handbook of leadership theory and practice: A Harvard Business School Centennial Colloquium* (pp. 265-290). Boston, MA: Harvard Business Press.

Chapter 3 References

Association to Advance Collegiate Schools of Business (AACSB). 2006. *A World of Good: Business, Business Schools, and Peace.* Report of the AACSB International Peace Through Commerce Task Force. Available from: https://www.aacsb.edu/-/media/aacsb/publications/research-reports/peace-english.ashx?la=en&hash=E0728523E447276A5C4E677E7990D4EBDABE354C [Accessed 19 July 2019].

Alper, S., Tjosvold, D. & Law, K. 2000. Conflict management, efficacy, and performance in organizational teams. *Personnel Psychology, 53*(3): 625-642.

Ancona, D., Backman, E. & Isaacs, K. 2019. Nimble Leadership: Walking the line between creativity and chaos. *Harvard Business Review, 97*(4): 74-83.

Anstey, M. 1991. *Negotiating Conflict.* Cape Town: Juta and Co Ltd.

Armor, D.A. & Taylor, S.E. 2003. The Effects of Mindset on Behavior: Self-Regulation in Deliberative and Implemental Frames of Mind. *Personality and Social Psychology Bulletin, 29*(1): 86-95.

Barki, H. & Hartwick, J. 2004. Conceptualizing the construct of interpersonal conflict. *International Journal of Conflict Management, 15*(3): 216-244.

Bonchek, M. 2016. *Why the Problem with Learning Is Unlearning.* Available from: https://hbr.org/2016/11/why-the-problem-with-learning-is-unlearning [Accessed 19 July 2019].

Bower, J.L. & Paine, L.S. 2017. The Error at the Heart of Corporate Leadership. *Harvard Business Review, 95*(3): 50–60.

Brauer, J. & Marlin, J.T. 2009. *Defining Peace Industries and Calculating the Potential Size of a Peace Gross World Product by Country and by Economic Sector*. Available from: https://www.files.ethz.ch/isn/126268/definingpeaceindustrieandcalculatingapeacewgp.pdf [Accessed 18 July 2019].

Browning, M. 2018. Self-Leadership: Why It Matters. *International Journal of Business and Social Science, 9*(2): 14-18.

Bryant, A. & Kazan, L. 2012. *Self Leadership*. New York: McGraw-Hill.

Carmeli, A., Meitar, R. & Weisberg, J. 2006. Self-leadership skills and innovative behavior at work. *International Journal of Manpower, 27*(1): 75-90.

Chartered Management Institute. 2015. *Paul Polman: Unilever's clean winner in leadership*. Available from: https://www.managers.org.uk/insights/news/2015/february/paul-polman-unilevers-clean-winner-in-corporate-governance [Accessed 28 July 2019].

Cloke, K. & Goldsmith, J. 2003. *The Art of Waking People Up: Cultivating Awareness and Authenticity at Work*. San Francisco: Jossey Bass/Wiley.

Cloke, K. & Goldsmith, J. 2011. *Resolving Conflicts at Work: Ten Strategies for Everyone on the Job*. San Francisco: Jossey-Bass.

Collins, J.C. 2001. *Good to Great*. London: William Collins.

Coleman, P.T. 2018. Conflict Intelligence and Systemic Wisdom: Meta Competencies for Engaging Conflict in a Complex, Dynamic World. *Negotiation Journal, 34*(1): 7-35.

Cronin, M.A. & Bezrukova, K. 2019. *Conflict Management Through the Lens of System Dynamics*. Briarcliff Manor, NY: Academy of Management Annals, p. 1-84.

D'Intino, R.S., Goldsby, M.G., Houghton, J.D. & Neck, C.P. 2007. Self-Leadership: A Process for Entrepreneurial Success. *Journal of Leadership and Organizational Studies, 13*(4): 105-120.

Doz, Y. & Kosonen, M. 2008. The dynamics of strategic agility: Nokia's rollercoaster experience. *California Management Review, 50*(3): 95–118.

Draganski, B., Gaser, C., Busch, V., Schuierer, G., Bogdahn, G.Y. & May, A. 2004. Neuroplasticity: changes in grey matter induced by training. *Nature, 427*: 311-312.

Dweck, C.S. & Ehrlinger, J. 2006. Implicit Theories and Conflict Resolution. In M. Deutsch, P. Coleman & E. Marcus (Eds.). *The Handbook of Conflict Resolution, Vol. 2*. San Francisco: Jossey-Bass.

Dweck, C.S. 2007. *Mindset: The New Psychology of Success*. New York: Random House.

Eisenhardt, K.M., Kahwajy, J.L. & Bourgeois, L.J. 1997. How management teams can have a good fight. *Harvard Business Review, 75*(4): 77-85.

Elgoibar, P., Euwema, M. & Munduate, L. (Eds.). 2016. *Building Trust and Constructive Conflict Management in Organisations*. Cham, Switzerland: Springer International Publishing.

Finkelstein, S. 2003. *Why smart executives fail*. London: Penguin.

Frankl, V. 1992. *Man's Search for Meaning*. Boston: Beacon Press.

Holsapple, C. & Li, X. 2008. *Understanding Organizational Agility: A Work-Design Perspective*. Available from: https://www.researchgate.net/publication/278006905_Understanding_Organizational_Agility_A_Work-Design_Perspective [Accessed 13 July 2019].

Houghton, J.D., Neck, C.P. & Many, C.C. 2006. Self-leadership and superleadership: The heart and art of creating shared leadership in teams. In C.LM. Pearce & J.A. Conger (Eds.). *Shared Leadership: Reframing the How's and Why's of Leadership*. Thousand Oaks, CA: Sage Publications.

Institute for Economics and Peace. 2019. *Business and Peace Report*. Available from: http://visionofhumanity.org/app/uploads/2018/09/Business-and-Peace-Report.pdf [Accessed 24 July 2019].

Jehn, K., Greer, L., Rispens, S. & Jonsen, K. 2013. Conflict contagion: A temporal perspective on the development of conflict within teams. *International Journal of Conflict Management, 24*(5): 352-373.

Jensen, M.C. & Meckling, W.H. 1976. Theory of the Firm: Managerial Behavior, Agency Costs and Ownership Structure. *Journal of Financial Economics, 3*(4): 305-360.

Jones, N.A., Ross, H., Lynam, T., Perez, P. & Leitch, A. 2011. Mental models: an interdisciplinary synthesis of theory and methods. *Ecology and Society, 16*(1): 46.

Jordaan, B. & Cilliè, G. 2016. Building a collaborative workplace culture: a South African perspective. In M. Euwema, L. Munduate & P. Elgobar (Eds.). *Building Trust and Constructive Conflict Management in Organizations*. Cham, Switzerland: Springer.

Jordaan, B. 2019. Leading Organisations in Turbulent Times: Towards a Different Mental Model. In J. Kok & S.C. Van den Heuvel (Eds.). *Leading in a VUCA World: Integrating Leadership, Discernment and Spirituality*. Cham, Switzerland: Springer Nature.

Katsos, J.E. & Fort, T.L. 2006. Leadership in the promotion of peace: Interviews with the 2015 Business for Peace honorees. *Business Horizons, 59*: 463-470.

Koestler, A. 1972. *The roots of coincidence*. New York: Vintage Books.

Laloux, F. 2014. *Reinventing Organisations*. Available from: http://www.reinventingorganizations.com/uploads/2/1/9/8/21988088/140305_laloux_reinventing_organizations.pdf [Accessed 12 July 2019].

Lash, R. 2012. *The collaboration imperative*. Available from: http://iveybusinessjournal.com/publication/the-collaboration-imperative/ [Accessed 12 July 2019].

Leathes, M. 2009. *Conflict leadership*. Presentation made to 24th meeting of General Counsel and Legal Directors of International Companies in Frankfurt, Germany. Available from: https://imimediation.org/conflict-leadership [Accessed 12 July 2019].

Leavitt, H. 1989. Educating MBA's: On teaching what we haven't taught. *California Management Review, 31*(3): 38-50.

McKinsey and Co. 2009. *Conversations with global leaders*. Available from: www.mckinsey.com/business-functions/strategy-and-corporate-finance/our-insights/mckinsey-conversations-with-global-leaders-paul-polman-of-unilever [Accessed 28 July 2019].

McKinsey and Co. 2015. *The science of organizational transformations*. Available from: https://www.mckinsey.com/business-functions/organization/our-insights/the-science-of-organizational-transformations [Accessed 12 July 2019].

Miklian, J. 2016. *Mapping business-peace interactions: five assertions for how businesses create peace*. Available from: SSRN: https://ssrn.com/abstract=2891391 [Accessed 19 July 2019].

Milliken, F., Schipani, C.A., Bishara, D. & Prado, A.M. 2015. Linking workplace practices to community engagement: The case for encouraging employee voice. *Academy of Management Perspectives, 29*(4): 405–421.

Neck, C.P. & Manz, C.C. 1992. Thought self-leadership: The influence of self-talk and mental imagery on performance. *Journal of Organizational Behavior, 13*(7): 681-699.

Nicholson, N. 2001. *Managing the Human Animal*. Knutsford: Texere Publishing.

Pearce, G.L. & Manz, C.C. 2005. The New Silver Bullets of Leadership: The Importance of Self- and Shared Leadership in Knowledge Work. *Organizational Dynamics, 34*(2): 130–140.

Pfeffer, R. 2005. Changing mental models: HR's most important task. *Human Resource Management, 44*(2): 123 - 128.

Prussia, G.E., Anderson, J.S. & Manz, C.C. 1998. Self-leadership and performance outcomes: the mediating influence of self-efficacy. *Journal of Organizational Behavior, 19*: 523-538.

Reeves, M. & Deimler M. 2011. Adaptability: the new competitive advantage. *Harvard Business Review, 89*(7): 134-141.

Rigby, D.K., Sutherland, J. & Takeuchi, H. 2016. *Embracing agile*. Available from: https://hbr.org/2016/05/embracing-agile [Accessed 13 July 2019].

Reger, R.K., Mullane, J.V., Gustafson, L. & DeMarie, S.M. 1994. Creating earthquakes to change organizational mindsets. *Academy of Management Executive, 8*(4): 31–43.

Rima, S. 2000. *Leading From the Inside Out: The Art of Self-Leadership*. Grand Rapids: Bake Brooks.

Saeed, T., Almas, S., Anis-ul-Haq, M. & Niazi, G.S.K. 2014. Leadership styles: relationship with conflict management styles. *International Journal of Conflict Management, 25*(3): 214-226.

Schmidt, S.M. & Kochan, T. 1972. Conflict: Toward Conceptual Clarity. *Administrative Science Quarterly, 17*(3): 359-370.

Seligman, M.E.P. 1991. *Learned optimism*. New York: Alfred Knopf.

Senge, P.M. 1990. *The fifth discipline: The art and practice of the learning organization*. New York: Doubleday.

Sisodia, R.S., Wolfe, D.B. & Sheth, J.N. 2007. *Firms of endearment: How world class companies profit from passion and purpose*. Upper Saddle River, NJ: Wharton School Publishing.

Spreitzer, G. 2007. Giving peace a chance: Organisational leadership empowerment and peace. *Journal of Organisational Behaviour, 28*: 1077-1095.

Sull, D. 2010. *Competing through organizational agility*. Available from: https://www.researchgate.net/publication/289616104_Competing_through_organizational_agility |[Accessed 13 July 2019].

Swanepoel, B.J. (Ed.). 1999. *The Management of Employment Relations: Conceptual and Contextual Perspectives*. Durban: Butterworths.

The Economist Intelligence Unit. 2009. Organisational agility: How business can survive and thrive in turbulent times. *The Economist*. Available from: http://static1.1.sqspcdn.com/static/f/447037/22518673/1366674874460/TheEconomist_organisational_agility.pdf?token=w6AVyV73sAKBQO3ViCbglFaVils%3D [Accessed 15 July 2019].

Thompson, D.S., Butkus, G., Colquitt, A. & Boudreau, J. 2016. *The Right Kind of Conflict Leads to Better Products*. Available from: https://hbr.org/2016/12/the-right-kind-of-conflict-leads-to-better-products [Accessed 15 July 2019].

Thomas, K.W. 1992. Conflict and conflict management: Reflections and update. *Journal ofOrganizational Behavior, 13*: 265-274.

Tjosvold, D. 1997. Conflict within interdependence: its value for productivity, in K.W. De Dreu & E. Van de Vliert (Eds.). *Using Conflict in Organisations*. London: Sage.

Tjosvold, D. 2008. The conflict-positive organization: it depends upon us. *Journal of Organizational Behavior, 29*: 19–28.

Tjosvold, D., Yu, Z. & Wu, P. 2009. Empowering Individuals for Team Innovation in China: Conflict Management and Problem Solving. *Negotiation and Conflict Management Research, 2*(2): 185-205.

UN Global Compact. 2008. *Corporate Sustainability in the World Economy*. Available from: https://www.unglobalcompact.org/library/240 [Accessed 24 July 2019].

Van Boven, L. & Thompson, L. 2003. A Look into the Mind of the Negotiator: Mental Models in Negotiation. *Group Processes and Intergroup Relations, 6*(4): 387–404.

Van den Broeck, H. & Jordaan, B. 2018. *The Agile Leader's Scrapbook*. Leuven: Lannoo Campus.

Van Saane, J. 2019. Personal Leadership as Form of Spirituality. In J. Kok & S.C. Van den Heuvel (Eds.). *Leading in a VUCA World: Integrating Leadership, Discernment and Spirituality*. Cham, Switzerland: Springer.

Van Velsor, E., McCauley, C.D. & Ruderman, M.N. 2010. *CCL Handbook of Leadership Development*. San Francisco: Jossey-Bass.

Weingart, L.R., Behfar, K.J., Bendersky, C., Todorva, G. & Jehn, K.A. 2015. The directness and oppositional intensity of conflict expression. *Academy of Management Review, 40*(2): 235–262.

World Development Report. 2015. *Thinking with mental models*. Available from: http://pubdocs. worldbank.org/en/504271482349886430/Chapter-3.pdf [Accessed 12 July 2019].

World Economic Forum. 2018. *The Future of Jobs Report*. Available from: http://www3.weforum. org/docs/WEF_Future_of_Jobs_2018.pdf [Accessed 12 July 2019].

Zhang, X., Cao, Q. & Tjosvold, D. 2011. Linking Transformational Leadership and Team Performance: A Conflict Management Approach. *Journal of Management Studies, 48*(7): 1586-1611.

Chapter 4 References

Arendt, H. 1998. *Vom Leben des Geistes. Das Denken. Das Wollen*. München: Piper.

Arendt, H. 2016. *Sokrates. Apologie der Pluralität*. Berlin: Matthes & Seitz.

Bachtin, M. 1985. *Probleme der Poetik Dostoevskijs*. Frankfurt a.M./Berlin/Wien: Ullstein Materialien.

Bar-On, D. 2001. *Die „Anderen" in uns. Dialog als Modell der interkulturellen Konfliktbewältigung*. Hamburg: Körber.

Böhme, G. 2002. *Der Typ Sokrates*. Frankfurt a.m.: Suhrkamp.

Bosch, R. 1957. *Ausätze, Reden und Gedanken*. Stuttgart: Bosch Schriftenreihe.

Daniels, C. 2018. *Socratic Management Techniques For the Modern Leader*. Available from: https://medium.com/swlh/socratic-management-techniques-for-the-modern-leader-f43d9a50caad [Accessed 12 June 2019].

Dietrich, W. 2017. Friedensarbeit im 21. Jahrhundert: Transrationale Philosophie, elicitive Praxis und das Psychodrama. *Zeitschrift für Psychodrama und Soziometrie, 1*(16): 81-92.

Foucault, M. 2005. *The Hermeneutics of the Subject. Lectures at the Collége de France, 1981-82*. New York: Palgrave. Macmillan.

Foucault, M. 2015. *Die Sorge um sich. Sexualität und Wahrheit, 3*. Frankfurt a.M.: Suhrkamp.

Griese, C. & Marburger, H. (eds.). 2012. *Interkulturelle Öffnung. Ein Lehrbuch*. München: Oldenburg Verlag.

Hamm, I., Seitz, H. & Werding, M. (Eds.). 2008. *Demographic Change in Germany. The Economic and Fiscal Consequences*. Berlin/Heidelberg: Springer.

Hermans, H., Konopka, A., Oosterwegel, A. & Zomer, P. 2017. Fields of Tension in a Boundary-Crossing World: Towards a Democratic Organization of the Self. *Integrative Psychological and Behavioral Science, 51*(4): 505-535.

Laing, R. 1977. *Phänomenologie der Erfahrung*. Frankfurt a.M.: Suhrkamp.

Lederach, J.P. 1995. *Preparing for Peace. Conflict Transformation Across Cultures*. Syracuse, NY: Syracuse University Press.

Mall, R.A. & Peikert, D. 2017. *Philosophie als Therapie. Eine interkulturelle Perspektive*. Freiburg/München: Alber.

Nussbaum, M. 1994. *The Therapy of Desire. Theory and Practice in Hellenistic Ethics*. Princeton, NJ: Princeton University Press.

Platon. 2002. *Sämtliche Werke, I* (Eds. Wolf, U.). Reinbek bei Hamburg: Rowohlt.

Schellhammer, B. 2018. The philosophy of Self-Care, Individuation and Psychodrama. Exploring creative means to Encountering the "unknown Other" in Self. *British Journal of Guidance & Counselling, 48*(1): 114-124.

Schellhammer, B. 2019. *An Konflikten wachsen. Konflikt-Coaching und die Sorge um sich selbst.* Weinheim: Beltz.

Schulz von Thun, F. 2003. *Miteinander Reden 3. Das „Innere Team" und situationsgerechte Kommunikation.* Reinbek bei Hamburg: Rowohlt.

Stavemann, H. 2015. *Sokratische Gesprächsführung in Therapie und Beratung.* Weinheim/ Basel: Beltz.

Straub, J. 2012. Personale Identität als Politikum. In B. Henry & A. Pirni (Eds.). *Der asymmetrische Westen. Zur Pragmatik der Koexistenz pluralistischer Gesellschaften,* Bielefeld: transcript, p.41-78.

The Guardian. 2010. Socrates – a man for our times. *The Guardian.* Available from: https://www. theguardian.com/books/2010/oct/17/socrates-philosopher-man-for-our-times [Accessed 28 February 2019].

Theiner, P. 2017. *Robert Bosch. Unternehmer im Zeitalter der Extreme. Eine Biografie.* München: C.H. Beck.

Welsch, W. 1991. Subjektsein heute. Überlegungen zur Transformation des Subjekts. *Deutsche Zeitschrift für Philosophie, 39*(4): 347-365.

Wisniewski, R. & Niehaus, M. 2016. *Management by Sokrates. Praktische Philosophie für Mitarbeiterführung, Beratung, Coaching und Training.* Norderstedt: BoD Books.

Chapter 5: References

Arendt, H. 1963. *Eichmann in Jerusalem: A report on the banality of evil.* New York: Penguin.

Aurelius, M. 2013. *Meditations.* Available from: https://www.gutenberg.org/files/2680/2680-h/2680-h.htm (Accessed 25 May 2019).

Beck, D. & Cowan C. 2006. *Spiral dynamics. Mastering values, leadership, and change.* Malden, MA: Blackwell Publishing.

Buber, M. 1970. *I and thou.* Trans. by Walter Kaufmann. New York: Touchstone Rockefeller Center.

Crowe, D. 2004. *Oskar Schindler. The untold account of his life, wartime activities, and the true story behind the list.* Cambridge, MA: Westview Press.

Damasio, A. 2010. *Self comes to mind. Constructing the conscious brain.* New York: Vintage Books.

Encyclopaedia Britannica. 1938. *Munich agreement.* Available from: https://www.britannica. com/event/Munich-Agreement (Accessed 25 April 2019).

Facing History and Ourselves. 1943. *Himmler speech in Posen (Poland) in October 4, 1943.* Available from: https://www.facinghistory.org/holocaust-human-behavior/himmler-speech-posen-1943 (Accessed 22 May 2019).

Fackenheim, E. 2003. *Glaube an Gott und „Idee Mensch" nach Auschwitz.* Jewish Christian relations. Insights and issues in the ongoing Jewish-Christian dialogue. Available from: http://www.jcrelations.net/Glaube_an_Gott_und__Idee_Mensch__nach_ Auschwitz.2738.0.html?L=3&pdf=1 (Accessed 10 June 2019).

General Assembly. 1999. *Declaration and programme of action on a culture of peace.* General Assembly Resolution 53/243, 6 October. Available from: https://undocs.org/en/A/ RES/53/243 (Accessed 9 July 2019).

General Assembly. 2015. *Transforming our world: the 2030 agenda for sustainable development.* General Assembly Resolution 70/1, 25 September. Available from: https://www.un.org/ga/ search/view_doc.asp?symbol=A/RES/70/1&Lang=E (Accessed 9 July 2019).

George, B. & Sims, P. 2007. *True North. Discover your authentic leadership.* San Francisco: Jossey-Bass.

Gergen, K. 2009. *Relational being. Beyond self and community.* Oxford: Oxford University Press.

Greenleaf, R.K. 1977. *Servant leadership: A journey into the nature of legitimate power and greatness.* New York: Paulist Press.

Hart, H.L.A. 1961. *The concept of law.* Oxford: Clarendon Press.

International Organization for Standardization. 2017. *Annual report: Building for a better future.* Geneva: ISO.

Kahneman, D. 2011. Thinking, fast and slow. New York: Doubleday Canada.

Kant, I. 1991. *The metaphysics of morals.* Translated by Mary J. Gregor. New York: Cambridge University Press.

Kant, I. 2017. *Groundwork for the metaphysics of morals.* Available from: https://www.earlymoderntexts.com/assets/pdfs/kant1785.pdf. (Accessed 4 June 2019).

Pico Della Mirandola, G. 1956. *Oration on the dignity of man.* Translated by A. Robert Caponigri. South Bend, IN: Gateway Editions, Ltd.

Keneally, T. 1982. *Schindler's List.* New York: Touchstone.

Levinas, E. 1998. *On thinking-of-the-other entre nous.* Translated by Michael B. Smith. New York: Columbia University Press.

Levinas, E. 1999. *Alterity and transcendence.* Translated by Michael B. Smith. New York: Columbia University Press.

Lipman-Blumen, J. 1996. *Connective leadership. Managing in a changing world.* Oxford: Oxford University Press.

Longerich, P. 2010. *The Nazi prosecution and murder of the Jews.* Oxford: Oxford University Press.

Majer, D. 2003. *"Non-Germans" under the Third Reich: The Nazi judicial and administrative system in Germany and occupied Eastern Europe with special regard to occupied Poland, 1939–1945.* Baltimore: John Hopkins University.

McNab, C. 2009. *The SS: 1923-1945.* London: Amber Books.

Northouse, P. 2016. *Leadership. Theory and practice.* 7th edition. Los Angeles: Sage.

Oxford University Press. 1973. *The Shorter Oxford English Dictionary.* 3rd edition. Oxford: Clarendon Press.

Pico Della Mirandola, G. 1956. *Oration on the dignity of man.* Translated by A. Robert Caponigri. South Bend, IN: Gateway Editions, Ltd.

Pryor, Z. 1979. Czechoslovak fiscal policies in the Great Depression. *The Economic History Review, 32*(2): 228-240.

Rifkin, J. 2009. *The empathic civilization: The Race to Global Consciousness in a World in Crisis.* New York: Penguin Group.

Roberts, J. 1996. *The importance of Oskar Schindler.* San Diego: Lucent.

Roberts, J. 2000. *Oskar Schindler: Righteous gentile.* Costa Messa: SaddleBack Pub.

SDG Tracker. 2018. *Measuring progress towards the sustainable development goals.* Available from: https://sdg-tracker.org/ (Accessed 9 July 2019).

Stuttgarter Zeitung. 1999. *Schindlers Koffer: Berichte aus dem Leben eines Lebensretters.* Stuttgart: Stuttgarter Zeitung Verlagsgesellschaft Eberle GmbH&Co.

The Giving Pledge. 2019. *A commitment to philanthropy.* Available from: https://givingpledge.org/ (Accessed 10 July 2019).

United Nations. 1948. *Universal declaration of human rights.* Available from: https://www.un.org/en/universal-declaration-human-rights/ (Accessed 5 June 2019).

Walzel, V., Polak, F. & Solar, J. 1960. *T. G. Masaryk – champion of liberty*. New York: Research and Studies Center of CFTUF.

Wilber, K. 2007. *The integral vision*. Boston and London: Shambhala.

Chapter 6 References

Allen, T.D., Henderson, T.G., Mancini, V.S. & French, K.A. 2017. Mindfulness and Meditation Practice as Moderators of the Relationship between Age and Subjective Wellbeing among Working Adults. *Mindfulness, 8*(4): 1055–1063.

Anālayo, B. 2019. Adding historical depth to definitions of mindfulness. *Current Opinion in Psychology, 28*(28): 11–14.

Antoine De Saint-Exupery. 2000. *Wind, Sand, And Stars*. London: Penguin Classic.

Benefiel, M. 2019. *Conscious Leadership as a Spiritual Journey*. Available from: https://shalem.org/2019/05/01/conscious-leadership-as-a-spiritual-journey [Accessed 18 February 2020].

Berkley Center for Religion, Peace and World Affairs at Georgetown University. 2011. *The Business of Spirit: A Conversation on Meditation and Leadership*. Available from: https://berkleycenter.georgetown.edu/events/the-business-of-spirit-a-conversation-on-meditation-and-leadership [Accessed 18 February 2020].

Blanchard, K.H. & Broadwell, R. 2018. *Servant leadership in action: how you can achieve great relationships and results*. Oakland, CA: Berrett-Koehler Publishers, Inc.

DeWees, B.R. 2019. *Essays on Judgment and Decision Making*. [PhD Dissertation] pp.1–178. Available from: https://dash.harvard.edu/handle/1/42029732 [Accessed 18 February 2020].

Eliot, T.S. 1971. *Complete Poems and Plays*. New York: Harcourt, Brace & World.

Fine, S. 2018, January 13. How Beverley McLauchlin found her bliss. Where she came from and what she leaves behind. *The Globe and Mail*. Available from: https://newstral.com/en/article/en/1084721978/how-beverley-mclachlin-found-her-bliss-where-she-came-from-and-what-she-leaves-behind [Accessed 18 February 2020].

Frankl, V.E. n.d. *Viktor E. Frankl Quotes*. Available from: https://www.brainyquote.com/quotes/viktor_e_frankl_160380 [Accessed 20 February 2020].

Frankl, V.E., Lasch, I., Kushner, H.S. & Wnislade, W.J. 2015. *Man's search for meaning*. Boston, MA: Beacon Press.

Freeman, L. 2015. *The Selfless Self: Meditation and the Opening of the Heart*. Norwich: Canterbury Press.

Freeman, L. 2019. *Good Work: Meditation for Personal and Organisational Transformation*. Singapore: Meditatio.

Friedland, D. 2016. *Leading well from within: a neuroscience and mindfulness-based framework for conscious leadership*. San Diego, CA: Supersmarthealth.

Fry, L. & Kriger, M. 2009. Towards a theory of being-centered leadership: Multiple levels of being as context for effective leadership. *Human Relations, 62*(11): 1667–1696.

George, B. 2003. *Authentic leadership: rediscovering the secrets to creating lasting value*. San Francisco: Jossey-Bass.

George, B. 2010. *Mindful Leadership: Compassion, Contemplation and Meditation Develop Effective Leaders*. Available from: https://www.billgeorge.org/articles/mindful-leadership-compassion-contemplation-and-meditation-develop-effective-leaders/ [Accessed 19 February 2020].

Goyal, M., Singh, S., Sibinga, E., Gould, N., Rowland-Seymour, A. Sharma, R. Berger, Z. Sleicher, D. Maron, D. Shihab, H. Ranasinghe, P. Linn, S. Saha, S. Bass, E. & Haythornthwaite, J. 2014. Meditation Programs for Psychological Stress and Well-being: A Systematic Review and Meta-analysis. *Deutsche Zeitschrift für Akupunktur, 57*(3): 26–27.

Gurney, M. 2020. *Lessons from SARS Part 3: The Public-health officer.* Available from: https://www.tvo.org/article/lessons-from-sars-part-3-the-public-health-officer. [Accessed 19 February 2020].

Hayes, M.C. & Flower, A. 2019. *The serenity passport: a world tour of peaceful living in 30 words.* London: White Lion Publishing.

Heider, J. 2015. *The Tao of leadership: Lao Tzu's Tao te ching adapted for a new age.* Palm Beach Florida: Green Dragon Books.

Holiday, R. 2019. *Stillness is the key: an ancient strategy for modern life.* London: Profile Books.

Khobragade, Y., Khobragade, S. & Abbas, A. 2016. Hypertension and meditation: can meditation be useful in preventing hypertension? *International Journal of Community Medicine and Public Health, 3*(7): 1685–1694.

Kirste, I., Nicola, Z., Kronenberg, G., Walker, T.L., Liu, R.C. & Kempermann, G. 2013. *Is silence golden? Effects of auditory stimuli and their absence on adult hippocampal neurogenesis.* Available from: https://www.ncbi.nlm.nih.gov/pmc/articles/PMC4087081/ [Accessed 19 February 2020].

Lane, B.C. 1998. *The solace of fierce landscapes : exploring desert and mountain spirituality.* New York; Oxford: Oxford University Press.

Lazar, S.W., Kerr, C.E., Wasserman, R.H., Gray, J.R. Greve, D.N., Treadway, M.T., McGarvey, M., Quinn, B.T., Dusek, J.A., Benson, H., Rauch, S.L., Moore, C.I. & Fischld, B. 2005. *Meditation experience is associated with increased cortical thickness.* Available from: https://www.ncbi.nlm.nih.gov/pmc/articles/PMC1361002/. [Accessed 19 February 2020].

Meditatio. 2012. *The Business of Spirit.* London: World Community for Christian Meditation.

Montero-Marin, J., Kuyken, W., Gasión, V., Barceló-Soler, A., Rojas, L., Manrique, A., Esteban, R. & Javier García Campayo. 2020. Feasibility and effectiveness of a workplace-adapted mindfulness-based programme to reduce stress in workers at a private sector logistics company: An exploratory mixed methods study. *International Journal of Environmental Research and Public Health, 17*(5): 1643.

Pascoe, M.C., Thompson, D.R. & Ski, C.F. 2020. Meditation and Endocrine Health and Wellbeing. *Trends in Endocrinology & Metabolism* (in press).

Picard, A. 2020, March 9. Bonnie Henry a calming voice in a sea of coronavirus madness. *The Globe and Mail.* Available from: https://www.theglobeandmail.com/opinion/article-bonnie-henry-is-a-calming-voice-in-a-sea-of-coronavirus-madness/ [Accessed 19 February 2020].

Rakoczy, S. 2006. *Great mystics and social justice: walking on the two feet of love.* New York: Paulist Press.

Randerson A.K. 2020. Mindfulness, Wellness, and Spirituality in the Workplace. In S. Dhiman (Ed.). *The Palgrave Handbook of Workplace Well-Being.* Randerson A.K. 2020. Mindfulness, Wellness, and Spirituality in the Workplace. In S. Dhiman (Ed.). The Palgrave Handbook of Workplace Well-Being. Palgrave Macmillan: Cham: Palgrave Macmillan: Cham.

Reitz, M., Waller, L., Chaskalson, M., Olivier, S. & Rupprecht, S. 2020. Developing leaders through mindfulness practice. *Journal of Management Development, 39*(2): 223-239.

Rolheiser, R. 1994. *The Insufficiency of Everything Attainable.* Available from: https://ronrolheiser.com/the-insufficiency-of-everything-attainable/#.Xk4rcBd7nRY [Accessed -21 September 2019.

Rolheiser, R. 2019. *A Spirituality for Steadiness and Sanity*. Conference, St. Mark's College, Vancouver, British Columbia.

Rowland, D. 2017. *Still moving: how to lead mindful change*. New York: John Wiley & Sons.

Rowland, D. 2018, February 1. Leadership development today requires that faculty act less as experts, more as Sherpas. *Leadership Development Today*. Available from: https://www. deborahrowland.com/new-blog/2018/2/1/leadership-development-today-my-lse-article [Accessed 18 February 2020].

Saleem, M. & Samudrala, P. 2017. Meditation Experience Associated with Structural Neuroplasticity. *Annals of International Medical and Dental Research, 3*(4):1-6.

Song, P. N. K. 2018. *GIC Insights: Ng Kok Song on what most surprised him about China in the last 5 years*. Available from: https://www.youtube.com/watch?v=yv1JrxF_j7E [Accessed 18 February 2020].

Strait, J.E., Strait, G.G., McClain, M.B., Casillas, L., Streich, K., Harper, K. & Gomez, J. 2020. Classroom Mindfulness Education Effects on Meditation Frequency, Stress, and Self-Regulation. *Teaching of Psychology, 47*(2): 162–168.

Talbot-Zorn, J. & Marz, L. 2017. *The Busier you are, the More you need Quiet Time*. Available from: https://hbr.org/2017/03/the-busier-you-are-the-more-you-need-quiet-time [Accessed 19 February 2020].

Tan, C. 2019. Rethinking the Concept of Mindfulness: A Neo-Confucian Approach. *Journal of Philosophy of Education, 53*(2): 359–373.

Taylor, C. 1991. *The malaise of modernity*. Toronto, ON: House of Anansi Press.

Taylor-Vaiser, N. 2020. Does Theresa Tam ever get a day off? *MacLeans*. Available from: https://www.macleans.ca/politics/ottawa/does-theresa-tam-ever-get-a-day-off/ [Accessed 19 February 2020].

Vella, E. & McIver, S. 2019. Reducing stress and burnout in the public-sector work environment: A mindfulness meditation pilot study. *Australian Health Promotion Journal, 30*(2): 219-227.

Viswanathan, M., Golin, C.E., Jones, C.D., Ashok, M., Blalock, S.J., Wines, R.C.M., Coker-Schwimmer, E.J.L., Rosen, D.L., Sista, P. & Lohr, K.N. 2012. Interventions to improve adherence to self-administered medications for chronic diseases in the United States: a systematic review. *Annals of Internal Medicine, 157*(11): 785–95.

Walumbwa, F.O., Hartnell, C.A. & Oke, A. 2010. Servant leadership, procedural justice climate, service climate, employee attitudes, and organizational citizenship behavior: A cross-level investigation. *Journal of Applied Psychology, 95*(3): 517–529.

Warneka, T.H. 2008. *Black belt leader, peaceful leader: an introduction to Catholic servant leadership*. Cleveland, OH: Asogomi Pub. International.

Ying Gao, C. 2018. *A Narrative Inquiry into Contemplative Leadership: Concepts, Characteristics, Challenges, Opportunities*. pp.1–269. Available from: https://scholar.google.ca/scholar?cluster=5419158117977677381&hl=en&as_sdt=0,5&as_vis=1 [Accessed 20 September 2020].

Chapter 7 References

Bachkirova, T., Jackson, P., Gannon, J., Iordanou, I. & Myers, A. 2017. Reconceptualising coach education from the perspectives of pragmatism and constructivism. *Philosophy of Coaching: An International Journal, 2*(2): 29-50.

Botha, D. 2017. *The Fourth Industrial Revolution and Knowledge Management: Early-stage conceptualisation*. South African Knowledge Management Summit, 29-31 August.

Bhalla, V., Dyrcks, S. & Strack, R. 2017. *Twelve forces that will radically change how organizations work*. The New Way of Working Series. Available from: www.bcg.com/en-us/publications/2017/people-organization-strategy-twelve-forces-radically-change-organizations-work.aspx/ [Accessed 20 March 2020].

Brown, D.R. 2012. The BGR contingency model for leading change. *International Journal of Learning and Change*, 6(2): 66-78.

Britt, T.W., Shen, W., Sinclair, R.R., Grossman, M.R., and Klieger, D.M. 2016. How much do we know about employee resilience? *Industrial and Organizational Psychology*, 9(2): 378-404.

Burke, W.W. 2017. *Organization change: Theory and practice*. Los Angeles: Sage Publications.

Chimbganda, T. 2015. *Traumatic pedagogy: When epistemic privilege and white privilege collide. Racial battle fatigue in higher education: Exposing the myth of post-racial America.* Lanham, MD: Rowman & Littlefield Publishers.

Collinson, D. 2012. Prozac leadership and the limits of positive thinking. *Journal of Leadership*, 8(2): 87-107.

Crane, M.F. 2017. *Managing for resilience: A practical guide for employee wellbeing and organizational performance*. New York: Routledge.

Crocitto, M. & Youssef, M. 2003. The human side of organizational agility. *Industrial Management and Data Systems, 103*(6): 388-397.

Dobbs, R., Manyika, J. & Woetzel, J.R. 2015. *No Ordinary Disruption: The Four Global Forces breaking all the Trends*. New York: Public Affairs.

Grant, H. & Gelety, L. 2009. *Goal content theories: Why differences in what we are striving for matter*. New York: Guilford Press.

Garwe, E.C. 2015. Student voice and quality enhancement in higher education. *Journal of Applied Research in Higher Education, 30*(2): 232-251.

Gray, A. 2016. *The 10 skills you need to thrive in the Fourth Industrial Revolution*. Available from: www.weforum.org/agenda/2016/01/the-10skills-you-need-to-thrive-in-the-fourth-industrial-revolution/ [Accessed 21 May 2019].

Ivtzan, I., Lomas, T., Hefferon, K. & Worth, P. 2016. *Second Wave Positive Psychology*. New York: Routledge.

Kinsinger, P. & Walch, K. 2012. *Living and leading in a VUCA world*. Phoenix, USA: Thunderbird University.

Kotzé, M. & Nel, P. 2013. Psychometric properties of the adult resilience indicator. *SA Journal of Industrial Psychology*, 39(2): 1-11.

Kurasha. P. 2015. Peeling the Onion: Public Policy Challenges, Hotspots and Gaps in Contentious Educational Policy Areas. *Journal of Scientific Research*, 4(30): 614-621.

Lucas, H.C. 2012. *The Search for Survival: Lessons from Disruptive Technologies*. Santa Barbara: Praeger Publishing.

Mutenga, T. 2012. *Zimbabwe: Higher Education in Crisis*. Available from: www.allafrica.com/stories/201208021111.html?page=2 [Accessed 6 April 2018].

Madzimure, J. 2016. *Zimbabwean university education system: a survival of the fittest*. Available from: www.nehandaradio.com/2016/10/04/zimbabwean-university-education-system-survivial-fittest/ [Accessed 21 July 2019].

Meyer, P. 2016. *Agility shift: Creating agile and effective leaders, teams, and organizations*. New. York: Routledge.

Mhlanga, T. 2017. *A study to investigate the attitude of customers towards electronic banking: The case of a South African-based company*. Available from: http://etd.uwc.ac.za/bitstream/handle/11394/6321/Mhlanga_MCOM_EMS_2017.pdf?sequence=1&isAllowed=y [Accessed 22 May 2019].

Pandor, N. 2019. *National Skills Authority Conference, Department of Higher Education and Training.* Available from: www.gov.za/speeches/minister-naledi-pandor-opens-national-skills-conference-and-officiates-skills-awards-gala/ [Accessed 22 May 2019].

Reb, J., Narayanan, J. & Ho, Z.W. 2015. Mindfulness at work: Antecedents and consequences of employee awareness and absent-mindedness. *Mindfulness Review, 6*(1): 111-122.

Rodney-Gumede, Y. 2019, March 8. Africa needs to think differently and embrace 4IR. *Mail and Guardian.* Available from: https://mg.co.za/article/2019-03-08-00-south-africa-needs-to-think-differently-and-embrace-4ir [Accessed 23 May 2019].

Simpson, G. & Jones, K. 2013. How important is resilience among family members supporting relatives with traumatic brain injury or spinal cord injury? *Clinical rehabilitation, 27*(4): 367-377.

Sharifi, H. & Zhang, Z. 1999. A methodology for achieving agility in manufacturing organisations: An introduction. *International Journal of Production Economics, 62*(1-2): 7-22.

Uzhenyu, D. 2017. Perennial challenges facing the Government of Zimbabwe on paying salaries and other benefits to its workers. *International Open and Distance Learning Journal, 3*(2): 2013-2016.

World Economic Forum (WEF). 2016. *The Future of Jobs: Employment, Skills and Workforce Strategy for the Fourth Industrial Revolution.* Available from: https://www.weforum.org/agenda/2016/01/the-future-of-jobs [Accessed 17 July 2019].

York. G. 2018. Under New Leadership Zimbabwe Still faces Educational Crisis. *The Globe and Mail.* Available from: www.theglobeandmail.com/news/world/under-new-rulers-zimbabwe-still-faces-education-crisis/article37517003 [Accessed 19 July 2019].

Zauszniewski, J.A., Bekhet, A.K. & Suresky, M.J. 2010. Resilience in family members of persons with serious mental illness. *Journal of Nursing, 45*(4): 613-626.

Zimbabwe Open University (ZOU). 2014. *Towards Achieving Quality Education through Distance Learning. Challenges and opportunities.* Available from: www.eiseverywhere.com/ereg/popups/speakerdetails.php?eventid=142986&language=eng&speakerid=474747 [Accessed 23 January 2020].

Chapter 8 References

Ackerman, C. 2020. *What is Self-Regulation? (+95 Skills and Strategies).* Available from: https://positivepsychology.com/self-regulation/ [Accessed 14 May 2020].

Ackley, D. 2016. Emotional intelligence: A practical review of models, measures, and applications. *Consulting Psychology Journal: Practice and Research, 68*(4): 269-286.

Artuch-Garde, R., González-Torres, M.D.C., de la Fuente, J., Vera, M.M., Fernández-Cabezas, M. & López-García, M. 2017. Relationship between resilience and self-regulation: a study of Spanish youth at risk of social exclusion. *Frontiers in Psychology, 8,* Article 612: 1-11.

Badat, S. 2010. *The challenges of transformation in higher education and training institutions in South Africa.* Paper commissioned by Development Bank of South Africa. Available from: https://www.dbsa.org/EN/Pages/default.aspx/ [Accessed 2 February 2020].

Bandura, A., 1991. Social cognitive theory of self-regulation. *Organizational behavior and human decision processes, 50*(2): 248-287.

Baumeister, R.F. & Vohs, K.D. 2007. Self-Regulation, ego depletion, and motivation. *Social and personality psychology compass, 1*(1): 115-128.

Bennett, N. & Lemoine, J. 2014. What VUCA really means for you. *Harvard Business Review, 92*(1/2): 27.

Bergland, C. 2016. *Your Brain Can Be Trained to Self-Regulate Negative Thinking*. Available from: https://www.psychologytoday.com/za/blog/the-athletes-way/201601/your-brain-can-be-trained-self-regulate-negative-thinking [Accessed 14 May 2020].

Brown, K.W. & Ryan, R.M. 2003. The benefits of being present: mindfulness and its role in psychological well-being. *Journal of Personality and Social psychology, 84*(4): 822-848.

Bryant, A. & Kazan, A.L. 2012. *Self-leadership: how to become a more successful, efficient, and effective leader from the inside out*. New York: McGraw Hill Professional.

Buitenweg, J.I., van de Ven, R.M., Prinssen, S., Murre, J.M. & Ridderinkhof, K.R. 2017. Cognitive flexibility training: A large-scale multimodal adaptive active-control intervention study in healthy older adults. *Frontiers in human neuroscience, 11* Article 529: 1-11.

De Carvalho, J. & Florez-Florez, J. 2014. The meeting of knowledge: A project for the decolonisation of the university in Latin America. *Postcolonial Studies, 17*(2): 122–139.

D'Intino, R.S., Goldsby, M.G., Houghton, J.D. & Neck, C.P. 2007. Self-leadership: A process for entrepreneurial success. *Journal of leadership and organizational studies, 13*(4): 105-120.

ENCA. 2016, September 19. No more than 8% increase – Nzimande. *ENCA*. Available from: https://www.enca.com/south-africa/catch-it-live-minister-nzimande-announces-higher-education-fees-adjustments/ [Accessed 2 February 2020].

Goleman, D. 1995. *Emotional Intelligence: Why it can matter more than IQ*. New York: Bantam Books.

Jamieson, S.D. & Tuckey, M.R. 2017. Mindfulness interventions in the workplace: A critique of the current state of the literature. *Journal of Occupational Health Psychology, 22*(2): 180-193.

Jansen, J. 2004. Changes and continuities in South Africa's higher education system, 1994 to 2004. In L. Chisholm (Ed.). *Changing class: Education and social change in post-apartheid South Africa*. Pretoria: Human Science Research Council Press, pp 293–314.

Kail, E.G. 2010. *Leading in a VUCA environment: V is for volatility*. Available from: https://hbr.org/2010/11/leading-in-a-vuca-environment [Accessed June 2019].

Kamga, G.E.K. 2019. The #FeesMustFall protest: when the camp (u) s becomes the matrix of a state of emergency. *Acta Academica, 51*(1): 88-108.

Kgatle, M.S. 2018. The role of the church in the# FeesMustFall movement in South Africa: Practical Theological reflection. *HTS Teologiese Studies/Theological Studies, 74*(1): 1-8.

King, L.A. 2001. The health benefits of writing about life goals. *Personality and Social Psychology Bulletin, 27*: 798–807.

Kolzow, D.R. 2014. *Leading from within: Building organizational leadership capacity. International Economic Development Council*. Available from: https:// www.iedconline.org/clientuploads/Downloads/edrp/Leading_from_Within.pdf/ [Accessed: 5 May 2020].

Korsakova, T.V. 2019. Higher Education in VUCA-World: New Metaphor of University. *European Journal of Interdisciplinary Studies, 5*(2): 31-35.

Langa, M., Ndelu, S., Edwin, Y. & Vilakazi, M. 2017. *# Hashtag: An analysis of the# FeesMustFall movement at South African universities*. Johannesburg: Centre for the Study of Violence and Reconciliation.

Le Grange, L. 2016. Decolonising the university curriculum: Leading article. *South African Journal of Higher Education, 30*(2): 1-12.

Madia, T. 2016. Hard to predict the next step for Fees Must Fall. *News24*. Available from: https://www.news24.com/SouthAfrica/News/hard-to-predict-the-next-step-for-fees-must-fall-20160814/ [Accessed 10 May 2020].

Malouff, J.M. & Schutte, N.S. 2017. Can psychological interventions increase optimism? A meta-analysis. *The Journal of Positive Psychology, 12*(6): 594–604.

Manz, C.C. & Neck, C.P. 2004. Mastering self-leadership: Empowering yourself for personal excellence (3rd ed.). Upper Saddle River, NJ: Prentice Hall

Mavunga, G. 2019. #FeesMustFall protests in South Africa: A critical realist analysis of selected newspaper articles. *Journal of Student Affairs in Africa, 7*(1): 81-99.

Morrell, R. 2019. Rebels and Rage: reflecting on# FeesMustFall by Adam Habib. *Transformation: Critical Perspectives on Southern Africa, 100*(1): 209-219.

Mutekwe, E. 2017. Unmasking the ramifications of the fees-must-fall-conundrum in higher education institutions in South Africa: a critical perspective. *Perspectives in Education, 35*(2): 142-154.

Naicker, C. 2016. From Marikana to #feesmustfall: The praxis of popular politics in South Africa. *Urbanisation, 1*(1): 53–61.

Ndlovu-Gatsheni, S.J. 2014. Global coloniality and the challenges of creating African futures. *Strategic Review for Southern Africa, 36*(2): 181-202.

Ngqakamba, S. 2019. Fees Must Fall was a progressive struggle, we just differed on tactics' - Adam Habib. *News24*. Available from: https://www.news24.com/SouthAfrica/News/fees-must-fall-was-a-progressive-struggle-we-just-differed-on-tactics-adam-habib-20190807 [Accessed 5 December 2019].

Orejarena, H., Zambrano, O. & Carvajal, M. 2019. Emotional intelligence and its influence on organizational leadership in the VUCA world. In *4th International Conference on Social, Business, and Academic Leadership (ICSBAL October 2019)*. Prague: Atlantis Press.

Padesky, C.A. & Mooney, K.A. 2012. Strengths-based cognitive–behavioural therapy: A four-step model to build resilience. *Clinical Psychology & Psychotherapy, 19*(4): 283-290.

Penprase, B.E. 2018. The fourth industrial revolution and higher education. In N.W. Gleason (Ed.). *Higher education in the era of the fourth industrial revolution*. Singapore: Palgrave Macmillan, pp. 207–229.

Postma, D. 2016. An educational response to student protests. Learning from Hannah Arendt. *Education as Change, 20*(1): 1-9.

Prati, G. & Pietrantoni, L. 2009. Optimism, social support, and coping strategies as factors contributing to posttraumatic growth: A meta-analysis. *Journal of Loss and Trauma, 14*: 364–388.

Samoilov, A. & Goldfried, M.R. 2000. Role of emotion in cognitive-behavior therapy. *Clinical Psychology: science and practice, 7*(4): 373-385.

Sanaghan, P. 2016. *Building leadership resilience in higher education*. Available from: https://www.academicimpressions.com/sites/default/files/0116-leadership-resilience-md.pdf. [Accessed 2 February 2019].

Saunders S.T. 2019. *Rebels and rage: Reflecting on #FeesMustFall – A review*. Available from: http://www.scielo.org.za/pdf/sajs/v115n7-8/03.pdf [Accessed 14 May 2020].

Seligman, M.E. 2006. *Learned optimism: How to change your mind and your life*. New York: Vintage Books.

Spencer, L.M. & Spencer, P.S.M. 1993. *Competence at Work models for superior performance*. New York: John Wiley and Sons.

Stenger, M. 2017. *7 Ways to Develop Cognitive Flexibility*. Available from: https://www.opencolleges.edu.au/informed/features/7-ways-develop-cognitive-flexibility/ [Accessed 14 May 2020].

Sugay, C. 2020. *What is Positive CBT? A Look at Positive Cognitive Behavioral Therapy*. Available from: https://positivepsychology.com/positive-cbt/ [Accessed 14 May 2020].

Sullivan, J. 2012. *Talent Strategies for a Turbulent VUCA World — Shifting to an Adaptive Approach*. Available from https://drjohnsullivan.com/uncategorized/talent-strategies-for-a-turbulent-vuca-world-shifting-to-an-adaptive-approach/ [Accessed 15 June 2019].

Weatherspoon-Robinson, S. 2013. *African American female leaders: Resilience and success.* (Doctoral dissertation, Pepperdine University, Malibu, California). Available from https://pqdtopen.proquest.com/doc/1426825313.html?FMT=ABS [Accessed 2 February 2019].

Chapter 9 References

Ajala, E.M. 2013. Quality of work life and workers wellbeing: The industrial social workers approach. *IFE PsychologIA: An International Journal, 21*(2): 46-56.

Bettencourt, L.A. & Brown, S.W. 1997. Contact employees: relationship among workplace fairness, job satisfaction and prosocial service behaviours. *Journal of Retailing, 73*(1): 39–61.

Bornman, D.A.J. & Puth, G. 2017. Investigating employee perceptions of leadership communication: a South African study. *Journal of Contemporary Management, 14*: 1-23.

Brunetto, Y., Teo, S. T., Shacklock, K. & Farr-Wharton, R. 2012. Emotional intelligence, job satisfaction, well-being and engagement: explaining organisational commitment and turnover intentions in policing. *Human Resource Management Journal, 22*(4): 428-441.

Carley, K.C. 2000. Organizational adaptation in volatile environments. In C.L. Hulin & D.R. Ilgen (Eds.). *Computational modelling in organizational behaviour: The Third Scientific Discipline*. Washington DC: American Psychological Association (p. 241-268).

de Wet, W. 2019. Surviving in a VUCA world - last but not least. *AFMA Matrix, 28*(2): 48.

Deci, E.L. & Ryan, R.M. 2000. The "What" and "Why" of goal pursuits : Human needs and the self-determination of behavior. *Psychological Inquiry, 11*(4): 227–268.

Dhurup, M. & Dibihlela, J. 2013. Role ambiguity and job satisfaction: prevalence, relationships and gendered comparison through workplace experiences of employees in sport organisations. *African Journal for Physical Health Education, Recreation and Dance, 2*: 223-235.

Greenberg, J. 2011. *Behavior in organisations* (10th ed.). Cape Town, South Africa: Pearson.

Hartman, A. 2019. Students risk missing exams due to loan delays. *The Namibian Newspaper.* Available from: https://www.nambian.com.na/165230/archive-read/students-risk-missing-exams-due-to-loan-delays [Accessed 20 August 2019].

Ileka, S. 2017. Lack of funds delays payments- NSFAF. *The Namibian Newspaper.* Available from: https://www.namibian.com.na/169176/archive-read/lack-of-funds-delays-payments---NSFAF [Accessed 20 August 2019].

Men, L.R. 2015. The internal communication role of the chief executive officer: communication channels, style and effectiveness. *Public Relations Review, 41*: 461-471.

Nakale, A. 2019. Unam subsidy falls short of budgetary needs. *New Era Newspaper.* Available from: https://neweralive.na/posts/unam-subsidy-falls-short-of-budgetary-needs [Accessed 15 December 2019].

Naude, R., Kruger, S. & Saayman, M. 2012. Does leisure have an effect on employee quality of work life? *South African Journal of Research in Sport, Physical Education and Recreation, 34*(2): 153-171.

Pieters, W.R. 2018a. Assessing organisational justice as a predictor of job satisfaction and employee engagement of employees in Windhoek. *South African Journal of Human Resource Management, 16*: 1-11.

Pieters, W.R. 2018b. *The effect of job attitudes, job embeddedness and work engagement on turnover intention of academic staff at the University of Namibia.* Unpublished Doctoral Dissertation. University of the Free State, Bloemfontein, South Africa.

Pieters, W.R., Van Zyl, E. & Nel, P. 2019. Job attitudes as a predictor of work engagement of the lecturing staff at the University of Namibia. *South African Journal of Human Resource Management, 17*: 1-11.

Pincus, J.D. & Rayfield, R.E. 1987. The relationship between top management communication performance and job satisfaction. *Communicare, 6*(2): 14-26.

Rothmann, S., Diedericks, E. & Swart, J.P. 2013. Managers relations, psychological need satisfaction and intention to leave in the agricultural sector. *South African Journal of Industrial Psychology, 39*(2): 1-11.

Rothmann, S. & Jordaan, G.M.E. 2006. Job demands, job resources and work engagement of academic staff in South African higher education institutions. *South African Journal of Industrial Psychology, 32*(4): 87-96.

Shikololo, A. 2019. Rejected NSFAF applicants face turbulent times. *New Era Newspaper.* Available from: https://www.google.com/amp/s/neweralive.na/amp/rejected-nsfaf-applicants-face-turbulent-times [Accessed 20 August 2019].

Soltis, S.M., Agneessens, F., Sasovova, Z. & Labianca, G. 2013. A social network perspective on Turnover intentions: The role of distributive justice and social support. *Human Resource Management, 52*(4): 561-584.

Verstuyf, J., Vansteenkiste, M., Soenens, B., Boone, L. & Mouratidis, A. 2013. Daily ups and downs in women's binge eating symptoms: The role of basic psychological needs, general self-control and emotional eating. *Journal of Social and Clinical Psychology, 32*(3): 335-361.

Chapter 10 References

Africa Growth Initiative. 2019. *Foresight Africa: Top priorities for the continent in 2019.* Washington: Brookings Institution.

Anon. 2013. Tutu leads Mandela memorial at Centre of Memory. *Media Club South Africa.* Available from: www.mediaclubsouthafrica.com/nelsonmandela/3597-tutu-leadsmandela-memorial-at-centre-of-memory#ixzz3sNWyV52E. [Assessed 24 November 2015].

Blanchard, K. 2007. *Leading at a higher level.* Edinburgh: Pearson.

Burns, J.M. 1978. Leadership. New York: Harper & Row.

Bushe, G.R. & Marshak, R.J. 2016. The dialogic mindset: leading emergent change in a complex world. *Organization Development Journal, 34*(1): 37-65.

Churchill, O., Mai, J., Lee, A., Zhou, C. & Tang, F. 2019. China and U.S. 'agree to phased rollback' of extra trade war tariffs. *Politico.* Available from: www.politico.com›2019/11/07›us-china-trade-war-tariffs-067287 [Accessed 7 November 2019].

Cloete, F. 1999. *The discipline of public administration and management at South African universities.* Mt. Grace 2 Conference, Magaliesburg, North-West Province. 23–26 November.

Covey, S. 1996. *Principle centered leadership.* Sydney: Simon & Schuster.

Department of Finance. 1996. *Growth, Employment and Redistribution. A Macroeconomic Strategy.* Pretoria: Government Printers.

Duggan, J. 2014. *Archival Collections of South African Heads of State Part Two.*

Department of Social Anthropology, University of Cape Town. Available from: www.archivalplatform.org [Accessed 3 September 2019].

Hartley, J. 2018. Ten propositions about public leadership. *International Journal of Public Leadership, 14*(4): 202-217.

Johanson, B. 2017. *The New Leadership Literacies. Thriving in a future of extreme disruption and distributed everything.* Milwaukee: Berrett-Koehler Publishers.

Landsberg, C. 2007. The AU, Nepad and Mbeki's progressive African agenda. *Mail & Guardian.* Available from: https://mg.co.za/article/2007-06-18-the-au-nepad-and-mbekis-progressive-african-agenda [Accessed 4 September 2019].

Lues, L. 2016. The dynamic and changing work environment. In: E.J. van der Westhuizen (Ed.). *Human Resource Management in Government: A South African perspective on theories, politics and processes.* Cape Town: Juta and Company.

Lues, L. 2019a. Peace leadership in the public and private sectors, In: E. van Zyl and A. Campbell (Eds.). *Peace Leadership. Self-Transformation to Peace.* Randburg: KR Publishing.

Lues, L. 2019b. *How can public sector leadership advance peace, justice and strong institutions in a VUCA environment?* International Association of Schools and Institutes of Administration. Portugal, July 2019.

Mandela, N. 1994. *Long walk to freedom: The autobiography of Nelson Mandela.* New York, NY: Liveright Publishing.

Maxwell, J.C. 2007. *21 Irrefutable Laws of Leadership: Follow them and people will follow you.* New York: Nelson Thomas Publishers.

Myburgh, P. 2019. *Gangster state: Unravelling Ace Magashule's web of capture.* Cape Town: Penguin Books.

Ngambi, H.C. 2011. RARE leadership: An Alternative Leadership Approach for Africa. *International Journal of African Renaissance Studies – Multi-, Inter- and Transdisciplinary, 6*(1): 6-23.

Rimita, K. 2019. *Leader Readiness in a volatile, uncertain, complex, and ambiguous (VUCA) business environment.* Available from: https://scholarworks.waldenu.edu/dissertations/7727/ [Accessed 15 July 2019].

Statistics South Africa. 2019. *Youth graduate unemployment rate increases in 1Q of 2019.* Available from: www.statssa.gov.za/?p=12121 [Accessed 4 June 2019].

United Nations. 2018. *Sustainable developmental goals.* Available from: www.un.org/sustainabledevelopment/sustainable-development-goals/ [Accessed 4 June 2019].

University of Cambridge Institute for Sustainability Leadership. 2017. Global Definitions of Leadership and Theories of Leadership Development: Literature Review. Cambridge, UK: Cambridge Institute for Sustainability Leadership.

Venter, A. & Landsberg, C. 2011. *Government and politics in the new South Africa.* Pretoria: Van Schaik.

Winters, M.S. 2019. Trump may make America great again after all -- when we show how out of step he is. *The National Catholic Reporter Publishing Company.* Available from: https://www.ncronline.org/.../trump-may-make-america-great-again-after-all-when-we... [Accessed 22 April 2019].

Yang, Y., Peng, F., Wang, R., Guan, K., Jiang, T., Xu, G., Sun, J. & Chang, C. 2020. The deadly coronaviruses: The 2003 SARS pandemic and the 2020 novel coronavirus epidemic in China. *Journal of Autoimmunity, 109*: 1-16.

Chapter 11 References

Albrecht, S. 2005. Leadership climate in the public sector: Feelings matter too! *International Journal of Public Administration, 28*: 397–416.

Auditor-General South Africa. 2019. *Consolidated General Report on local government audit outcomes 2017-2018*. Pretoria: Auditor-General South Africa.

Bass, B.M. & Avolio, B.J. (Eds.). 1994. *Improving Organizational Effectiveness through. Transformational Leadership*. Thousand Oaks, CA: Sage.

Bass, B.M. & Riggio, R.E. 2006. *Transformational leadership* (2nd ed.). New York, NY: Psychology Press.

Bodla, M.A. & Nawaz, M.M. 2010. Comparative study of full range leadership model among faculty members in public and private sector higher education institutes and universities. *International Journal of Business and Management, 5*(4): 208–214.

Bogason, P. & Musso, J.A. 2006. The Democratic Prospects of Network Governance. *American Review of Public Administration, 36*(1): 3-18.

Breakfast, N. 2019. Violent Service Delivery Protests in Post-apartheid South Africa, 1994–2017. A Conflict Resolution Perspective. *African Journal of Public Affairs, 11*(1): 107-126.

Browning, M. 2018. Self-Leadership: Why It Matters. *International Journal of Business and Social Science, 9*(2): 14-18.

Burns, J.M. 1978. *Leadership*. New York: Harper Torchbooks.

Cajaiba-Santana, G. 2014. Social Innovation: Moving the Field Forward. A Conceptual Framework. *Technological Forecasting and Social Change, 82*: 42–51.

Chawla, S. & Lenka, U. 2018. Leadership in a VUCA Environment. In S. Dhir. *Flexible Strategies in VUCA Markets*. Singapore: Springer.

Cipolla, C. & Moura, H. 2012. Social innovation in Brazil through design strategy. *Design Management Journal, 6*(1):40–51.

CNBC Africa. 2020. *South Africa confirms first case of COVID-19*. Available from: https://www.cnbcafrica.com/news/2020/03/05/south-africa-confirms-first-case-of-covid-19/ [Accessed 27 March 2020].

Ramaphosa, C. 2020. Covid-19: Ramaphosa declares national state of disaster, imposes travel bans. *Daily Maverick*. Available from: https://www.dailymaverick.co.za/article/2020-03-15-covid-19-ramaphosa-declares-national-state-of-disaster-imposes-travel-bans/ [Accessed 26 March 2020].

Department of Cooperative Governance and Traditional Affairs. 2009. *State of Local Government in South Africa: National State of Local Government Assessment. Working Document*. Pretoria: Government Printers.

Department of Co-operative Governance and Traditional Affairs. 2010. *Min Mec Briefing: The Local Government Turnaround Strategy. Report*. Pretoria: Government Printer.

Department of Health. 2020a. *COVID-19 Corona Virus South African Resource Portal*. Available from: https://sacoronavirus.co.za/ [Accessed 26 March 2020].

Department of Health. 2020b. *Minister Zweli Mkhize confirms total of 927 cases of Coronavirus COVID-19* Department of Health. Available from: https://www.gov.za/speeches/minister-zweli-mkhize-confirms-total-927-cases-coronavirus-covid-19-26-mar-2020-0000 [Accessed 26 March 2020].

De Vries, M. 2016. *Understanding Public Administration*. London and New York: Palgrave Macmillan.

Dilts, R. 1996. *Visionary Leadership Skills: Creating a World to Which People Want to Belong.* Capitola, CA: Meta Publications.

Dubrin, A. 2007. *Leadership Research Findings, Practice, and Skills.* Boston; New York: Houghton Mifflin Company.

Dunoon, D. 2002. Rethinking leadership for the public sector. *Australian Journal of Public Administration, 61*(3): 3-18.

Ensor, L. 2019. Municipal debt is more than municipalities' debt to Eskom. *BusinessDay.* Available from: https://www.businesslive.co.za/bd/national/2019-10-29-municipal-debt-is-more-than-municipalities-debt-to-eskom/ [Accessed 26 March 2020].

Evans, S. 2018. 24 municipalities now under administration. *News24.* Available from: www.news24.com/SouthAfrica/News/24-municipalities-now-under-administration-20181118 [Accessed 18 March 2020].

Grimm, R., Fox, C., Baines, S. & Albertson, K. 2013. SI, an answer to contemporary societal challenges? Locating the concept in theory and practice. *The European Journal of Social Science Research, 26*(4), 436–455.

Hambley, L.A., O'Neill, T.A. & Kline, T.J.B. 2007. Virtual team leadership: The effects of leadership style and communication medium on team interaction styles and outcomes. *Organizational Behavior and Human Decision Processes, 103*(1): 1-20.

Hart, T., Jacobs, P., Ramoroka, K., Mangqalazah, H., Mhula, A., Ngwenya, M. & Letty, B. 2014. *Social innovation in SA's rural municipalities: Policy implications.* Policy brief. Pretoria: Human Science Research Council.

Hautala, T.M. 2006. The relationship between personality and transformational leadership. *Journal of Management Development, 25*(8): 777-794.

Haxeltine, A. et al. 2017. *TRANSIT WP3 Deliverable D3.4-Consolidated Version of TSI Theory; Deliverable no. D3.4.* Oakland, CA: TRANSIT.

House, R.J. 1976. *Leadership: The Cutting Edge.* Carbondale: Southern Illinois University Press.

Hunt, J.G. 1999. Transformational/charismatic leadership's transformation of the field: An historical essay. *The Leadership Quarterly, 10*(2): 129-144.

Kirkman, B.L., Chen, G., Farh, J.L., Chen, Z. & Lowe, K.B. 2009. Individual power distance orientation and follower reactions to transformational leaders: A cross-level, cross-cultural examination. *Academy of Management Journal, 52*(4): 744-764.

Javidan, M. & Waldman, D.A. 2003. Exploring charismatic leadership in the public sector: Measurement and consequences. *Public Administration Review, 63*(2): 229–242.

Joiner, W.B. & Josephs, S.A. 2007. *Leadership agility: Five levels of mastery for anticipating and initiating change.* San Francisco, CA: Jossey-Bass/Wiley.

Joiner, B. 2009. Creating a culture of agile leaders. *People and Strategy, 32*(4): 28–35.

Joiner, B. 2018. Leadership agility for strategic agility. In C. Prange & L. Heracleuos (Eds.). *Agility.X: How organizations thrive in unpredictable times.* Cambridge, UK: Cambridge University Press.

Jung, D., Wu, A. & Chow, C.W. 2008. Towards understanding the direct and indirect effects of CEOs' transformational leadership on firm innovation. *The Leadership Quarterly, 19*(5): 582-594.

Kerr, S. & Jermier, J.M. 1978. Substitutes for leadership: their meaning and measurement. *Organization Behavior and Human Performance, 2*: 375-403.

Kingsinger, P. & Walch, K. 2012. *Living and leading in a VUCA world.* Glendale, AZ: Thunderbird University.

Kotze, K. 2020. Cyril's style is to inspire the nation. *Mail and Guardian*. Available from: https://mg.co.za/article/2020-02-14-cyrils-style-is-to-inspire-the-nation/ [Accessed 25 May 2020].

Leslie, K. & Canwell, A. 2010. Leadership at all levels: Leading public sector organisations in an age of austerity. *European Management Journal, 28*(4): 297–305.

Lowndes, V. & Roberts, M. 2013. *Why Institutions Matter: The New Institutionalism in Political Science*. Hampshire, UK: Palgrave Macmillan.

Magubane, K. 2019. Municipal debt to Eskom grows by over R1bn in a month. *Fin24*. Available from www.fin24.com/Economy/South-Africa/council-debt-to-eskom-grows-by-over-r1bn-in-a-month-20191203 [Accessed 18 March 2020].

Manz, C.C. 1983. *The Art of Self-Leadership: Strategies for Personal Effectiveness in your Life and Work*. Prentice-Hall, Englewood Cliffs, NJ.

Manz, C.C. 1986. Self-leadership: toward an expanded theory of self-influence processes in organizations. *Academy of Management Review, 11*: 585-600.

Masiya T., Davids Y.D. & Mangai M.S. 2019. Assessing Service Delivery: Public Perception Of Municipal Service Delivery in South Africa. *Theoretical and Empirical Research in Urban Management, 14*(2): 20-40.

McCleskey, J.A. 2014. Situational, Transformational, and Transactional Leadership and Leadership Development. *Journal of Business Studies Quarterly, 5*(4): 117-130.

Moulaert, F., MacCallum, D., Mehmood, A. & Hamdouch, A. (Eds.) 2013. *The International Handbook on Social Innovation: Collective Action, Social Learning and Transdisciplinary Research*. Cheltenham, UK: Edward Elgar Publishing.

Municipal Data and Intelligence (Municipal IQ). 2020. *Increasing violence diminishes protesters' often legitimate grievances*. Available from: www.municipaliq.co.za/index.php?site_page=article.php&id=113 [Accessed 18 March 2020].

Nandram, S.S. & Bindlish, P.K. 2017. *Managing VUCA through Integrative Self-Management How to Cope with Volatility, Uncertainty, Complexity and Ambiguity in Organizational Behavior*. Switzerland: Springer International Publishing.

Nanus, B. 1992. *Visionary Leadership: Creating a Compelling Sense of Direction for Your Organization*. San Francisco, CA: Jossey-Bass.

Ndevu, Z.J. 2019. Trust and organisational performance: A grounded theory approach for a South African district municipality. *SA Journal of Human Resource Management, 17*(0): 1-11.

Neck, P. & Houghton, J.D. 2006. Two decades of self-leadership theory and research Past developments, present trends, and future possibilities. *Journal of Managerial Psychology, 21*(4): 270-295.

Orazi, D.C., Turrini, A., and Valotti, G. 2013. Public sector leadership: new perspectives for research and practice. *International Review of Administrative Sciences, 79*(3): 486–504.

Organisation for Economic Cooperation and Development (OECD). 2014. *OECD public governance reviews: Together for better public services – Partnering with citizens and civil society*. Available from: http://browse.oecdbookshop.org/oecd/pdfs/product/4211131e.pdf. [Accessed 23 February 2015].

Paarlberg, L.E. & Lavigna, B. 2010. Transformational leadership and public service motivation: Driving individual and organizational performance. *Public Administration Review, 70*(5): 710–718.

Pearce, C.L. & Manz, C.C. 2005. The New Silver Bullets of Leadership: The Importance of Self- and Shared Leadership in Knowledge Work *Organizational Dynamics, 34*(2): 130-140.

Rainey, H.G. & Bozeman, B. 2000. Comparing public and private organizations: Empirical research and the power of the 'a priori'. *Journal of Public Administration Research and Theory, 10*(2): 447–470.

Ramaphosa, C. 2018. *President Cyril Ramaphosa: SALGA National Members Assembly.* Available from: https://www.gov.za/speeches/address-president-cyril-ramaphosa-salga-national-members-assembly-inkosi-albert-luthuli-11 [Accessed 25 May 2020].

Ramaphosa, C. 2020. *President Cyril Ramaphosa: 2020 State of the Nation Address.* Available from: https://www.gov.za/speeches/president-cyril-ramaphosa-2020-state-nation-address-13-feb-2020. [Accessed 20 May 2020].

Reddy, P.S. 2015. Post 1994 local governance and development in South Africa: Quo vadis? In: P.S. Reddy & M. De Vries (Eds.). Quo Vadis: Local Governance and Development in South Africa Post 1994. Belgium (Brussels): Bruylant Publishers, pp. 323–340.

Reddy, P.S. 2018. Evolving local government in post conflict South Africa: Where to? Local Economy, *33*(7): 710–725.

Republic of South Africa. 1996. *Constitutions Act 108 of 1996.* Pretoria: Government Printers.

Satpathy, J. & Hejmadi, A. 2019. Managerial decision uncertainties in vuca spectrum. *International Journal of Advance and Innovative Research, 6*(1) (XXXIII): 1-8.

Sarros, C.J. & Santora C.J. 2001. The transformationtransactional leadership model in practice. *Leadership and organisation Development Journal, 22*(8): 383-393.

Saz-Carranza, A. & Ospina, S.M. 2010. The behavioral dimension of governing interorganizational goal-directed networks: Managing the unity–diversity tension. *Journal of Public Administration Research and Theory, 21*(2): 327–365.

Shokane, M.S., Stanz, K.J. & Slabbert, J.A. 2004. Description of leadership in South Africa: organisational context perspectivesa. *Journal of Human Resource Management, 2*(3): 1-6.

Singh, N. & Krishnan, V.R. 2008. Self-sacrifice and transformational leadership: Mediating role of altruism. *Leadership and Organization Development Journal, 29*(3): 261-274.

Sørensen, E. & Torfing, J. 2011. Enhancing collaborative innovation in the public sector. *Administration and Society, 43*(8): 842–868.

Statistics South Africa (StatsSA). 2018. *Four facts about indigent households.* Available from: www.statssa.gov.za/?p=11722 [Accessed 18 March 2020].

Statistics South Africa (StatsSA). 2019. *Statistics South Africa releases 2018 Non-financial Census of Municipalities Report.* Available from: www.gov.za/speeches/non-financial-census-municipalities-2018-29-aug-2019-0000 [Accessed 18 March 2020].

Stewart, G.L., Courtright, S.H. & Manz, C.C. 2011. Self-Leadership: A Multilevel Review. *Journal of Management, 37*(1): 185-222.

Sullivan, J. 2012. *VUCA: The new normal for talent management and workforce planning.* Available from: www.ere.netvuca-the-new-normal-for-talent-management-and-workforce-planning/. [Accessed 18 March 2020].

The Presidency. 2012. *National Development Plan 2030. Our Future - make it work.* Pretoria: Sherino printers.

The Presidency. 2020. *President Cyril Ramaphosa: Escalation of measures to combat Coronavirus COVID-19 pandemic.* Available from: www.gov.za/speeches/president-cyril-ramaphosa-escalation-measures-combat-coronavirus-covid-19-pandemic-23-mar [Accessed 26 March 2020].

Thornhill, C. & Cloete, J.J.N. (Eds.). 2014. *South African Municipal Government and Administration.* Pretoria: JL Van Schaik Publishers.

Tshishonga, N. 2015. The increased politicization of human resources recruitment. In: P.S. Reddy & M. De Vries (Eds.). *Quo Vadis? Local Governance and Development in South Africa Post 1994.* Brussels: Bruylant Publishers, pp. 129–146.

van der Waldt, C., Venter, A., Phutiagae, K., Nealer, E., Khalo T. & Vyas-Doorgapersad. 2018. *Municipal Management Serving the people* (3rd ed.). Juta: Cape Town.

World Economic Forum (WEF). 2020. *The IMF explains the economic lessons from China's fight against coronavirus*. Available from: www.weforum.org/agenda/2020/03/imf-economic-lessons-from-china-fight-against-coronavirus/ [Accessed 26 March 2020].

World Health Organisation (WHO). 2020. *Coronavirus disease 2019 (COVID-19) Situation Report – 63*. Geneva: WHO.

Wright, B.E. & Pandey, S.K. 2010. Transformational leadership in the public sector: Does structure matter? *Journal of Public Administration Research and Theory, 20*(1): 75–89.

Yukl, G. 2011. Contingency theories of effective leadership. In A. Bryman, D. Collinson, K. Grint, B. Jackson & M. Uhl-Bien (Eds.). *The SAGE handbook of leadership* (pp. 286-298). Thousand Oaks, CA: Sage.

Chapter 12 References

Bandura, A. 1986. Social foundations of thought and action: A social cognitive theory. Englewood Cliffs, NJ: Prentice-Hall, Inc.

Baumeister, R.F. 1999. The nature and structure of the self: An overview. In R. Baumeister (Ed.). The self in social psychology (pp. 1-20). Philadelphia, PA: Psychology Press (Taylor & Francis).

Business Insider. 2019, November 8. Rajat Gupta is out of jail but still has some high-profile grudges. The ex-McKinsey head's book reveals his beefs with Lloyd Blankfein and Preet Bharara and celebrates his former life among the global elite. *Latest Nigerian News.* Available from: https://www.latestnigeriannews.com/news/7860140/rajat-gupta-is-out-of-jail-but-still-has-some-highprofile-grudges-the-exmckinsey.html [Accessed 22 April 2019].

Cooley, C.H. 1902. *Human nature and the social order.* New York: Charles Scribner's Sons.

Csikszentmihalyi, M. 1990. Flow: The Psychology of Optimal Experience. New York: Harper and Row.

Dyer, W.W. 1976. *Your erroneous zones.* New York, Funk & Wagnalls.

Frankl, V.E. 2006. Man's Search for Meaning. Boston: Beacon Press.

Goodreads. (n.d.). Alvin Toffler Quotes. Available from: https://www.goodreads.com/quotes/8800-the-illiterate-of-the-21st-century-will-not-be-those [Accessed 22 April 2019].

Khanna, S. & Sood, V. 2019. *I was a big fish and an easier target: Rajat Gupta.* Available from: https://www.livemint.com/companies/people/i-was-a-big-fish-and-an-easier-target-rajat-gupta-1553455806681.html [Accessed 22 April 2019].

Kinsinger, P. & Walch, K. 2019. *Living and Leading in a VUCA World.* Available from: http://www.forevueinternational.com/Content/sites/forevue/pages/1482/4_1__Living_and_Leading_in_a_VUCA_World_Thunderbird_School.PDF [Accessed 22 April 2019].

Mukerjea, D.N. 2019. Rajat Gupta's memoir is the biggest gamble of all. *Telegraph India.* Available from: https://www.telegraphindia.com/opinion/rajat-guptas-memoir-is-the-biggest-gamble-of-all/cid/1688431 [Accessed 22 April 2019].

Rosenberg, M. 1979. *Conceiving the Self.* New York, NY: Basic.

Sarao, K.T.S. & Long, J. 2017. *Encyclopedia of Indian Religions: Buddhism and Jainism*. New York: Springer.

Seligman, M.E.P. 1990. Learned Optimism: How to Change Your Mind and Your Life. New York: Vintage.

Skinner, B.F. 1991. *The Behavior of Organisms*. Acton, MA: Copley Pub Group.

Sri Sankaracharya. 1988. *Bhagavad Gita with the commentary of Sri Sankaracharya.* Twin Lakes, WI: Lotus Press (WI).

Stiehm, J. & Townsend, N. 2002. *The U.S. Army War College: Military Education in a Democracy.* Philadelphia: Temple University Press.

Wikipedia. 2020. *Rajat Gupta.* Available from: https://en.wikipedia.org/wiki/Rajat_Gupta [Accessed 22 April 2019].

Chapter 13 References

Bakshi, V. 2017. *The forward-looking manager in a VUCA world.* New Delhi: Sage Publications.

Baltici, A. & Balci, A. 2017. Complexity leadership: A theoretical perspective. *International Journal of Educational Leadership and Management, 5*(1): 30-58.

Betz, F. 2016. *Strategic thinking: A comprehensive guide.* London: Emerald Group.

Brand-Jacobsen, K., Curran, D., Demarest, L., Annan, N., Wolter, S., Tanase, A., Tunney, E. & Shiroka, S. 2018. *The peace training handbook.* Available from: www.peace.edu (Accessed 24 April 2020).

Campbell, A.B. 1993. *Applied chaos theory: A paradigm for complexity.* Boston, MA: Academic Press.

Cohen, T. & Insko, C. 2008. War and peace: Possible approaches to reducing intergroup conflict. *Perspectives on Psychological Science, 3*(87): 93.

Cole, B. 2009. *Guidelines principals for stabilization and reconstitution.* Washington DC: United States Institute of Peace Press.

Cseh, M., Davis, E. & Khilji, S. 2013. Developing a global mindset: Learning of global leaders. *European Journal of Training and Development, 37*(5): 489-499.

Ferch, S.R. 2012. *Forgiveness and power in the age of atrocity.* Plymouth, UK: Lexington Books.

Fukuyama, F. 2006. *The end of history and the last man.* New York, NY: Simon and Schuster.

Goleman, D., Boyatzis, R.E., McKee, A. & Finkelstein, S. 2015. *HBR's 10 Must Reads on Emotional Intelligence.* Boston, MA: Harvard Business Review Press.

Goleman, D., Kaplan, R. S., David, S. & Eurich, T. 2019. *Self-awareness: HBR Emotional intelligence series.* Boston, MA: Harvard Business Review.

Heifetz, R. A., Grashow, M. & Lindsey, A. 2009. *The practice of adaptive leadership: Tools and tactics for changing your organization and the world.* Boston, MA: Harvard Press.

Joiner, B. & Josephs, S. 2007. *Leadership agility: Five levels of mastery for anticipating and initiating change.* New York, NY: Jossey Bass.

Kethledge, R.M. & Erwin, M.S. 2017. *Leading yourself first: Inspiring leadership though solitude.* London: Bloomsbury Publishing.

Mack, O., Khare, A., Kramer, A. & Burgartz, T. 2016. *Managing in a VUCA world.* Cham, Switzerland: Springer Publishing.

Mandela, N. 1994. *Long walk to freedom: The autobiography of Nelson Mandela.* New York, NY: Liveright Publishing.

Mandela, N. 2010. *Conversations with myself.* New York, NY: Liveright Publishing.

Mandela, N. & Langa, M. 2017. *Dare to linger-The presidential years.* New York, NY: Liveright Publishing.

Mandela, N. & Venter, S. 2018. *Prison letters of Nelson Mandela.* New York, NY: Liveright Publishing.

Mendenhall, M.E., Osland, J.S., Bird, A., Oddou, G.R., Maznevski, M.L., Stevens, M.J. & Stahl, G.K. 2013. *Global leadership: Research, practice, and development* (2nd ed.). New York, NY: Routledge.

Rayment, J. & Smith, J. 2011. *Misleadership: Prevalence, causes, and consequences.* Burlington, VT: Ashgate Publishing.

Redmond, M.V. 2015. *Uncertainty reduction theory.* English Technical Reports and White Papers, 3. Available from: http://lib.dr.iastate.edu/engl_reports/3.

Rimita, K. 2019. *Leader Readiness in a volatile, uncertain, complex, and ambiguous (VUCA) business environment.* Available from: https://scholarworks.waldenu.edu/dissertations/7727/

Sieman, G., Dawson, S. & Eshleman, K. 2018. *Complexity: A leader's framework for understanding and managing change in higher education.* Available from: https://er.educause.edu/articles/2018/10/complexity-a-leaders-framework-for-understanding-and-managing-change-in-higher-education

Stein, S. & Brooks, H. 2011. *The EQEdge: Emotional Intelligence and your success* (3rd ed.). Mississauga, ON: Jossey-Boss.

Tutu, D. 2000. *No future without forgiveness.* New York, NY: Random House Press.

Uhl-Bein, M. & Arena, M. 2017. Complexity leadership: Enabling people and organizations for adaptability. *Organizational Dynamics, 46*: 9-20.

Uhl-Bien, M. & Arena, M. 2018. Leadership for organizational adaptability: A theoretical synthesis and integrative framework. *The Leadership Quarterly, 29*(1): 89–104.

Van Zyl, E. & Campbell, A. 2019. *Peace leadership: Self-transformation to peace.* Randburg, South Africa: KR Publishing.

Veldsman, T.H. & Johnson, A.J. 2016. Leadership: Perspectives from the front line, Randburg, South Africa: KR Publishing.

Worthington, E.L. 2013. Forgiveness and justice. *The power of forgiveness*, 1-3. Available at: http://www.thepowerofforgiveness.com/pdf/Worthington.pdf

Chapter 14 References

Arango, T. 2017, 15 July. Iran dominates in Iraq after US 'handed the country over' *New York Times.* Available from: https://www.nytimes.com/2017/07/15/world/middleeast/iran-iraq-iranian-power.html (Accessed 10 March 2020).

Bateson, N. 2017. *Liminal leadership.* Available from: https://www.thebeyondpartnership.co.uk/events/nora-bateson-liminal-leadership/ (Accessed 10 March 2020).

Bawany, S. 2018, 16 January. *What is VUCA? Leadership in a VUCA World.* [video file]. Available from: https://www.youtube.com/watch?v=eC_mik3DOGo (Accessed 10 March 2020).

Beck, D.E. & Cowan, C. 1996. *Spiral Dynamics: Mastering values, leadership, and change.* Oxford, England: Blackwell Publishing.

Better Help. 2018. *Understanding how liminal space is different from other places.* Retrieved from https://www.betterhelp.com/advice/general/understanding-how-liminal-space-is-different-from-other-places/ (Accessed 14 September 2019).

Brown, B.C. 2006. *An overview of developmental stages of consciousness.* Available from: rhttps://integralwithoutborders.net/sites/default/files/resources/Overview%20of%20Developmental%20Levels.pdf (Accessed 1 September 2019).

Curran, K. 2018. Global Resonance. In: R.J. Thompson & J. Storberg-Walker (Eds.). *Leadership and power international development: Navigating the intersections of gender, culture, context, and sustainability.* London: Emerald Publishing, pp. 311-329.

Hawkins, B. & Edwards, G. 2017. Facing the monsters: Embracing liminality in leadership development. In S. Kempster, A.F. Turner & G. Edwards. *Field Guide to Leadership Development.* [Kindle edition] Cheltenham, UK: Edgar Elgar Publishing, pp. 203-217.

Horvath, A., Thomassen, B. & Wydra, H. 2015. *Breaking boundaries: Varieties of liminality.* New York: Berghahn.

Jordaan, B. 2019. Leading organisations in turbulent times: Towards a different mental model. In: J. Kok & J. van den Heuval. *Leading in a VUCA world: Integrating leadership, discernment, and spirituality.* [Kindle edition]. New York, NY: Springer Open Publishers.

Joubert, S. 2019. A well-played life: Discernment as the constitutive building block of selfless leadership. In: J. Kok & J. van den Heuval. *Leading in a VUCA world: Integrating leadership, discernment, and spirituality.* [Kindle edition]. New York, NY: Springer Open Publishers.

Kegan, R. 1982. *The evolving self: Problem and process in human development.* Cambridge, MA: Harvard University Press.

Kegan, R. & Lahey, L. 2001. *How the way we talk can change the way we work.* San Francisco: Jossey-Bass.

Kok, J. & van den Heuval, P. 2019. *Leading in a VUCA world: Integrating leadership, discernment, and spirituality.* [Kindle edition]. New York, NY: Springer Open Publishers.

Leslie, J.B., Li, P.P. & Zhao, S. 2015. *Managing paradox: Blending east and west philosophies to unlock its advantages and opportunities.* White Paper, Center for Creative Leadership.

Mannherz, T. 2017. *New leadership models for the VUCA world: Five leadership approaches to cope with uncertainty.* Available from: https://www.grin.com/document/377619 (Accessed 14 April 2020).

Nullens, P. 2019. From spirituality to responsible leadership: Ignatian self-discernment and theory-u. In: J. Kok & J. van den Heuval. *Leading in a VUCA world: Integrating leadership, discernment, and spirituality.* [Kindle edition]. New York, NY: Springer Open Publishers.

Orton, A. & Withrow, L. 2015. Transformative potentials of liminal leadership. *Journal of Religious leadership, 14*(1): 23-44.

Rohrm, R. 1999. *Everything Belongs: The Gift of Contemplative Prayer.* Editora, USA: Crossroad Publishing Company

Scharmer, O. 2016. *Theory U: Leading from the future as it emerges.* San Francisco, CA: Berrett-Koehler Publishers.

Smith, P. 1991. Codes and conduct: Toward a theory of war as ritual. *Theory and Society, 21*(1): 103-138.

Van-Buskirk, L., Lim, D.O. & Leong, S. 2019. Liminal leadership: Leading betwixt and between. *European Journal of Training and Development, 43*(78): 643-660.

Van Zyl, E. 2019. A peace-leadership-in-action model: Self-transformation to the creation of peace. In: E. Van Zyl & A. Campbell, A. (Eds.). *Peace leadership: Self transformation to peace.* [Kindle edition]. Bryanston, SA: KR Publishers.

Van Zyl, E. & Campbell, A. (Eds.). 2019. *Peace leadership: Self transformation to peace.* [Kindle edition]. Bryanston, SA: KR Publishers.

Wigglesworth, C. 2011. *Spiritual intelligence and why it matters.* Available from: http://www.godisaserialentrepreneur.com/uploads/2/8/4/4/2844368/spiritual_intelligence__emotional_intelligence_2011.pdf (Accessed 14 April 2020).

Wilber, K. 2000. *Integral psychology: Consciousness, spirit, psychology, therapy.* Boston, MA: Shambala.

Chapter 15 References

Allison, S.T., Kocher, C.T. & Goethals, G.R. 2017. *Frontiers in spiritual leadership: Discovering the better angels of our nature.* New York: Palgrave Macmillan.

Ammerman, N.T. 2003. Religious identities and religious institutions. In: M. Dillon (Ed.). *A handbook of the sociology of religion*. Cambridge: Cambridge University Press, pp.207–24.

Bangura, J.B. 2018. African charismatic movements, the Bible and Bible schools. In: K. Fitschen, M. Schröter, C. Spehr & E-J. Waschke (Eds.). *Kulturelle Wirkungen der Reformation / Cultural impact of the Reformation*. Leipzig: Evangelische Verlagsanstalt, pp.299–310.

Barentsen, J. 2014. Spirituality and innovation: New faces of leadership? In: J. Barentsen & P. Nullens (Eds.). *Leadership, spirituality and innovation. Christian perspectives on leadership and social ethics 1*. Leuven: Peeters, pp.3–11.

Barentsen, J. 2015. Church leadership as adaptive identity construction in a changing social context. *Journal of Religious Leadership, 15*(2): 49–80.

Barentsen, J. 2016. Practising religious leadership. In: J. Storey, J. Hartley, J-L. Denis, P. Hart & D. Ulrich (Eds.). *Routledge companion to leadership*. London: Routledge, pp.260-277.

Barentsen, J. 2018. *The pastor as innovator? Religious leadership in a post-truth world*. Inaugural lecture, September 2018. Leuven: Evangelische Theologische Faculteit.

Barentsen, J., Kessler, V. & van den Heuvel, S. (Eds.). 2018. *Increasing diversity: Loss of control or adaptive identity construction. Christian perspectives on leadership and social ethics 5*. Leuven: Peeters.

Bauman, Z. 2000. *Liquid modernity*. Malden, MA: Polity Press.

Berghuijs, J. 2017. Multiple religious belonging in the Netherlands: An empirical approach to hybrid religiosity. *Open Theology, 3*(1):19–37.

Boy, J. 2015. *Blessed disruption: Culture and urban space in a European church planting network*. (PhD Dissertation). New York: City University of New York.

Brugmann, J. 2009. *Welcome to the urban revolution: How cities are changing the world*. New York: Bloomsbury.

Carrette, J.R. & King, R. 2005. *Selling spirituality: The silent takeover of religion*. London: Routledge.

Carroll, J.W. 2011. *As one with authority: Reflective leadership in ministry* (2nd and revised ed.). Eugene, OR: Cascade.

Christerson, B. & Flory, R. 2017. *The rise of network Christianity: How independent leaders are changing the religious landscape*. Oxford: Oxford University Press.

Cornille, C. (Ed.). 2010. *Many mansions? Multiple religious belonging and Christian identity*. Eugene, OR: Wipf and Stock.

Elliott, A. 2016. *Identity troubles: An introduction*. New York: Routledge.

Faucett, J.M., Corwyn, R.F. & Poling, T.H. 2013. Clergy Role Stress: Interactive effects of role ambiguity and role conflict on intrinsic job satisfaction. *Pastoral Psychology, 62*(3): 291–304.

Fry, L.W. 2003. Toward a theory of spiritual leadership. *The Leadership Quarterly, 14*(6): 693–727.

Geloven in Spangen. 2020. *Dit is Geloven in Spangen*. Available from: https://geloveninspangen.nl/over-ons/ [Accessed March 3, 2020].

Goodhew, D., Roberts, A. & Volland, M. 2012. *Fresh! An introduction to fresh expressions of church and pioneer ministry*. London: SCM Press.

Haslam, S.A., Reicher, S. & Platow, M.J. 2011. *The new psychology of leadership: Identity, influence and power*. New York: Psychology Press.

Herriot, P. 2007. *Religious fundamentalism and social identity*. New York: Routledge.

Hogg, M.A., van Knippenberg, D. & Rast, D.E. 2012a. The social identity theory of leadership: Theoretical origins, research findings, and conceptual developments. *European Review of Social Psychology, 23*(1): 258–304.

Hogg, M.A., van Knippenberg, D. & Rast, D.E. 2012b. Intergroup leadership in organizations: Leading across group and organizational boundaries. *Academy of Management Review, 37*(2): 232–255.

Hornikx, R. 2002. *Spiritualiteit als motor tot vernieuwing: Een model voor parochie en gemeente*. Kampen: Kok.

Johnson, B.C. & Dreitcer, A. 2001. *Beyond the ordinary: Spirituality for church leaders*. Grand Rapids: Eerdmans.

Kollontai, P., Yore, S. & Kim, S. (Eds.). 2018. *The role of religion in peacebuilding: Crossing the boundaries of prejudice and distrust*. London: Jessica Kingsley.

Lee, S. & Sinitiere, P.L. 2009. *Holy mavericks: Evangelical innovators and the spiritual marketplace*. New York: NYU Press.

Manz, C.C. & Sims, H.P. 2001. *The new superleadership: Leading others to lead themselves*. San Francisco, CA: Berrett-Koehler.

McIntyre-Miller, W. 2016. Toward a scholarship of peace leadership. *International Journal of Public Leadership, 12*(3): 216–226.

Meijer, H. 2019. In Spangen horen de kapper en zwemles bij kerk-zijn. *Nederlands Dagblad*. NDzeven, 8–9.

Neck, C.P. & Houghton, J.D. 2006. Two decades of self-leadership theory and research: Past developments, present trends, and future possibilities. *Journal of Managerial Psychology, 21*(4): 270–295.

Powell, N. & James, J. 2019. *Together for the city: How collaborative church planting leads to citywide movements*. Downers Grove: IVP.

Quinn, R.E. 1996. *Deep change: Discovering the leader within*. San Francisco: Jossey-Bass.

Root, A. 2019. *The pastor in a secular age: Ministry to people who no longer need a God*. Grand Rapids: Baker Academic.

Roxburgh, A.J. 2010. *Missional: Joining God in the neighborhood*. Grand Rapids: Baker.

Saroglou, V. 2006. Religious bricolage as a psychological reality: Limits, structures and dynamics. *Social Compass, 53*(1): 109–115.

Stanton, G.D. 2019. A theology of complexity for Christian leadership in an uncertain future. *Practical Theology, 12*(2): 147–157.

Stewart, G.L., Courtright, S.H. & Manz, C.C. 2011. Self-leadership: A multilevel review. *Journal of Management, 37*(1): 185–222.

Tomic, W., Tomic, D.M. & Evers, W.J.G. 2004. A question of burnout among reformed church ministers in the Netherlands. *Mental Health, Religion and Culture, 7*(3): 225–247.

Van Zyl, E. & Campbell, A. (Eds.). 2018. *Peace leadership: Self-transformation to peace*. Randburg: KR Publishing.

Vellekoop, M. 2015. *Pionieren vanuit de Protestantse Kerk*. Utrecht: PKN.

Vertovec, S. 2015. *Routledge international handbook of diversity studies*. London: Routledge.

Warren, R. 1995. *The purpose-driven church: Growth without compromising your message and mission*. Grand Rapids: Zondervan.

Warren, R. 2012. *The purpose driven life: What on earth am I here for?* (Expanded ed.). Grand Rapids: Zondervan.

Westjohn, S.A., Singh, N. & Magnusson, P. 2012. Responsiveness to global and local consumer culture positioning: A personality and collective identity perspective. *Journal of International Marketing, 20*(1): 58–73.

Chapter 16 References

Bass, B.M. & Bass, R. 2008. *The handbook of leadership: Theory, research, and managerial applications* (4th ed.). New York, NY: Free Press.

Bawany, S. 2016. NextGen Leaders for a VUCA World: Transforming Future Leaders for Success. *Leadership Excellence Essentials, 33*(8), 43-44.

Cheah, S.L. 2020. *Strategic Foresight: Accelerating Technological Change*

HBR Guide to thinking strategically. Boston, MA: Harvard Press Publishing.

Chevallier, A. 2016. *Strategic Thinking in Complex Problem Solving*. New York, NY: Oxford Press.

Dufour, Y. & Steane, P. 2014. Creative strategic thinking and sustainable leadership: Lessons from Picasso. *Journal of Global Responsibility, 5*(2): 219-225.

Fuchs, M., Messner, J. & Sok, R. 2018. *Leadership in a VUCA World: The Jedi path to agile mastery*. Freiburg, Germany: Haufe-Lexware Publishing.

Harvard Business Review. 2019. *Guide to Thinking Strategically*. Boston, MA: Harvard Business Review Press.

Hambert, D., Finkelstein, S. & Cannella, A. 2009. *Strategic leadership: Theory and research on executives, top management teams, and boards*. New York, NY: Oxford Press.

Kok, J. & van den Heuvel, S. 2019. *Leading in a VUCA world: Integrating leadership discernment and spirituality*. Cham, Switzerland: Springer Publisher.

Maleka, S. 2014. *Strategic Management and Strategic Planning Process*. Available from: https://www.researchgate.net/profile/Stevens_Maleka/publication/273757341_Strategic_Management_and_Strategic_Planning_Process/links/550a8c7f0cf26198a63b0fb1/Strategic-Management-and-Strategic-Planning-Process.pdf (Accessed 24 April 2020).

Mannhez, T. 2017. *New leadership models for a VUCA world. Five leadership approaches to cope with uncertainty*. Norderstedt, Germany: Open Publishing.

Shoemaker, P., Krupp, S. & Holwand, S. 2019. Strategic leadership: The essential skills. HBR Guide to Thinking Strategically. Boston, MA: Harvard Business Review Press.

Tavakoli I. & Lawton J. 2005. Strategic thinking and knowledge management, *Handbook of Business Strategy, 6*(1),155-160.

Tiefenbacher, W. 2019. *Strategic management: how and why to redefine organizational strategy in today's VUCA world*. Available from: https://www.ckju.net/en/blog/strategic-management-how-and-why-redefine-organizational-strategy-todays-vuca-world/58699 (Accessed 24 April 2020).

Chapter 17 References

Abelli, H. 2020. *The 6 truths of modern leadership development*. Available from: https://www.skillsoft.com (Accessed 4 June 2020).

Church, J. n.d. *A circle of caring*. Available from: https://www.pinterest.co.uk (Accessed 4 June 2020).

History.com. 2020. *Franklin D Roosevelt*. Available from: https://www.history.com (Accessed 4 June 2020).

Kornelsen, J. 2019. The quest to led (with) millennials in a VUCA-world: Bridging the gap between generations. In: J. Kok & S.C. van den Heuvel (Eds.). *Leading in a VUCA world* (pp. 27-43). Cham, Switzerland: Springer.

Moore, S. 2019. *Jacinda Ardern is showing the world what real leadership is*. Available from: https://www.the guardian.com/commentisfree/2019/mar/18/jacinda-adern-is-showing-the-world—what-real-leadership-is-sympathy-love-and-integrity (Accessed 4 June 2020).

Morse, S. 2017. *Emmanuel Macron says this is the secret to leadership*. Available from: https://thriveglobal.com/stories/emmanuel-macron-says-this-the-secret-to-leadership/ (Accessed 4 June 2020).

Nullens, P. 2019. From spirituality to responsible leadership: Ignatian discernment and theory–U. In J. Kok & S.C. van den Heuvel (Eds.). *Leading in a VUCA world* (pp. 185-206). Cham, Switzerland: Springer.

Oxford Learners University Press. 2020. *Oxford University Dictionary*. Available from: https://www.oxfordlearnersdictionary (Accessed 4 June 2020).

Van Zyl, E.S. & Campbell, A. 2019. *Peace leadership: Self-transformation to peace*. Randburg: KR Publishers.

Veldsman, T.H. & Johnson, A.J. 2016. *Leadership in context: Perspectives from the frontline*. Johannesburg: KR Publishers.

Wittenberg-Cox, A. 2020. *What do countries with the best coronavirus responses have in common? Women leaders*. Available from: https://forbes.com/sites/avivahwittenbergcox/2020/04/13/what-do-countries--with-the-best-coronavirus-repsonses-have-in-common--women-leadership (Accessed 4 June 2020).

INDEX

CPSIA information can be obtained
at www.ICGtesting.com
Printed in the USA
BVHW011837160622
639995BV00015B/149

9 781869 228606